Other titles in the Cognitive Strategy Training Series

Cognitive Strategy Instruction for Middle and High Schools
Eileen Wood, Vera Woloshyn & Teena Willoughby

Implementing Cognitive Strategy Instruction Across the School:
    The Benchmark Manual for Teachers
Irene Gaskins & Thorne Elliott

Helping Students Become Strategic Learners:
    Guidelines for Teaching
Karen Scheid

Helping Young Writers Master The Craft:
    Strategy Instruction and Self-Regulation in the Writing Process
Karen Harris & Steve Graham

Teaching Students Ways To Remember:
    Strategies for Learning Mnemonically
Margo Mastropieri & Thomas Scruggs

Teaching Test-Taking Skills:
    Helping Students Show What They Know
Thomas Scruggs & Margo Mastropieri

Textbooks and the Students Who Can't Read Them:
    A Guide for the Teaching of Content
Jean Ciborowski

Cognitive Strategy Instruction that *Really* Improves Children's Academic Performance

Second Edition

Michael Pressley
State University of New York–Albany

Vera Woloshyn
Brock University

& Associates
Jacquelyn Burkell
Teresa Cariglia-Bull
Linda Lysynchuk
Jacqueline A. McGoldrick
Brynah Schneider
Barbara L. Snyder
Sonya Symons

Brookline Books

Library of Congress Cataloging-in-Publication Data
Pressley, Michael.
      Cognitive strategy instruction that really improves children's academic performance / Michael Pressley, Vera Woloshyn & associates. -- 2nd ed.
            p. 266   cm. -- (Cognitive strategy training series)
      Includes bibliographic references and indexes.
      ISBN 1-57129-005-2 (paper) :
      1. Thought and thinking--Study and teaching (Elementary)
2. Cognitive learning. 3. Language arts (Elementary)
4. Mathematics--Study and teaching (Elementary)   I. Woloshyn, Vera.
II. Title. III. Series.
LB1590.3.P76   1995
372.13--dc20   95-2310
Reprinted, 2000.   CIP

Part of the Cognitive Strategy Training Series
Series Editor: Michael Pressley, SUNY–Albany

ISBN 1-57129-005-2
Printed in USA by McNaughton & Gunn, Saline, Michigan.
10 9 8 7 6 5 4 3 2

Brookline Books
P.O. Box 1047
Cambridge, Massachusetts 02238-1047

CONTENTS

Series Preface i

Foreword to the Second Edition
Barak Rosenshine, University of Illinois iii

Authors' Preface vi

Chapter 1: Introduction to Cognitive Strategy Instruction
Barbara Snyder & Michael Pressley 1

Chapter 2: Decoding and the Beginnings of Reading
Michael Pressley & Teresa Cariglia-Bull 19

Chapter 3: Reading Comprehension Strategies
Michael Pressley, Sonya Symons,
Jacqueline A. McGoldrick & Barbara L. Snyder 57

Chapter 4: Vocabulary
Michael Pressley & Linda Lysynchuk 101

Chapter 5: Spelling
Vera E. Woloshyn & Michael Pressley 116

Chapter 6: Writing
Michael Pressley, Jacqueline A. McGoldrick,
Teresa Cariglia-Bull & Sonya Symons 153

Chapter 7: Mathematical Problem Solving
Michael Pressley, Jacquelyn Burkell & Brynah Schneider 184

Chapter 8: Science
Vera Woloshyn & Michael Pressley 213

Chapter 9: Learning Facts: The Value of Always
Asking Yourself Why And Other Mnemonic Strategies
Michael Pressley & Vera Woloshyn 234

Chapter 10: Getting Started Teaching Strategies
Michael Pressley 244

Appendix: Additional Sources of Information About Strategies 254

Author Index 257
Subject Index 261
About the Authors 265

Series Preface

This volume is the flagship volume in a series of short paperbacks published by Brookline Books on the topic of cognitive strategy instruction. The goal of the series is to provide the very best and most up-to-date information about strategy instruction and related topics to the educator community.

Two types of books are featured in the series:

(a) Most are written by educational researchers who are doing work that directly relates to school performance. Their work is reviewed by the general editor, Michael Pressley, before an invitation to submit a book is delivered to them. The editor only provides invitations to scholars whose research is sound methodologically and unambiguously relevant to education. One clear goal of the series is to make the very best research on cognitive strategy instruction more readily available to teachers. Pressley and Milton Budoff, the publisher of Brookline Books, are proud that the series has attracted, and continues to attract, outstanding scholars and educators.

(b) A few books in the series are by scholars who are supervising outstanding demonstration projects in strategy instruction or who have done outstanding integrative work. A few well-known schools and institutes have or will contribute. Bibliographic scholars who can provide definitive commentary on how to do strategy instruction or who can provide input about changes in curriculum or educational practices that foster better information processing in children will also appear in the series.

All those involved with the series are extremely excited about bridging the gap between the researcher/scholar community and the teaching profession. The contributors to this series are all committed to make high quality work accessible to teaching professionals who can translate research findings into telling educational practices.

Because strategy instruction is particularly appropriate for intellectually handicapped populations, and because of the commitment of the publisher to provide materials to educators servicing students who experience difficulties in school, the series especially features outstanding contributions to the learning disabilities literature. But strategy instruction is highly appropriate for normal learners, especially inner city and minority children. The series will focus on conveying these methods for use with those students. Special education is not the exclusive focus of the series.

It is our strong desire to publish books about a variety of cognitive strategy interventions that are worthwhile for children—handicapped, average, and gifted. Authors who feel they might contribute to this effort should contact Milton Budoff at Brookline Books or Michael Pressley at the Department of Educational Psychology and Statistics, University at Albany, State University of New York, Albany, NY 12222.

Foreword to the Second Edition

This book is an important collection and review of the research on the teaching of cognitive strategies appropriate for instruction. Cognitive strategies are procedures that students can use to help them understand and address higher-order tasks in areas such as reading comprehension and writing. The concept of cognitive strategies, and the studies that have been conducted in this area, represent the most important instructional advance of the past 15 years.

Until the late 1970s, students were seldom provided with any help in completing higher-level tasks. In a classic observational study of reading comprehension instruction, Durkin (1975) noted that of the 4,469 minutes she observed in reading instruction in grade 4, only 20 minutes were spent in comprehension instruction by the teacher. Durkin noted that teachers spent almost all of the instructional time asking students questions, but little time teaching students comprehension strategies they could use to *answer* the questions. Duffy, Lanier, and Roehler (1980) noted a similar lack of comprehension instruction in elementary classrooms:

> There is little evidence of instruction of any kind. Teachers spend most of their time assigning activities, monitoring to be sure the pupils are on task, directing recitation sessions to assess how well children are doing, and providing corrective feedback in response to pupil errors. Seldom does one observe teaching in which a teacher presents a skill, a strategy, or a process to pupils, shows them how to do it, provides assistance as they initiate attempts to perform the task and assures that they can be successful (Duffy et al., 1980, p. 4).

As a result of these astonishing findings, and as a result of emerging research on cognition and information processing, investigators began to develop and validate specific cognitive strategies, such as for question-generation or summarization, that students could use to help improve their reading comprehension. Other research focused on developing and testing cognitive strategies that are specific to writing, mathematical problem solving, and science comprehension. This volume is an important summary of those studies.

Cognitive strategies are heuristics. A cognitive strategy is not a direct procedure; it is not an algorithm to be followed precisely. Rather, a cognitive strategy is a *heuristic*: it serves to support or facilitate learners as they develop internal procedures that enable them to perform the higher-level operations. Teaching students to generate questions about their reading is an example of a cognitive strategy. Generating questions does not directly lead, in a step-by-step manner, to comprehension. Rather, in the process of generating questions, students need to search the text and combine information, and these processes serve to help students comprehend what they read.

The concept of cognitive strategies represents at least two instructional advances. First, the concept itself provides us with a general approach that can be applied to the teaching of higher-order skills in the content areas. When teachers are faced with difficult areas, they can now ask, "What cognitive strategies might I use or develop that can help students complete these tasks?" Second, there have now been a large number of studies in which students who were taught various cognitive strategies obtained significantly higher post-test scores than did students in the control groups. The cognitive strategies that were taught in these studies, and the procedures by which these strategies were taught, can now be used as part of regular instruction. These cognitive strategies, together with a description of the studies in which they appeared, have been assembled in this volume and are now available for teachers to use.

Let me describe a few of the cognitive strategies that are in this volume. The chapter on reading contains the prompts students were given to help them generate questions. The chapter on writing describes a number of prompts, such as "think sheets" that students have used to help organize and revise their writing. The chapter on science describes the use of "concept maps" that can help students organize their thinking. The chapter on spelling describes three spelling strategies: an imagery strategy, a word analogy strategy, and a proofreading strategy.

Pressley and Woloshyn describe not only strategies that students can use, but strategies that teachers have used successfully which have been validated by controlled research. Thus, the chapter on vocabulary describes the use of semantic mapping, and the chapter on science describes instructional procedures for promoting conceptual change. In each chapter, the authors provide a general framework for instruction in these areas and descriptions of the research studies which show the benefits of these procedures.

We can be proud of our progress as a profession. In place of Durkin's observation that there was little evidence of cognitive strategy instruction in reading, we now have a large number of studies that demonstrate that cognitive strategies can successfully improve instruction in a number of domains as reflected by improved student scores. This book is a celebration of that progress.

Barak Rosenshine, Ph.D.
University of Illinois at Urbana-Champaign
January 1995

REFERENCES

Duffy, G., Lanier, J.E., & Roehler, L.R. (1980). *On the need to consider instructional practice when looking for instructional implications.* Paper presented at the Conference on Reading Expository Materials, Wisconsin Research and Development Center, University of Wisconsin–Madison.

Durkin, D. (1979). What classroom observations reveal about reading comprehension. *Reading Research Quarterly, 14,* 581-544.

Authors' Preface

My students and I have been doing research on various aspects of cognitive strategy instruction for two decades. During that time, we have written a number of overview papers as well as reported many empirical studies. In recent years we became especially impressed by the need to communicate to the educator community exactly what is known about cognitive strategy instruction. The need follows from the fact that a large number of commercial ventures have emerged that feature cognitive strategy instruction. Few of these are well validated, although they are widely disseminated and recommended by educator professional associations. Most of these products consist of recommendations to teach a number of strategies, some of which enjoy research support and some of which do not. In addition, most of these products are silent about *how* to teach strategies. A book that separated the wheat from the chaff seemed appropriate, and thus, the first edition of this book and its revision. We summarize here what we view as the best validated cognitive strategies for teaching academic content to children in grades 1 through 8 as well as some commentary about how strategy instruction should proceed. We believe the teaching professional who knows the strategies in this volume will be in a better position to teach effective cognitive strategies than the many teachers who have bought expensive strategy instructional kits.

Our perspective is definitely not that cognitive strategy instruction can or should be a "quick fix" for children who are experiencing difficulties in school. Rather, cognitive strategy instruction consists of teaching students procedures that sometimes take a while to master, but are worth acquiring because they reflect the processes that people who are good at academic tasks routinely employ. Moreover, we believe that cognitive strategy instruction is not an "add-on," but rather should be routinely included in ongoing instruction and that the specific strategies that are taught should address academic tasks that children are currently confronting in school. Thus, what is offered here are well validated strategies that fit well with the elementary curriculum. There is an emphasis on long-term and thorough teaching of these procedures rather than quick teaching. Finally, cognitive strategy instruction is not suggested as a substitute for content teaching, but rather a complement to it. Our view is that good thinking consists not only of using the right procedures but coordinating use of effective strategies with a well-developed knowledge base. This model of good thinking—good information processing, as it is referred to in the literature—is elaborated in the first chapter.

This book was first developed between September 1987 and January 1989 at the University of Western Ontario. Author Pressley hung his professional hat there from 1979 to 1989, and all of the student associates were enrolled as graduate students in psychology when they participated in the writing of this book. The student associates earned graduate course credit for their participation in the project, a graduate course that was nominally headed by Pressley. There was a great deal of cooperation and interaction between the contributors as the book was developed. Ultimately particular individuals took responsibility for certain sections of the volume. Thus, each chapter is listed with the names of those associates who were principally responsible for the contribution in their order of impact. Pressley appears as the last author of several chapters, reflecting his role in those chapters as chief devil's advocate, critic, editor, and the person who kept saying, "It seems to me that there might be some work on .... Go look in the *Journal of ...*, maybe between 197? and 198?." In 1994, Michael Pressley and Vera Woloshyn took on the task of revising and updating.

A few others deserve mention for both tangible and intangible support they provided. Carla J. Johnson and Janice A. Kurita of the University of Western Ontario were involved in a major project (independent of this volume) to summarize what is known about reading comprehension strategy instruction. Their thinking and perspectives clearly influenced the direction of chapter 3. We are indebted to many colleagues at a number of universities who provided helpful input about their own projects and patiently answered our inquiries. A partial list includes Lynette Bradley (Oxford), Carol Sue Englert (Michigan State), Jill Fitzgerald (North Carolina), Steve Graham (Maryland), Karen Harris (Maryland), Annemarie S. Palincsar (Michigan State), and Taffy Raphael (Michigan State). We thank the Department of Psychology of the University of Western Ontario for providing the course credit opportunity to permit the completion of this work.

Mike Pressley particularly acknowledges Donna Forrest-Pressley's patience for those occasions when working on chapters for the book prevented getting other things done. Tim Pressley often played quietly in Daddy's home office as MP reworked parts of the first edition manuscript. As Pressley worked on the revision, there were many breaks for Dad and Tim to practice Tim's pitching. Father is now teaching his son strategies for striking out opponents.

We also acknowledge the contributions of the teachers from the Peel Board of Education who commented on the first chapter: Dawn Coulter, Greta Blance, Elaine Jackson, Jack Uchida, Lavar Snyder.

Michael Pressley was supported by an operating grant from the Natural Sciences and Engineering Research Council of Canada during the period when the first edition of book was written. The student associates were supported partially by the Natural Sciences and Engineering Research Council of Canada and partially through funds administered by the Faculty of Social Sciences and the Graduate School of the University of Western Ontario. During the revising process, Pressley received support from the National Reading Research Center; Woloshyn was supported by the Social Sciences Research Council of Canada.

CHAPTER 1

Introduction to Cognitive Strategy Instruction

Over the past several years, cognitive strategy instruction has emerged as a hot topic in educational research. Nonetheless, strategy instruction has not been incorporated into the curriculum on a large scale (e.g., Applebee, 1984, 1986; Durkin, 1979; Thompson, 1985). This discouraging state of affairs is largely because strategy instruction is not always easy for educators to understand or to implement (Pressley, Goodchild, Fleet, Zajchowski, & Evans, 1989). Even so, recent theory and research should do much to increase the likelihood that strategy instruction will be deployed in classrooms (Pressley with McCormick, 1995; Pressley, Symons, Snyder, & Cariglia-Bull, 1989; Symons, Snyder, Cariglia-Bull, & Pressley, 1989).

First, new theoretical models of competent thinking are more complete and educationally relevant than their predecessors. Autonomous strategy use is characterized in these models as a complex interaction of many factors, most of which are potentially modifiable through instruction. The complexity of these new models makes them more realistic, which should appeal to educators. Second, educational tasks are also being analyzed carefully so that the processing required to carry them out can be specified. These detailed analyses are an important prerequisite to the development of strategy instruction programs. They also assist in explaining to teachers how strategies match the tasks their students face. Third, more complete models of instruction have emerged as a result of both the current models of good thinking and more detailed knowledge of what constitutes competent performance on specific tasks. These instructional models address the important and modifiable components of the thinking process in general and the relevant aspects of some important instructional tasks (e.g., reading comprehension, problem solving).

In this chapter, we elaborate on the ways that research and theory are contributing to the development of strategy instruction that can be deployed in actual classrooms. We also indicate in this introductory chapter how this volume attempts to bridge the gap between the researcher and educator communities.

EDUCATIONALLY RELEVANT MODELS OF COMPETENT THINKING

For the most part, the theoretical roots of current models of competent thinking lie in the general information-processing approach to cognition. Accordingly, current models assume that people initially register information from the environment in their sensory organs (i.e., the eyes, ears, nose etc.). Some of that information is filtered out (ignored) at the sensory level, while the remainder enters short-term memory (consciousness). Short-term memory has a limited capacity to maintain information and thus its contents must be processed in some way (e.g., rehearsed), or they will fade quickly. If processed, information from short-term memory may transfer into long-term memory. The long-term store contains factual information (i.e., declarative knowledge) as well as information about how to do things (i.e., procedural knowledge) (e.g., Anderson, 1983).

Contemporary models of thinking (e.g., Baron, 1985; Brown, Bransford, Ferrara, & Campione, 1983; Sternberg, 1985) are pertinent to educators because they emphasize the aspects of information processing that can be modified through instruction (i.e., the contents of long-term memory) as opposed to the instructionally unmodifiable "architectural" components (i.e., the sensory organs per se or the neurological elements of short- and long-term memory). According to recent models, for instance, the important features of thinking include strategies (procedural knowledge), knowledge about those strategies and about one's own thinking processes (metacognition), knowledge about the world in general (the knowledge base; e. g., elements of cultural and scientific literacy), motivational beliefs, and overall cognitive style (e.g., Baron, 1985; Borkowski, Carr, Rellinger, & Pressley, 1990; Meichenbaum, 1977; Nicholls, 1990). These components operate in interaction. Whereas older models of thinking emphasized the "hardware" and/or a few "critical" cognitive processes (e.g., Atkinson & Shiffrin, 1968), these recent conceptualizations address the cognitive, metacognitive, and social-emotional aspects of thinking that both affect classroom functioning and can be altered using instruction. Thus, recent models of thinking are both more complete and more educationally relevant than their predecessors.

The Components of Good Information Processing

We are partial to one particular description of thinking: the good information processor model (e.g., Pressley, 1986; Pressley, Borkowski, & Schneider, 1987, 1989; Pressley with McCormick, 1995). According to this framework, a good strategy user is one who possesses a variety of strategies and uses these procedures to meet cognitive challenges. These strategies include "tricks" that aid in the performance of very specific tasks. For example, the name "ROY G. BIV" can be used to remember the order of the colors in the spectrum (i.e., Red, Orange, Yellow, Green, Blue, Indigo, and Violet). This is an example of a first-letter mnemonic strategy (Morris, 1979). There are also more generally applicable strategies including procedures for reading (e.g., self-questioning, constructing representational images, activating prior knowledge, and rereading difficult-to-understand sections of text), problem solving (e.g., means-ends analysis, working forward), writing (e.g., plan, draft, review, & revise tactics), and memorizing (e.g., repetition; relating to previously acquired, associated material). There are also strategies for regulating and promoting the use of other strategies. These include allocating attention to a task, monitoring performance, and searching for relationships between the present task and others that were previously accomplished via strategic mediation. Some more general strategic processes like monitoring sometimes generate information about whether a particular strategy is facilitating task performance (i.e., metacognitive knowledge). In turn, this knowledge permits decisions about whether to continue with a strategy currently in use or abandon it in favor of a potentially more effective approach.

Strategies are rarely used in isolation. Rather, they are integrated into higher-order sequences that accomplish complex cognitive goals. For example, good reading may begin with previewing, activation of prior knowledge about the topic of a to-be-read text, and self-questioning about what might be presented in the text. These prereading activities are then followed by careful reading, reviewing, and rereading as necessary. General strategies (e.g., self-testing) are used to monitor whether subgoals have been accomplished, prompting the reader to move on when it is appropriate to do so or motivating reprocessing when subgoals have not been met. That is, good information processors evaluate whether the strategies they are using are producing progress toward goals they have set for themselves. With years of practice, these repertoires of processes are used automatically and flexibly (Pressley & Afflerbach, 1995).

Such proficiency depends on knowing when and where to use the strategies a person knows, the benefits that follow from using the procedures, and the amount of effort required to carry out strategies. This metacognitive knowledge about strategies enables the good information processor to recognize when particular strategies are appropriate and to decide whether the potential benefits of strategy use are worth the costs in terms of effort. Eventually such "sizing up" can be done quickly and without much thought.

Appropriate motivational beliefs also can facilitate competent thinking. Good information processors see themselves as able to control their own cognitive performance and, thus, they are motivated to devote effort and attention to strategic processing (Clifford, 1984; McCombs, 1980). Particular cognitive styles can also benefit performance. Good information processors tend to shield strategic processing from competing behaviors, distractions, and emotions (e.g., Kuhl, 1985). They are neither impulsive nor reflective to the point of inaction, but rather, they are appropriately reflective (Baron, 1985; Meichenbaum, 1977). Although they may experience appropriate anxiety when work is not complete (i.e., enough anxiety to motivate doing the work), they are not highly anxious and certainly not to the point that anxiety disrupts cognition (e.g., Tobias, 1979).

Finally, the nonstrategic knowledge base also plays an important role in competent thinking. Sometimes this knowledge base diminishes the need to execute strategies. For instance, serious baseball fans might watch an inning of the game and remember how every out was made—without exerting any strategic effort. For these fans, the knowledge base is so well developed with respect to baseball that they can readily assimilate new information about the game (e.g., Spilich, Vesonder, Chiesi, & Voss, 1979). On the other hand, baseball fans, most of whom are not specialists in neurology or medicine, would remember the names of the twelve cranial nerves more quickly if they used a mnemonic strategy than if they simply read over a list of the twelve names.

A broad knowledge base is often advantageous because it enables the use of particular strategies. For instance, there is evidence to suggest that the prereading strategy of activating prior knowledge about a topic only improves retention of unfamiliar prose material if the reader possesses a good deal of knowledge about the topic. Child soccer experts, for example, process prose about soccer more effectively when they intentionally activate their knowledge about soccer before reading than when they do not activate this knowledge. The same strategy, however, does not benefit students who know little about soccer (e.g., Hasselhorn & Körkel, 1980).

The Good Information Processor

Although we have discussed the components of good information processing separately, they operate interactively. When confronted with a task, the good information processor attends to it and exerts effort toward meeting the goal in the belief that appropriately expended effort will lead to competent performance. For many familiar tasks, the situation automatically elicits appropriate strategic procedures. For example, an experienced journalist may unconsciously use a plan-draft-review-revise sequence of strategies to prepare an article (e.g., Flower & Hayes, 1981), while consciously attending only to the content of the piece that is being written. When faced with not-so-familiar tasks, on the other hand, the good information processor analyzes the situation and attempts to identify similarities between the current problem and more familiar tasks. A student may notice, for example, that a problem now being tackled is much like the time-distance problems studied in algebra class (Mayer, Larkin, & Kadane, 1984).

When similarities are identified, strategies associated with the previous situation are triggered (e.g., "I'll try to work this out like problems that are solved with distance = speed X time"). An orderly strategic plan is then formed (e.g., identify the distance, speed, and time elements of the problem, and organize them into the d = st equation). Use of the strategy and generation of a solution is facilitated by the knowledge base (e.g., mastery of the basic "math facts"). Next, performance is monitored as the strategy is being executed to determine whether there is progress toward the goal. If the problem is only superficially similar to those encountered previously, the strategies that are generated may be inappropriate (e.g., if there is more than one speed mentioned in the problem at hand and several seem necessary to solve the problem, the inadequacy of the d = st procedure would become obvious). The student might then try to substitute other strategies until one is identified that works (e. g., this is a problem that should be set up as speed X time = speed X time). See Table 1-1 for a summary of these elements of good information processing.

Selection, conscious execution, and monitoring of strategies consume short-term memory capacity (e. g., Baddeley, 1980; Case, 1985; Kahnemann, 1973); that is, they are carried out using the consciousness that is short-term memory capacity. Selection, execution, and monitoring of strategies all become more automatic with practice, however, and hence require less capacity with additional experience (e.g., Logan, 1985; Schneider, Dumais, & Shiffrin, 1984). Consider a child who is learning to use reading comprehension strategies. The child might

Table 1-1
Elements of Good Information Processing

Use of efficient strategies to accomplish important tasks.

Knowing when and where to use particular strategies, eventually to the point that procedures are used appropriately and automatically.

Coordination of strategies to accomplish complex goals (e.g., skilled reading involves a sequence of reading comprehension strategies), eventually to the point that this occurs automatically and flexibly.

Monitoring use of strategies to determine if progress is being made toward cognitive goals.

Possession of extensive world knowledge, especially about cultural and scientific categories of information that are important to know in order to comprehend events and function competently in contemporary society.

Motivational beliefs that promote good thinking (e.g., believing that it is possible to become a better thinker by learning and using appropriate strategies and acquiring relevant world knowledge).

A cognitive style that supports competent thinking (i.e., appropriately reflective and attentive; not overly anxious).

practice procedures such as directing attention to relevant parts of text, self-testing, and summarizing. At first, the use of these strategies may be clumsy, and consume most, if not all, of the child's short-term memory capacity, leaving few cognitive resources (i.e., little consciousness) available for the other demands of reading (e.g., integrating what is being read with prior knowledge). With practice, however, the strategies can be carried out more quickly and efficiently, with much less short-term capacity being consumed in the process. That is, strategy use gets easier and more effective with practice (see Pressley & Afflerbach, 1995).

Task Analysis of Important Educational Tasks

Many tasks that students commonly encounter in the classroom have been carefully analyzed by educational researchers in order to determine the steps or processes involved in successful performance—that is, the strategies students need to execute to do the task well. This type of research, known as *task analysis*, has been carried out in various educational domains such as mathematics (Derry, Hawkes, & Tsai, 1987; Mayer, 1986a), problem-solving (Gick, 1980), reading comprehension (Bereiter & Bird, 1985; Garner, 1987), and writing (Hayes & Flower, 1980; Scardamalia & Bereiter, 1986a, 1986b). Successful writers, for instance, follow a sequence that involves planning the composition, writing a draft, reviewing the draft to determine whether the goals set in the planning stage have been met, and finally, performing revisions. Each step in this general sequence can be broken down further into component processes on the basis of additional task analysis (Englert, Raphael, Anderson, Anthony, & Stevens, 1991), and the entire cycle or parts of it are repeated a number of times as writing proceeds.

Task analysis is an important step in the development of new strategies and strategy instruction. This information is necessary to develop maximally efficient strategies. Strategies developed on the basis of task analysis emphasize the steps that are necessary and sufficient to complete a task successfully. Indeed, many powerful strategies have been derived from task-analytic research (see Gagné, 1985; Mayer, 1986a, 1987), including procedures for vocabulary learning (e.g., Pressley, Levin, & McDaniel, 1987), communication (e.g., Elliott-Faust, Pressley, & Dalecki, 1986), and problem solving (e.g., Butterfield, 1989). In general, each strategy presented in this book is nothing more than a listing of the processes required to accomplish a particular task efficiently, although again and again it will be emphasized that learning to use strategies is not the mechanized sequencing of processes, but rather a *flexible, constructive execution of the processes* needed to carry out important academic tasks.

OVERVIEW OF THIS VOLUME'S ORGANIZATION

Each of the succeeding chapters covers a different part of the elementary school curriculum. Some chapters are longer than others, with length determined by the number of well-studied strategies more than by any other factor. Some of these areas are of greater concern to contemporary researchers than are others. The large number of recent references in the reading comprehension, writing, and mathematics chapters reflects great interest in these areas by contemporary researchers.

Each chapter begins with a conceptual overview. We present this information because of a conviction that the reflective teaching practitioner will want to know why the particular strategies are being proposed. These short reviews are not meant to substitute for more in-depth treatments of the issues. The reference list directs interested readers to more extensive coverage of the topics, with references placed at the end of each chapter (rather than having a composite list for the entire volume). We did this to provide reading lists of what we regard as the best available strategy-instructional research for each of the instructional areas covered in the book.

Three types of strategies are presented in this book. Some strategies are principally ones that teachers can use in presenting material. Thus, presenting mnemonic pictures to aid memory of letter-sound associations is a teaching strategy. So is a type of decoding instruction that is conveyed with a computer program. These will be identified with a [T] when first introduced in the text. Then there are strategies that students could acquire and use on their own. Teaching students a procedure to increase memory of vocabulary, a procedure which they can carry out on their own, is one example of this type of strategy. Each of these, designated as a strategy that can be student self-regulated, will be identified with an [SSR] when first presented in the text. Those strategies that teachers can use to improve their presentations and which eventually can lead to student self-regulated strategy use are marked [T & SSR]. One example would be writing instruction that begins with a teacher providing prompts to improve writing and leads to students eventually prompting themselves.

Student self-regulated strategies are particularly important, but must be taught in a particular way if students are eventually to control the procedures. How to teach such strategies so that students eventually do self-regulate their use of them is becoming better understood, and is covered in detail in the next section.

TEACHING FOR SELF-REGULATED STRATEGY USE

Both researchers and educators are studying the issue of *how* to teach strategies most effectively in order to increase the likelihood that students will use strategies autonomously, that is, in a self-regulated fashion. Recent interest in this issue has led to the emergence of several new models of instruction, including the good information processor perspective on instruction (Pressley, 1986), the Kansas strategy intervention model (Deshler, Schumaker, & Lenz, 1984; Deshler & Schumaker, 1988), direct explanation (e.g., Duffy & Roehler, 1986, 1987; Duffy, Roehler, & Putnam, 1987), and the training arithmetic problem-solving skills model (TAPS) (e.g., Derry, et al., 1987). The first two examples are general prescriptions for instruction across domains, whereas the second two address strategy instruction within the domains of reading and mathematical problem-solving, respectively.

While these models differ superficially with respect to terminology and emphasis, they also have many similarities. Rather than review each one in detail, we have chosen to focus on commonalities. In general, there is a common pedagogical perspective in these models: All of the components of good information processing receive instructional attention. That is, metacognitive information about strategies (e.g., when and where to use them), nonstrategic knowledge, and appropriate motivational beliefs are imparted as strategies are taught. Moreover, the teaching is decidedly constructivist—the teacher explanations and modeling are the start of a process by which students construct understanding of the strategy by using it (Moshman, 1982; Pressley, Harris, & Marks, 1992).

Strategies

Recent instructional prescriptions suggest that students should be taught effective strategies that are well-matched to the actual tasks that are presented in school. Current models favor teaching only a few strategies at a time and teaching them well, as opposed to teaching many strategies concurrently and superficially. New strategies are introduced once old ones are well known. Strategy instruction is perceived as a long-term endeavor because the learning of individual strategies takes time (more later in this chapter about this), and there are a number of important strategies that can be taught (Pressley et al., 1989), although a main theme of this volume is that the number is not insurmountable.

Monitoring

Recent models of strategy instruction emphasize that students should be taught to monitor how they are doing. As students execute strategies, they should be taught to check performance in order to keep track of their progress. They should also be encouraged to try to remediate any problems they experience. On-line checking of cognitive progress needs to be taught since even good students sometimes fail to monitor performance adequately and/or fail to take corrective measures when problems are spotted (e.g., Garner, 1987; Markman, 1981; Schneider &

Pressley, 1989, Ch. 7).

Metacognition about Strategies

Making certain that students know when and where to use strategies is another important aspect of strategy instruction. This information may be explained to students directly, or it may be abstracted by students during extensive practice across settings where strategies can be employed. The former tactic is preferable since children are not efficient at discovering metacognitive information on their own (Pressley, Borkowski, & O'Sullivan, 1984, 1985; Pressley, Levin, & Ghatala, 1984), nor do they automatically apply it even if it is independently discovered (e.g., Pressley, Ross, Levin, & Ghatala, 1984). Abstracting metacognitive information during strategy practice is more likely to work if students are taught methods for noting when and whether the strategies they are using work (e.g., if they are taught to compare how they do with a strategy versus how they do when not using the strategy) (Pressley, Borkowski, & O'Sullivan, 1984; Pressley & Ghatala, 1990). Opportunities that make clear when strategies work are essential if metacognition about strategies is to develop (Pressley, Levin, & Ghatala, 1988).

It is necessary to impart metacognitive information about strategies because of the critical role it plays in the generalization and maintenance of strategies. In order to deploy strategies broadly and appropriately, students must possess knowledge about when and where strategies should be used—that is, teaching metacognitive information about strategies boils down largely to making certain that students know when the strategies they are learning should be deployed.

Student Motivation

Students are most likely to be motivated to use strategies if they are aware that strategic procedures do in fact enhance performance. Thus, strategy instruction should include explicit information about the utility of the strategies being taught. Explanations as to how strategies can be helpful, feedback about strategy-mediated performance, and having students chart their progress while using strategies may all serve to increase motivation.

In a more global sense, children also need to be made aware that competent functioning is often a result of using appropriate strategies rather than superior innate ability or just trying hard. Students should be taught that they can become competent thinkers by employing the strategies used by successful learners. It should be emphasized to students that strategies are processes that resemble what really good students do when they tackle tasks in school. Students who believe that they can become more intellectually competent by learning the procedures used by competent people should have high motivation to learn the strategies described in later chapters of this book.

Styles

Students need to be encouraged to adopt a general intellectual style that is consistent with good strategy use. The instructional setting should promote a comfortable, reflective pace and calm academic activity rather than anxiety. When given an academic task, students need to know that it is appropriate to reflect upon what is required in that particular situation. Make students aware of the need to shield themselves from distractions when doing academic work. Let them know the importance of attention to tasks and encourage appropriate reflection on what *ways* they can approach the task.

Teaching in Context

Strategies should not be taught as a separate topic in the curriculum. Rather, they should be taught throughout the curriculum as part of the actual academic tasks that students encounter. Important strategies are best learned when they are practiced with the kinds of materials that students are expected to master when using the strategies. Thus, when students are given a writing assignment as part of a social studies unit, this is an opportunity to teach strategic procedures for producing high quality written compositions.

Interactions Between Strategies and the Knowledge Base

The teaching of strategies alone is not sufficient. The competent thinker possesses many pieces of knowledge, and strategy use is often dependent on this knowledge. Successful performance is not attributable to either strategies or knowledge independently (e.g., Glaser, 1984) but rather, to strategies and nonstrategic knowledge operating together. Thus, instructional attention should be given to expanding the student's knowledge base in addition to expanding his or her repertoire of strategies. But if students master effective strategies (e.g., reading comprehension strategies), it should be easier for them to learn more and to do so more efficiently than they would otherwise. Thus, strategy instruction can promote the goal of content learning and is in no way antagonistic to it.

Interactive Direct Teaching

Contemporary models of instruction advocate direct explanation and/ or modeling of strategic procedures. There is gradual releasing of control from the teacher to the student, with teachers resuming greater control as needed. Thus, teachers describe and model strategies initially, and then allow a great deal of student practice in order for students to master those strategies. This practice is monitored by the teacher, who provides individually tailored corrective feedback and encouragement. It is to be expected that mastery of a strategy will take some time and a lot of re-explanations. It takes a while for students to construct knowledge of a strategy, its adaptive use, and its appropriate application. Generalization of strategies is promoted by explicitly providing guidance and reminders to students about when and how strategies can be extended to new situations. This direct explanation approach contrasts with alternative models that view the teacher as someone who should explain procedures briefly and then assign unsupervised practice, or as someone who should supervise discovery learning procedures (see Brainerd, 1978; Pressley, Snyder, & Cariglia-Bull, 1987).

Summary

A general outline of how to teach a strategy can be drawn from the common pedagogical perspective of current instructional models. The first step in teaching a strategy is to describe the strategy to students. This can be accomplished by the teacher modeling actual use of the strategy, particularly with "thinking aloud" statements about how to execute the procedure. Descriptions of the strategy include important metacognitive information such as why the strategy should be used, what it accomplishes, and specific situations in which the strategy is applicable.

Once students know the steps that comprise a strategy, they should be given plenty of guided practice, during which the teacher provides reinforcement as well as feedback about how to improve execution of the strategy. Practice should begin with fairly simple materials and progress to grade-appropriate work. Because instruction is given until students can execute the strategy proficiently, there is a great deal of responsibility on the teacher to monitor student progress, diagnose student difficulties, and adjust instruction accordingly. A lot of teacher and student effort is required for students to construct knowledge of strategies.

Strategy generalization and adaptive application of strategies are encouraged by having students practice strategies with different types of materials (e.g., a summarizing strategy could be practiced with social studies, science, and general interest articles). Strategy use should also be prompted during the course of the school day when situations arise in which the procedure can be used. Students should be taught to be alert for cues in the instructional environment indicating that a strategy might apply. Throughout instruction, the teacher emphasizes the utility of the strategy itself as well as the importance of strategy use in general.

Strategy instruction should be explicit, intensive, and extensive. The ultimate goal is to have students using the trained strategies autonomously, skillfully, appropriately, and creatively. Strategies should be taught to students directly over an extended period of time as part of the existing curriculum. Other components of effective thinking such as metacognition, motivation, and the nonstrategic knowledge base must also be addressed by instruction. That is, students are provided input about when and where to use the strategies they are learning; they are shown how their performance improves by using the right strategies, with a lot of emphasis on the theme that learning how to do important tasks is a critical part of intellectual development. *Teaching of important content is not sacrificed in order to teach strategies, but rather teaching of strategies is integrated with teaching of content.* By attending to both the strategic and nonstrategic elements of competent performance, contemporary models of strategy instruction are more complete than

---

Table 1-2
General Model of How to Teach Strategies

Teach a few strategies at a time, intensively and extensively, as part of the ongoing curriculum; in the beginning, teach only one at a time, until students are familiar with the "idea" of strategy use.

Model and explain each new strategy.

Model again and re-explain strategies in ways that are sensitive to aspects of strategy use that are not well understood. (The students are constructing their understanding of the strategy, refining the understanding a little bit at a time.)

Explain to student where and when to use strategies, although students will also discover some such metacognitive information as they use strategies.

Provide plenty of practice, using strategies for as many appropriate tasks as possible. Such practice increases proficient execution of the strategy, knowledge of how to adapt it, and knowledge of when to use it.

Encourage students to monitor how they are doing when they are using strategies.

Encourage continued use of and generalization of strategies, for example, by reminding students throughout the school day about when they could apply strategies they are learning about.

Increase students' motivation to use strategies by heightening student awareness that they are acquiring valuable skills that are at the heart of competent functioning with learning tasks.

Emphasize reflective processing rather than speedy processing; do all possible to eliminate high anxiety in students; encourage students to shield themselves from distraction so they can attend to the academic task.

previous ones, which emphasized brief instruction of strategies and focussed only on teaching the steps required to carry out the strategic procedures. The most important teaching recommendations are summarized in Table 1-2.

CLOSING THE GAP BETWEEN RESEARCH AND PRACTICE

Strategy instruction that addresses the elements of good information processing is clearly not a simple matter. It is a long-term endeavor that cuts across all areas of the school curriculum. Thus, widespread practice of strategy instruction may require changes in teacher training, instructional methods, and the current curriculum (Pressley et al., 1989). Given these obstacles to implementation, it is not very surprising that strategy instruction is not widespread at this point in time. It is our perspective, however, that changes in the ways that information about strategy instruction is disseminated may increase teachers' abilities and willingness to teach strategies. That was the greatest motivation for writing this book!

There are a number of obstacles to the dissemination of information about strategies and strategy instruction. These include the large number of strategies, the lack of evaluation data for many strategies, and the inaccessability to practitioners of existing research that is normally published in academic journals. Essentially, these obstacles boil down to poor communications between researchers and those for whom their work has direct implications. Unless information produced in educational research is available, manageable, and appealing to practitioners, it will have no impact. We feel that researchers would do well to create a positive regard for strategy instruction on the part of educators. To this end, researchers must demonstrate they have something concrete to offer in the way of effective, teachable strategies.

The current instructional literature is filled with strategy suggestions (e.g., Chipman, Segal, & Glaser, 1985; Segal, Chipman, & Glaser, 1985; Nickerson, Perkins, & Smith, 1985). Such a large volume of strategies would be overwhelming if a teacher had to to teach all or most of them. Moreover, the literature would be difficult to sort through for someone who wishes to select only a few strategies to present in the classroom. This state of affairs may discourage educator interest from the very beginning, and does little to encourage a positive regard for strategy instruction.

To complicate matters, many of the strategies that are advocated in the curriculum literature have not been adequately evaluated. Often, strategies are promoted on the basis of meagre evidence or their theoretical and intuitive appeal. Some strategies are offered commercially and adapted by educators only because they "seem like they should work" or they "sound good." This is a serious problem because resources are wasted when the strategies that are taught are ineffective or, worse yet, harmful to students. In addition, when educators recognize that a strategy does not lead to the gains it was supposed to produce, there may be a sense that all of strategy instruction is a hoax. In short, it is a real challenge for educators to obtain sufficient information to separate strategies that have not been evaluated from those that have been tested, and then to separate the ones that produce important educational gains from those that do not.

This book should alleviate some of the problems related to the dissemination of information about strategies. Specifically, we have identified teachable strategies for many areas of the elementary school curriculum. Most strategies presented here have been tested in true experiments (Campbell & Stanley, 1966); a few are the products of qualitative evaluations (e.g., Strauss & Corbin, 1990). A few, however, have yet to prove their worth in true experiments, either because the validation studies have not been completed at the time of this writing, or they were evaluated in a nonexperimental fashion. In every case, however, there is at least some data-based analysis suggesting the method improves student performance, though in a few cases uncontrolled pretest-posttest designs were used so that whether strategy instruction is causing the performance gains cannot be determined with confidence. (Strategies not yet evaluated in true experiments will be cited as such when they are presented.) This book is not an exhaustive catalogue of strategies that can be taught to children, but rather, a selective presentation of procedures that have the most evidence to support their use with elementary school-age children.

This book contains a small, but well-substantiated, list of strategies that any teacher of elementary children can use to begin a strategy instruction program encompassing many areas of the curriculum. Most of the strategies are ones that many students can learn to execute on their own (i.e., they have the potential to become student self-regulated strategies [SSRs]). These strategies should be taught according to the guidelines for instruction presented earlier in this chapter.

We reiterate the strong recommendation to try teaching only a few strategies at a time, to model and to explain those few strategies a lot, to re-explain them as necessary, and to be prepared to do a lot of re-explanation. Make certain that students know when and where to use the strategies that they learn. All of this is part of student construction of good information processing abilities.

Teaching strategies in the context of social studies, science, and literary tasks that children are expected to accomplish as part of the elementary curriculum increases the likelihood children will learn the applicability of strategies to actual educational tasks.

Although a clear focus of this volume is the development of students who know and use strategies, we are also including teaching strategies (the [T] strategies) because they complement well the main goal of teaching students to use strategies: Teaching students to execute effective strategies makes good student performance more likely; so should the use of teaching strategies. In summary, there are a lot of suggestions in this volume for improving student performance on academic tasks, including both ways of increasing students' self-directed use of efficient processing and ways of improving teachers' presentation of materials.

REFERENCES

Anderson, J.R. (1983). *The architecture of cognition*. Cambridge, MA: Harvard University Press.

Applebee, A.N. (1984). *Contexts for learning to write*. Norwood, NJ: Ablex.

Applebee, A.N. (1986). Problems in process approaches: Toward a reconceptualization of process instruction. In A.R. Petrosky, P. Bartholomae, & K.J. Rehage (Eds.), *The teaching of writing; Eighty-fifth Yearbook of the National Society for the Study of Education* (pp. 95-113). Chicago: University of Chicago Press.

Atkinson, R.C., & Shiffrin, R.M. (1968). Human memory: A proposed system and its control processes. In W. Spence & J.T. Spence (Eds.), *The psychology of learning and motivation* (Vol. 2). New York: Academic Press.

Baddeley, A. (1980). *Working memory*. New York: Oxford University Press.

Baron, J. (1985). *Rationality and intelligence*. Cambridge, England: Cambridge University Press.

Bereiter, C., & Bird, M. (1985). Use of thinking aloud in identification and teaching of reading comprehension strategies. *Cognition and Instruction, 2*, 91-130.

Borkowski, J.G., Carr, M., Rellinger, E., & Pressley, M. (1990). Self-regulated cognition: Interdependence of metacognition, attributions, and self-esteem. In B.F. Jones & L. Idol (Eds.), *Dimensions of thinking and cognitive instruction* (pp. 53-92). Hillsdale, NJ: Lawrence Erlbaum Associates.

Brainerd, C.J. (1978). Learning research and Piagetian theory. In L.S. Siegel & C.J. Brainerd (Eds.), *Alternatives to Piaget: Critical essays on the theory* (pp. 69- 109). New York: Academic Press.

Brown, A.L., Bransford, J.P., Ferrara, R.A., & Campione, J.C. (1983). Learning, remembering, and understanding. In J.H. Flavell & E.M. Markman (Eds.), *Handbook of child psychology: vol. 3. Cognitive development* (pp. 177-206). New York: John Wiley & Sons.

Butterfield, E. C. (1989). On solving the transfer problem. In M. Gruneberg, M., Sykes, R.N., & Morris, P.E. (Eds.), *Proceedings of the second conference on the practical aspects of memory*. London: John Wiley & Sons.

Campbell, P.T., & Stanley, J.C. (1966). *Experimental and quasiexperimental designs for research*. Chicago: Rand McNally.

Case, R. (1985). *Intellectual development*. Orlando, FL: Academic Press.

Chipman, S F., Segal, J.W., & Glaser, R. (Eds.) (1985). *Thinking and learning skills: Vol. 2. Research and open questions*. Hillsdale, NJ: Lawrence Erlbaum Associates.

Clifford, M.M. (1984). Thoughts on a theory of constructive failure. *Educational Psychologist, 19*, 108-120.

Derry, S.J., Hawkes, L.W., & Tsai, C-J. (1987). A theory for remediating problem-solving skills of older children and adults. *Educational Psychologist, 22*, 55-87.

Deshler, P.P., & Schumaker, J.B. (1988). An instructional model for teaching students how to learn. In J.L. Graden, J.E. Zins, & M.J. Curtis (Eds.), *Alternative educational delivery systems: Enhancing instructional options for all students* (pp. 391-411). Washington, DC: National Association of School Psychologists.

Deshler, D.P., Schumaker, J.B., & Lenz, B.K. (1984). Academic and cognitive interventions for LD adolescents (Part I). *Journal of Learning Disabilities, 17*, 108-117.

Duffy, G.G., & Roehler, L.R. (1986). *Improving classroom reading instruction: A decision-making approach*. New York: Random House.

Duffy, G.G., & Roehler, L.R. (1987). Improving reading instruction through the use of responsive elaboration. *The Reading Teacher, 40*, 514-520.

Duffy, G.G., Roehler, L.R., & Putnam, J. (1987). Putting the teacher in control: Basal textbooks and teacher decision making. *Elementary School Journal, 87*, 357-366.

Durkin, D. (1979). What classroom observations reveal about reading comprehension instruction. *Reading Research Quarterly, 14*, 481-538.

Elliott-Faust, D.J., Pressley, M., & Dalecki, L.B. (1986). Process training to improve children's referential communication: Asher and Wigfield (1981) revisited. *Journal of Educational Psychology, 78*, 22-26.

Englert, C.S., Raphael, T.E., Anderson, L.M., Anthony, H.M., & Stevens, D.D. (1991). Making strategies and self-talk visible: Writing instruction in regular and special education classrooms. *American Educational Research Journal, 28*, 337-372.

Flower, L.S., & Hayes, J.R. (1981). A cognitive process theory of writing. *College Composition and Communication, 32*, 305-387.

Gagné, E.D. (1985). *The cognitive psychology of school learning*. Boston: Little, Brown, & Co.

Garner, R. (1987). *Metacognition and reading comprehension*. Norwood, NJ: Ablex.

Gick, M. L. (1980). Problem-solving strategies. *Educational Psychologist, 21*, 99-120.

Glaser, R. (1984). Education and thinking: The role of knowledge. *American Psychologist, 39*, 93-104.

Hasselhorn, M., & Körkel, J. (1980). Metacognitive versus traditional reading instructions: The mediating role of domain-specific knowledge on children's text processing. *Human Learning, 5*, 75-90.

Hayes, J.R., & Flower, L.S. (1980). Identifying the organization of writing processes. In L.W. Gregg & E.R. Steinberg (Eds.), *Cognitive processes in writing* (pp. 3-30). Hillsdale, NJ: Lawrence Erlbaum Associates.

Kahnemann, P. (1973). *Attention and effort.* Englewood Cliffs, NJ: Prentice Hall.

Kuhl, J. (1985). Volitional mediators of cognition-behavior consistency: Self-regulatory processes and action control versus state orientation. In J. Kuhl & J. Beckmann (Eds.), *Action control: From cognition to behavior* (pp. 101-128). New York: Springer-Verlag.

Logan, G.P. (1985). Skill and automaticity: Relations, implications, and future directions. *Canadian Journal of Psychology, 39*, 367-386.

Markman, E.M. (1981). Comprehension monitoring. In W.P. Dickson (Ed.), *Children's oral communication skills* (pp. 61-84). New York: Academic Press.

Mayer, R.E. (1986a). Mathematics. In R.F. Dillon & R.J. Sternberg (Eds.), *Cognition and instruction* (pp. 127-154). Orlando FL: Academic Press.

Mayer, R.E. (1986b). Teaching students how to think and learn: A look at some instructional programs and the research: A review of J.W. Segal, S.F. Chipman, & R. Glaser's (1985) *Thinking and learning skills: Vol. 1. Relating instruction to research* and S.F. Chipman, J.W. Segal, & R. Glaser's (1985) *Thinking and learning skills: Vol. 2. Research and open questions. Contemporary Psychology, 31* 753-756.

Mayer, R.E. (1987). *Educational psychology: A cognitive approach.* Boston, MA: Little, Brown, & Co.

Mayer, R.E., Larkin, J.H., & Kadane, J. (1984). A cognitive analysis of mathematical problem solving ability. In R. Sternberg (Ed.), *Advances in the psychology of human intelligence,* (Vol. 2, pp. 231-273). Hillsdale, NJ: Lawrence Erlbaum Associates.

McCombs, B.L. (1986). The role of the self-system in self-regulated learning. *Contemporary Educational Psychology, 11*, 314-332.

Meichenbaum, P.M. (1977). *Cognitive behavior modification.* New York: Plenum.

Morris, P.E. (1979). Strategies for learning and recall. In M.M. Gruneberg & P.E. Morris (Eds.), *Applied problems in memory* (pp. 25-57). London: Academic Press.

Moshman, D. (1982). Exogenous, endogenous, and dialectical constructivism. *Developmental Review, 2*, 371-384.

Nicholls, J.G. (1990). What is ability and why are we mindful of it? A developmental perspective. In R J. Sternberg & J. Kolligian, Jr. (Eds.), *Ccompetence reconsidered* (pp. 11-40). New Haven, CT: Yale University Press.

Nickerson, R.S., Perkins, D.N., & Smith, E.E. (Eds.), (1985). *The teaching of thinking.* Hillsdale, NJ: Lawrence Erlbaum Associates.

Pressley, M. (1986). The relevance of the good strategy user model to the teaching of mathematics. *Educational Psychologist, 21*, 139-161.

Pressley, M., & Afflerbach, P. (in press). *Verbal protocols of reading: The nature of constructively responsive reading.* Hillsdale, NJ: Erlbaum.

Pressley, M., Borkowski, J.G., & O'Sullivan, J.T. (1984). Memory strategy instruction is made of this: Metamemory and durable strategy use. *Educational Psychologist, 19*, 94-107.

Pressley, M., Borkowski, J.G., & O'Sullivan,

J.T. (1985). Children's metamemory and the teaching of memory strategies. In D.L. Forrest-Pressley, G.E. MacKinnon, & T.G. Waller (Eds.), *Metacognition, cognition, and human performance* (pp. 111-153). Orlando, FL: Academic Press.

Pressley, M., Borkowski, J.G., & Schneider, W. (1987). Cognitive strategies: Good strategy users coordinate metacognition and knowledge. In R. Vasta & G. Whitehurst (Eds.), *Annals of Child Development* (Vol. 5, pp. 89-129). New York: JAI Press.

Pressley, M., Borkowski, J.G., & Schneider, W. (1989). Good information processing: What it is and what education can do to promote it. *International Journal of Educational Research, 13,* 857-867.

Pressley, M., Cariglia-Bull, T., & Snyder, B.L. (1984). Are there programs that can really teach thinking and learning skills: A review of Segal, Chipman, & Glaser's *Thinking and learning skills: Vol. 1. Relating instruction to research. Contemporary Education Review, 3,* 435-444.

Pressley, M., & Ghatala, E.S. (1990). Self-regulated learning: Monitoring learning from text. *Educational Psychologist, 25,* 19-34.

Pressley, M., Goodchild, F., Fleet, J., Zajchowski, R., & Evans, E.D. (1989). The challenges of classroom strategy instruction. *Elementary School Journal, 89,* 301-342.

Pressley, M., Harris, K.R., & Marks, M.B. (1992). But good strategy instructors are constructivists! *Educational Psychology Review, 4,* 3-31.

Pressley, M., Johnson, C.J., Symons, S.E., McGoldrick, J., Kurita, J., & Pressley, M. (1988). *Reading comprehension strategies that can be taught efficiently.* Manuscript submitted for publication. London, Ontario: Department of Psychology, University of Western Ontario.

Pressley, M., Levin, J.R., & Ghatala, E.S. (1984). Memory strategy monitoring in adults and children. *Journal of Verbal Learning and Verbal Behavior, 23,* 270-288.

Pressley, M., Levin, J.R., & Ghatala, E.S. (1988). Strategy comparison opportunities promote long-term strategy use. *Contemporary Educational Psychology, 13,* 137-168.

Pressley, M., Levin, J.R., & McDaniel, M.A. (1987). Remembering versus inferring what a word means: Mnemonic and contextual approaches. In M. McKeown & M.E. Curtis (Eds.), *The nature of vocabulary acquisition* (pp. 107-127). Hillsdale, NJ: Lawrence Erl-

baum Associates.

Pressley, M. (with C.B. McCormick) (1995). *Advanced educational psychology for researchers, educators, and policymakers.* New York: HarperCollins.

Pressley, M., Ross, K.A., Levin, J.R., & Ghatala, E.S. (1984). The role of strategy utility knowledge in children's strategy decision making. *Journal of Experimental Child Psychology, 38,* 491-504.

Pressley, M., Snyder, B.L., & Cariglia-Bull, T. (1987). How can good strategy use be taught to children?: Evaluation of six alternative approaches. In S. Cormier & J. Hagman (Eds.), *Transfer of learning: Contemporary research and applications* (pp. 81-121). Orlando, FL: Academic Press.

Pressley, M., Symons, S.E., Snyder, B.L., & Cariglia-Bull, T. (1989). Strategy instruction research is coming of age. *Learning Disabilities Quarterly, 12,* 16-30.

Scardamalia, M., & Bereiter, C. (1986a). Research on written composition. In M.C. Wittrock (Ed.), *Handbook of research on teaching.* New York: Macmillan.

Scardamalia, M., & Bereiter, C. (1986b). Writing. In R.F. Dillon & R.J. Sternberg (Eds.), *Cognition and instruction* (pp. 59-81). Orlando, FL: Academic Press.

Schneider, W., Dumais, S.T., & Shiffrin, R.M. (1984). Automatic and control processing and attention. In R. Parasuraman & D.R. Davies (Eds.), *Varieties of attention* (pp. 1-27). Orlando, FL: Academic Press.

Schneider, W., & Pressley, M. (1989). *Memory development between 2 and 20.* New York & Berlin: Springer-Verlag.

Segal, J.W., Chipman, S.F., & Glaser, R. (Eds.) (1985). *Thinking and learning skills: Vol. 1. Relating research to instruction.* Hillsdale, NJ: Lawrence Erlbaum Associates.

Spilich, G.J., Vesonder, G.T., Chiesi, H.L., & Voss, J.F. (1979). Text processing of domain-related information for individuals with high and low domain knowledge. *Journal of Verbal Learning and Verbal Behavior, 18,* 275-290.

Sternberg, R.J. (1985). *Beyond IQ: A triarchic theory of human intelligence.* London & New York: Cambridge University Press.

Strauss, A., & Corbin, J. (1990). *Basics of qualitative research: Grounded theory procedure and research.* Newbury Park, CA: Sage Publications.

Symons, S.E., Snyder, B.L., Cariglia-Bull, T., & Pressley, M. (1989). Why be optimistic about cognitive strategy instruction? In C.B. McCormick, G.E. Miller, & M. Pressley (Eds.), *Cognitive strategy research: From basic research to educational applications*. New York & Berlin: Springer-Verlag.

Thompson, A.G. (1985). Teachers' conceptions of mathematics and the teaching of problem solving. In E.A. Silver (Ed.), *Teaching and learning mathematical problem solving* (pp. 281-294). Hillsdale, NJ: Lawrence Erlbaum Associates.

Tobias, S. (1979). Anxiety research in educational psychology. *Journal of Educational Psychology, 71*, 573-582.

CHAPTER 2

Decoding and the Beginnings of Reading

Decoding involves "making sense" out of printed words. It involves learning to discriminate letters from each other, as well as identifying letters and letter clusters. In order to decode successfully, a child must understand how symbols relate to sounds. Word decoding is an important component of early reading skill (Calfee, Lindamood & Lindamood, 1973; Curtis, 1980; Just & Carpenter, 1987; Perfetti & Hogaboam, 1975; Torgeson, 1986), and for many children, decoding is the major skill to be learned during early reading instruction (Just & Carpenter, 1987).

Current theories of reading stress the interactive nature of the components of reading: reading is an information-processing task which changes according to the skills of the reader (Underwood, 1985). According to Perfetti's verbal efficiency theory, decoding skills must be automatic, so that the execution of this process of reading will not require much attentional capacity. By reducing the amount of capacity required for the execution of the decoding process, more capacity is made available for the execution of other higher-order processes, such as comprehension (Lesgold & Perfetti, 1981; Perfetti, Finger & Hogaboam, 1978; Perfetti & Hogaboam, 1975; Perfetti & Roth, 1981).

Whole-Word or Phonics?

Most educators would agree that decoding skills are important in reading. However, there is little consensus with respect to how these skills should be taught. Two historically opposed views to reading instruction are the whole-word and phonics approaches. Whole-word programs stress the importance of reading for meaning and enjoyment (Beck, 1981). Children learn to read words by looking at their global shape. To remember a word, the child is encouraged to think of the meaning of the word while looking at it. There is little emphasis on the specific letters that make up the word. Contextual cues are to be used to recognize unknown words. With continued practice, the child develops his or her sight word vocabulary (Beck, 1981; Just & Carpenter,

1987). In contrast, the phonics approach emphasizes the teaching of symbol-sound correspondences. Phonics instruction precedes the reading lesson: the to-be-read story is made up of words that can be decoded using the phonics skills taught up to that point (Beck, 1981).

Despite unambiguous theoretical distinctions between the two approaches, many programs used today cannot be defined as solely "phonics" or "whole-word": most programs incorporate aspects of both, and it becomes a difference in emphasis (Barr, 1984; Beck, 1981). For example, some programs which emphasize reading for meaning may include a short phonics lesson as a supplement to instruction. Conversely, many phonics-emphasis programs also encourage reading for meaning. Beck (1981) suggests that the difference between the two approaches has dwindled to a difference in the timing of letter-sound instruction: phonics approaches teach these correspondences early in instruction, whereas whole-word programs tend to delay this aspect of instruction until later years of schooling.

Both whole-word and phonics programs have their strengths and weaknesses, and there have been many attempts to determine the "superior method" of instruction. In general, phonics instruction has proven to be superior to the whole-word method with respect to word attack skills (Barr, 1984; Beck, 1981; Gettinger, 1986; Johnson & Baumann, 1984; Just & Carpenter, 1987; Pflaum, Walberg, Karegianes & Rasher, 1980; Vellutino & Scanlon, 1986). Children seem to need to be taught directly the relations between letters and sounds in order to become good, independent readers (Bradley, 1987: Ehri & Wilce, 1983). Early, fairly intensive phonics instruction helps produce readers that are able to pronounce new words accurately (Johnson & Baumann, 1984).

Gettinger (1986) compared the effectiveness of the whole-word and phonics approaches and produced typical results. She found that although the whole-word approach resulted in slightly better performance on trained words, the phonics approach produced far superior performance on transfer words. Imagine how difficult the task of learning to read would be to a child if he/she had to be taught how to read each and every word. Awareness of the relation between graphemes and phonemes encourages the child to be more discriminating in his/her processing of printed words and facilitates the detection of letter-sound patterns which will make learning new words easier (Vellutino & Scanlon, 1986).

Taylor and Taylor (1983) summarized this point in their review of the literature:

> Phonics is necessary for secure decoding of many new words. And it cannot be left entirely to children to induce by themselves, for not all children are bright and not all materials are optimal for induction (p. 384).

What About Whole Language Approaches?

One popular contemporary model of beginning reading instruction, the whole language approach, emphasizes language processes and the creation of learning environments in which children experience authentic reading and writing (Weaver, 1990). Both linguistic and cognitive development are presumed to be stimulated by experiencing excellent literature and attempting to compose new meanings (e.g., Y.M. Goodman, 1990). Whole language opposes explicit, systematic teaching of reading skills, especially elements of decoding. According to whole language theorists, any skills instruction that occurs—including decoding instruction—should be in the context of natural reading and only as needed by individual readers. Whole language advocates believe that the development of literacy is a natural by-product of immersion in high-quality literacy environments.

The evidence is growing that whole language experiences stimulate literate activities and positive attitudes toward literacy in children, as well as increased understanding about the nature of reading and writing (e.g., Graham & Harris, 1994; Morrow, 1990, 1991, 1992; Neuman & Roskos, 1990, 1992). Even so, a disturbing finding is that whole language programs do not seem to make much impact on early reading achievement compared to conventional instruction, as measured by standardized tests of decoding, vocabulary, comprehension, and writing (Graham & Harris, 1994; Stahl, McKenna & Pagnucco, 1994; Stahl & Miller, 1989).

In contrast, programs explicitly teaching phonics and letter-sound analysis have promoted standardized performances and, in particular, have proven superior to programs emphasizing meaning-making, such as whole language (Adams, 1990; Pflaum, Walberg, Karegianes & Rasher, 1980). Thus, we recommend strongly the systematic teaching of decoding skills to primary readers.

This chapter includes a number of strategies that can be used to teach decoding. The list is by no means exhaustive, but rather represents approaches receiving at least some empirical support. First, however, we present important ideas about early literacy which make clear that primary-grade literacy depends on activities that start in the home during the preschool years.

DEVELOPMENT OF EARLY READING COMPETENCE

Literacy development starts during the preschool years, the period of emergent literacy (Sulzby & Teale, 1991). Emergent literacy is reflected in the reading and writing behaviors during the preschool years that precede and develop into conventional literacy.

Nature of Home Environments Supporting Emergent Literacy [T]

The home environment can and should support and facilitate literacy activities. Environments that support emerging literacy include

a) rich interpersonal experiences with parents, brothers and sisters, and others;

b) literacy materials, ranging from plastic refrigerator letters to story books to writing materials; and

c) high positive regard by parents and others for literacy and its development in children (Leichter, 1984; Morrow, 1989).

What are homes like that stimulate emergent literacy? Parents read to the children, helping them with their "reading" and "writing." Parents frequently read themselves, valuing reading as a source of pleasure. There are books everywhere around the home. Parents take their children to libraries and bookstores. Television viewing is limited. For in-depth analyses of home environments supporting emergent literacy, see Clark (1976), Durkin (1966), Morrow (1983), Plessas and Oakes (1964), and Teale (1978). In short, literacy often begins with plastic "bathtub" books. These early beginnings expand into a rich array of literacy experiences, from scribbling letters to Grandma to experiencing stories on her lap.

That experiences during the preschool years can make a difference is supported by a variety of evidence, including an impressive experiment conducted by Whitehurst et al. (1988). In that study, the parents of 14 children between $1^{3}/_{4}$ years and 3 years of age participated in a 1-month intervention designed to improve interactions between parents and children during storybook reading. Parents were taught to ask more open-ended questions and more questions about the functions and attributes of objects in stories as they read stories with their preschoolers. The parents were also given instruction about how to respond appropriately to their children's comments during story reading and how to expand on what the children had to say. They were also taught to reduce the amount of straight reading they did, and to eliminate questions that the child could answer simply by pointing to something in an illustration. Fifteen other children and their parents served as control participants in the study, with control families encouraged to continue reading storybooks as they normally did with their children.

The intervention parents were able to implement the treatment. That is, they could learn to increase the quality of interactions with their children during storybook reading. Although there had been no differences between intervention and control children at the beginning of the study with respect to language variables, there were clear differences at the end of the treatment, favoring the intervention participants. At the end of the study, the intervention participants outscored the control subjects on a standardized measure of psycholinguistic ability and on two vocabulary tests. What was most striking was that when the same measures were repeated 9 months later, the intervention subjects still had an advantage over the control participants, although the differences were not as large on the 9-month follow-ups as at immediate posttesting. In general, however, the results were consistent with the hypothesis that high-quality storybook reading can positively impact long-term language development, which is a critical emergent literacy ability. Valdez-Menchaca and Whitehurst (1992) replicated and extended the Whitehurst et al. (1988) finding with Mexican children. Preschoolers learn a great deal about reading books, what is in books, and how to interact with book content if they are in an environment supportive of emergent literacy. The more parents interact verbally with their children, the more verbally competent the children are (e.g., Huttenlocher, Haight, Bryk, Seltzer & Lyons, 1991).

Sesame Street [T]

Since fall 1969, American preschoolers have had Sesame Street in their living rooms. Every evaluation ever conducted of Sesame Street (e.g., Anderson & Collins, 1988; Ball & Bogatz, 1970; Bogatz & Ball, 1971) has concluded that children learn a great deal about the alphabet and language from watching the program, much more so than entertainment television, with Sesame Street making contributions to the development of literacy over and above family interactions and other sources of stimulation (e.g., Rice, Huston, Truglio & Wright, 1990). Sesame Street is designed to grab children's attention through use of elements such as animated films, second-person address, and lively music (Campbell, Wright & Huston, 1987), resulting in substantial learning of the material featured on the show. Watching Ernie, Bert, Big Bird, and Cookie Monster can stimulate some fundamental literacy understandings.

TEACHING OF LETTERS AND THEIR SOUNDS TO PRESCHOOLERS: PRESCHOOL DEVELOPMENT OF PHONEMIC AWARENESS

Not surprisingly, 5-year-olds who demonstrate emergent literacy—reflected by greater competence in reenacting stories, writing individual words, "writing" stories, and "reading"—tend to outperform less emergent-literate 5-year-olds in reading during the primary grades, which can be interpreted as a validation for emergent literacy experiences (Barnhart, 1991). That is, emergent literacy competence at age 5 predicts later, more conventional reading competence.

Even so, emergent literacy experiences such as book reading do not produce all of the competencies that are essential for success at reading during the elementary years. One such critical competency is phonemic awareness, which is awareness that words are composed of separable sounds (i.e., phonemes) and that phonemes combine to make words.

Phonemic awareness is one of the best predictors of success in early reading in school (e.g., Adams, 1990; Bond & Dykstra, 1967; Scarborough, 1989). Children who fail to learn to read during the first several years of schooling often lack phonemic awareness (e.g., Pennington, Groisser & Welsh, 1993; Stanovich, 1986). Children who lack phonemic awareness have a difficult time learning to spell and developing understanding of letter-sound relationships (Griffith, 1991; Juel, Griffith & Gough, 1986). Poor phonemic awareness at 4 to 6 years of age is predictive of reading difficulties throughout the elementary years (Juel, 1988; Stuart & Masterson, 1992). Poor readers at all age levels often are less phonemically aware than same-age good readers (e.g., Pratt & Brady, 1988). Low phonemic awareness is almost certain in dyslexic readers (e.g., Bruck, 1992; Bruck & Treiman, 1990; Pennington, Van Orden, Smith, Green & Haith, 1990).

For phonemic awareness to develop in normal readers, formal instruction in reading seems essential; only a very small proportion of children develop phonemic awareness in the absence of such instruction (e.g., Lundberg, 1991). Notably, the one emergent literacy experience that predicts phonemic awareness is parental teaching of letters and their sounds (Crain-Thoreson & Dale, 1992). Unfortunately, many parents do not engage in such teaching, so that there is a need for schools to stimulate the children's phonemic awareness. We review three important approaches here.

DEVELOPMENT OF PHONEMIC AWARENESS THROUGH FORMAL INSTRUCTION

Sound Categorization Training [T]

Much research has been conducted examining the relation between rhyming and reading skill (Bradley & Bryant, 1983; Calfee, Chapman & Venezky, 1972). The ability to categorize words on the basis of common sounds, that is, knowledge of rhyme and alliteration, seems to be related to later reading and spelling skill (Bradley & Bryant, 1983, 1985). This connection would seem to be important since both activities involve breaking words and syllables into phonological segments. Understanding the relation between the visual or graphemic segments and the sound produced is vital to decoding. Bradley and Bryant (1985) have developed a training program that is based on teaching children to categorize according to sound. The program improves both decoding and spelling skill.

Two principles underlie the technique. The first principle is that the

Table 2-1
Sample sets of words used in Sound Categorization Training.

First Sounds				Middle Sounds			End Sounds					Rhyming Groups		
b	c	h	n	a	e	i	o	u	t	n	g			
bag	cat	hat	net	bag	bed	pig	box	bus	hat	man	bag	bat	hen	band
band	car	hand	nut	cat	hen	fish	cot	cup	nut	hen	leg	mat	men	hand
bat	cot	hen	nest	man	leg	hill	doll	gun	net	gun	dog	cat	pen	land
bed	cup	hair	nail	tap	net	pin	sock	nut	coat	pin	pig	rat	ten	sand
box	coat	hill		mat	peg		fox	sun	rat	sun	peg	hat		
ball	cake	hook		rat	ten		dog		cot	ten				
book	cook													
bus														

same word can be categorized in the same way in different sets of words. For example, the children are taught that "*hen* starts with the same sound as *hat* and *hand*, and it also starts with the same sound as *hill* and *hair*" (Bradley & Bryant, 1985, p. 80).

The second principle taught is that the same word can be categorized in different ways in successive sets of words. For example, the child is taught that "*hen* starts with the same sound as *hat* and *hand*, ends with the same sound as *men* and *sun*, and has the same middle sound as *bed* and *leg*" (Bradley & Bryant, 1985, p. 80). Examples of the types of sets used in sound categorization training by Bradley and Bryant (1985) are reproduced in Table 2-1.

The program involves 40 ten-minute sessions. In their early work, these sessions were spread out over 2 years; more recent research has examined the effectiveness of training when the sessions are grouped over 4 months (Bradley, 1988). In the first half of the sessions, 6-year-old children were taught to categorize words on the basis of common sounds using pictures of familiar objects.

The first category of introduced words begins with the letter *b*. A selection of pictures from this group are spread out in front of the child, and the child is asked to name the objects in the pictures. The child is asked to repeat the names and listen care-fully to them. This is repeated, and the child is asked if he/she can hear anything the same about them. The child is encouraged to discover the sound common to the objects in the set. The child is to say what sound it is, in this case, the sound /*buh*/.

In order to reinforce the concept, the task is repeated with different picture cards. The child is then required to pick out pictures that start with the same sound as *bus*, for example, and is also asked to pick out pictures of things that start with the letter *b*. Next, the child is required to pick out the pictures that do not start with the target letter or sound. The child is asked which pictures go together, and is required to provide reasons for the choice. When the child is consistently correct in giving reasons for his/her decision, the next sound category is introduced. This increases the difficulty level of the task, since the child is required to choose between more and more categories (Bradley & Bryant, 1985).

The child also plays "*the odd-one-out-game*" (Bradley & Bryant, 1985). During this task, the child is presented with a number of cards with pictures whose names start with the same letter and one card with a picture whose name starts with another letter. The child is required to pick out the card that does not belong, and to explain the choice.

The next stage involves presenting the child with sets of words. The child has to decide whether the words rhyme or whether they share the same first sound (alliteration). Once the child has mastered this stage, he/she is ready to learn about differences in the end sounds of words. For example, the child is presented with the set "*hat, cat, rat, man.*" *Man* is the odd word because it has a different end sound. Task difficulty is increased by introducing the child to words which only share a common final sound, for example, *man* and *pin* (Bradley and Bryant, 1985).

The last sets to be introduced are characterized by words that share a common middle vowel sound. For example, the child is presented with the set "*hat, mat, rat, cot,*" and is asked to pick the odd word. In this example, the child would choose *cot*, since it has a different vowel sound from the rest of the words in the set. The task is made more difficult by presenting sets of words which only have common middle vowel sounds, such as *man* and *cat*.

As training progresses, the use of pictures is phased out; thus, the task becomes an aural one. The child is asked to produce words which share a common sound; identify the sound that is common to the words in the set; choose the "*odd one out*" of four spoken words, given the sound in common; choose the "*odd one out*" of four spoken words, not given the common sound; and identify the sound common to three out of four spoken words (Bradley & Bryant, 1985).

During the second half of the training sessions, the use of plastic alphabet letters is introduced. A new sound category is introduced first with the picture cards, as previously described, and then the child is required to make each word in the set with the plastic letters. When the child does not know how to spell the word, the teacher makes the word for him/her. The child is told to look at the word carefully, and then the teacher scrambles the letters. The child is then asked to make the word. This cycle continues until the child spells the word correctly (Bradley, 1988). After successfully spelling the first word, the child is asked to spell the second word in the set. During the first few trials with the plastic letters, the child usually puts away all of the letters before starting on the next word, but as training progresses the child soon learns that many of the letters used for the first word are needed for the rest of the words in the set. In other words, the child learns to keep the sequence common to the words in the set in place and only alter the changing letters.

Evaluation Data Produced by Bradley and Colleagues

Bradley and her associates evaluated the efficacy of the sound categorization training program. Children trained in sound categorization were reading at levels 8 months ahead (Schonell Reading Test) and 10 months (Neale Reading Test) ahead of children trained to categorize words conceptually (i.e., *rat, bat, cat* are all animals). Sound categorization training also resulted in gains in spelling skill: these children were 17 months ahead in Schonell Spelling than children who were taught to categorize words conceptually. The comparisons with control group children who received no instruction outside of their regular classroom are even more convincing. Sound categorization trained children were 11 months (Schonell) and 14 months (Neale) ahead in reading, and 23 months ahead in spelling (Schonell).

Bradley has also collected longitudinal data (Bradley, 1987). Four years after sound categorization training, these children were still 10 months ahead of conceptual categorization trained children in reading and 14 months ahead in spelling: gains were maintained. Very few children in the experimental group required remedial reading instruction, whereas many of the control group children required the extra help.

The program has also undergone componential analysis (Bradley & Bryant, 1985; Bradley, 1988). It was found that the largest gains resulted from the use of both phonological (sound categorization) and visual orthographic (plastic letters) strategies. Although the instruction of both strategies separately or either strategy alone resulted in some gains in reading and spelling, the direct instruction of the connection between phonological and orthographic features of language seems to optimize progress in reading and spelling (Bradley, 1988).

Evaluations of Phonemic Awareness Training by Other Researchers

The evidence is overwhelming that providing instruction to increase phonemic awareness in primary-level children improves their reading, in both the short term and the long term. In several experiments, kindergarten and grade-1 children have been provided phonemic awareness training, with positive results immediately and well after training ended (e.g., Ball & Blachman, 1988, 1991; Blachman, 1991; Lundberg, Frost & Peterson, 1988; Tangel & Blachman, 1992; Treiman & Baron, 1981). Typically the instruction has been long-term, for example, occurring daily over the course of a school year. Training involves a variety of elements, including rhyming exercises, dividing words into syllables, identifying phonemes, segmenting words into phonemes, and synthesizing phonemes into words. Students are exposed to letter names and their associated sounds and perform categorization tasks like the ones used in Bradley and Bryant's work.

Cunningham (1990) provided an exceptional analytical study of the impact of phonemic awareness instruction on primary-grade students' reading. She compared two approaches to increasing the phonemic awareness of kindergarten and grade-1 children. One was "skill and drill," with emphasis on segmentation and blending of phonemes. In the second, there was discussion of the value of decoding and phonemic awareness and how learning to segment and blend phonemes could be applied in reading. This latter condition was metacognitively rich, providing children with a great deal of information about when, where and why to use the knowledge of phonemes they were acquiring. Although both forms of instruction were effective, the metacognitively rich instruction was more effective at the grade-1 level. We view this as an especially important study because it demonstrates the importance of metacognitive embellishment of strategy instruction. (Segmentation and blending are strategic procedures for young readers.)

These training studies clearly permit the conclusion that phonemic awareness training has a causal impact on young children's reading: such training causes them to read better in the short and longer terms.

Encouraging Student Use of Computer Programs
Aimed at Increasing Phonemic Awareness [T]

Computer programs are now on the market that are designed to increase the phonemic awareness of prereaders. Because of our commitment in this book to favor research-supported instruction, we single out here *The Daisy Quest Program* (available from Blue Wave Software), which has been validated in studies conducted by Joseph Torgeson and his colleagues (e.g., Torgeson & Morgan, 1992; Torgeson, Morgan & Davis, 1992).

Daisy Quest is designed to train children to be able (a) to identify individual sounds in intact words (analytical phonological skills) and (b) to blend individual sounds into recognizable real words (synthetic phonological skills). For the former, the program requires the student to identify rhyming words, to make comparisons of words based on first, middle, and last sounds, and to count the number of phonemes in short words. There are also two activities in the program to stimulate blending skills. The program "talks" and the graphics are colorful as the children "search" for clues where Daisy the Dragon is hiding.

After 20 sessions of the program, *Daisy Quest* players outperformed control subjects (all players were 4-1/2 to 6-1/2 years of age) on tasks involving matching words on the basis of first sounds and identifying which of four words has a different last sound. They could also segment and blend words better. In short, the program seemed to promote phonemic awareness. Qualitative data collected by the researchers suggested that this program might be an inviting way for prereaders to experience exercises aimed at increasing phonemic awareness. Torgeson et al. (1992) reported that children enjoyed interacting with *Daisy Quest* and its graphics, could follow the directions, and understood and liked the speech used in the program. Only one of the youngest children in the study did not want to finish the 20 sessions. *Daisy Quest* is engaging instructional material that works.

Increasing Phonemic Awareness by Encouraging Children to Read More [T]

Both Wimmer, Landerl, Linortner and Hummer (1991) and Perfetti (1992) have presented evidence that phonemic awareness can be increased by reading, with the implication that these gains facilitate subsequent reading. Specifically, Perfetti (1992) argues that children develop phonemic awareness through experiences with the alphabet—that is, experiences with printed text. Children are ready to develop phonemic awareness when they recognize that words contain separate elements. Phonemic awareness is the realization that these separate elements are represented by letters which have corresponding speech sounds. Associated with such awareness is the potential for reading gain. For instance, Wimmer and his colleagues found that nonreaders' abilities to substitute one vowel in a given word with another (e.g., substitute the *a* in *back* with an *i* to form the nonword *bick*) was predictive of their reading and spelling performances at the end of grade one. In order to complete the vowel substitution task, students needed to deconstruct established phonological and articulatory patterns. Children in Wimmer et al. (1991) who possessed such high phonemic awareness prior to formal reading instruction, demonstrated similarly high reading and spelling achievement at the end of grade one. By contrast, some of the children who demonstrated low phonemic awareness prior to instruction experienced difficulties learning to read and to spell.

The relationship between phonemic awareness and reading and spelling skills is circular—not only do gains in phonemic awareness enhance reading, expertise in reading and spelling may further facilitate phonemic awareness (Perfetti, Beck, Bell & Hughes, 1987). When children are exposed to text, they are simultaneously increasing their knowledge of letters and phonemes that constitute words. Thus, there are many positive effects of encouraging children to read and read and read! Additional information about the value of extensive reading is presented in the next section, specifically addressing decoding instruction.

BEYOND PHONEMIC AWARENESS: DECODING OF WORDS

Before embarking on a review of the various strategies for teaching students to decode words, it makes sense to outline the version of decoding theory that we most favor based on available scientific analyses. According to *dual-route theory* (e.g., Ehri, 1992; Just & Carpenter, 1987), good readers can read many words by sight, but for those words not known by sight, they can use knowledge of letter-sound associations, blending, and word parts (e.g., *orthographs* such as familiar prefixes, root words, and suffixes). The visual sight word route, of course, is faster and less effortful than the phonological-orthographic route, not requiring linear processing of the letter and sound relationships. Because learning sight words logically first requires being able to decode them—sight word knowledge is built up from repeated successful decodings—teaching children to decode is paramount according to dual-route theory. In addition, Ehri (1992) believes that the faster visual route probably still involves some phonological decoding, so that even sight word reading depends in part on decoding competence, making even stronger the case for explicit decoding instruction.

Additional evidence for decoding instruction comes from recognition of one of the most important discoveries in reading research during the past 15 years (see Adams, 1990, Chapter 6): When good readers read, they process the words in a text very thoroughly. Studies of eye movement during skilled reading have established that not only are good readers reading every single word when they are trying to learn what is in text (e.g., McConkie, Zola, Blanchard & Wolverton, 1982; for a discussion, see Carver, 1990, Chapter 5), but they are processing every single letter of every single word (e.g., Rayner, Inhoff, Morrison, Slowiaczek & Bertera, 1981; Stanovich, 1986)! It makes good conceptual sense to teach students how to process words so thoroughly.

In contrast to good readers, poor readers have deficient decoding skills. For example, the good reader/poor reader distinction is maximized in situations that rely heavily on decoding skill—for example, during the reading of pseudowords and low-frequency words (i.e., Perfetti & Hogaboam, 1975). Good readers are able to rely on their knowledge of letter-sound patterns, whereas for poor readers, "code-breaking" is a slow and laborious process (Perfetti & Hogaboam, 1975). Good readers are able to decode on the basis of multiletter units (e.g., -tion, -ing, -ance) that have fairly simple pronunciation rules and can be carried out quickly. In contrast, poor readers decode letter-by-letter, which involves more complex rules and results in slower decoding (Frederiksen, 1981). Thus, it makes sense that interventions should be aimed at improving word attack skills.

We make the case for explicit decoding instruction so emphatically in what follows, not just because it is consistent with dual-route theory and related positions and evidence, but because of very strong opposition to explicit decoding instruction by some whole language theorists. In particular, some whole language theorists favor a form of instruction that we cannot endorse because it has not been well supported by research. A popular hypothesis with whole language theorists and enthusiasts (e.g., Goodman, 1967; Smith, 1971) is that when words are read in context, decoding is really a "psycholinguistic guessing game." Consequently, rather than teaching students how to sound out words, they should be taught to analyze semantic context clues as the primary means of decoding. One classic study which whole language advocates interpret as supportive of this assumption was Goodman (1965), who demonstrated that children's reading accuracy for words improved 60% to 80% when the words were in text, compared to when the same words were presented on lists. Supposedly, the children's use of context clues provided them with information about the meaning of the to-be-decoded words. Unfortunately, follow-up investigations have failed to confirm the strong advantage of context that Goodman (1965) claimed (e.g., Nicholson, 1991; Nicholson, Bailey & McArthur, 1991; Nicholson, Lillas & Rzoska, 1988). Indeed, contemporary analyses favor the conclusion that analyzing context clues as the principal means of decoding is an immature strategy, one favored by weaker readers (e.g., Corley, 1988; Goldsmith-Phillips, 1989; Schwantes, 1991). That is, poor readers rely on context in an attempt to compensate for poor decoding skills (Stanovich, 1986). Thus, we do not favor teaching students to analyze semantic context clues as an exclusive approach to decoding instruction, but rather as one strategy among a number of strategies, and not one of the more powerful ones at that. The research on the semantic-context strategy provided strong evidence in favor of more explicit teaching of decoding.

Dual-route theory is a good way to organize the processes covered in what follows in this section: When readers engage in alphabetic reading or phonics rule application, their processing is phonological. When readers engage in sight word reading or orthographic reading, their processing is based on visual recognition of whole words and part words stored in long-term memory. A number of approaches to decoding instruction are now well validated, largely due to a great deal of basic research, complemented by classroom studies. The end result is a number of effective strategies that can be meshed into a teaching repertoire, ones permitting a variety of reading and learning experiences that promote decoding competency.

A Phonological Approach for Developing Initial Knowledge of Letters and Their Sounds: Integrated Picture Training [T]

A mnemonic method for learning letter-sound associations, one involving the use of pictorial memory aids, was developed by Ehri, Deffner and Wilce (1984). It is intended for prereaders, usually children in preschool and kindergarten. During the first phase of training, the phonemic segmentation pretraining phase, the children are taught to segment and pronounce the five target sounds they are going to learn. Five common names of people are pronounced, and the children are required to repeat each name and then pronounce the initial sound alone (i.e., Bob, /buh/) to a criterion of 2 flawless trials in a row on 2 sets of names. The children are then given the five object names that serve as mnemonics during letter-sound training, and are taught to segment their initial sounds to a criterion of one perfect trial.

The next phase of training, the letter-sound training phase, involves the training of consonant letters. Objects having names beginning with the response sounds to be associated with the letters are identified (i.e., *f*, *flower*). All letters are taught in the lowercase form, except for the letter *t*, which is taught in the capital form because of its greater resemblance to *table*, its mnemonic picture. Children view integrated pictures, that is, drawings of pictures with the letter responsible for the initial sound embedded in it (e.g., a flower with the *f* as part of the stem). Examples of the types of integrated pictures used during this type of training are shown in Figure 2-2.

Five trials (one per day) are administered. Children are told they will be learning some letters and the sounds that they make, and that they will see pictures that will give them clues about the sounds of the letters. They are also told that the shapes of the pictures will tell them what the letters look like.

The procedure for teaching each letter is as follows. Children are shown a detailed picture of the object. They hear and repeat the object name plus its initial sound. The attention of the children is directed towards the relevant part of the picture. The children are then given a simplified drawing of the object with the appropriate embedded letter, and are told to notice how the picture was drawn to have the shape of the letter. The children are required to name the object, point to the letter, and pronounce its sound. The children are then required to print the letter, and convert their letter into the simplified drawing by adding the relevant details. The final step involves having the children look at the letters again and say the sound it makes. If necessary, the children may be prompted to think of the object name, but they are told not to vocalize the word, just the sound. Corrective feedback is provided during this phase.

A test trial follows each study trial. The children are shown each letter and are told to say the sound it makes. They are encouraged to think of the picture to help remember the sound, but they are to vocalize only the sound and not the word. After each letter has been presented and the child has vocalized the sound, the children are asked to name the picture associated with the letter. If necessary, the children are given the name and are asked to give the initial sound in the name that went with the letter.

Ehri, Deffner and Wilce (1984) found that children receiving integrated-pictures training recalled significantly more letter-sound relations. The authors concluded that integrated-picture mnemonics are helpful for teaching letter-sound relations to prereaders. They also

Figure 2-2
Sample pictures used during Integrated-Picture Training.

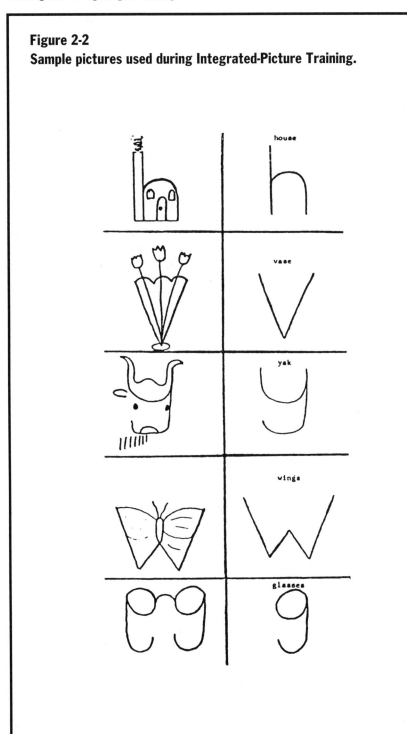

suggested the need to determine if this knowledge can then be used to begin reading words.

A Phonological Approach: Alphabetic Reading and Blending [SSR]

Traditional decoding instruction emphasizes sounding out words using letter-sound relations and blending them as part of sounding out the word. The data are quite clear that most children can learn to decode by learning to sound out words (see Adams, 1990, Chapter 4; Harris & Sipay, 1990, Chapter 12). An important prerequisite to sounding out is learning all of the letter-sound relationships. Children need to acquire what Gough and his colleagues (e.g., Gough, Juel & Griffith, 1992) refer to as the *cipher*, which is a code mapping the sounds of a language (i.e., *phonemes*) onto its alphabet. Beyond learning the sounds associated with each letter, there are a number of specific decoding "rules" that must be acquired as part of cipher learning. Some are easy, for they require only one piece of information. For example, the letter *b* is pronounced the same regardless of context; the same is true for *d, f, l, n, r, v, z*. Other letters sound differently depending on other letters in the word, with the most common example being that vowels are long if there is a final *-e* in a syllable, short if there is not. Another example is that *c* is pronounced differently if followed by an *e* or an *i* than if followed by an *a, o,* or *u* (compare the pronunciation of the *c* sounds in *celestial, city, cat, cot,* and *cut*). In general, conditional rules, involving consideration of more than one letter to determine the sound of a particular letter, are acquired later than rules involving one letter-sound association (e.g., Venezky & Johnson, 1973).

An important point to emphasize is that phonemic awareness (i.e., thorough understanding that words are composed of sequences of sounds) is critical in learning to decode by sounding out and blending. Thus, Tunmer, Herriman and Nesdale (1988) observed that grade-1 children were especially likely to make good progress in decoding instruction if they possessed both phonemic awareness and high levels of letter-name knowledge. Byrne and Fielding-Barnsley (1990, 1991) reported that preschoolers with phonemic awareness, who also knew the sounds associated with letters, were particularly adept at decoding unfamiliar words. Analyzing the sounds in words and putting them together to sound out words seems to depend on understanding first that there is a sequence of sounds in each word that can be separated! Thus, instruction to develop phonemic awareness, as described earlier in this chapter, makes sense, followed by instruction to sound out and blend.

A Phonological Approach: Using Phonics Rules [SSR]

Students can be taught phonics rules (e.g., "When two vowels go walking, the first does the talking," "When there is an *-e* at the end of a syllable…"). There are a manageable number of such rules (see Table 2-1 for a 45-rule list produced by Clymer, 1963). Although termed rules, phonics generalizations rarely hold 100% of the time. For example, "Two vowels go walking…" works about 66% of the time according to Clymer. Thus, it almost always works when *oa* is the vowel combination, as in *boat*; it rarely works for *ui* (i.e., it works for *suit* but not for most other *ui* words like *build*, *quill*). The final -*e* rule really is a host of rules of varying utility: "When there is one *e* in a word that ends in a consonant, the *e* usually has a short sound" works about 76% of the time (e.g., for *leg* but not *blew*). "In many two- and three-syllable words, the final *e* lengthens the vowel in the last syllable" works 46% of the time (e.g., for *invite* but not *gasoline*).

Teaching children phonics rules does improve early reading (Adams, 1990; Anderson, Hiebert, Scott & Wilkinson, 1985; Ehri, 1991). For example, successful sounding out of words is more likely among children receiving explicit phonics rule instruction than among children receiving no such instruction (e.g., Barr, 1974-75). The value of phonics instruction is in giving students a good start. Therefore, we recommend that teachers provide students with information about meaningful phonics rules—ones relating to frequently encountered spelling patterns, given the reader's current reading abilities. (Beware—many of the rules identified by Clymer as being highly reliable relate to infrequent spelling patterns!)

On the down side, phonics rule instruction requires substantial instructional time. In order to be useful for decoding, phonics rules must be instantly and effortlessly available to the reader. For rules to be overlearned, they must be extensively reviewed and practiced (Adams, 1990). Most importantly, students need to be instructed about the limitations associated with phonics rules: while rules may work in many instances, there are exceptions to every case.

A Visual Recognition Approach: Development of Sight Word Knowledge [T]

How do young children acquire sight words? Ehri (1991) describes three phases which children undergo when learning sight words. Each of these phases is defined by the kind of connections that students form between the visual text and the information stored in memory about that word.

During the first phase, children have very little knowledge about letters. Therefore, they form arbitrary connections between the letters in a word and the word's meaning and pronunciation, with these connections being learned by rote. As children learn more about letter names and sounds, they form more systematic connections between letters in words and letter sounds. These connections are incomplete, however, because only a few sounds in words are directly represented by their corresponding letter names (usually beginning and ending consonants). As students continue to acquire sophisticated phonemic

Table 2-1
The Utility of Forty-Five Phonic Generalizations

	Generalization	No. of Words Conforming	No. Of Exceptions	%of Utility
1	When there are two vowels side by side, the long sound of the first one is heard and the second is usually silent.	309 (bead)**	377 (chief)	45
2	When a vowel is in the middle of a one-syllable word, the vowel is short.	403	249	62
	- middle letter	191 (dress)	84 (scold)	69
	- one of the middle two letters in a word of four letters	191 (rest)	135 (told)	59
	- one vowel within a word of more than four letters	26 (splash)	30 (fight)	46
3	If the only vowel letter is at the end of a word, the letter usually stands for a long sound.	23 (he)	8 (to)	74
4	When there are two vowels, one of which is final E, the first vowel is long and the E is silent.	180 (bone)	108 (done)	63
*5	The R gives the preceding vowel a sound that is neither long nor short.	484 (horn)	134 (wire)	78
6	The first vowel is usually long and the second silent in the digraphs AI, EA, OA and UI.	179	92	66
	AI	43 (nail)	24 (said)	64
	EA	101 (bead)	51 (head)	66
	OA	34 (boat)	1 (cupboard	97
	UI	1 (suit)	16 (build)	6
7	In the phonogram IE, the I is silent and the E has a long sound	8 (field)	39 (friend)	17
8	Words having double E usually have the long E sound.	85 (seem)	2 (been)	98
9	When words end with silent E, the preceding A or I is long.	164 (cake)	108 (have)	60
*10	In AY the Y is silent and gives A its long sound.	36 (play)	10 (always)	78
11	When the letter I is followed by the letters gh, the i usually stands for its long sound, and the gh is silent.	22 (high)	9 (neighbor)	71
12	When A follows W in a word, it usually has the sound A as in was.	15 (watch)	32 (swam)	32
13	When E is followed by W, the vowel sound is the same as represented by OO.	9 (blew)	17 (sew)	35
14	The two letters OW make the long O sound.	50 (own)	35 (down)	59
15	W is sometimes a vowel and follows the vowel digraph rule.	50 (crow)	75 (threw)	40
*16	When Y is the final letter in a word, it usually has a vowel sound.	169 (dry)	32 (tray)	84
17	When Y is used as a vowel in words, it sometimes has the sound of long I.	29 (fly)	170 (funny)	15
18	The letter A has the same sound (au) when followed by L, W and U.	61 (all)	65 (canal)	48
19	When A is followed by R and final E, we expect to hear the sound heard in "care".	9 (dare)	1 (are)	90
*20	When C and H are next to each other, they make only one sound	103 (peach)	0	100

* Generalizations marked with an asterisk were found "useful" according to the criteria.
** Words in parentheses are examples — either of words which conform or of exceptions, depending on the column.

Reproduced from Clymer (1963) with permission of the International Reading Association.

Table 2-1cont'd.
The Utility of Forty-Five Phonic Generalizations

	Generalization	No. of Words Conforming	No. Of Exceptions	%of Utility
*21	CH is usually pronounced as it is in "kitchen," "catch" and "chair," not like SH.	99 (catch)	8 (machine)	95
*22	When C is followed by E or I, the sound of S is likely to be heard.	66 (cent)	3 (ocean)	96
*23	When the letter C is followed by O or A, the sound of K is likely to be heard.	143 (camp)	0	100
24	The letter G often has a sound similar to that of J in "jump" when it precedes an I or E.	49 (engine)	28 (give)	64
*25	When GHT is seen in a word, GH is silent.	30 (fight)	0	100
26	When a word begins KN, the K is silent.	10 (knife)	0	100
27	When a word begins with WR, the W is silent.	8 (write)	0	100
*28	When two of the same consonant are side by side, only one is heard.	334 (carry)	3 (suggest)	99
*29	When a word ends in CK, it has the same last sound as in "look."	46 (brick)	0	100
*30	In most two-syllable words, the first syllable is accented.	828 (famous	143 (polite)	85
*31	If A, IN, RE, EX, DE, or BE is the first syllable in a word, it is usually unaccented.	86 (belong)	13 (insect)	87
*32	In most two-syllable words that end in a consonant followed by Y, the first syllable is accented and the last is unaccented.	101 (baby)	4 (supply)	96
33	One vowel letter in an accented syllable has its short sound.	547 (city)	356 (lady)	61
*34	When Y or EY is seen in the last syllable that is not accented, the long sound of E is heard.	157 (baby)	0	100
35	When TURE is the final syllable in a word, it is unaccented.	4 (picture)	0	100
36	When TION is the final syllable in a word, it is unaccented.	5 (station)	0	100
37	In many two- and three-syllable words, the final E lengthens the vowel in the last syllable.	52 (invite)	62 (gasoline)	46
38	If the first vowel sound in a word is followed by two consonants, the first syllable usually ends with the first of the two consonants.	404 (bullet)	159 (singer)	72
39	If the first vowel sound in a word isfollowed by a single consonant, that consonant usually begins the second syllable.	190 (over)	237 (oven)	44
*40	If the last syllable of a word ends in LE, the consonant preceding the LE usually begins the last syllable.	62 (tumble)	2 (buckle)	97
*41	When the first vowel element in a word is followed by TH, CH or SH, these symbols are not broken when the word is divided into syllables and may go with either the first or second syllable.	30 (dishes)	0	100
42	In a word of more than one syllable, the letter V usually goes with the preceding vowel to form a syllable.	53 (cover)	20 (clover)	73
43	When a word has only one vowel letter, the vowel sound is likely to be short.	433 (hid)	322 (kind)	57
*44	When there is one E in a word that ends in a consonant, the E usually has a short sound.	85 (leg)	27 (blew)	76
*45	When the last syllable is the sound R, it is unaccented.	188 (butter)	9 (appear)	95

* Generalizations marked with an asterisk were found "useful" according to the criteria.
** Words in parentheses are examples — either of words which conform or of exceptions, depending on the column.

segmentation and coding skills, their visual-phonological connections also become more complete: individual letters are linked to individual phonemes, letter sequences are linked to phonological blends. Real sight word learning can begin to occur at this point.

Many trials of successfully sounding out a word increases the connections between the letter pattern defining the word and the word in memory (Adams, 1990, Chapter 9; Ehri, 1980, 1984, 1987, 1992). Thus, on initial exposure to a word like *frog*, the word is sounded out. Such sounding out begins a process in which the connections between each letter and adjacent letters are strengthened (e.g., between *f-r* and *o-g*) as are the connections between the entire sequence of letters and letter combinations in the word (between *fr-* and *-og*). Eventually the word is represented in memory as a whole. By repeated reading, there is also a strengthening of the connections between this visual stimulus and the conceptual understanding in long-term memory that defines a frog, so that eventually even the briefest exposure to the word *frog* elicits thoughts of a little green animal that lives in water and jumps.

A Visual Recognition Approach: Orthographic Recognition [T]

As a child experiences alphabetic reading, letter strings that are encountered often are eventually perceived as wholes (i.e., repeated co-occurrence of *i*, *n* and *g*, in that order, results eventually in *-ing* being perceived as a unit; Stanovich & West, 1989). Prefixes and suffixes are obvious examples, but there are other recurring combinations, many of which are root words (e.g., *-take*, *mal-*, *ben-*, *rog-*, *do-*). When familiar orthographic patterns are encountered, it is not necessary to decode alphabetically. It makes good sense to increase children's awareness of prefixes, suffixes and root words and to teach them to make use of orthographic units to decode words.

There are tremendous advantages when words can be read by sight and orthographic chunks can be processed as wholes, with these advantages summarized in *automaticity theory* (LaBerge & Samuels, 1974; Samuels, Schermer & Reinking, 1992). According to this perspective, two tasks are required to understand a word: (a) it must be decoded; (b) it must be comprehended. Both require use of short-term memory, that extremely limited resource which can be thought of as one's attentional capacity. Decoding operations and comprehension processes can be thought of as competing for such capacity.

Alphabetic decoding and/or phonics rule application consumes a great deal of short-term memory. If all of the attentional capacity is consumed by decoding, there is nothing left over for comprehension, with the result that words may be pronounced but not understood. *Automatic* sight word reading and *automatic* recognition of orthographic chunks, by contrast, require little effort or attention. Thus there is substantial mental capacity left over for comprehension when decoding is automatic. Indeed, for many sight words and orthographic chunks, there are probably automatic connections between the sight words and the chunks, the phonological representation of the word and the chunks, and the meanings of the words and the chunks (e.g., Baron, 1977). The result is faster, more accurate, and less effortful reading with experience and development (e.g., Horn & Manis, 1987). All of this supports the next strategy.

A Visual Recognition Approach: The Method of Repeated Readings [T]

LaBerge and Samuels (1974) argue that basic processes in reading, such as decoding, must be automatic before more in-depth processing, such as comprehension, can occur. A fluent reader decodes text automatically, and therefore can devote his/her attention to comprehending what is read (LaBerge & Samuels, 1974). A beginning reader devotes his/her attention to decoding, and therefore cannot devote attention to the comprehension of what is read. For the beginning reader, then, the process of what is read is much more slow and laborious (Samuels, 1979). This theory parallels the verbal efficiency theory put forth by Perfetti and Lesgold (1977), which also states that underlying processes must be conducted efficiently in order for there to be sufficient residual processing capacity for comprehension to take place. Theories such as these stress the importance of good decoding skills. In order to achieve automaticity in decoding, a lot of practice is required. A cost-efficient way of providing extensive practice is through the method of repeated readings.

The method of repeated readings can be easily implemented in any classroom. It simply involves having a child repeatedly read a short, meaningful passage until a predetermined level of fluency is reached. Fluency is defined by the accuracy of word recognition as well as reading speed (Samuels, 1979). Once fluency is achieved, the procedure is repeated with a new passage. The passages increase in length as the child's reading skills improve. As the number of passages successfully read increases, fewer rereadings are required before the criterion fluency level is reached. Practice with many passages is more effective than practice with only one story (Dowhower, 1987). Keeping a graph of individual reading scores is usually a good idea, since it makes obvious to the child that he or she is making progress in reading, which should affect motivation positively.

The method of repeated readings can be conducted with or without audio support. Children begin the training by reading a passage along with a tape recording. The audio support is gradually removed with progressive readings. Dowhower (1987) suggests that audio support be used for extremely slow readers (under 45 words per minute), since it reduces the amount of monitoring and encouragement these readers require. She claims that after one or two error-free readings with the tape recording, these children are ready to read without audio support.

The method of repeated readings is an appealing method of

instruction, since it can be used with the materials already available in any classroom. It is adaptable to virtually any reading material, as long as the passages chosen are short at first and then increase in length as training progresses. The method is meant to be an adjunct to the regular reading curriculum; it is not meant to replace direct reading instruction (Samuels, 1979). While the teacher is instructing one group of children, the remaining children can be practicing repeated reading, either on their own or with the help of other students. It can be used with tutors, peer partners or teachers' aides (Dowhower, 1987), whose roles are to provide feedback and encouragement (Carver & Hoffman, 1981).

Adaptations of The Method of Repeated Readings

This method has also been attempted using phrases and lists of words during training (Fleisher, Jenkins and Pany 1979). The 30-minute training sessions involve one-to-one instruction and testing. Each child is given a flash card drill on the words from a 100-word passage. The order of the words in the list is random on each trial, and practice is terminated after the child is able to read the list of words at a rate of 90 wpm or faster. When the child has mastered the list of words, he or she is presented with a story that is made up of the same words. The child is then required to read the story out loud. It is stressed that the child is to read for understanding.

A similar procedure is used when training phrases: the child is given repeated practice on reading phrases from the story until the fluency criterion is reached, that is, the child is reading at a rate of 160 words per minute without error. The child is then allowed to read the story from which the trained phrases were extracted.

Caution is warranted in using the method of repeated readings, since the effects do not generalize well. Training in words or phrases improves decoding speed during reading only when the passage is made up of the trained words or phrases (Fleisher et al., 1979). Repeated reading of passages results in faster and more accurate reading of new passages, but only when the new passages are very similar to the trained passages (Dowhower, 1987). Computerized versions of the method (see Carver & Hoffman, 1981, for a description of Programmed Prose) show a similar lack of generalizability of gains to other types of reading tasks.

Repeated reading does not result in improvements in comprehension (Fleisher et al., 1979; Spring, Blunden & Gatherall, 1981). Children trained to automaticity may perceive the task of reading to be fluent word recognition, rather than comprehension of what is read. O'Shea, Sindelar and O'Shea (1985) examined this possibility and found that when comprehension was emphasized to students, both fluency and comprehension increased as the number of repeated readings increased. Thus, the optimal way to use the method of repeated readings is to have students practice reading passages about four times while cueing them to read for understanding. It is likely that asking comprehension questions after reading will encourage children to maintain the desired focus.

A Method for Promoting Both Phonological and Visual Recognition Competencies: Encourage Students to Read More [T]

When children read more, their phonological decoding skills increase as their knowledge of sight words and orthographs improves (see Allen, Cipielewski & Stanovich, 1992; Cipielewski & Stanovich, 1992; Cunningham & Stanovich, 1990, 1991; Juel, 1988; Samuels et al., 1992; Stanovich, 1986; Taylor, Frye & Maruyama, 1990). Cipielewski and Stanovich (1992) found that individual differences in 3rd- through 5th-graders' reading ability were positively correlated to the amount of their experiences with print. Similar results were obtained by Taylor and her colleagues (1990) who had 5th- and 6th-graders keep daily reading journals over a 17-week interval. In these journals, students recorded the number of pages and amount of time spent reading. Students were instructed to record their activities for both teacher-assigned basal or book readings and pleasure readings, and for readings completed both at school and at home. The amount of time spent reading during the observational session contributed significantly to gains in students' reading achievement, with those students who read more being better readers. Juel (1988) also concluded that good readers read considerably more often (both inside and outside the classroom) than do poor ones, with this difference in text exposure increasing with each grade. For example, 4th-grade good readers reported reading at home about four nights a week, whereas poor readers reported reading only once a week. Experience with text, in turn, contributes to reading growth and writing skill.

We encourage teachers to implement silent reading sessions (e.g., DEAR: Drop Everything And Read; USSR: Unrestricted Sustained Silent Reading) into their daily classroom routines, with these sessions lasting for at least 20 minutes. During these sessions, teachers should serve as reading models, sharing their reading experiences with their students. Teachers should also consider having students read aloud to one another (Allington, 1977).

Without proper supervision and assistance, however, not all readers will benefit from such programs. Many poor readers fail to benefit from these sessions because they spend their time surreptitiously avoiding reading (Biemiller, 1994). For these students, monitoring and assistance during DEAR and USSR is extremely important. Such assistance can take a variety of forms, ranging from reading with the assistance of an adult or peer-coach to having the student read with a speed-controlled tape recording of the text. With these types of support mechanisms, even poor and at-risk readers can benefit from sustained reading.

A Visual Recognition Approach: Reading by Analogy [SSR]

Words that sound the same often have the same spelling patterns. Thus, a child who knows how to pronounce *beak* could make a good guess at *peak* the first time it is encountered simply by decoding by analogy ("This is like *beak* only it starts with a *p*!"). That same *beak*-knower would also have a fighting chance with *bean*, *bead* and *beat* using the analogy strategy.

For the most part, analogy has been considered an advanced strategy used only by children who have been reading awhile or by adults, with Marsh and his colleagues especially strong advocates of this position (e.g., Marsh, Desberg & Cooper, 1977; Marsh, Friedman, Desberg & Saterdahl, 1981; Marsh, Friedman, Welch & Desberg, 1981). Others, notably Goswami and Bryant (1992), have made the case that analogy is a strategy possible even with beginning readers. In one study (Goswami, 1986), 5- to 8-year-olds were asked to read words that were either analogous or not analogous to "clue" words such as *beak*, which were shown and pronounced for the child. Although children were not instructed how to use the clue words, they were better able to read words that were analogues to the clue words than words that were not analogues. Even nonreaders were able to do this in some cases (i.e., with respect to words sharing simple endings such as -*at*). In a subsequent study, Goswami (1988) found that young children were especially adept at decoding by using analogues based on word endings (i.e., decoding of words that rhyme).

Use of this visual recognition strategy probably depends on phonological decoding skills, however. Ehri and Robbins (1992) found that only children who already had some phonological decoding skills were able to decode words by analogy. Peterson and Haines (1992) produced results complementary to the Ehri and Robbins outcome. In addition, Bruck and Treiman (1992) demonstrated that even when young children can use analogies, they rely greatly on decoding of individual phonemes and orthographs in decoding new words they encounter. In short, teaching students to decode by analogy is a sensible strategy, but it *complements* phonological decoding rather than replacing it. Teaching students to use decoding by analogy makes sense, but only as one of a repertoire of strategies.

Benchmark School's Word ID Program: A Specific Analogy Approach to Decoding [SSR]

Benchmark School's students have often failed to learn to decode given the types of decoding instruction considered thus far. In response to these children's needs, Irene Gaskins and her colleagues have developed a program based on decoding by analogy (Gaskins & Elliot, 1991; Gaskins, Downer, Anderson, Cunningham, Gaskins, Schommer &

Teachers of Benchmark School, 1988; Gaskins, Gaskins, Anderson & Schommer, 1994; Gaskins, Gaskins & Gaskins, 1991, 1992). At the heart of the program are 120 key words that capture the key letter patterns associated with the six English-language vowels. There are also key words for the two sounds of *g* (i.e., *girl, giraffe*) and the two sounds of *c* (i.e., *can, city*). Some word parts that always sound the same (e.g., *-tion*) are taught as wholes. In addition, students are introduced to about 30 high-frequency words (e.g., *was, were, where, who, are, do*). Although none of these words contain a phonogram helpful in decoding, they are important for students to know because of their extensive use in the English language. All the key words in the program are summarized in Table 2-2.

The program extends over several years at Benchmark. Five to six new key words are introduced each week, over daily 15- to 20-minute word lessons. The most extensive instruction occurs on the first day, usually a Monday. Prior to any study, the students generate a rationale for learning the target words and for using the analogy strategy. The teacher also directs students' attention to the application and value of the strategy outside of the classroom. For instance, students could use the analogy strategy to read information on a billboard or street sign. The teacher then models using the analogy strategy to decode an unfamiliar word. Consider the following dialogue, during which the teacher used previously acquired words to decode the word *prepayment* in the sentence, "You must make a prepayment to get the TV."

Teacher: I'm gonna look at this and I'm gonna say, "You must make a BLANK, to get the TV." So, I know the word *he* [writes *he* on the board]. I know the word *day* [writes *day*]. And I know the word *tent* [writes *tent*]. So I would say to myself, "If this is *he*, this is *pre*. If this is *day*, this is *pay*. If this is *tent*, this is *ment*. *Prepayment*." Am I finished, Michael?

Michael: No, you have to go back and read the sentence over. Because reading always has to make sense.

Teacher: Reading has to make sense, good for you. OK, let's see. "You must make a prepayment to get the TV." Adam, you know prepayment?

Adam: Mm-hmm!

Teacher: What?

Adam: It means you have to pay something to get TV.

(Illinois Center for the Study of Reading, 1991, pp. 22-23)

After demonstrating how to use the strategy, including checking the word in context for meaning, the new target words are presented. Each word is printed across the top of chart paper, with students instructed to identify two to three other words that share the same spelling pattern. When students produce a rhyming word with a different spelling pattern, the word is differentially recorded (e.g., bracketed, circled, placed in a margin). For the remainder of the lesson, the teacher will have the students participate in a number of activities designed to promote mastery of the new words. For example, students

Table 2-2
Benchmark School Word Identification/Vocabulary Development Program
KEY PATTERNS

-a	-e	-i	-o	-u	-y
grab	he	hi	go	club	my
place	speak	mice	boat	truck	baby
black	scream	kick	job	glue	gym
had	year	did	clock	bug	
made	treat	slide	frog	drum	
flag	red	knife	broke	jump	
snail	see	pig	old	fun	
rain	bleed	right	from	skunk	
make	queen	like	on	up	
talk	sleep	smile	phone	us	
all	sweet	will	long	use	
am	tell	swim	zoo	but	
name	them	time	good		
champ	ten	in	food		
can	end	find	look		
and	tent	vine	school		
map	her	king	stop		
car	yes	think	for		
shark	nest	ship	more		
smart	let	squirt	corn		
smash	flew	this	nose		
has		wish	not		
ask		it	could		
cat		write	round		
skate		five	your		
brave		give	scout		
saw			cow		
day			glow		
			down		
			boy		

	g		g=i	an i mals	drag on
girl		grab	gym	con test	ex cite ment
go		dragon	giraffe	crea ture	pres i dent
bug		glow		choc o late	ques tion
				dis cover	re port
				thank ful	un happy
				va ca tion	

	c=k		c=s		
can		club	city	excitement	
corn		discover	princess	centipede	

may be asked to generate a story using the new words (placing them in a meaningful context), or to spell other words using the rhyming principle.

After the key words are mastered, lessons in their use continue. During these lessons, teachers continue to model use of the key words to decode new ones. Students review words learned previously in the Word ID program, and they practice decoding new words—with many exercises included in the instruction to produce overlearning of the key words and overlearning of decoding using them (e.g., compare/contrast, tongue twisters, rhyming games). Throughout these lessons, care is taken to ensure that every student participates (e.g., using cue cards to respond to the teacher's questions) and is provided with immediate feedback regarding their decoding skills. See the Illinois Center for the Study of Reading (1991) film *Teaching Word Identification* for memorable examples of Benchmark teaching.

Correlational data generated at Benchmark School support the efficacy of the program, with several experiments at other sites supportive of the approach now in the analysis stage (I. Gaskins, personal communication, July 1994). The goal of developing students who have excellent word attack skills and can use them autonomously seems to be achieved both at Benchmark and in other settings. Thus, when an older Benchmark student is presented a word like *caterpillar*, they can sound out an approximate pronunciation through analogy with the component words *cat*, *her*, *will*, and *car*. The older Benchmark students can use the key words they know to decode words they do not know. The entire Word ID program can be purchased from Benchmark School (2107 N. Providence, Media, PA 19063).

A Phonological And Visual Recognition Approach: Computer Programs that Teach Decoding Skills [T]

Because of the need for lots of practice and controlled feedback, computers are being used as instructional tools to teach decoding skills. "Computers have the capacity to deliver motivating, carefully monitored, individualized and speed-oriented practice in concentrations far beyond those available in traditional instructional formats" (Torgeson, 1986, p. 159). Two programs in particular have been well-researched (i.e., Roth and Beck, 1987) relative to others.

Construct-A-Word

In this program, the student is required to compose words from sets of subword letter strings. The student is shown a matrix of subword letter strings, and is required to select the appropriate word beginnings and word endings in order to form real words. Figure 2-3 shows an example screen from the program. The task has a gamelike quality in that the object of the activity is to construct more words in less time. *Construct-*

Figure 2-3
Sample screen from Construct-a-Word.

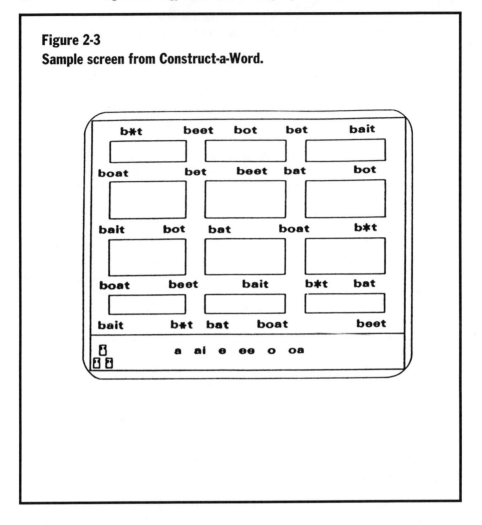

a-Word provides corrective feedback when the student makes a selection that does not form a real word. The pseudoword is presented aurally and visually, and the student is informed that the string does not spell a word. A student may also request HELP. In response to this command, the computer will aurally present a word that the student has not used. If this hint is not enough to enable the student to construct a word, the program will flash the correct word beginning, and if necessary, the appropriate word ending.

There are 20 levels in the *Construct-a-Word* program, progressing from common CVC combinations found in early reading material, to endings using a long vowel/silent -*e* combination, to beginning and ending consonant clusters and vowel digraphs in increasingly longer words. The goal of the program is to create a pool of approximately 50 word parts that when combined across all 20 levels of materials would produce several thousand words. In short, the program is designed to develop generalizable decoding skills.

Hint and Hunt

This program involves attending to subword letter strings during word recognition by encouraging vowel discrimination. The specific goal is to increase the accuracy and efficiency with which vowels and vowel digraphs are used to identify words. A word or pseudoword is presented aurally, and the student must either find or compose a letter string that matches the spoken one. Figure 2-4 illustrates a typical screen of the program.

At each new level of the program, the HINT phase occurs. This is a 5- to 10-minute introduction to the words and vowel discriminations that are covered in that level. The students are aurally and visually presented with examples of strings where the initial and final sounds remain constant while the vowel sound changes. After several examples are presented, the student will see the initial and final letters of the string with the vowels missing. The student will then hear a word, and must fill in the blank with the appropriate vowel or vowel digraph.

The main phase of the program is the HUNT phase. The student is required to match a spoken version of a word or pseudoword to a visual one. This phase has a gamelike structure as well, since the student is required to move a ban-shaped cursor through a maze to the nearest letter string that matches the spoken one. Some of the letter strings match the spoken "word" directly, whereas others require the vowel sound to be filled in. Points are accumulated based on the time that elapses before the word is found and selected. The "game" continues until the maze is cleared or the student has lost three "men". Men are lost when an incorrect choice is made or when the time limit is exceeded. The program provides corrective feedback when an incorrect choice is made. The feedback consists of the visual and aural presentation of both the correct and incorrect words. The corrective feedback may be repeated as often as the student desires.

There are 20 levels of materials within *Hint and Hunt*. The first 10 levels focus on the five short vowels and introduce discriminations between these and several digraphs, whereas the later levels focus on vowel digraphs, emphasizing discrimination between the various digraphs.

Both *Construct-a-Word* and *Hint and Hunt* have been evaluated by Roth and Beck (1987). They found that grade 4 children who received 20-24 hours of instruction with these programs experienced substantial increases in the accuracy and efficiency of decoding and word recognition processes for both laboratory tasks and standardized achievement tests. Decoding improvements were found in tasks that were different from the activities of the instruction. In addition, the effects were not limited to a specific set of words (i.e., those used in instruction). Students' ability to comprehend phrases and sentences increased

Figure 2-4
Sample screen from Hint and Hunt.

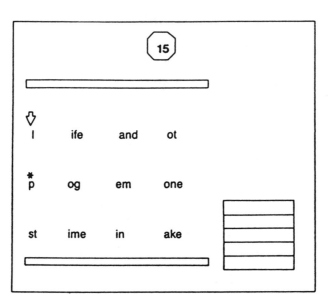

substantially on laboratory tasks and standardized achievement tests as well. (Experimental students gained more than a year relative to controls on the standardized tests.)

Other Computer Programs

A number of other decoding instructional programs are now marketed, with all of them including a variety of components. Programs such as *Reader Rabbit I, II* and *III* (The Learning Company) and *Daisy's Castle* (Blue Wave Software) are intended to develop sounding out, blending, and orthographic skills. Although more research, evaluation and validation of these particular programs would build the case in their favor, the fact that they incorporate state-of-the-science knowledge about decoding inspires confidence in them. These programs' availability in many software stores may increase their appeal relative to *Construct-a-Word* and *Hint and Hunt*, which are not marketed widely.

Concluding Comment

The scientific study of beginning reading has blossomed in the last decade and a half. One result is that it is clearly understood better than ever that explicit decoding instruction improves reading both during the primary years and in the long term. A second result is that a rich array of teaching strategies has emerged.

This work has not occurred in a vacuum. In particular, it occurred in an educational context that heavily favored whole language instruction, a theory of teaching and learning which rejected explicit, systematic teaching of decoding. As the evidence accumulated that whole language was not effective in promoting reading, at least as measured by conventional tests (see the entire December 1994 issue of *Educational Psychologist*, for example), many educators made efforts to preserve the strengths of the whole language approach while importing systematic instruction of phonemic awareness and decoding.

In 1992-93, Pressley, Rankin, and Yokoi (1994; see also Pressley & Rankin, 1994) surveyed 83 primary-level teachers who were nominated by their supervisors as outstanding literacy teachers—in that high proportions of their students became readers. Rankin and Pressley (1994) surveyed 31 special education teachers from across the country who were similarly purported to be outstanding literacy teachers. Many of the teachers reported that explicit decoding instruction occurs in their classrooms. However, this is in the context of other instructional practices, many of which are consistent with whole language philosophy, including the following:

- Both outstanding general and special education teachers reported that they attempt to surround students with a literate environment, including chart stories, in-classroom libraries, and displays of student work.
- They model the love of reading.
- They use themes to organize reading and writing instruction.
- Many types of reading occur in the class: the teachers use rhyming books and pattern books; they read stories to their students; students read along as the teacher reads.
- Teachers report developing background knowledge before students read stories.
- Students write, typically stories and journal writing, and usually have an editing conference with a teacher.
- The teachers do much to motivate reading and writing in

their students, including encouraging an "I can read, I can write" attitude; reading of student-selected materials in class; providing positive feedback; creating a "risk-free" environment with respect to reading and writing; encouraging student ownership of writing by letting them write about their interests; accepting where the child is right now and working to improve literacy from that point; attempting to let students know why their lessons are important and why reading and writing are critical in life; and setting an exciting mood for reading and writing.

The teachers also report a number of instructional practices that are not consistent with whole language. These elements were reported as especially prevalent with weaker readers in the regular classrooms and emphatically reported as present in the special education classes. There is a very clear concern with the development of decoding and related skills (e.g., concepts of print, phonemic awareness). Consistent with the presentation in this chapter, there was definitely a commitment to a variety of methods for enhancing students' decoding.

Gone are the days when it made sense to argue over phonics or whole-word instruction. The strategies suggested in this chapter are aimed at development of both phonological-decoding skills and whole-word recognition. Implicit in the old phonics versus whole-word debate (see Chall, 1967) was the idea that not much else mattered in primary-level literacy instruction. The message from the exceptional teachers surveyed by Pressley, Rankin, and their colleagues is that there is much else that matters. The excellent teachers who use the strategies recommended in this chapter will do so along with other comprehension, spelling, and writing strategies, integrating teaching of strategies into a complex setting that stimulates literacy in many ways.

REFERENCES

Adams, M. J. (1990). *Beginning to read*. Cambridge, MA: Harvard University Press.

Allen, L., Cipielewski, J., & Stanovich, K. E. (1992). Multiple indicators of children's reading habits and attitudes: Construct validity and cognitive correlates. *Journal of Educational Psychology, 84*, 489-503.

Allington, R. (1977). If they don't read much, how they ever gonna get good? *Journal of Reading, 21*, 57-61.

Anderson, D. R., & Collins, P. A. (1988). *The impact on children's education: Television's influence on cognitive development* (Office of

Research Working Paper No. 2). Washington, DC: U.S. Department of Education, Office of Educational Research and Improvement.

Anderson, R. C., Hiebert, E. H., Scott, J. A., & Wilkinson, I. A. G. (1985). *Becoming a nation of readers*. Washington, DC: National Institute of Education.

Ball, E.W., & Blachman, B.A. (1988). Phoneme segmentation training: Effect on reading readiness. *Annals of Dyslexia, 38*, 203-225.

Ball, E. W., & Blachman, B. A. (1991). Does phoneme segmentation training in kindergarten make a difference in early word recognition and developmental spelling? *Reading Research Quarterly, 26,* 49-66.

Ball, S., & Bogatz, G. A. (1970). *The first year of "Sesame Street": An evaluation.* Princeton, NJ: Educational Testing Service.

Barnhart, J. E. (1991). Criterion-related validity of interpretations of children's performance on emergent literacy tasks. *Journal of Reading Behavior, 23,* 45-444.

Baron, J. (1977). Mechanisms for pronouncing printed words: Use and acquisition. In D. LaBerge & S. J. Samuels (Eds.), *Basic processes in reading: Perception and comprehension* (pp. 175-216). Hillsdale, NJ: Erlbaum & Associates.

Barr, R. (1984). Beginning reading instruction: From debate to reformation. In P. D. Pearson, R. Barr, M. Kamil, & P. Mosenthal (Eds.), *Handbook of reading research* (pp. 545-581). New York: Longman.

Barr, R. C. (1974-75). The effect of instruction on pupil reading strategies. *Reading Research Quarterly, 10,* 555-582.

Beck, I. L. (1981). Reading problems and instructional practices. In G. E. MacKinnon & T. G. Waller (Eds.), Reading research: *Advances in theory and practice* (Vol. 2; pp. 53-95). New York: Academic Press.

Biemiller, A. (1994). Some observations on beginning reading instruction. *Educational Psychologist.*

Blachman, B. A. (1991). Phonological awareness: Implications for prereading and early reading instruction. In S. A. Brady & D. P. Shankweiler (Eds.), *Phonological processes in literacy: A tribute to Isabelle Y. Liberman* (pp. 29-36). Hillsdale, NJ: Erlbaum & Associates.

Bogatz, G. A., & Ball, S. (1971). *The second year of "Sesame Street": A continuing evaluation.* Princeton, NJ: Educational Testing Service.

Bond, G. L., & Dykstra, R. (1967). The cooperative research program in first-grade reading instruction. *Reading Research Quarterly, 2,* 5-142.

Bradley, L. (1987). *Categorizing sounds, early intervention and learning to read: A follow-up study.* Paper presented at the British Psychological Society conference, December, 1987.

Bradley, L. (1988). Making connections in learning to read and to spell. *Applied Cognitive Psychology, 2,* 3-18.

Bradley, L. & Bryant, P. E. (1983). Categorizing sounds and learning to read—a causal connection. *Nature, 301* 419-421.

Bradley, L., & Bryant, P. E. (1985). *Rhyme and reason in reading and spelling.* International Academy for Research in Learning Disabilities Series. Michigan: University of Michigan Press.

Bruck, M. (1992). Persistence of dyslexics' phonological awareness deficits. *Developmental Psychology, 28,* 874-886.

Bruck, M., & Treiman, R. (1990). Phonological awareness and spelling in normal children and dyslexics: The case of initial consonant clusters. *Journal of Experimental Child Psychology, 50,* 156-178.

Bruck, M., & Treiman, R. (1992). Learning to pronounce words: The limits of analogies. *Reading Research Quarterly, 27,* 374-398.

Byrne, B., & Fielding-Barnsley, R. (1990). Acquiring the alphabetic principle: A case for teaching recognition of phoneme identity. *Journal of Educational Psychology, 82,* 805-812.

Byrne, B., & Fielding-Barnsley, R. (1991). Evaluation of a program to teach phonemic awareness to young children. *Journal of Educational Psychology, 83,* 451-55.

Calfee, R. C., Chapman, R., & Venezky, R. (1972). How a child needs to think to learn to read. In L. W. Gregg (Ed.), *Cognition in learning and memory.* New York: Wiley.

Calfee, R. C., Lindamood, P., & Lindamood, C. (1973). Acoustic-phonetic skills and reading—kindergarten through twelfth grade. *Journal of Educational Psychology, 64,* 293-298.

Campbell, T. A., Wright, J. C., & Huston, A. C. (1987). Form cues and content difficulty as determinants of children's cognitive processing of televised educational messages. *Journal of Experimental Child Psychology, 43,* 311-327.

Carver, R. P. (1990). *Reading rate: A review of research and theory.* San Diego, CA: Academic Press.

Carver, R. P., & Hoffman, J. V. (1981). The effect of practice through repeated reading on reading ability using a computer-based instructional system. *Reading Research Quarterly, 16,* 374-390.

Chall, J. S. (1967). *Learning to read: The great debate.* New York: McGraw-Hill.

Cipielewski, J., & Stanovich, K. E. (1992). Predicting growth in reading ability from children's exposure to print. *Journal of Experimental Child Psychology, 54,* 74-89.

Clark, M. M. (1976). *Young fluent readers: What can they teach us?* London: Heinemann.

Clymer, T. (1963). The utility of phonic generalizations in the primary grades. *Reading Teacher, 16*, 252-58.

Corley, P. J. (1988). A developmental analysis of sentence comprehension abilities in good and poor readers. *Educational Psychologist, 23*, 57-75.

Crain-Thoreson, C., & Dale, P. S. (1992). Do early talkers become early readers?: Linguistic precocity, preschool language, and emergent literacy. *Developmental Psychology, 28*, 421-29.

Cunningham, A. E. (1990). Explicit versus implicit instruction in phonemic awareness. *Journal of Experimental Child Psychology, 50*, 429-444.

Cunningham, A. E., & Stanovich, K. E. (1990). Assessing print exposure and orthographic processing skill in children: A quick measure of reading experience. *Journal of Educational Psychology, 82*, 733-740.

Cunningham, A. E., & Stanovich, K. E. (1991). Tracking the unique effects of print exposure in children: Associations with vocabulary, general knowledge, and spelling. *Journal of Educational Psychology, 83*, 264-274.

Curtis, M. E. (1980). Development of components of reading skill. *Journal of Educational Psychology, 72*, 656-669.

Dowhower, S. L. (1987). Effects of repeated reading on second-grade transitional readers' fluency and comprehension. *Reading Research Quarterly, 22*, 389-406.

Durkin, D. (1966). *Children who read early.* New York: Teachers College Press.

Ehri, L. C. (1980). The development of orthographic images. In U. Frith (Ed.), *Cognitive processes in spelling* (pp. 311-338). London: Academic Press.

Ehri, L. C. (1984). How orthography alters spoken language competencies in children learning to read and spell. In J. Downing & R. Valtin (Eds.), *Language awareness and learning to read* (pp. 119-147). New York: Springer-Verlag.

Ehri, L. C. (1987). Learning to read and spell words. *Journal of Reading Behavior, 19*, 5-31.

Ehri, L. C. (1991). Development of the ability to read words. In R. Barr, M. L. Kamil, P. B. Mosenthal & P. D. Pearson (Eds.), *Handbook of reading research*, Vol. 2 (pp. 383-417). New York: Longman.

Ehri, L. C. (1992). Reconceptualizing the development of sight word reading and its relationship to decoding. In P. B. Gough, L. C. Ehri & R. Treiman (Eds.), *Reading acquisition* (pp. 107-143). Hillsdale. NJ: Erlbaum & Associates.

Ehri, L. C., Deffner, N. D. & Wilce, L. S. (1984). Pictorial mnemonics for phonics. *Journal of Educational Psychology, 76*, 880-893.

Ehri, L. C., & Robbins, C. (1992). Beginners need some decoding skill to read words by analogy. *Reading Research Quarterly, 27*, 12-27.

Ehri, L. C., & Wilce, L. S. (1983). Development of word identification speed in skilled and less skilled beginning readers. *Journal of Educational Psychology, 75*, 3-18.

Fleisher, L. S., Jenkins, J. R. & Pany, D. (1979). Effects on poor readers' comprehension of training in rapid decoding. *Reading Research Quarterly, 15*, 30-48.

Frederiksen, J. R. (1981). Sources of process interactions in reading. In A. M Lesgold & C. A. Perfetti (Eds.), *Interactive processes in reading* (pp. 361-386). Hillsdale: Lawrence Erlbaum.

Gaskins, I. W., Downer, M. A., Anderson, R. C., Cunningham, P. M., Gaskins, R. W., Schommer, M., & Teachers of Benchmark School (1988). A metacognitive approach to phonics: Using what you know to decode what you don't know. *Remedial and Special Education, 9*, 36-41, 66.

Gaskins, I.W., & Elliot, T.T. (1991). *Implementing cognitive strategy instruction across the school: The Benchmark manual for teachers.* Cambridge, MA: Brookline Books.

Gaskins, R. W., Gaskins, I. W., Anderson, R. C., & Schommer, M. (1994). *The reciprocal relationship between research and development: An example involving a decoding strand for poor readers.* Media, PA: Benchmark School.

Gaskins, R. W., Gaskins, J. C., & Gaskins, I. (1991). A decoding program for poor readers—and the rest of the class, too! *Language Arts, 68*, 213-225.

Gaskins, R. W., Gaskins, J. C., & Gaskins, I. (1992). Using what you know to figure out what you don't know: An analogy approach to decoding. *Reading and Writing Quarterly: Overcoming Learning Disabilities, 8*, 197-221.

Gettinger, M. (1986). Prereading skills and achievement under three approaches to teaching word recognition. *Journal of Research and Development in Education, 19*, 1-9.

Goldsmith-Phillips, J. (1989). Word and context in reading development: A test of the interactive-compensatory hypothesis. *Journal of Educational Psychology, 81*, 299-305.

Goodman, K. S. (1965). A linguistic study of cues and miscues in reading. *Elementary English, 42,* 639-642.

Goodman, K. S. (1967). Reading: A psycholinguistic guessing game. *Journal of the Reading Specialist, 6,* 126-135.

Goodman, Y. M. (Ed.) (1990). *How children construct literacy: Piagetian perspectives.* Newark, DE: International Reading Association.

Goswami, U. (1986). Children's use of analogy in learning to read: A developmental study. *Journal of Experimental Child Psychology, 42,* 73-83.

Goswami, U. (1988). Orthographic analogies and reading development. *Quarterly Journal of Experimental Psychology, 40,* 239-268.

Gough, P. B., Juel, C., & Griffith, P. L. (1992). Reading, spelling, and the orthographic cipher. In P. B. Gough, L. C. Ehri & R. Treiman (Eds.), *Reading acquisition* (pp. 35-48). Hillsdale, NJ: Erlbaum & Associates.

Graham, S., & Harris, K. R. (1994). The effects of whole language on children's writing: A review of literature. *Educational Psychologist.*

Griffith, P. L. (1991). Phonemic awareness helps first graders invent spellings and third graders remember correct spellings. *Journal of Reading Behavior, 23,* 215-233.

Harris, A. J., & Sipay, E. R. (1990). *How to increase reading ability: A guide to developmental and remedial methods.* White Plains, NY: Longman.

Horn, C. C., & Manis, F. R. (1987). Development of automatic and speeded reading of printed words. *Journal of Experimental Child Psychology, 44,* 92-108.

Huttenlocher, J., Haight, W., Bryk, A., Seltzer, M., & Lyons, T. (1991). Early vocabulary growth: Relation to language input and gender. *Developmental Psychology, 27,* 236-248.

Illinois Center for the Study of Reading (1991). *Teaching word identification.* Champaign, IL: University of Illinois.

Johnson, D. D., & Baumann, J. F. (1984). Word identification. In P. D. Pearson, R. Barr, M. Kamil & P. Mosenthal (Eds.), *Handbook of reading research* (pp. 583-608). New York: Longman.

Juel, C. (1988). Learning to read and write: A longitudinal study of 54 children from first through fourth grades. *Journal of Educational Psychology, 80,* 417-477.

Juel, C., Griffith, P. L., & Gough, P. B. (1986). Acquisition of literacy: A longitudinal study of children in first and second grade. *Journal of Educational Psychology, 78,* 243-255.

Just, M. A., & Carpenter, P. A. (1987). *The psychology of reading and language comprehension.* Newton: Allyn & Bacon.

King, D. F., & Goodman, K. S. (1990). Whole language: Cherishing learners and their language. *Language, Speech, and Hearing Services in Schools, 21,* 221-27.

LaBerge, D., & Samuels, S. J., (1974). Toward a theory of automatic information processing in reading. *Cognitive Psychology, 6,* 293-323.

Leichter, H. P. (1984). Families as environments for literacy. In H. Goelman, A. Oberg & F. Smith (Eds.), *Awakening to literacy.* Exeter, NH: Heinemann.

Lesgold, A. M., & Perfetti, C. A. (1981). Interactive processes in reading: Where do we stand? In A. M. Lesgold and C. A. Perfetti (Eds.), *Interactive processes in reading.* Hillsdale: Lawrence Erlbaum.

Lundberg, I. (1991). Phonemic awareness can be developed without reading instruction. In S. A. Brady & D. P. Shankweiler (Eds.), *Phonological processes in literacy: A tribute to Isabelle Y. Liberman* (pp. 47-53). Hillsdale, NJ: Erlbaum & Associates.

Lundberg, I., Frost, J., & Peterson, O. (1988). Effects of an extensive program for stimulating phonological awareness in preschool children. *Reading Research Quarterly, 23,* 263-84.

Marsh, G., Desberg, P., & Cooper, J. (1977). Developmental strategies in reading. *Journal of Reading Behavior, 9,* 391-394.

Marsh, G., Friedman, M., Desberg, P., & Saterdahl, K. (1981). Comparison of reading and spelling strategies in normal and reading-disabled children. In M. P. Friedman, J. P. Das & N. O'Connor (Eds.), *Intelligence and learning* (pp. 363-67). New York: Plenum.

Marsh, G., Friedman, M., Welch, V., & Desberg, P. (1981). A cognitive-developmental theory of reading acquisition. In G. E. MacKinnon & T. G. Waller (Eds.), *Reading research: Advances in theory and practice,* Vol. 3 (pp. 199-221). New York: Academic Press.

McConkie, G. W., Zola, D., Blanchard, H. E., & Wolverton, G. S. (1982). Perceiving words during reading: Lack of facilitation from prior peripheral exposure. *Perception & Psychophysics, 32,* 271-281.

Morrow, L. M. (1983). Home and school correlates of early interest in literature. *Journal of Educational Research, 76,* 221-230.

Morrow, L. M. (1989). *Literacy development in the early years: Helping children read and write.* Boston: Allyn & Bacon.

Morrow, L. M. (1990). Preparing the classroom environment to promote literacy during play. *Early Childhood Research Quarterly, 5,* 537-554.

Morrow, L. M. (1991). Relationships among physical designs of play centers, teachers' emphasis on literacy during play, and children's literacy behaviors in play. In J. Zutell & S. McCormick (Eds.), *Learner factors/teacher factors: Issues in literacy research and instruction: Fortieth yearbook of the National Reading Conference* (pp. 127-140). Chicago: National Reading Conference.

Morrow, L. M. (1992). The impact of a literature-based program on literacy achievement, use of literature, and attitudes of children from minority backgrounds. *Reading Research Quarterly, 27,* 251-275.

Neuman, S. B., & Roskos, K. (1990). The influence of literacy-enriched play settings on preschoolers' engagement with written language. In J. Zutell & S. McCormick (Eds.), *Literacy theory and research: Analyses from multiple paradigms* (pp. 179-188). Chicago: National Reading Conference.

Neuman, S. B., & Roskos, K. (1992). Literacy objects as cultural tools: Effects on children's literacy behaviors in play. *Reading Research Quarterly, 27,* 203-225.

Nicholson, T. (1991). Do children read words better in context or on lists? A classic study revisited. *Journal of Educational Psychology, 83,* 444-450.

Nicholson, T., Bailey, J., & McArthur, J. (1991). Context cues in reading: The gap between research and popular opinion. *Journal of Reading: Writing and Learning Disabilities, 7,* 33-41.

Nicholson, T., Lillas, C., & Rzoska, A. (1988). Have we been misled by miscues? *The Reading Teacher, 42,* 6-10.

O'Shea, L. J, Sindelar, P. T. & O'Shea, D. J, (1985). The effects of repeated readings and attentional cues on reading fluency and comprehension. *Journal of Reading Behavior, 17,* 129-142.

Pennington, B. F., Groisser, D., & Welsh, M. C. (1993). Contrasting cognitive deficits in attention deficit hyperactivity disorder versus reading disability. *Developmental Psychology, 29,* 511-523.

Pennington, B. F., Van Orden, G. C., Smith, S. D., Green, P. A., & Haith, M. M. (1990).

Phonological processing skills and deficits in adult dyslexics. *Child Development, 61,* 1753-1778.

Perfetti, C. A. (1992). The representation problem in reading acquisition. In P. B. Gough, L. C. Ehri & R. Treiman (Eds.), *Reading acquisition* (pp. 145-174). Hillsdale, NJ: Erlbaum & Associates.

Perfetti, C.A., Beck, I., Bell, L., & Hughes, C. (1987). Children's reading and the development of phonological awareness. *Merrill-Palmer Quarterly, 33,* 39-75.

Perfetti, C. A., Finger, E. & Hogaboam, T. (1978). Sources of vocalization latency differences between skilled and less skilled young readers. *Journal of Educational Psychology, 70,* 730-739,

Perfetti, C. A., & Hogaboam, T. (1975). Relationship between single word decoding and reading comprehension skill. *Journal of Educational Psychology, 67,* 461-469.

Perfetti, C. A., & Lesgold, A. M. (1977). Discourse comprehension and sources of individual differences. In M. A. Just & P. A. Carpenter (Eds.), *Cognitive processes in comprehension.* Hillsdale: Lawrence Erlbaum.

Perfetti, C. A., & Roth, S. (1981). Some of the interactive processes in reading and their role in reading skill. In A. M. Lesgold & C. A. Perfetti (Eds.), *Interactive processes in reading* (pp. 269-297). Hillsdale: Lawrence Erlbaum.

Peterson, M. E., & Haines, L. P. (1992). Orthographic analogy training with kindergarten children: Effects of analogy use, phonemic segmentation, and letter-sound knowledge. *Journal of Reading Behavior, 24,* 109-127.

Pflaum, S. W., Walberg, H. J., Karegianes, M. L. & Rasher, S. P. (1980). Reading instruction: A quantitative analysis. *Educational Researcher, 9* (7), 12-18.

Plessas, G. P., & Oakes, C. R. (1964). Prereading experiences of selected early readers. *Reading Teacher, 17,* 241-45.

Pratt, A. C., & Brady, S. (1988). Relation of phonological awareness to reading disability in children and adults. *Journal of Educational Psychology, 81,* 101-108.

Pressley, M., & Rankin, J. (1994). More about whole language methods of reading instruction for students at risk for early reading failure. *Learning Disabilities Research & Practice, 9,* 157-168.

Pressley, M., Rankin, J., & Yokoi, L. (1994). *A survey of instructional practices of outstanding primary-level literacy teachers.* Manuscript submitted for publication review. Albany, NY: University at Albany, SUNY, Department of Educational Psychology and Statistics.

Rankin, J., & Pressley, M (1994). Manuscript in preparation.

Rayner, K., Inhoff, A. W., Morrison, R. E., Slowiaczek, M. L., & Bertera, J. H. (1981). *Journal of Experimental Psychology: Human Perception and Performance, 7,* 167-179.

Rice, M. L., Huston, A. C., Truglio, R., & Wright, J. (1990). Words from "Sesame Street": Learning vocabulary from viewing. *Developmental Psychology, 26,* 421-28.

Roth, S. F. & Beck, I. L. (1987). Theoretical and Instructional implications of the assessment of two microcomputer word recognition programs. *Reading Research Quarterly, 22,* 197-218.

Samuels, S. J, (1979). The method of repeated readings. *The Reading Teacher, 32,* 403-408.

Samuels, S. J., Schermer, N., & Reinking, D. (1992). Reading fluency; Techniques for making decoding automatic. In S. J. Samuels & A. E. Farstrup (Eds.), *What research has to say about reading instruction* (pp. 124-144). Newark, DE: International Reading Association.

Scarborough, H. S. (1989). Prediction of reading disability from familial and individual differences. *Journal of Educational Psychology, 81,* 101-108.

Schwantes, F. M. (1991). Children's use of semantic and syntactic information for word recognition and determination of sentence meaningfulness. *Journal of Reading Behavior, 23,* 335-350.

Smith, F. (1971). *Understanding reading: A psycholinguistic analysis of reading and learning to read.* New York: Holt, Rinehart & Winston.

Spring, C., Blunden, D. & Gatherall, M. (1981). Effect on reading comprehension of training to automaticity in word-reading. *Perceptual and Motor Skills, 53,* 779-786.

Stahl, S. A., McKenna, M. C., & Pagnucco, J. R. (1994). The effects of whole language instruction: An update and reappraisal. *Educational Psychologist.*

Stahl, S., & Miller, P. D. (1989). Whole language and language experience approaches for beginning reading: A quantitative research synthesis. *Review of Educational Research, 59,* 87-116.

Stanovich, K. (1986). Matthew effects in reading: Some consequences of individual differences in the acquisition of literacy. *Reading Research Quarterly, 21,* 360-407.

Stanovich, K. E., & West, R. F. (1989). Exposure to print and orthographic processing. *Reading Research Quarterly, 24,* 402-433.

Stuart, M., & Masterson, J. (1992). Patterns of reading and spelling in 10-year-old children related to prereading phonological abilities. *Journal of Experimental Child Psychology, 54,* 168-187.

Sulzby, E., & Teale, W. (1991). Emergent literacy. In R. Barr, M. L. Kamil, P. B. Mosenthal & P. D. Pearson (Eds.), *Handbook of reading research,* Vol. II (pp. 727-758). New York: Longman.

Tangel, D. M., & Blachman, B. A. (1992). Effect of phoneme awareness instruction on kindergarten children's invented spellings. *Journal of Reading Behavior, 24,* 233-261.

Taylor, B. M., Frye, B. J., & Maruyama, G. M. (1990). Time spent reading and reading growth. *American Educational Research Journal, 27,* 351-362.

Taylor, I., & Taylor, M. M. (1983). *The psychology of reading.* New York: Academic Press.

Teale, W. (1978). Positive environments for learning to read: What studies of early readers tell us. *Language Arts, 55,* 922-932.

Torgeson, J. K. (1986). Computers and cognition in reading: A focus on decoding fluency. *Exceptional Children, 53,* 157-162.

Torgeson, J. K., & Morgan, S. (1992, April). *Effects of two types of phonological awareness training on word learning in kindergarten children.* Presented at the annual meeting of the American Educational Research Association, San Francisco.

Torgeson, J. K., Morgan, S. T., & Davis, C. (1992). Effects of two types of phonological awareness training on word learning in kindergarten children. *Journal of Educational Psychology, 84,* 364-370.

Treiman, R. A., & Baron, J. (1981). Segmental analysis ability: Development and relation to reading ability. In G. E. MacKinnon & R. G. Walker (Eds.), *Reading research: Advances in theory and practice,* Vol. 3. San Diego, CA: Academic Press.

Tunmer, W. E., Herriman, M. L., & Nesdale, A. R. (1988). Metalinguistic abilities and beginning reading. *Reading Research Quarterly, 23,* 134-158.

Underwood, G. (1985). Information processing in skilled readers. In G. E. MacKinnon & T. G. Waller (Eds.), *Reading research: Advances in theory and practice* (vol. 4, pp. 139-181). Orlando: Academic Press.

Valdez-Menchaca, M. C., & Whitehurst, G. J. (1992). Accelerating language development through picture book reading: A systematic extension to Mexican day care. *Developmental Psychology, 28,* 1106-1114.

Vellutino, F. R. & Scanlon, D. M. (1986). Experimental evidence for the effects of instructional bias on word identification. *Exceptional Children, 53,* 145-155.

Venezky, R. L., & Johnson, D. (1973). The development of two letter-sound patterns in grade 1-3. *Journal of Educational Psychology, 64,* 109-115.

Weaver, C. (1990). *Understanding whole language: From principles to practice.* Portsmouth, NH: Heinemann.

Whitehurst, G. J., Falco, F. L., Lonigan, C. J., Fischel, J. E., DeBaryshe, B. D., Valdez-Menchaca, M. C., & Caulfield, M. (1988). Accelerating language development through picture book reading. *Developmental Psychology, 24,* 552-559.

Wimmer, H., Landerl, K., Linortner, R., & Hummer, P. (1991). The relationship of phonemic awareness to reading acquisition: More consequence than precondition but still important. *Cognition, 40,* 219-249.

CHAPTER 3

Reading Comprehension Strategies

In recent years, the Pressley group has focused on strategies that promote children's comprehension and memory of what they read, because of the importance of learning from text. Consistent with information processing theory, this group has never contended that teaching of comprehension strategies alone could produce skilled reading, thinking, or memory (Pressley, Borkowski & Schneider, 1987, 1989; Schneider & Pressley, 1989). Rather, their perspective is that students must be taught strategies for use in conjunction with their other knowledge. For strategies to be coordinated with factual and conceptual knowledge, the learner must possess metacognitive knowledge, so that she can understand when, where, and how to use the strategies she knows. In addition, the active use of strategies and other knowledge is very much dependent on student motivation to learn from text.

In brief, the Pressley group contends that effective strategy instruction must be long-term and aimed at developing coordinated use of strategies in conjunction with knowledge of other sorts, the strategies serving as learning tools. Such instruction must be metacognitively rich, including information about where and when to use the strategies taught. Extensive practice is necessary to promote strategy efficiency and automaticity. Such practice also permits additional opportunities to discover how, where and when to use strategies. Effective instruction develops in students the sense that they can be effective thinkers—that is, effective strategy instruction motivates students to learn and use strategies with other information.

Most research on comprehension strategy instruction has had the following form: A researcher believes that if students would construct particular types of text representations (e.g., mental images representing the story told in a narrative, summaries), or react to texts in a particular way (e.g., relating them to prior knowledge, explicitly seeking clarifications when unsure of meaning), comprehension and long-term memories of text would improve. These researchers believed that students were not already engaging in such thinking when reading, or they were doing so less systematically and completely than they could. Thus, the researcher created instruction to stimulate the desired thinking processes. The reading comprehension of students receiving such instruction, measured by some type of objective test of understanding (e.g., multiple-choice items over literal and inferred messages in text), was compared to the reading comprehension of students not receiving such instruction (e.g., control subjects permitted to read as they normally would in preparation for an objective test). When strategy-trained students outperformed control students, the researcher concluded that the students (a) probably had not been using the trained strategy(-ies) on their own or were not using it (them) systematically, but more positively, (b) students could be taught to do so. That is, students were production-deficient (Flavell, 1970), in that they were capable of producing the strategies but did not unless they were instructed to do so.

Many such experiments in the 1970s and 1980s produced evidence that students could benefit from instructions to use a number of thinking strategies aimed at improving learning from text (see Pearson & Dole, 1987; Pressley, Johnson, Symons, McGoldrick & Kurita, 1989). We summarize that research in the first section of this chapter. The strategies discussed in this first section can typically be taught to children in grades 3 through 8, usually in 10 hours or less (including time to practice applying the strategies). Our discussion of each strategy begins with a brief rationale and description of the strategy. When there are variations of the strategy, these are presented. The scientific evidence supporting the effectiveness of each strategy is reviewed, with gaps in knowledge also cited.

The section on teaching individual strategies is followed by a section on how teachers can teach repertoires of comprehension strategies so that students can react to text flexibly, effectively applying strategies to particular parts of text and adapting these strategies as needed. The chapter concludes with a section summarizing the nature of sophisticated comprehension and reiterating the importance of teaching students to use the strategies summarized in this chapter.

INSTRUCTION OF INDIVIDUAL COMPREHENSION STRATEGIES

Summarization [SSR]

A single reading rarely permits recall of all information in a text. Mature readers usually abstract the gist, or macrostructure, of what they read (Kintsch & van Dijk, 1978). This macrostructure resembles a summary of the passage in that trivial details are not included and generalizations are made that sum up the passage. Summarization, or abstraction of the macrostructure, is thought to be an integral part of competent reading (Kintsch & van Dijk, 1978). Children, however, have difficulty producing summaries of text passages unless they are taught how to do so (Brown & Day, 1983; Brown, Day, & Jones, 1983). Thus, a number of investigators have provided summarization instruction to children.

There have been many approaches to instructing summarization. The simplest involves producing single sentences that capture the meaning of entire paragraphs (Doctorow, Wittrock, & Marks, 1978; Jenkins, Heliotis, Stein, & Haynes, 1987). The simplicity of this approach is appealing. Although this basic form of summarization has been effective in improving memory of isolated facts, the general utility of this approach has not been established since it has not been evaluated using more general comprehension or memory measures.

A more complex and theoretically well-grounded approach includes instruction of the rules that Kintsch and van Dijk (1978) identified as the basis for summaries constructed by mature readers. These rules include (e.g., Brown & Day, 1983):

(1) Delete trivial information.
(2) Delete redundant information.
(3) Substitute superordinate terms for lists of items.
(4) Integrate a series of events with a superordinate action term.
(5) Select a topic sentence.
(6) Invent a topic sentence if there is none.

Bean and Steenwyk (1984) successfully taught grade-6 children to apply these rules to single paragraphs. Summarization instruction improved the children's recall of paragraphs. More impressive, however, was the finding that the children trained to use the summarization rules did better on a standardized reading comprehension test than did children who were not instructed to summarize paragraphs.

Summarization instruction has also been extended to prose that is longer than single paragraphs. Children have been taught to construct summaries of passages that are as long as those commonly contained in middle-grade science and social studies texts (i.e., 800- to 2500-word passages). For example, Taylor and Beach (1984) taught seventh-grade children to summarize 6-10 page (approximately 2500-word) social studies passages. During 7 one-hour sessions, the children were taught how to produce and study a hierarchical summary of a reading passage. A hierarchical summary consists of a thesis statement at the top of the page that is followed by main idea statements; each main idea statement has two or three supporting ideas for each section of the text, and topic headings are written in the margins to connect the sections (see Table 3-1 for an example of a hierarchical summary). Taylor and Beach taught the students to outline each sub-section before constructing the thesis statement for the entire passage. The teacher helped students generate the summaries for the first four sessions, and the students produced summaries independently for the remaining three sessions. During each session, the class discussed their summaries with the teacher and compared their summaries to the prototypical summaries provided by

Table 3-1
Hierarchical Summary for a Three-Page Social Studies Passage

1. Johnson developed programs to fight injustice and poverty.

Civil Rights

    A. *Lyndon Johnson became President of the U.S. after Kennedy was assassinated.* hard worker, tried to carry out some of Kennedy's programs.

    B. *Johnson fought for civil-rights law.* to protect blacks from discrimination in hotels and restaurants, blacks had not been allowed in some hotels or restaurants in the South.

    C. *Johnson persuaded Congress to pass a law ensuring all people the right to vote.* protected black people's right to vote, literacy tests now illegal.

    D. *Johnson started a "war on poverty."* job training, education for poor people, plans for a "Great Society".

Great Society Programs

    E. *Johnson persuaded Congress to develop Medicare.* for people at least 65 years old, hospital bills paid, doctor's bills paid in part.

    F. *Johnson persuaded Congress to pass a law giving money to schools.* to improve education for poor families, one billion dollars in aid to schools.

Adapted from Taylor and Beach (1984).

Taylor and Beach (1984). After producing the summaries, the students were instructed to study them for five minutes to try to remember as much of the content as possible. This summarization training proved successful in that recall of subsequent passages was improved compared to that of students not trained in summary production.

Rinehart, Stahl, and Erickson (1986) used a similar method to train grade-school children to produce summaries that include main ideas with supporting information so that the summary reflected the organization of the original text. The instruction was based on two of Kintsch and van Dijk's (1978) rules—delete trivial information and delete redundant information— and another summarization technique— relate main to supporting information. Instruction was provided over the course of five 45-50 minute sessions.

First, the teacher defined a summary as *"the important information from a reading"* (p. 429) and explained its utility in reading and studying. The teacher modeled how to write down only main ideas and supporting information by *"talking through"* four sample paragraphs and having individual children do similar *"talk-throughs."* Next, the teacher modeled use of the following checklist to be used by students during the first three lessons:

- Have I found the overall idea that the paragraph or group of paragraphs is about?
- Have I found the most important information that tells more about the overall idea?
- Have I used any information that is not directly about the overall idea?
- Have I used any information more than once?

During the second lesson, students practiced summarizing single paragraphs while the teacher provided individual and class feedback. The third lesson consisted of summarizing groups of paragraphs. The students were taught to summarize individual paragraphs first and then to summarize the summaries. Again, teacher modeling and discussion was followed by teacher-monitored student practice. The fourth step involved summarizing passages of several paragraphs without first summarizing individual paragraphs. The students were instructed to write the overall idea for the passage, then to add the most important supporting ideas from the passage in as few sentences as possible. The final lesson included practice of the passage length version of the summarization strategy. Students practiced writing summaries of each section of a textbook chapter. Table 3-2 provides an outline of the principles and procedures used by Rinehart et al. (1986). Use of this strategy by the trained students improved their recall of main ideas from passages compared to students not trained to use the summarization strategy.

Summarization training can also include spatial components. Baumann (1984) included graphic metaphors as part of his summarization instruction with sixth-grade students. For example, students were taught to think of the main idea as a table top supported by details as represented by the legs of the table. This training improved children's summary writing, but not their recall of text. However, Baumann (1984) did not emphasize the Kintsch and van Dijk (1978) rules of summarization or the utility of graphic metaphors.

Berkowitz (1986), on the other hand, emphasized use of summarization rules and spatial outlining in her research. Grade-6 students were taught to construct maps of passages over the course of six 45-minute sessions. Students were taught to write the title of the passage in the center of a sheet of paper. They then surveyed the text for four to six main ideas. These ideas were placed in a circle around the title. Then, students wrote two to four important supporting details under each main idea. Students were taught to use the graphic summary as a test until they could recite the main ideas and the supporting details. Overall recall of passages was improved by use of this graphic summarizing strategy.

Armbruster, Anderson, and Ostertag (1987) taught fifth-grade children about the problem/solution structure that characterizes many social studies passages. This structure includes statement of a problem, actions taken to solve the problem, and the results of the actions. Students learned to use this structure to organize summaries of problem/solution passages into three-box diagrams depicting problems, actions, and results. The instruction proceeded over eleven 45-minute sessions in which the children were told that summarizing in this way would facilitate learning of text. The children were given a lot of practice summarizing social studies passages using the problem/solution framework. Again, the summarization training resulted in improved recall of text.

We recommend instructing students to produce summaries while they read. Summarization instruction improves children's recall of what they read compared to children who are taught using traditional reading comprehension instruction (Armbruster et al., 1987; Berkowitz, 1986; Taylor & Beach, 1984). Summarization training is a powerful intervention, with many variations of the technique improving long-

---

Table 3-2
Summarization Instruction

A. Teach four rules for producing summaries:
    (1) Identify main information.
    (2) Delete trivial information.
    (3) Delete redundant information.
    (4) Relate main and supporting information.

B. Base teaching on principles of direct instruction and self-control training:
    (1) Use explicit explanation—teach why, when, and where to apply the skill.
    (2) Model skills—talk through examples, showing how the skill is applied.
    (3) Provide practice with feedback.
    (4) Break complex skills down—summarize short paragraphs before proceeding to longer passages.
    (5) Use scripted lessons to provide guidance to your instruction.
    (6) Program self-control—phase out teacher direction and phase in student control throughout instruction.

C. Three steps to follow in summarizing multiple-paragraph essays:
    (1) Write summaries of each paragraph.
    (2) Create a summary of the paragraph summaries.
    (3) Apply the four summarization rules to this paragraph.

From Rinehart, Stahl, and Erickson (1986)

term memory of text.

There are several cautionary notes that should be added to this generally positive evaluation. First, research has not been conducted on summarization with normal children younger than 10 years of age. The only data on children younger than 10 were produced by Jenkins et al. (1987) who trained grade-3 and grade-4 learning disabled children to write brief restatements of single paragraphs. Second, teachers need to monitor students' progress in acquiring the strategy. In her investigations with grade-5 students, Taylor (1982) found that when students had not mastered the strategy, there was little evidence of improved performance. Third, there has been little study of how much training time is required to teach summarization. Most studies provided at least six hours of instruction, suggesting that students require ample opportunity for practice to master the strategy. Finally, successful summarization interventions seem to require active student involvement in generating summaries. For instance, Berkowitz (1986) observed only small effects when prepared summaries were provided to elementary-school students. There are clear benefits, however, when students master the strategy of summarization and generate summaries themselves.

Mental Imagery [SSR]

Construction of mental images while reading is another strategy that has been demonstrated to improve children's memory for prose (Pressley, 1977). The use of imagery in reading has a sound theoretical base in dual-coding theory (Paivio, 1971). According to this theory, imagery should aid reading comprehension because both a verbal memory code and an imaginal memory code are activated. Dual coding of prose should aid later recall in that the two codes could be expected to leave a stronger memory trace than a verbal code alone, making it easier to recall the information later.

Two different approaches to construction of images have been investigated. The first is representational imagery in which the images represent precisely the content of the prose. Consider the sentence, *"The kitten clung to the clothesline while the dog glared at it from below."* A representational image for that sentence would include a kitten hanging by its paws with a dog on the ground below. It is possible to construct a representational image of this sentence because the elements (kitten, clothesline, dog) are all easily imaginable. Most readers possess concrete images for these objects.

Sometimes, however, prose contains elements that are not as easily imagined. Consider the sentence, *"Mr. McGoldrick planted potatoes in a large field."* While most people could construct an image of a man planting potatoes in a large field, few people would have a concrete image of someone named Mr. McGoldrick. In this case, a proxy, or keyword mnemonic, for McGoldrick could be generated—that is, a word that can be linked to the concept for which an image cannot be generated. Readers might notice that the name *McGoldrick* contains the word *gold*. Imagining a man who is planting potatoes suddenly unearthing gold would make the sentence memorable. When asked later, "What did Mr. McGoldrick do?", the name *McGoldrick* could cue the mnemonic element *gold*, which would lead back to the image of a man planting potatoes in a large field.

Representational Imagery

Representational imagery facilitates children's learning of text after the age of eight, at least when children are reading concrete stories. Representational imagery has a positive effect on short-answer recall tests (Pressley, 1977; Pierce, 1980). Sadoski (1983, 1985) also demonstrated that children in grades 3, 4, and 5 who report spontaneous use of representational imagery have a better understanding of complex relationships in prose than do children who do not report imagery use. Although the effects produced by representational imagery are relatively small, the evidence is consistent and, hence, we recommend teaching this strategy to elementary school children. Our enthusiasm for this strategy is also fueled by the fact that children can be taught to use representational imagery quickly and easily.

Pressley (1976) taught third-grade children to construct representational images for prose material in approximately 20 minutes. Training began by having children practice forming images with sentences. The children were taught in groups of four to six. After forming an image of a sentence like *"The man sat in his chair and smoked his pipe,"* the children were shown a picture representing the contents of the sentence to demonstrate what their images might look like. It was stressed that the children's images did not have to look exactly like the instructor's pictures. The training proceeded from practice with sentences to practice with paragraphs and a short story. The children were instructed not to try to read and construct images at the same time since both involve the visual system and could interfere with each other. The children were taught to read a section of the text and then to stop reading and to imagine what was conveyed in the text. Children who were taught this strategy could recall more of a 950-word story—one not accompanied by any pictures—than could children who were not taught the strategy.

Gambrell and Bales (1986) provided evidence that representational imagery has a larger effect when measures other than short-answer recall are obtained. They used detection of text inconsistencies as their outcome measure. They taught poor readers from the 4th and 5th grades to construct images representing prose, with instruction proceeding from sentence-length to paragraph-length material. The entire training took 30 minutes and consisted of telling children, *"One good way to understand and remember what you read is to make pictures in your mind. I want you to make pictures in your mind to help you understand and remember what you read"* (p. 458).

To test whether representational imagery aided detection of text inconsistencies, children read two passages containing inconsistencies after being told that someone was attempting to write short stories for children. They were asked to read the stories to see if they made sense and were prompted to "make pictures in your mind to determine if there is anything that is not clear and easy to understand about the story" (p. 459). One of the passages contained the following sentences, *"The blindfolded pigeons could not use their eyes. All of the pigeons were able to find their way home. They were able to use the sun to find their way home"* (p. 437). After reading a passage, the student was questioned to determine if the inconsistencies had been detected. The questioning began without any hint that there might be a problem. Thus, the child was asked, "What do you think about the passage about pigeons? Do you have any suggestions? Did the author forget to put in any information?" (p. 458). If the child did not detect the inconsistency with these questions, they were asked questions that contained hints (e.g., "Was there anything that was not clear and that was not easy to understand? Could blindfolded pigeons use their eyes?").

The main finding in this study was that children trained to use representational imagery detected more inconsistencies than did children who were not trained to use imagery. The untrained children were given the same prose and asked to do whatever would help them remember it. Again, representational imagery was demonstrated to improve reading comprehension with minimal investment of instructional time and effort. Children's reading comprehension was improved by having them construct images that represented the content of the written material. It should be emphasized that the instruction outlined here began with sentence-length material before proceeding to longer passages.

Mnemonic Imagery [T & SSR]

Research on mnemonic imagery as a reading comprehension strategy has largely been restricted to the study of an intervention known as the *keyword method* (McCormick & Levin, 1984; Shriberg, Levin, McCormick, & Pressley, 1982). For instance, Levin, Shriberg, and Berry (1983) read passages to eighth-grade students describing the attributes of fictitious towns (e. g., the town of "Fostoria" was noted for its abundant natural resources, advances in technology, considerable wealth, and growing population). Students were first taught a *keyword* for the town name, that is, a well-known word that sounded like part of the town name (e.g., *frost* for Fostoria). Then, the students were provided with a picture in which frost covered all of the town attributes (i.e., oil pumps representing natural resources, computers for advanced technology, money for wealth, and many people with young children for the growing population). Figure 3-1 is a black-and-white line-drawn version of the colored picture shown to students as an example of what

Figure 3-1
Keyword mnemonic picture
for learning the characteristics
of the town "Fostoria"

Reprinted from Levin, Shriberg, & Berry (1983) by permission of the authors and the American Educational Research Association.

their image might look like. In other words, during instruction the students were provided with an interactive picture of the keyword (representing the town) and all of the to-be-remembered attributes. Compared to students who were not given keyword mnemonic pictures, these students recalled more of the attributes when later presented with the town names.

In Levin et al. (1983), the descriptions of the towns were read to the students. Peters and Levin (1986) extended the mnemonic representational approach by having the students read 200-word descriptions of famous people. They conducted two experiments in which grade-8 students learned about famous people using the keyword method. In the first experiment, the famous people were fictitious with names that were easily convertible to keywords (e.g., Charlene Fidler and Larry Taylor). The children successfully learned to generate keywords as well as mnemonic images in which the keyword referent interacted with the accomplishments of the famous people. Training in the keyword method improved recall of the accomplishments of the "famous" people.

The second experiment involved teaching eighth-grade students to use the keyword method to learn the accomplishments of actual famous people. Generating keywords required some transformation of the names since the names were not created to be easily convertible to keywords (e.g., the keywords for James Smithson were *jam* and *smile*, respectively). The experimenters provided the students with keywords in this experiment (i.e., students were not expected to generate their own keywords). The students practiced using the keyword method with two passages before being tested on eight other 200-word passages. The instructor provided pictures to which students could compare their images during practice. The students spent only 2 minutes 45 seconds on each passage, including reading and generating keyword mnemonics. Despite the small amount of time, the effects produced by the keyword method were large. The small amount of instructional time expended was well-rewarded in terms of student recall.

Mnemonic imagery is useful when trying to learn information about totally unfamiliar concepts, such as the accomplishments of unfamiliar people or information about unknown countries. It seems especially useful when there are a great many previously unknown concepts that must be learned in a short time.

More work is required to determine precisely the types of text for which mnemonic imagery is appropriate, the utility of the method for younger children, and whether children can be taught to generate their own keywords. However, we are optimistic that the keyword method will prove to be a potent strategy that can be taught quickly and efficiently. As a final note, recent evidence suggests that students seem struck by the effectiveness of mnemonic imagery when they use it, with their enthusiasm related to future use of the strategy (Beuhring & Kee, 1987). Enthusiasm for use of a strategy increases the probability of long-term benefits of instruction.

Question Generation and Answering of Self-Generated Questions [SSR]

Students can be asked to generate think-type questions, ones that integrate the material covered in a text. The strategy is hypothesized to work either by making readers more active while reading (Singer & Donlan, 1982) or by increasing student awareness of whether they are comprehending (Davey & McBride, 1986). Generating good think-type questions may highlight problems in comprehension and prompt the reader to engage in actions to compensate for comprehension failure.

The instructional effectiveness of this strategy with children is difficult to assess because most question-generation research has been conducted with high school or college students. When the approach has been used with children, it has been as one of several strategies in an effective instructional package (e.g., Palincsar & Brown, 1984), making it difficult to discern the worth of question generation alone. The data with children that can be interpreted suggest modest effects: Wong (1985) reported that the gains produced by question generation are modest when they are obtained at all. More recently, Denner and Rickards (1987) and McDonald (1986) found that very brief instruction in question generation does not improve memory of what is read.

Thus far, our assessment of the effects of question generation has been fairly negative. However, several recent, well-controlled studies with grade-school children (Davey & McBride, 1986; King, 1994) permit optimism about question generation as a strategy to improve comprehension and memory for what is read. Most other research on question generation with children has only asked children to generate questions or included very brief instruction about how to generate questions. Davey and McBride (1986) and King (1994), on the other hand, showed that reading comprehension and memory for prose are improved if grade-school children are actually taught *how* to generate questions as they read.

Davey and McBride (1986) trained grade-6 children to generate questions over five 40-minute sessions. The instruction provided in this study was successful. First, children who received the full instructional procedure learned to generate better think-type questions than any of the groups to which they were compared. Second, there were moderate to large differences favoring the question-trained group for memory of inferential information. The effect was not as dramatic for memory of literal information but this is not surprising given the focus on inferential information during question-generation training.

The training approach used by Davey and McBride (1986) is summarized in Table 3-3. During the first lesson, students were given a general overview of the activities they would be engaged in during instruction, and an explanation of the value of using question generation while reading. According to our perspective, this is an important step in any strategy instruction. If learners are expected to use strategies, they must understand that the strategies will help. Students were also taught the difference between locate (literal) and think-type (inferential) questions during this first session.

The second lesson consisted of a review of the distinction between think and locate questions and the rationale for generating good think-type questions after reading was further developed. For example, students were told that asking themselves questions would help them know if they need to re-read, help them to remember, and help them predict test questions. Students were also taught how to generate question stems to relate information from one part of a passage to information from another part of the passage. The teacher discussed important words for question stems. For example, they were taught that signal words such as "what," "why" and "how" can be used to construct questions requiring integration over parts of text (e.g., *What did the author describe previously about ... ?*). Teachers also discussed how to respond to such questions.

During the third lesson, the teacher reviewed what was taught in previous sessions, and students practiced generating questions related to the most important ideas of a passage. The teacher demonstrated how to decide what is most important in a passage and how to generate questions related to this content.

Table 3-3
Principles of Davey and McBride's (1986)
Question-Generation Instructional Procedure

Explain the Rationale and Basics
Explain why generating 'think-type' questions will help comprehension. Explain and practice identifying the distinction between think and locate questions.

Teach How to Generate Questions
Have students practice generating questions while you provide feedback regarding whether they are good 'think-type' questions.

Teach How to Identify Important Information
Demonstrate and have students practice identifying the most important information in passages. Have students practice generating questions related to this content.

Teach Students How to Monitor their own Strategy Use
Provide children with questions to be used to monitor their own use of the question generation strategy, e.g. "How well did I identify important information?"

Provide Practice and Feedback
Provide ample opportunity to practice generating questions, identifying important information, and monitoring strategy use. Provide feedback on each of these aspects during instruction.

Children were taught to evaluate their use of the question generation strategy in the fourth lesson. They were given five monitoring questions to answer as they generated their own questions:

"How well did I identify important information?"
"How well did I link information together?"
"How well could I answer my question?"
"Did my 'think' question use different language from the text?"
and
"Did I use good signal words?" (p.258).

The final training session provided students with additional opportunity to practice generating questions. Throughout instruction, students were given the opportunity to practice generating questions, answering questions, and responding to the self-evaluation questions designed to promote student monitoring of their strategy use. Practice was always integrated with teacher feedback regarding student progress and success using the strategy.

King (1994) has also generated exceptionally important work on the effects of teaching grade-4 students how to ask and then answer questions about text content. King recognized that children often do not know how to construct questions about text, especially inferential ones that prompt deep thinking about how the various parts of the text are related (i.e., how to construct questions using such signal words as *what*, *why* and *how*). Her solution is to provide students with general question frames that can be used to construct questions requiring inferential responses, with students supplied cards reminding them of the various frames. The question frames are summarized in Table 3-4.

Teachers in King's research met with students to discuss effective question generation and answering over three 60-minute sessions. During the first session, students were taught to differentiate "describing" from "explaining" responses. Specifically, they were told that an explanation is more than just providing information about *what* something is, it also includes providing *how* and *why* information about the concept; that good explanations were ones that paraphrased, rephrased using the students' words, and connected two pieces of information (e.g., text ideas, procedures); and that when people make explanations, they often use their prior knowledge to help make new concepts more meaningful.

In order to help students differentiate between descriptive and explanatory responses, students were provided with examples of each response type (e.g., *descriptive response:* "The circulatory system is made up of the heart, veins, arteries and blood"; *explanatory response:* "We need a circulatory system in our bodies to move the blood around to all parts of the body, because the blood carries oxygen which is food for the cells of the body"). The teacher shared her thoughts (i.e., think aloud) about how the two statements differed and provided a rationale about why the latter was explanatory in nature. The students were also

Table 3-4
Question Frames Students Can Be Taught

Comprehension:
Describe ... in your own words.
What does ... mean?
Why is ... important?

Connection questions:
Explain why ...
Explain how ...
How are ... and ... similar?
What is the difference between ... and ... ?
How does ... affect ... ?
What are the strengths and weaknesses of ... ?
What causes ... ?
How could ... be used to ... ?
What would happen if .... ?
How does ... tie in with ... that we learned before?

Adapted from King (1994).

provided opportunities to practice distinguishing the sentence types, first as a class under the guidance of the teacher, and then with a partner as the teacher provided help on an as-needed basis.

For the second session, students were instructed about the differences between "memory" and "thinking" questions. The teacher explained that memory questions are those that simply require students to remember and repeat information they heard in a lesson. Thinking questions require learners not only to remember information from the lesson, but to use that information in a new way (i.e., to really have to think about it!). Examples of each type of question were presented to the students (*memory questions:* "What are the main parts of the digestive system?" and "Where does food go when it leaves the stomach?"; *thinking questions:* "How is the digestive system similar to the respiratory system?" and "What is the difference between the small intestine and the large intestine?"). Students were also taught how to transform memory questions into thinking ones, with the teacher modeling this process. For example, the question "What are the main parts of the circulatory system?" can be transformed into, "Describe in your own words how the circulatory system works."

Thinking questions were subclassified into comprehension and connection questions (see Table 3-4), with the critical difference being that connection questions linked ideas that were separated in the text. Students were told that asking and answering their own and other people's thinking questions would help them understand and remember material presented in lessons. For the remainder of the second and third lessons, the teacher modeled these question generation and answering procedures. Students were also provided opportunities to practice generating and answering questions using the frames. Students practiced with a partner, providing feedback to each other about the quality of the questions posed and the answers generated. This practice was supported by the teacher, who provided individualized assistance to the student pairs.

Following such question generation training, students could better pose and respond to questions, compared to control students who met to "discuss" text. In general, the discussion of the text was richer and more conceptually advanced for the trained children than for students not receiving question generation and response instruction. Finally, trained students' performances on several types of comprehension tests were improved relative to control students.

In short, King's (1994) work highlights that children need to be taught both how to ask questions and how to respond to them. The approach still requires much validation. An especially critical question is whether such training can increase students' spontaneous generation of questions as well as their understanding of what they read on their own. Long-term internalization of questioning strategies, and use of them when reading independently, were not studied by King (1994).

Others have developed question-asking/-answering strategies similar to King's approach. In particular, Lyman (e.g., 1987) and his colleagues (e.g., Coley & DePinto, 1989) have developed a set of question-answer cues (Think Trix)—symbols designed to remind students about the different types of questions that can be asked about a text. (See Table 3-5.) Similar to King's research, students are taught how to answer such questions at the same time that they are taught how to pose them, with many opportunities to practice using the cues to discuss text content with other children. Teachers using the Think Trix often have a poster in their classroom to remind students of the questions that can be generated in reaction to text, just as King's students were provided cue cards summarizing the question frames. We encourage readers to compare the question frames developed by King (1994) and the Think Trix question-response cues (i.e., compare Tables 3-4 and 3-5). It should be apparent that there is quite a bit of overlap between the two approaches.

In recommending question-generation training, we emphasize the comprehensive nature of the described training procedures. Davey and McBride tested the components of their model and found that the full instructional package was more effective than less comprehensive approaches at improving the quality of questions generated and increasing the amount of information recalled from reading passages. Thus, in recommending teaching this strategy to grade-school children, we suggest that the strategy be taught using such a complete format.

Question-generation training should include an explanation of why it is good to self-question while reading, practice using the strategy, feedback regarding students' use of the strategy, and information about how to monitor the use of the strategy. In addition, students must be provided with information about what constitutes a good response to a question, with responses being differentiated as a function of question type. While most researchers have used expository text in their investigations of self-questioning, there is no obvious reason why the strategy would not have the same potential benefits with narrative text.

Question-Answering Strategies [SSR]

Teachers and textbooks frequently provide children with questions based on text, with the expectation that answering questions will improve learning. Questions are usually provided after children have read a narrative or a textbook chapter. Questions are thought to help by

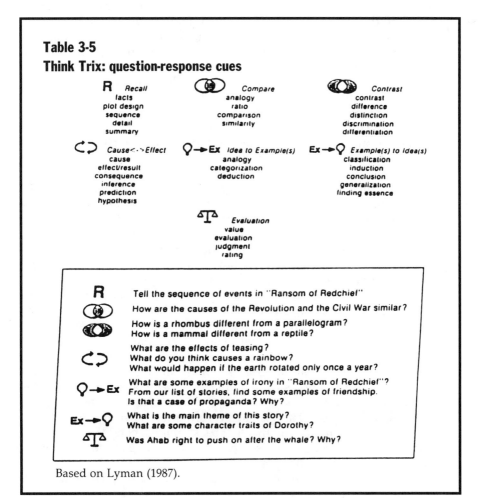

Table 3-5
Think Trix: question-response cues

Based on Lyman (1987).

leading to reprocessing of text, especially when the answers to the questions are not known. Such post-questions have been effective in improving learning by adults (Anderson & Biddle, 1975), but the effects of post-questions with children are much less consistent (e.g., Levin & Pressley, 1981; Pressley & Forrest-Pressley, 1985; Rowls, 1976). However, recent evidence suggests a reason for the inconsistent findings— children may not reprocess text when they do not know the answers to questions. That is, many children do not look back to the text when they have difficulty answering questions (Garner, Hare, Alexander, Haynes, & Winograd, 1984). This is especially true of young children and poor readers in the upper elementary grades. Hence, it has been suggested that children need to be taught strategies to improve their use of questions.

Lookbacks

One such strategy is the "lookback" strategy, which involves looking back to the text only for questions that might be answered in the text, focusing on parts of the text that might contain the answer, and integrating across sentences and phrases to produce an answer. Garner, McCready, and Wagoner (1984) reported that a minority of their grade-5 subjects used such a mature lookback strategy.

Garner et al. (1984) have conducted initial work to determine if children who do not use the text lookback strategy can be trained to do so. They taught 12 children between 9 and 13 years of age who were experiencing reading difficulties to look back when they could not answer post-questions. The children were taught the lookback strategy in three 20-minute sessions over a period of three days. During the first session, children read two 200-word expository passages and answered three questions. They were told *why* looking back at the text to find the answers should help (*"You cannot remember everything you read"*). During the second session, the *why* hint was reviewed and another expository passage with three questions was read. Children were then told *when* looking back at the text should help (*"for questions that ask about what specific articles or authors said, not about what you think"*). On the third day, children were given another passage with three questions and the lookback strategy was modeled by the teacher to show the children *where* to look for the answers (*"skim the whole article to find the part that might have the answer"*). The instruction of this strategy is summarized in Table 3-6.

The results of Garner et al.'s (1984) training are clear. Students trained to use lookbacks were more likely than control subjects to use lookbacks when they did not know the answer to a question that was located in the text. The probability of correct answers to the post-questions was higher in the lookback trained condition, with the advantage due to lookback subjects being more likely to find correct answers when they did look back.

As optimistic as these results may seem, we emphasize that this

Table 3-6
Question-Answering Strategies

A. Text Lookback
  Successful readers know these three things about looking back to text to
  answer questions:
  1. *Why look back?*
     You cannot remember everything you read.
  2. *When should you look back?*
     When questions ask about what articles or authors said, not about what
     you think.
  3. *Where should you look?*
     Skim the whole article to find the part that might have the right answer.

B. Question-Answer Relationships (Raphael and colleagues)
  1. *Right There*: words used to create the question and words used for the
     answer are "right there" in the same sentence. .
  2. *Think and Search*: the answer is in the text, but words used to create the
     question and those used for an appropriate answer would be found in
     two or more sentences.
  3. *On My Own*: the answer is not found in the text; rather, you would think
     to yourself that you have to find the answer "on your own."

strategy is recommended provisionally, given that more detailed
investigation of this strategy is warranted. First, Garner et al. (1984) did
not include measures of memory or comprehension for text after
children had answered questions on the passage. Second, the questions
were worded such that it was obvious when the passage would provide
the answer to the question (i.e., questions contained phrases like, "in
the article" and "what did the author write"). Real-world questions are
often less explicit about where to find the answers.

Question-Answer Relationships [SSR]

Where to find answers to questions is the focus of another question-
answering strategy investigated by Raphael and her colleagues (Raphael
& McKinney, 1983; Raphael & Pearson, 1985; Raphael & Wonnacott,
1985). Because some children do not know where to find answers to
questions, these researchers have taught elementary students question-
answer relationships (QARs). The children in these studies were taught
to analyze questions to decide if they could be answered by information
stated in the text ("right there" questions), by information that could be
inferred by combining pieces of information in text ("think and search"
questions), or by information in the reader's knowledge base ("on my
own" questions).

There was clear evidence that instruction about the relationships between questions and answers increased correct responding to questions following a reading selection. In general, the results were more striking with younger children (fourth graders) than with older students (eighth graders) and with average- and lower-ability children than with high-ability children. It should also be pointed out that the effects produced by this strategy are not very large. As with the lookback strategy, it is also not possible to make the case that improved responding to the questions improved comprehension or long-term memory of the passage, since there has been no clear test of this possibility to date.

Raphael and colleagues have used both teachers and researchers to instruct QARs. In general, QAR instruction was conducted in groups within classrooms as follows. Students received four days of instruction, each session lasting approximately 40 minutes. On the first day, students were introduced to the concept of QAR, being given definitions and visual presentations of the three types of QARs. For example, a picture of a child thinking with an open book might accompany the teacher's explanation of "think and search" questions. Following the introduction, students were given brief passages (2-3 sentences) with three questions (one of each QAR type). The three types of QARs are described in Table 3-6. At first, students were provided with answers to the questions as well as justifications for why the question fit the QAR category. Over the next three sessions, the passages became longer (400 words) with more questions and the students were expected to answer the questions, identify the QAR classification, and justify their QAR choice themselves. Teachers provided feedback on accuracy of answers, QAR category, and justification for QAR choice.

To summarize the data on the question-answering strategies, we emphasize that children's question answering can be improved by training in how to answer comprehension questions that accompany text. Children can be taught to look back to text to find answers to questions and they can be taught to discriminate opinion questions from those for which answers would be stated explicitly in text. Although we might expect improved question answering to increase long-term learning from text, we cannot make this conclusion based on the research to this point. Therefore, we emphasize our provisional recommendation of the question-answering strategies.

Story Grammar [SSR]

Conventional stories share a general structure (Stein & Glenn, 1979). They begin with a setting that may include information about the time of the story, where it took place, and the central characters. An initiating event then sets a goal or problem. This is followed by an internal response by the characters which, in turn, is followed by actions, or attempts to achieve the goal or solve the problem. Finally, there are consequences of the characters' actions and the characters' reactions to the resolutions. Skilled, mature readers definitely know this story grammar and use it automatically to facilitate comprehension and memory of stories (Mandler, 1984). There is evidence to suggest that poor elementary-school readers possess less well-developed knowledge of story grammar than do their good-reader peers (Rahman & Bisanz, 1986). This leads to the hypothesis that poor readers would benefit from training in story-grammar elements.

Support for this hypothesis comes from a study reported by Short and Ryan (1984). They trained grade-4 boys to use story grammar while reading stories. Following training, the text recall of poor readers was comparable to that of skilled fourth-grade readers. Short and Ryan (1984) trained the children to ask themselves (and answer) the following five questions as they read stories:

(1) Who is the main character?
(2) Where and when did the story take place?
(3) What did the main character do?
(4) How did the story end?
(5) How did the main character feel?

Instruction proceeded through three 30-35 minute individual instructional sessions conducted by the experimenter. The first session included modeling of the story grammar strategy by the experimenter through a taped example. Story grammar was introduced as a game called *Clue*, with a Story-Teller who provided clues that enabled predictions about what would happen in the story and a Detective Reader who searched for the clues in the story to answer the five story-grammar questions. During the second and third training sessions, the story-grammar strategy was reviewed and children practiced using it with three stories. Children were prompted to use the strategy while reading and to underline and label the answers to the questions.

Story grammar has also been taught using story maps (Idol, 1987; Idol & Croll, 1987). Nine- to twelve-year-old children were taught to construct maps that recorded the setting, problem, goal, action, and outcome information (see Figure 3-2). The story-map training was administered by teachers in classrooms containing 22 children. The teacher modeled use of the strategy and children practiced constructing maps. Story-map training is an extension of the Short and Ryan (1984) training to classroom instruction, with essentially the same questions being asked in both types of training. Idol's story-map training improved poor readers' memory for a story. However, the story-grammar training was not necessary for normal readers, a finding that is consistent with the hypothesis that good readers already possess story-grammar knowledge (Dreher & Singer, 1980).

The studies reviewed thus far indicate that story-grammar training is effective only for below-average readers. However, Nolte and Singer (1985) reported that a slight variation on story-grammar training improved recall of story facts by normal fourth- and fifth-grade readers.

Figure 3-2
Components of the Story Map

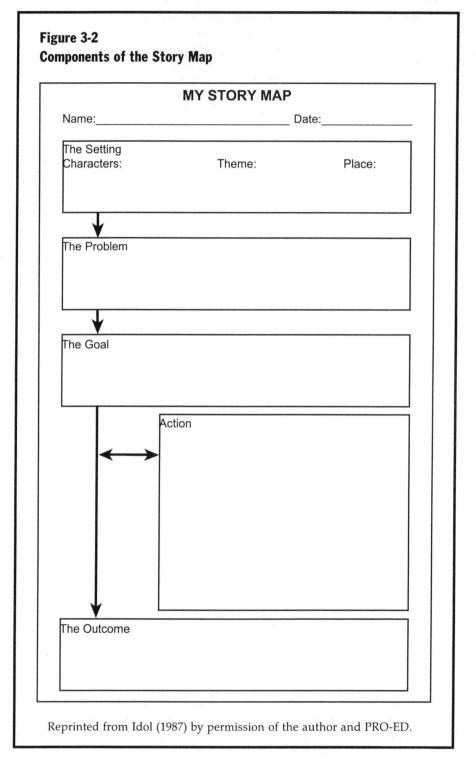

Reprinted from Idol (1987) by permission of the author and PRO-ED.

Children were taught to ask themselves questions about the setting, the main characters, the goals of the characters, and the obstacles encountered on the way to the goal. This training differs from other story-grammar training in that the students generated their own questions. Short and Ryan (1984) and Idol's group (Idol, 1987; Idol & Croll, 1987) provided questions to the students. Nolte and Singer (1985) combined question-generation and story-grammar training. Teaching of this strategy occurred over ten 40-minute sessions. As in most strategy instruction, instruction began with teacher explanations and modeling. Guidance was faded until all students were using the strategy autonomously.

To summarize, we recommend story-grammar training, especially for poor readers who may not have sufficient knowledge about narrative structure. Teaching poor readers to identify story-grammar elements helps students remember what they read.

When teaching story grammar, the teacher should model and explain the approach followed by student practice. Teacher prompting and feedback is gradually faded as the students' proficiency in strategy execution increases. The story-grammar strategy appears to be relatively easy to teach in that there are gains after only a few sessions of instruction with poor readers. The story grammar strategy is also easily adapted to classroom situations using story maps (Idol, 1987; Idol & Croll, 1987). Finally, for good readers the strategy may prove useful if students are taught to generate their own inferential questions aimed at story-grammar elements. Good readers may benefit from generating their own higher-level questions related to story structure.

Activating Prior Knowledge [SSR]

The reader's knowledge base, or prior knowledge of a topic, plays an important role in reading comprehension (Wilson & Anderson, 1986). The way in which text is interpreted or remembered depends on the prior knowledge the reader brings to the reading (e.g., Anderson, Reynolds, Schallert, & Goetz, 1977; Bransford & Johnson, 1973; Pearson, Hansen, & Gordon, 1979). The general finding is that readers who have a well-developed knowledge base recall more relevant information than do readers with less knowledge of the topic covered in the text (Chiesi, Spilich, & Voss, 1979). Activating prior knowledge of a topic while reading would appear to be a good strategy to improve reading comprehension. However, children often do not activate their prior knowledge spontaneously while reading even when they possess knowledge relevant to the topic (Paris & Lindauer, 1976).

Hansen and Pearson (1983) designed an instructional program to teach fourth-grade children to activate prior knowledge in hopes of improving inferential comprehension. The instruction consisted of pre- and post-reading group discussions. Hansen and Pearson (1983) rationalized that group discussion would be the best way to utilize prior knowledge because it is likely to increase the knowledge base of all children. For instance, children with less knowledge of a topic would benefit from the better-developed knowledge bases of their peers.

Hansen and Pearson (1983) provided instruction over the course of 10 weeks, with two sessions per week. The prereading discussion began with a rationale for why it was beneficial to discuss previous experiences that are similar to situations presented in text to be read. The teacher oriented the students with statements such as, "Today, pretend you are reading a science article about conservation. What might you be thinking about while you are reading the article?" (p. 823). Following the general discussion, the teacher provided three important ideas from each reading passage and asked students to relate previous experiences to the main ideas and to make predictions about the contents of the stories, based on the ideas. After reading the passages, the class discussed 10 literal and inferential questions. The students were required to use information not stated explicitly in the text to answer the questions. Instruction improved literal and inferential comprehension of poor readers but not of good readers.

Dewitz, Carr, and Patberg (1987) used a cloze procedure to teach fifth-grade students to integrate prior knowledge with material that they read. The students were taught to differentiate cloze questions that required use of prior knowledge from cloze questions that could be answered by using clues in the text. For example, if given only the sentence, "The car skidded out of control, and crashed through the railing over the _____" (p. 106), the students had to learn that the only way to answer this question was to use their prior knowledge.

After practicing with single sentences, the children were given social studies paragraphs with blanks inserted and had to use clues in the text or their prior knowledge to complete the sentences. Students were taught to distinguish between forward and backward clues. A forward clue is information that occurs after the blank that can be used to answer the inferential question (blank); a backward clue is one which was read prior to encountering the blank. The students were given feedback regarding their cloze answers and the teacher asked inferential questions based on the text. The final step in the process included transferring the procedure to intact social studies textbook passages by having students use their prior knowledge and clues in the text to answer inferential questions. Throughout instruction, students were provided the following list of questions to aid them in answering the cloze and inferential questions:

1. Does the answer make sense?
2. Does the answer make sense in the sentence?
3. Is the answer based on a combination of knowledge you had before you read the passage and the clues in the passage?
4. Is there a forward clue in the same sentence, paragraph, or passage?

5. Is there a backward clue in the same sentence, paragraph, or passage?
6. Did the clue make you change your answer, or is your answer the same?

Overall, the results of this study showed a positive effect of the cloze instruction on tests of literal and inferential comprehension. In addition, below-average readers tended to benefit more from the instruction than did average or above-average readers.

Activation of prior knowledge is especially recommended for poor readers who may not spontaneously relate their previous experience or knowledge to reading passages. Discussion of prior knowledge seems to be an effective way to increase the knowledge base of all readers in a classroom, given that many readers may not have well-developed knowledge bases relevant to topics in many classroom readings. Although activating prior knowledge seems to have a relatively small effect on reading comprehension, it might improve children's question-answering strategies in that it heightens children's awareness of where to find answers to questions (see discussion of question-answering strategies, this chapter).

As a final note of caution, some researchers have found that if text is incompatible with children's prior knowledge, activating that prior knowledge can actually be detrimental to children's comprehension (Lipson, 1982; Smith, Readence, & Alvermann, 1984). Teachers should probably attend to and attempt to correct errors in children's prior knowledge that may be incompatible with information presented in text while they are encouraging activation of prior knowledge.

Concluding Comments

If a student flexibly used all of the strategies summarized in this section, he or she would be a very strategic reader. We suspect that there are some teachers who teach all of these strategies, hoping that students will learn to coordinate and integratively adapt them. Other teachers take another approach, teaching a small repertoire of strategies, typically including most of the single strategies summarized in this section of the repertoire, with the overarching goal of teaching the development of readers who use the repertoire of strategies effectively. In order to teach such a repertoire of strategies, students need a complete understanding of each strategy in the repertoire. *It is perfectly appropriate and desirable to introduce strategies one at a time, following the guidelines given in this section. Moreover, when students experience difficulty with individual strategies, intensive teaching of the problematic strategy is entirely defensible.*

In short, we envision many lessons on single strategies, with the contents of this section intended as a strong support for teachers as they develop repertoires of strategies with their students.

TEACHING REPERTOIRES OF COMPREHENSION STRATEGIES [SSR]

By the early 1980s it was apparent that competent readers could and did carry out a variety of strategies before, during and after their reading of a text. The most telling data were generated in investigations in which readers thought aloud as they read (e.g., Bereiter & Bird, 1985; Johnston & Afflerbach, 1985; Lytle, 1982; Olshavsky, 1976-77; Olson, Mack & Duffy, 1981). What was apparent in these studies was that skilled reading did not involve use of a single potent strategy, but rather coordination of several strategies. Given this realization, it made good sense to teach children diverse strategies, making them aware that there are strategies that can be used in preparation for reading, strategies to increase the effectiveness of reading, and strategies to increase what is remembered from text after reading is completed.

Duffy et al. (1987) reported success with a year of instruction in which grade-3 teachers recast the skills taught during reading as strategies, providing many direct explanations about how to attack text and comprehend it. For example, if one of the prescribed skills was "comprehend words", teachers retaught and modeled this skill as a problem-solving strategy (i.e., identify known word parts and combine their meanings). This specific strategy was taught as part of a larger problem-solving approach where students stopped reading when they could not identify a word, searched for an appropriate strategy, and checked their solutions by referring back to the text content.

Collins (1991) produced improved comprehension in grades-5/6 students by providing a semester (3 days a week) of lessons on reasoning skills. Her students were taught to seek clarification when uncertain, look for patterns and principles, analyze decision-making that occurs during text processing, problem-solve (including the use of backward reasoning and visualization), summarize, predict, adapt ideas in text (including rearranging parts of ideas in text), and negotiate interpretations of texts in groups. Although the trained students did not differ from controls before the intervention with respect to standardized comprehension performance, there was a very substantial difference (3 standard deviations) between trained and untrained students on the posttest.

Bereiter and Bird (1985) demonstrated that students in grades 7/8 benefit from instructions to use a few comprehension strategies used by older, more sophisticated readers (i.e., restate difficult text, backtrack as necessary, watch for pertinent information in text, and resolve apparently anomalous information in text). These data could be combined with Duffy et al.'s (1987) and Collins' (1991) outcomes to produce optimism that instruction of multiple strategies is an intervention that is potentially effective during most of the elementary and middle-school years.

Notably, Duffy et al. (1987), Collins (1991), and Bereiter and Bird (1985) all involved extensive direct explanations of cognitive strategies by teachers to students. In all three cases, the teachers made visible otherwise invisible mental processes by thinking aloud (i.e., mental modeling; Duffy, Roehler & Herrmann, 1988). In all three cases, students were provided extensive practice opportunities, with teacher assistance provided during practice as required by students. In all three cases, there was opportunity for gradual acquisition of the repertoire of strategies and long-term instruction about the coordination of the strategic competencies acquired.

Reciprocal Teaching [SSR]

The best-known multiple-strategies intervention developed during the 1980s was reciprocal teaching of comprehension strategies, perhaps because it was the first report of classroom-deployed multiple-strategies intervention that seemed to promote reading comprehension (Palincsar & Brown, 1984). As part of this program, lower-ability students (i.e., those requiring supplementary or special reading instruction) were taught to use four effective comprehension strategies: prediction, seeking clarification, question generation, and summarization. Instruction lasted for approximately 20 weeks, with teachers meeting with small groups of students (2-3 children) daily for 30-minute sessions. These sessions started with the teacher introducing the target text passage. If the passage was a new one, the teacher would ask the students to make predictions about its content on the basis of its title. This was intended to activate students' relevant prior knowledge. If the passage was carried over from a previous day, the teacher asked the students to review the important text content covered so far, providing a review and stimulating reactivation of prior knowledge.

Instruction continued with the teacher assigning each student to be "the instructor" for a segment of text. Students were expected to ask questions, ask for clarification, and make summaries or predictions about the text. The role of the teacher was one of facilitator, providing guidance to students on an as-needed basis. For example, teachers provided students with prompts ("What questions do you think a teacher might ask?"), direct instructions ("Remember, a summary is a shortened version, it doesn't include detail"), and re-explanations ("If you're having a hard time thinking of a question, why don't you summarize first?"). Throughout the session, students were informed about the importance of using the reading strategies, with the teacher modeling strategy use. Students were encouraged to continue using the strategies during their silent reading.

In general, analyses of reciprocal teaching have been positive, with students continuing to use the strategies as they read. Although in some studies there has been evidence of improved performance on standardized measures of comprehension, such improvement has not always been observed. On other occasions the improvement on standardized comprehension measures has been small (Rosenshine & Meister, 1992).

Marks et al. (1993) analyzed the reciprocal teaching of a grade-1 teacher, a middle-school special education teacher, and a high school teacher. They observed that each adapted reciprocal teaching. The grade-1 and middle-grades students learned how to apply the four comprehension strategies over a long period of time. The student leader role was modified so that use of the four strategies occurred more as a discussion among students; by contrast, in Palincsar and Brown (1984), the student leader led and directed fellow students rather than dialoguing with them. All three teachers recognized that students needed additional instruction in question generation for interesting questions to be asked during the dialogues. Two of the teachers observed by Marks et al. (1993) taught their students to use the Think Trix reviewed in the last section in order to generate questions about materials being read by the group.

Our view is that reciprocal teaching is a sensible and relatively easy-to-implement intervention, although it may not be as flexible as other multiple-strategies teaching we have observed (e.g., transactional strategies instruction, covered in the next section). For teachers who wish to try this approach, there are, in our view, four key ingredients:

- Teach students to (a) make predictions about what is going to be in text, (b) generate questions about the text content, (c) seek clarification of points that are not well understood or are confusing, and (d) summarize what has been read.
- Encourage students in interaction to discuss text as they apply strategies to text. That is, encourage students to share their predictions with one another, ask questions of one another about the text, seek clarifications about text from fellow students, and summarize the text for one another.
- Have a student leader whose role is to orchestrate the discussion rather than "play teacher" as conceived in the original reciprocal teaching intervention.
- Teach students how to ask questions, since not knowing how to generate questions is a bottleneck that can undermine the effectiveness of the approach. Either King's (1994) approach or Lyman's (1987) Think Trix probably can be applied profitably to make question generation more certain.

Transactional Strategies Instruction [SSR]

Research on reciprocal teaching, and on Duffy et al.'s (1987) conceptualization of direct explanation of strategies, as well as the validations of the effectiveness of the individual comprehension strategies, motivated some educators to attempt comprehension strategies instruction in their own classrooms. That some educators seemed to be very successful in these instructional efforts in turn motivated Pressley and his colleagues to study such educator-developed instruction.

Three different educator-developed programs were studied: Benchmark School, which has a strategies-based curriculum for bright elementary-level underachievers (Gaskins & Elliot, 1991); and two comprehension strategies programs devised by separate Maryland public school systems (Coley, DePinto, Craig & Gardner, 1993; Pressley, El-Dinary et al., 1992; Schuder, 1993). The Pressley group has concluded that these effective reading comprehension strategies instructional programs are "transactional" in three senses of the term:

    a. Readers are encouraged to construct meaning by using strategies that encourage them to relate text content to prior knowledge.

    b. Much of the teaching of strategies occurs in reading groups, with the members of the group using the strategies to construct meaning jointly, meaning that none of the group members would construct on their own, especially if they did not use strategies (e.g., Hutchins, 1991).

    c. The teacher's or group members' actions and reactions cannot be anticipated when the reading group uses strategies to construct interpretations of text. Rather, the reactions and interpretations of individual members of the group (including the teacher) are determined in part by the interpretations and reactions of others in the group. Group members applying strategies to texts co-determine each other's reactions and thinking about text (e.g., Bell, 1968).

The long-term goal of transactional strategies instruction is the internalization and consistently adaptive use of strategic comprehension processes whenever students encounter demanding text. The short-term goal is deep understanding of the current reading assignments through the joint construction of text interpretations by group members.

How Strategies Are Taught Using Transactional Strategies Instruction

TSI entails teaching students to construct text meaning by emulating expert readers' use of comprehension strategies—to emulate how expert readers constructively respond to text as they try to understand it (e.g., Pressley & Afflerbach, 1995; Wyatt et al., 1993). Expert readers are planful and goal-oriented when they read, combine their background knowledge with text cues to create meaning, apply a variety of strategies (e.g., from seeking the important information in text to noting details), monitor their ongoing comprehension, attempt to solve comprehension problems they are experiencing, and evaluate what they read (e.g., Is the content believable? Is the piece well written?). The result is a personalized, interpretive understanding of text.

A variety of qualitative methods were used to study transactional

Table 3-7

Teaching Behaviors Associated With Transactional Strategies Instruction

- Strategy instruction is a long-term affair, with effective strategies instructors offering it in their classroom throughout the school year; the ideal is for high-quality process instruction to occur across school years.

- Teachers explain and model effective comprehension strategies. Typically, a few, powerful strategies are emphasized. Teacher explanations and modeling include the following teacher behaviors:

  (a) Use of strategy terms, including defining such terms when necessary.

  (b) Modeling of strategies by thinking aloud as he or she applies strategies during reading, including explaining the reasoning for applying particular strategies to particular parts of text—as well as how to apply the strategy to that part of text.

  (c) Emphasizing that strategies are coordinated with one another before, during and after reading a text, with different strategies appropriate at different points in a text.

  (d) Telling students the purpose of the strategies lesson (e.g., to understand stories by using the imagery strategy along with other strategies).

  (e) Telling students how they benefit from strategies use (i.e., how strategies help their comprehension), emphasizing that strategies are a means for obtaining comprehension and learning goals.

- The teachers coach students to use strategies, on an as-needed basis, providing hints to students about potential strategic choices they might make. There are many mini-lessons about when it is appropriate to use particular strategies. Coaching includes the following:

  (a) Encouraging students to use strategy terms.

  (b) Prompting students to think aloud as they apply strategies to text.

  (c) Cueing students to choose one of the strategies they know for application at a particular point in text, sometimes going so far as to suggest a particular strategy.

  (d) Explicitly reminding students to use bulletin board displays and cue cards summarizing strategies that can be applied during reading, with these prompts emphasizing that students should choose an appropriate strategy from ones they know.

  (e) Prompting students to evaluate how well they read and to evaluate the impact of strategy use on their reading.

Table 3-7 continued
Teaching Behaviors Associated With Transactional Strategies Instruction

- Teachers provide students with immediate feedback about their strategy-application attempts. Such responses include the following teacher reactions:

  (a) Asking students to explain reasoning behind their use of a particular strategy.

  (b) Restating students' strategic/interpretive responses.

  (c) Praising students for using strategies.

  (d) Pointing out when students are using strategies.

  (e) Using teachable moments to discuss strategies—that is, using an occasion when a particular strategy might be profitably applied as an occasion for a mini-lesson on that strategy.

  (f) Encouraging other students to make strategy-use sugges- tions to a student experiencing difficulties processing a text strategically.

- Throughout instruction, the usefulness of strategies is emphasized, with students reminded frequently about the comprehension gains that accompany strategy use. In addition to providing information about strategy benefits directly, sometimes teachers ask students whether use of a particular strategy helped them to understand/enjoy text. That is, prompting students to reflect on strategy benefits. Sometimes they explain how the student's use of strategy is probably benefiting him or her.

- Information about when and where various strategies can be applied is commonly discussed. Teachers consistently model flexible applica- tion of strategies in situations where the strategies can be appropriately applied; students explain to one another how they adapt strategies for use with particular texts.

- The strategies are used as a vehicle for coordinating dialogue about text. Thus, a great deal of discussion of text content occurs as teachers interact with students, reacting to students' use of strategies and prompting additional strategic processing (see especially Gaskins et al., 1993). In particular, when students relate text to their prior knowledge, construct summaries of text meaning, visualize relations covered in a text, and predict what might transpire in a story, they engage in personal interpretation of text, with these personal interpre- tations varying from child to child and from reading group to reading group (Brown & Coy-Ogan, 1993).

- A variety of conventional teaching behaviors are coordinated with teaching of strategies, for example, use of "wait time" (i.e., waiting for students to respond to questions that are posed as part of strategically- mediated discussions of text).

strategies instruction (Pressley, El-Dinary, Gaskins et al., 1992). These included ethnographies; teacher interviews; long-term case studies; and analyses of classroom discourse. Although the programs differed in their particulars, a number of conclusions about transactional instruction of comprehension strategies seem justified. Teaching as it occurs in TSI classrooms is summarized in Table 3-7.

What Strategies Are Taught in TSI Programs

Although the specific comprehension strategies taught to students vary from program to program, there are some that show up regularly. Typically, students receiving TSI are taught to use the processes summarized in Table 3-8.

In addition to comprehension strategies, TSI can include instruction in decoding and inferring the meanings of previously unknown words. The specific decoding strategies taught vary with the program, although the Pressley group has witnessed most of the decoding strategies discussed in Chapter 2 covered in TSI classrooms. In TSI classrooms, students typically have a variety of decoding strategies at their disposal, with the teacher prompting them to choose one that might be appropriate in order to understand a problematic word now being processed. The main vocabulary-meaning inference strategy that is

---

Table 3-8
Comprehension Strategies Typically Taught in
Transactional Strategies Instruction (TSI) Classrooms

- Predicting upcoming content, often by relating prior knowledge to ideas already encountered in text, including teaching students to check whether the predictions they made were consistent with text content.

- Reacting to text, again by relating ideas in text to prior knowledge, with this sometimes stimulated by encouraging students to activate background knowledge related to text (e.g., pre-reading discussion of what students know about the topic of a reading).

- Constructing images representing the ideas in text.

- Slowing down, reading more carefully, and checking back in text when meaning-making is unsure.

- Generating questions in reaction to text, perhaps by using specific question-asking methods (e.g. Think Trix), with the answers then pursued by reading group members when strategies are practiced in groups.

- Summarizing, including construction of notes capturing the important ideas in a text.

taught is to make use of external and internal context clues—that is, semantic context clues and word part clues, such as prefixes, suffixes, and root words. This approach is consistent with analyses of how effective readers infer the meanings of previously unknown vocabulary (e.g., Sternberg, 1987; Sternberg & Powell, 1983; see Chapter 4, this text).

Strategically Mediated Dialogues About Text As Part of Learning to Apply Strategies in TSI Classrooms

A good way to provide a feel for TSI is to analyze carefully the types of dialogues that occur in TSI classrooms as students read text. These discussions are critical because *so much of TSI is practice using strategies in interaction with classmates.* Student talk is very different during TSI instruction than during more conventional instruction (Gaskins, Anderson, Pressley, Cunicelli & Satlow, 1993; Brown & Coy-Ogan, 1993; Pressley, El-Dinary et al., 1992). In conventional classrooms, there are many rounds of a teacher posing a question, a student attempting a response, followed by a teacher evaluation of the response (i.e., initiate-respond-evaluate [IRE] cycles: Mehan, 1979). In contrast, in TSI classrooms, teachers have and use many other moves than questioning and evaluating student responses, resulting in extended conversations between students and teachers as students attempt to apply strategies to content they are reading. The various "moves" a teacher can make during a TSI lesson, as conceived by Gaskins and her colleagues at Benchmark School (see Gaskins & Elliot, 1991), are summarized in Table 3-9. Of course, these moves are consistent with the strategies teaching behaviors summarized in Table 3-7, providing yet another window on how teachers model, explain, and respond during transactional strategies instruction.

What follows is a dialogue that occurred in a Benchmark School classroom during a lesson on notetaking strategies. Readers of this text should think carefully about each part of the dialogue with respect to the moves represented in Table 3-9 as well as the instructional behaviors summarized in Table 3-7.

Teacher: What I want to concentrate on today is getting the correct information down in our notes, but more importantly, what? What do you have to think about as you look at the notes I am putting on the board, or as you look at your own notes? Having notes does nothing for you—it's just a bunch of words on a piece of paper. You have to be thinking something, too. Tom? *[The teacher asks about the "what" component of the strategy: What do you have to do when taking notes?]*

Student: See if you have the right information.

Teacher: That's one thing to do, but more importantly, what do I think? Do I just rattle off a bunch of points totally unconnected? *Rocky—forests—rivers—settlers.* No, what do I want to do when I see *rocky* in my book? What goes on in the brain as soon as you look at the word *rocky*? If I am taking notes,

Table 3-9
Definitions and Examples of Teacher Process Moves and Responsive Comments

Process Move	Definition	Example
Objective of lesson	Tells or asks what the objective or process is or what the class is learning.	"Our objective is to take notes on important ideas" (explicit). "Before beginning, we must analyze the task" (implicit).
Information about why	Tells or asks why objective or process is important.	"Putting notes in your own words is a way to check your understanding." "It's easier to remember if you attach it to something you know."
Information about when/where	Tells or asks when or where the objective or process can be used.	"Use notetaking when you will be accountable for remembering." "It is a good idea to analyze what you have to do before you begin doing it."
Information about what/how	Tells or asks what one does or should be aware of (w). Provides an explicit explanation for how to do the objective (h).	"Find the main ideas and write a sentence about each" (w). "To figure out cause and effect, ask what happened and why it happened" (h). "Stop and ask yourself: who, what, when, why, how. That's one way to self-question."
Modeling	Shares his or her thinking while using the objective or process.	"I'm picturing their boat, but I have a fuzzy picture of the scene they saw from the boat." "I just read the paragraph and I am thinking to myself, What was that mostly about?"
Personal experience	Tells story about how using the objective or process has proved helpful to self or others.	"Before I learned to write summary sentences about each paragraph, I used to study by reading each chapter five times." "It takes my son forever to tell about a movie because he doesn't know the strategy for summarizing."
Guided practice	Tells students to put the strategy to use while he or she gives feedback.	"Collect information about how they lived and put it on one piece of paper." "Turn the boldface type into a question, then read to answer it."
Cue	Tells student to use (or asks about) previously learned strategy.	"Be sure to ask for clarification." "Use the easy-reading books to increase your background knowledge."
Accept/reject	Explicitly tells that the response is correct or incorrect.	"Yes." "That's right." "Okay." "No." "That's not it."
Use	Uses what student says to continue the discussion on initiating comment or question, without guiding student thinking.	"You think that..." "That's one interpretation; what else could it mean?"
Tell	Tells correct response or answers student question regarding the initiating comment or question.	"One major idea is how they came to North America."
Guide	Provides support for student to formulate a response.	"Major ideas are often found in boldface type." "You are on the right track, look on page 56."
Explain thinking	Explains how one might think about situation being discussed.	"When I was looking for major ideas, I thought of the boldface type." "I was thinking that there was a lot about growing up in that chapter."

* Process moves may themselves be responsive. For example, a teacher may use what a student says by cueing the use of an explicit strategy related to the topic or theme.

Reproduced from Table 1 in Gaskins et al. (1993).

I might put something like *rocky* down, but there is a lot that goes on behind my putting that down in a piece of paper. I spent 5 minutes thinking about it, maybe, before I put *rocky* down. What questions do I ask myself about *rocky*? *[Teacher confirms the student response and then begins guiding the students to understand both the content of the lesson and the strategy involved.]*

Student: If you understand where *rocky* goes and what is rocky, you know—well....

Teacher: What does this mean? Rocky what? *[Seeks clarification.]*

Student: Rocky, where is it? Is it land or...

Teacher: You know that big question for the day, "So what?" So what if the place is rocky? Do I care if it is rocky? Is that important? I don't think it is very important right now. I am thinking to myself, "Big deal, it's rocky. Big deal, they had forests. I'm not even going to make a note on it." That's what I am thinking. I am pretending I'm a student. If you guys want to be a teacher, feel free to argue with me and point out, enlighten me what *rocky* has to do with anything. Because I would rather leave it out of my notes and save some time. *[Challenges students to elaborate and extend their thinking.]*

Student: Rocky is the land form and that is how they—that is the land form and it tells you what...

Teacher: The land is rocky. What does that tell you? *[Repeats the student response and seeks elaboration.]*

Student: It tells you how they lived.

Teacher: That tells me how they lived. *[Seeks confirmation.]*

Student: No, how people....

Teacher: How do they live because it is rocky? *[Seeks elaboration.]*

Student: Well, the different kinds of jobs the people do.

Teacher: I don't get it. It was rocky ground. Oh, big news. *[Seeks clarification.]*

Student: Well, then, they can't farm because of the rockiness. So it affects their way of life.

Teacher: I'm going to add that in there. Do you think I should add that to my notes? *[A guided practice move, as the teacher explicitly asks student to apply the strategy in the context of content.]*

(Gaskins et al., 1993, pp. 294-295)

Also consider this bit of dialogue produced by grade-2 students who are applying strategies to Maurice Sendak's book *Where The Wild Things Are*, strategies they have been learning throughout the year. Unlike the last lesson, this lesson does not emphasize one particular strategy):

Teacher: "That night Max wore his wool suit and made mischief of one kind and another..." Boy, I can really visualize Max. He's in this monster suit and he's chasing after his dog with a fork in his hand. I think he's really starting to act crazy. I wonder what made Max act like that... Hmm-m-m... I bet he was getting a little bored and wanted to go on an adventure. I think that's my prediction...

[Students take turns reading]

Marie: "And grew, until her..." [pause] Can I skip it? *[Skipping a hard word is one strategy for dealing with hard words in this TSI classroom.]*

Teacher: OK, Marie's at a big word, and she wants to skip it. Fine.

Marie: "Blank his. And grew until blank hunger with..." [long pause]

Teacher: OK, we have some problem-solving strategies we can use. [Points to the strategies bulletin board behind her as she thinks aloud about her options.] When we get to a word and we don't know the word, we can guess and substitute; we can ignore and read on; we can reread the sentence; we can look back in the story for clues; or we can use the picture clues.

Marie: Can I read this all over?

Teacher: You can decide. Marie says she wants to read it all over. I think that's a good decision.

[Reading continues]

Teacher: You know... I'm thinking to myself—I'm going to do a think-aloud—I'm thinking to myself, "Sailing over a year." That reminds me of Christopher Columbus sailing to America. A year is a very long time to go on an adventure.

Marie: He's probably just dreaming 'cause he can't sail in a boat for a year. 'Cause his mother would worry and she would look in his room and she would see a forest.

Teacher: So you think his mother would worry if he was gone for a year... OK... Deborah, can you think aloud too?

Deborah: A year is a whole 365 days!

Teacher: 365 days! And what do you need to stay alive that long?

Eric: Food and water.

Teacher: But you know, I'm looking at the picture clues, and I don't see any food and water.

Rico: I see lots of water.

Teacher: You see sea water.

Justin: I see a monster.

Teacher: You see a monster. What do you think is happening there, Justin?

Justin: For a long time, probably a monster grew up because all those years he's just been in the water.

Teacher: So the monster's been getting bigger as the time goes on?

Justin: Yeah.

Teacher: Oh, OK.

Marie: I just think he's dreaming now.

Teacher: You think he's dreaming. What makes you think that, Marie?

Marie: Because there's no such thing as monsters, and he can't sail for that long.

Deborah: But he might have a fishing rod in the boat that we can't see 'cause it's in the boat. And he might fish out fish and stuff to eat.

Teacher: Very good. You're bringing in a lot of background knowledge to give us some more understanding. OK, Rico, keep going. Let's really see if our predictions are right.

[Rico reads text]

Teacher: Anybody got any feeling about that?

Marie: I think he's not dreaming anymore.

Teacher: You don't think he's dreaming anymore. How come? That's changing your prediction.

Marie: Because he would wake up if somebody growled or something, maybe.

Teacher: A loud noise might wake him up. It certainly would startle me. What do you think, Ellen? You're shaking your head.

Ellen: I think Marie is right about that.

Teacher: Do you have any background knowledge that helped you make that prediction?

Ellen: No.

Teacher: Just a kind of feeling you have? Deborah?

Deborah: The noises they hear... oops! I was gonna say something at the end of the story.

Teacher: Oh, the noises might be what? That's OK.

Deborah: They might be his mother bringing in some food or something and putting it in his room. Maybe he might be dreaming like Marie said. And when he wakes up, he'll probably get it.

Teacher: So, do you think the wild things are—I'm not following you—do you think the wild things are real? Marie said in her prediction that she thinks they're real, now. Do you agree with that or disagree?

Deborah: I disagree.

Teacher: So, you're still thinking that...

Deborah: That he's dreaming.

Teacher: That he's still dreaming. OK, let's read on and find out. Justin.

[Justin reads]

Teacher: So they made him king. Why do you think they made him king, Justin?

Justin: Probably because [pause] he might be dreaming that he's the king.

Teacher: OK, so you think he wants to be the king.

Justin: Yeah, in his dreams.

[And the discussion continues...]

(Pressley, El-Dinary et al., 1992, pp. 518-520)

In short, a large part of TSI involves groups of children applying comprehension and decoding strategies as they read text, using the strategies as part of discussing the content of the text. What students are learning in these groups is how to be active readers in the same ways that skilled readers are active—they predict, question, make evaluative reactions, and draw conclusions. Sometimes their predictions are off, with this becoming apparent as text unfolds. Consistent with the Vygotskian idea that higher-order thinking skills develop during social interaction, TSI reading groups involve social interactions in which comprehension and decoding strategies are practiced with the long-term goal that group members will come to own the processes practiced.

Validation of Transactional Strategies Instruction

Does transactional strategies instruction work? The best test to date was carried out by Brown, Pressley, Van Meter, and Schuder (1994). They evaluated whether a year of transactional strategies instruction would promote the reading achievement of primary-level students who were experiencing difficulties in learning to read. Brown et al. (1994) expected that improvements might be detected on a variety of measures, from standardized test performances to interpretations-of-text and thinking-aloud measures. The evaluation involved contrasting the achievement of five reading groups of students receiving strategies instruction (with each group from a different classroom) and five matched reading groups receiving excellent, but more conventional reading instruction. Although the students participating in this study were assigned to grade 2, they were reading below grade level at the beginning of the year. Six students in each class were selected as participants, care being taken to match students in the strategies instruction and comparison reading groups as much as possible with respect to Chapter 1 status, ethnic background and minority affiliation.

Transactional strategies instruction began early in the 1991-92 school year and continued throughout the year. Standardized measurements of reading were administered early in the school year in both the strategies instruction and control conditions. End-of-year measures were collected in April and May 1992, with many informal observations made throughout the school year.

Strategies instruction had positive short-term and long-term impacts as expected. In the short term, students remembered more information about the stories they read in reading group. They also developed a richer, more personalized understanding of the stories, as reflected by interpretive recall of stories covered in reading group. In short, strategies instruction students learned more and richer story content from their daily reading group lessons than did students receiving more conventional grade-2 reading instruction.

Strategies instruction had long-term impacts as well. By the end of the year the strategies instruction students were much more conversant about strategic processes than were the comparison students, and used strategies more than did the comparison students. The standardized test performances of the strategies instruction students also were superior to the test scores of comparison students at the end of the year. Most critically, there was significantly greater improvement on standardized measures of reading comprehension from fall to spring in the strategies instruction versus the comparison classrooms. In short, all measures of student reading achievement collected in the study converged on the conclusion that a year of comprehension strategies instruction improves the reading of at-risk grade-2 students.

Whenever we have encountered what seems to be successful comprehension instruction, it resembles transactional strategies instruction. Those readers who would like more examples should consult the November 1993 issue of the *Elementary School Journal*, which can be purchased from the University of Chicago Press at a reasonable price. In that issue, Valerie Anderson and Marsha Roit (1993) detailed comprehension instruction that they taught to middle-school students experiencing reading difficulties. Anderson and Roit's instruction resembles the instruction just summarized in the last few subsections. Deshler and Schumaker (1993) discuss what it takes for students to become masterful strategies users in their nationally disseminated learning strategies curriculum, with all of the teaching in their program consistent with the transactional strategies instruction model. Cathy Collins Block (1993) details how she teaches thinking skills in a literature-based reading program, again consistent with transactional strategies instruction. In addition, there are several papers in the *Journal* expanding on the specific TSI research reviewed in this chapter.

Becoming a TSI Teacher

All who have studied the process of becoming a TSI teacher concur that it takes a while to feel comfortable with the approach. The teachers must learn the strategies and become familiar enough with them to model their articulated use for students. Teachers must learn to feel comfortable giving up control of discussions in favor of dialogues about text. Teachers must learn how to scaffold student strategy use, which involves monitoring students' use of strategies and providing appropriate assistance when needed. Such monitoring and support is very demanding. For those who want insights into the challenges of becoming a TSI teacher, see Duffy (1993), Schuder (1993), El-Dinary and Schuder (1993), and Brown and Coy-Ogan (1993).

What we emphasize at this point is that although it is challenging, the TSI teachers we have met are committed. Once teachers learn how to teach students to use a repertoire of comprehension and decoding strategies, they stick with the approach. In Chapter 10, we address in more detail how to begin teaching strategies. For the present, we urge that teachers who find this approach appealing begin by teaching students a small set of strategies—perhaps prediction, imagery generation, seeking clarification (including asking questions), relating text to prior knowledge (including evaluating the meaning and worth of what is being read), and summarization. They should be taught slowly, perhaps one at a time, beginning a new strategy only when students seem to understand the previous one, and then reviewing the strategies used earlier. When the students understand each strategy, make a wall card summarizing all the strategies, perhaps of the following form:

> Prediction
> Imagery
> Seeking clarification (Asking questions)
> Relating text to what we know (Making evaluations of whether
>   the text seems accurate)
> Summarization

Encourage students to use these strategies during reading groups and on their own. Model the use of these strategies. Have students model for each other. As students read a story in a group, have them generate their predictions, report their images and associations to text, ask questions about what is unclear, and eventually summarize what has been read. Something that is absolutely critical is that students *choose* which strategy to use when—rather than simply executing a strategy suggested by a teacher. Self-regulation depends on the ability to use sophisticated processes *appropriately*. This ability can only develop if students practice making processing choices on their own. The types of strategically mediated conversations described in the last part engage students—and more than that, introduce students to the processes that excellent readers use habitually as they read and the choices that excellent readers make as they make sense of text (Pressley & Afflerbach, 1995).

REFERENCES

Anderson, R., & Biddle, W. (1975). On asking people questions about what they are reading. In G.H. Bower (Ed.), *The psychology of learning and motivation*, Vol. 9 (pp. 90-132). New York, NY: Academic Press.

Anderson, R.C., Reynolds, R.E., Schallert, D.L., & Goetz, E.T. (1977). Frameworks for comprehending discourse. *American Educational Research Journal*, 14, 367-381.

Anderson, V., & Roit, M. (1993). Planning and implementing collaborative strategy instruction for delayed readers in grades 6-10. *Elementary School Journal*, 94, 121-137.

Armbruster, B.B., Anderson, T.H., & Ostertag, J. (1987). Does text structure/summarization instruction facilitate learning from expository text? *Reading Research Quarterly*, 22, 331-346.

Baumann, J.E. (1984). The effectiveness of a direct instruction paradigm for teaching main idea comprehension. *Reading Research Quarterly*, 20, 93-115.

Bean, T.W., & Steenwyk, F.L. (1984). The effect of three forms of summarization instruction on sixth graders' summary writing and comprehension. *Journal of Reading Behavior*, 16, 297-306.

Bell, R.Q. (1968). A reinterpretation of the direction of effects in studies of socialization. *Psychological Review*, 75, 81-95.

Bereiter, C., & Bird, M. (1985). Use of thinking aloud in identification and teaching of reading comprehension strategies. *Cognition and Instruction*, 2, 131-156.

Berkowitz, S.J. (1986). Effects of instruction in text organization on sixth-grade students' memory for expository reading. *Reading Research Quarterly*, 21, 161-178.

Beuhring, T., & Kee, D.W. (1987). Develop-

mental relationships among metamemory, elaborative strategy use, and associative memory. *Journal of Experimental Child Psychology*, 44, 377-400.

Block, C.C. (1993). Strategy instruction in a literature-based reading program. *Elementary School Journal*, 94, 139-151.

Bransford, J.D., & Johnson, M.K. (1973). Considerations of some problems of comprehension. In W.G. Chase (Ed.), *Visual information processing*. New York: Academic Press.

Brown, A.L., & Day, J.D. (1983). Macrorules for summarizing texts: The development of expertise. *Journal of Verbal Learning and Verbal Behavior*, 22, 1-14.

Brown, A.L., Day, J.D., & Jones, R.S. (1983). The development of plans for summarizing texts. *Child Development*, 54, 968-979.

Brown, R., & Coy-Ogan, L. (1993). The evaluation of transactional strategies instruction in one teacher's classroom. *Elementary School Journal*, 94, 221-233.

Brown, R., Pressley, M., Van Meter, P., & Schuder, T. (1994). *A quasi-experimental validation of transactional strategies instruction with previously low-achieving grade-2 readers*. Amherst, NY: University at Buffalo, SUNY, Department of Educational Psychology.

Chiesi, H.L., Spilich, G.J., & Voss, J.F. (1979). Acquisition of domain-related information in relation to high and low domain knowledge. *Journal of Verbal Learning and Verbal Behavior*, 18, 257-274.

Coley, J.D., & DePinto, T. (1989). Merging reciprocal teaching with question response cues. *Reading: Issues and Practice*, 6, 76-80.

Coley, J.D., DePinto, T., Craig, S., & Gardner,

R. (1993). From college to classroom: Three teacher's accounts of their adaptations of reciprocal teaching. *Elementary School Journal, 94,* 255-266.

Collins, C. (1991). Reading instruction that increases thinking abilities. *Journal of Reading, 34,* 510-516.

Davey, B., & McBride, S. (1986). The effects of question generation training on reading comprehension. *Journal of Educational Psychology, 78,* 256-262.

Denner, P.R., & Rickards, J.P. (1987). A developmental comparison of the effects of provided and generated questions on text recall. *Contemporary Educational Psychology, 12,* 135-146.

Deshler, D.D., & Schumaker, J.B. (1993). Strategy mastery by at-risk students: Not a simple matter. *Elementary School Journal, 94,* 153-167.

Dewitz, P., Carr, E.M., & Patberg, J.P. (1987). Effects of inference training on comprehension and comprehension monitoring. *Reading Research Quarterly, 22,* 99-121.

Doctorow, M., Wittrock, M.C., & Marks, C. (1978). Generative processes in reading comprehension. *Journal of Educational Psychology, 70,* 109-118.

Dreher, M.J., & Singer, H. (1980). Story grammar instruction unnecessary for intermediate grade students. *The Reading Teacher, 33,* 261-268.

Duffy, G.G. (1993). Rethinking strategy instruction: Four teachers' development and their low achievers' understandings. *Elementary School Journal, 93,* 231-247.

Duffy, G., Roehler, L., & Herrmann, G. (1988). Modeling mental processes helps poor readers become strategic readers. *Reading Teacher, 41,* 762-767.

Duffy, G.G., Roehler, L.R., Sivan, E., Rackliffe, G., Book, C., Meloth, M., Vavrus, L., Wesselman, R., Putnam, J., & Bassiri, D. (1987). Effects of explaining the reasoning associated with using reading strategies. *Reading Research Quarterly, 22,* 347-368.

El-Dinary, P.B., Pressley, M., Coy-Ogan, L., Schuder, T., & Strategies Instruction Teachers at Burnt Mills Elementary School (1994). *The teaching practices of transactional strategies instruction teachers as revealed through collaborative interviewing.* Manuscript submitted for publication consideration. College Park, MD: University of Maryland, National Reading Research Center.

El-Dinary, P.B., & Schuder, T. (1993). Seven teachers' acceptance of transactional strat- egies instruction during their first year using it. *Elementary School Journal, 94,* 207-219.

Flavell, J.H. (1970). Developmental studies of mediated memory. In H.W. Reese & L.P. Lipsitt (Eds.), *Advances in child development and behavior* (Vol. 5). New York: Academic Press.

Gambrell, L.B., & Bales, R.J. (1986). Mental imagery and the comprehension-monitoring performance of fourth- and fifth-grade poor readers. *Reading Research Quarterly, 21,* 454-464.

Garner, R., Hare, V., Alexander, P., V.C., Haynes, J., & Winograd, P. (1984). Inducing use of a text lookback strategy among unsuccessful readers. *American Educational Research Journal, 21,* 789-798.

Garner, R., McCready, G.B., & Wagoner, S. (1984). Readers' acquisition of the components of the text lookback strategy. *Journal of Educational Psychology, 76,* 300-309.

Gaskins, I.W., Anderson, R.C., Pressley, M., Cunicelli, E.A., & Satlow, E. (1993). Six teachers' dialogue during cognitive process instruction. *Elementary School Journal, 93,* 277-304.

Gaskins, I.W., & Elliot, T.T. (1991). *Implementing cognitive strategy instruction across the school: The Benchmark manual for teachers.* Cambridge, MA: Brookline Books.

Hansen, J., & Pearson, P.D. (1983). An instructional study: Improving the inferential comprehension of good and poor fourth-grade readers. *Journal of Educational Psychology, 75,* 821-829.

Hutchins, E. (1991). The social organization of distributed cognition. In L. Resnick, J.M. Levine, & S.D. Teasley (Eds.), *Perspectives on socially shared cognition* (pp. 283-307). Washington, DC: American Psychological Association.

Idol, L. (1987). Group story mapping: A comprehension strategy for both skilled and unskilled readers. *Journal of Learning Disabilities, 20,* 196-205.

Idol, L., & Croll, V.J. (1987). Story-mapping training as a means of improving reading comprehension. *Learning Disability Quarterly, 10,* 214-229.

Jenkins, J.R., Heliotis, J.D., Stein, M.L., & Haynes, M.C. (1987). Improving reading comprehension using paragraph restatements. *Exceptional Children, 54,* 54-59.

Johnston, P., & Afflerbach, P. (1985). The process of constructing main ideas from text. *Cognition and Instruction, 2,* 207-232.

King, A. (1994). Guiding knowledge construction in the classroom: Effects of teaching children how to question and how to explain. *American Education Research Journal, 31,* 338-368.

Kintsch, W., & van Dijk, T.A. (1978). Toward a model of text comprehension and production. *Psychological Review, 85,* 363-394.

Levin, J.R., & Pressley, M. (1981). Improving children's prose comprehension: Selected strategies that seem to succeed. In C.M. Santa & B.L. Hayes (Eds.), *Children's prose comprehension: Research and practice* (pp. 44-71). Newark, DE: International Reading Association.

Levin, J.R., Shriberg, L.K., & Berry, J.K. (1983). A concrete strategy for remembering abstract prose. *American Educational Research Journal, 20,* 277-290.

Lipson, M.Y. (1982). Learning new information from text; The role of prior knowledge and reading ability. *Journal of Reading Behavior, 14,* 243-261.

Lyman, F.T. (1987). The Think Trix: A classroom tool for thinking in response to reading. *Reading: Issues and Practices, 4,* 15-19.

Lytle, S.L. (1982). *Exploring comprehension style: A study of twelfth-grade readers' transaction with texts.* Doctoral dissertation: University of Pennsylvania (University Microfilms No. 82-27292).

Mandler, J.M. (1984). *Stories, scripts, and scenes: Aspects of schema theory.* Hillsdale, NJ: Lawrence Erlbaum Associates.

Markman, E.M. (1981). Comprehension monitoring. In W.P. Dickson (Ed.), *Children's oral communication skills* (pp. 61-84). New York, NY: Academic Press.

Marks, M., Pressley, M., in collaboration with Coley, J.D., Craig, S., Gardner, R., Rose, W., & DePinto, T. (1993). Teachers' adaptations of reciprocal teaching: Progress toward a classroom-compatible version of reciprocal teaching. *Elementary School Journal, 94,* 267-283.

McCormick, C.B., & Levin, J.R. (1984). A comparison of different prose-learning variations of the mnemonic keyword method. *American Educational Research Journal, 21,* 379-398.

McDonald, J.D. (1986). Self-generated questions and reading recall: Does training help? *Contemporary Educational Psychology, 11,* 290-304.

Mehan, H. (1979). *Social organization in the classroom.* Cambridge, MA: Harvard University Press.

Nolte, R.Y., & Singer, H. (1985). Active com-

prehension: Teaching a process of reading comprehension and its effects on reading achievement. *The Reading Teacher, 39,* 24-31.

Olshavsky, J.E. (1976-77). Reading as problem solving: An investigation of strategies. *Reading Research Quarterly, 12,* 654-674.

Olson, G.M., Mack, R.L., & Duffy, S.A. (1981). Cognitive aspects of genre. *Poetics, 10,* 283-315.

Paivio, A. (1971). *Imagery and verbal processes.* New York, NY: Holt, Rinehart, and Winston Co.

Palincsar, A.M., & Brown, A.L. (1984). Reciprocal teaching of comprehension fostering and comprehension monitoring activities. *Cognition and Instruction, 1,* 117-175.

Paris, S.G., & Lindauer, B.K. (1976). The role of inference in children's comprehension and memory. *Cognitive Psychology, 8,* 217-227.

Pearson, P.D., & Dole, J.A. (1987). Explicit comprehension instruction: A review of research and a new conceptualization of instruction. *Elementary School Journal, 88,* 151-165.

Pearson, P.D., Hansen, J., & Gordon, C. (1979). The effect of background knowledge on young children's comprehension of explicit and implicit information. *Journal of Reading Behavior, 11,* 201-209.

Peters, E.E., & Levin, J.R. (1986). Effects of a mnemonic imagery strategy on good and poor readers' prose recall. *Reading Research Quarterly, 21,* 179-192.

Pierce, J.W. (1980). Field independence and imagery-assisted prose recall of children. *Journal of Educational Psychology, 72,* 200-203.

Pressley, M. (1976). Mental imagery helps eight-year-olds remember what they read. *Journal of Educational Psychology, 68,* 355-359.

Pressley, M. (1977). Imagery and children's learning: Putting the picture in developmental perspective. *Review of Educational Research, 47,* 586-622.

Pressley, M., & Afflerbach, P. (1995). *Verbal protocols of reading: The nature of constructively responsive reading.* Hillsdale, NJ: Erlbaum.

Pressley, M., Borkowski, J.G., & Schneider, W. (1987). Cognitive strategies: Good strategy users coordinate metacognition and knowledge. In R. Vasta & G. Whitehurst (Eds.), *Annals of child development,* Vol. 4 (pp. 89-129). Greenwich, CT: JAI Press.

Pressley, M., Borkowski, J.G., & Schneider, W. (1989). Good information processing: What it is and what education can do to promote it. *International Journal of Educational Research, 13*, 857-867.

Pressley, M., & El-Dinary, P.B. (Guest Editors) (1993). Special issue on strategy instruction. *Elementary School Journal, 94* (2).

Pressley, M., in long-term collaboration with El-Dinary, P., Brown, R., Schuder, T., Pioli, M., Gaskins, I., & Benchmark School Faculty (1994). Transactional instruction of reading comprehension strategies. In J. Mangieri & C.C. Block (Eds.), *Creating powerful thinking in teachers and students: Diverse perspectives* (pp. 112-139). Fort Worth, TX: Harcourt Brace Jovanovich.

Pressley, M., El-Dinary, P.B., Gaskins, I., Schuder, T., Bergman, J.L., Almasi, J., & Brown, R. (1992). Beyond direct explanation: Transactional instruction of reading comprehension strategies. *Elementary School Journal, 92*, 511-554.

Pressley, M., & Forrest-Pressley, D.L. (1985). Questions and children's cognitive processing. In A.C. Graesser & J.B. Black (Eds.), *The psychology of questions* (pp. 277-296). Hillsdale, NJ: Lawrence Erlbaum Associates.

Pressley, M., Goodchild, F., Fleet, J., Zajchowski, R., & Evans, E.D. (1989). The challenges of classroom strategy instruction. *Elementary School Journal, 89*, 301-342.

Pressley, M., Johnson, C.J., Symons, S., McGoldrick, J.A., & Kurita, J.A. (1989). Strategies that improve memory and comprehension of what is read. *Elementary School Journal, 90*, 3-32.

Rahman, T., & Bisanz, G.L. (1986). Reading ability and the use of a story schema in recalling and reconstructing information. *Journal of Educational Psychology, 78*, 323-333.

Raphael, T.E., & McKinney, J. (1983). An examination of fifth- and eighth-grade children's question-answering behavior: An instructional study in metacognition. *Journal of Reading Behavior, 15*, 67-86.

Raphael, T.E., & Pearson, P.D. (1985). Increasing students' awareness of sources of information for answering questions. *American Educational Research Journal, 22*, 217-236.

Raphael, T.E., & Wonnacott, C.A. (1985). Metacognitive training in question-answering strategies: Implementation in a fourth-grade developmental reading program. *Reading Research Quarterly, 20*, 282-296.

Rinehart, S.D., Stahl, S.A., & Erickson, L.G. (1986). Some effects of summarization training on reading and studying. *Reading Research Quarterly, 21*, 422-438.

Rosenblatt, L.M. (1978). *The reader, the text, the poem: The transactional theory of the literary work.* Carbondale, IL: Southern Illinois University Press.

Rosenshine, B., & Meister, C. (1992). *Reciprocal teaching: A review of nineteen experimental studies.* Manuscript submitted for publication. Champaign-Urbana, IL: University of Illinois, Department of Educational Psychology.

Rowls, M.D. (1976). The facilitative and interactive effects of adjunct questions on retention of eighth graders across three prose passages: Dissertation in prose learning. *Journal of Educational Psychology, 68*, 205-209.

Sadoski, M. (1983). An exploratory study of the relationship between reported imagery and the comprehension and recall of a story. *Reading Research Quarterly, 19*, 110-123.

Sadoski, M. (1985). The natural use of imagery in story comprehension and recall: Replication and extension. *Reading Research Quarterly, 20*, 658-667.

Schneider, W., & Pressley, M. (1989). *Memory development between 2 and 20.* New York: Springer-Verlag.

Schuder, T. (1993). The genesis of transactional strategies instruction in a reading program for at-risk students. *Elementary School Journal, 94*, 183-200.

Short, E.J., & Ryan, E.B. (1984). Metacognitive differences between skilled and less skilled readers: Remediating deficits through story grammar and attribution training. *Journal of Educational Psychology, 76*, 225-235.

Shriberg, L.K., Levin, J.R., McCormick, C.B., & Pressley, M. (1982). Learning about "famous" people via the keyword method. *Journal of Educational Psychology, 74*, 238-247.

Singer, H., & Donlan, D. (1982). Active comprehension: Problem-solving schema with question generation for comprehension of complex short stories. *Reading Research Quarterly, 17*, 166-186.

Smith, L.C., Readence, J.E., & Alvermann, D.E. (1984). Effects of activating background knowledge on comprehension of expository prose. *33rd Yearbook of the National Reading Conference.* Rochester, NY: National Reading Conference.

Sternberg, R.J. (1987). Most vocabulary is learned from context. In M.G. McKeown & M.E. Curtis (Eds.), *Nature of vocabulary acquisition*. Hillsdale, NJ: Erlbaum & Associates.

Sternberg, R.J., & Powell, J.S. (1983). Comprehending verbal comprehension. *American Psychologist, 38,* 878-893.

Taylor, B.M. (1982). Text structure and children's comprehension and memory for expository material. *Journal of Educational Psychology, 74,* 323-340.

Taylor, B.M., & Beach, R.W. (1984). The effects of text structure instruction on middle-grade students' comprehension and production of expository text. *Reading Research Quarterly, 19,* 134-146.

Vygotsky, L.S. (1978). *Mind in society: The development of higher psychological processes.* Cambridge, MA: Harvard University Press.

Wilson, P.T., & Anderson, R.C. (1986). What they don't know will hurt them: The role of prior knowledge in comprehension. In J. Orasanu (Ed.), *Reading comprehension: From research to practice.* Hillsdale, NJ: Lawrence Erlbaum Associates.

Wong, B.Y.L. (1985). Self-questioning instructional research: A review. *Review of Educational Research, 55,* 227-268.

Wyatt, D., Pressley, M., El-Dinary, P.B., Stein, S., Evans, P., & Brown, R. (1993). Comprehension strategies, worth and credibility monitoring, and evaluations: Cold and hot cognition when experts read professional articles that are important to them. *Learning and Individual Differences, 5,* 49-72.

CHAPTER 4

Vocabulary

The following statement, two decades old, represents an almost universal attitude toward vocabulary held both by educators and those outside the field today:

> The importance of vocabulary is daily demonstrated in schools and out. In the classroom, the achieving students possess the most adequate vocabularies. Because of the verbal nature of most classroom activities, knowledge of words and ability to use language are essential to success in these activities. After schooling has ended, adequacy of vocabulary is almost equally essential for achievement in vocations and in society. (Petty, Harold & Stoll, 1968, p. 7)

Although vocabulary instruction appears to be needed in school, there is very little research examining the vocabulary instruction currently taking place in schools. When researchers have looked, however, they have found little teaching of vocabulary learning strategies. In one analysis of basal readers, Beck, Perfetti and McKeown (1982) examined vocabulary instruction presented in two third-grade through sixth-grade basal reading books, dividing their attention between pre-reading activities, during-reading activities, and post-reading activities. One basal series included no pre-reading activities; the other included words taught in sentences specifically designed to reveal their meaning. Both series assumed that students obtain meanings from natural contexts, contexts during reading, and failed to suggest effective teaching strategies. Students were also taught to look up words in the glossary. One series presented a set of words not previously taught for post-reading instruction; the other provided one review of the new words in the selection.

In a study of comprehension instruction in fourth grade classrooms, Durkin (1978-79) observed a total of 4,469 minutes of instruction. Durkin found that only 19 minutes were devoted to vocabulary instruction, with an additional 4 minutes devoted to vocabulary review. In short, little time was spent on teaching of vocabulary at all.

Shake, Allington, Gaskins, and Marr (1987) reported similar results. Twenty teachers were asked to present an exemplary vocabulary lesson. Although all teachers provided definitions and taught strategies on using context and semantic features (i.e., focusing on conceptual development), most instruction provided very few opportunities for students to use the words they were learning. Often there was a misunderstanding of the task requested by the teacher, as evidenced by the response the student supplied. For example, one teacher said, "Use *harpoon* in a sentence." The student's response was: "Well, it's long and sharp and used to kill whales."

In summary, it seems reasonable to conclude that the vocabulary instruction that students receive in schools is quite meager. Even those who are more optimistic about the amount of vocabulary instruction in school conclude that most of the teaching is not very good, and there is little teaching of strategies for acquiring word meanings or relating new words to familiar words (Blachowicz, 1987).

The issue addressed in this chapter is how to increase students' vocabulary. The first recommendations made here may seem obvious. We emphasize them, however, because they point to mechanisms so powerful that they should be the foremost components in any vocabulary instruction.

Read to Students and Encourage Them to Read Extensively [T & SSR]

The first and second recommendations we make for increasing student vocabulary is for teachers to read extensively to their students and encourage their students to read on their own. The evidence is simply overwhelming (and continues to increase!) that children learn new vocabulary by hearing and rehearing stories and other content that are rich in vocabulary, as well as talking about and retelling what they have heard. These generalizations hold from preschool through the elementary years (e.g., Dickinson & Smith, 1994; Elley, 1989; Leung, 1992; Leung & Pikulski, 1990; Nicholson & Whyte, 1992; Robbins & Ehri, 1994; Stahl, Richek & Vandevier, 1991). Once children can read on their own, the size of their vocabulary varies with the extent of their reading. The most likely explanation of this association is that students learn new vocabulary by experiencing the words during reading (e.g., Cunningham & Stanovich, 1991; Eller, Pappas & Brown, 1988; Stanovich & Cunningham, 1993). If students get hooked on reading excellent books and magazines, their vocabulary will continue to expand throughout their lives.

These recommendations are consistent with the general conclusion that most vocabulary words are acquired incidentally, in context, as part of reading and conversation (e.g., Sternberg, 1987). Indeed, some would argue that there is so much vocabulary for students to learn that vocabulary development from context is the only viable mechanism to explain the extensive vocabulary of adults. For example, Miller and Gildea (1987) estimated that children learn 13 new vocabulary words a day. Nagy and Anderson (e.g., 1984) propose that by the end of high school a student knows at least 40,000 words, and will need to continue learning 6 to 7 new words a day for life. Since it is certain that students are not being explicitly taught 6 to 7 or 13 new words a day for every day they are on the planet, incidental learning from context is the default explanation for vocabulary growth. The instructional implication of these analyses is that there are just too many words to attempt explicit teaching of vocabulary, and hence, that explicit instruction of vocabulary is futile.

Alternatively, D'Anna, Zechmeister, and Hall (1991) have made the case that previous estimates of the number of words known by young adults are inflated by various biases in the ways words have been counted in previous studies. Without getting into the technical details of their argument, they estimate that young adults (i.e., college students) know about 16,000 words, which means that they learn about 2 or 3 words a day. Given this number of words, explicit vocabulary instruction seems more viable. Our position is that vocabulary instruction makes good sense if teachers and students use powerful strategies for increasing student vocabulary.

Present Students with Definitions of Vocabulary Words [T]

One approach for increasing student learning of vocabulary words is to present the meanings of unknown words to them. Students, in fact, learn quite a bit from simply processing the word and its definition (Jenkins & Dixon, 1983). In general, the more students are exposed to the definitions, the better their vocabulary learning. That is, repeated presentations of a word and its meaning are more effective than single presentations (e.g., Jenkins, Matlock & Slocum, 1989; McKeown, Beck, Omanson & Pople, 1985).

With the advent of computer presentations of educational content, there is increasing opportunity to build in presentations of definitions for words students do not know. In fact, such computer presentations do increase vocabulary learning (e.g., Reinking & Rickman, 1990). Given a choice between materials that present definitions of likely unknown words and ones that do not present them, it makes sense to choose those that include the definitions. When developing new materials for students, it makes sense to make definitions of difficult words readily available.

The nature of the definitions presented to students, however, is critical. McKeown (1993) presented evidence that dictionary definitions are not as certain to lead to learning as rewritten definitions. For example, her rewritten definitions were aimed to provide greater differentiation between the new word and related words. In general, the rewritten definitions in her study were more elaborate than unrevised definitions. Consider the following examples:

Exotic: *Unrevised definition:* Foreign; strange; not native.

Revised definition: Describes something that is unusual and interesting because it comes from another country far away.

Vicarious: *Unrevised definition:* Felt by sharing in others' experience. *Revised definition:* Share the feeling of an experience by watching or reading about someone else doing it.

Thus, presenting dictionary definitions to children is likely to lead to confusion. This confusion can be avoided by writing definitions that clarify the meaning of the word more completely and in terms that children can understand.

Teach and Encourage Students to Derive Meanings from External Context Clues [SSR]

Because so much of vocabulary development depends on inferring the meanings of words in context, it is logically sensible to teach students to infer the meanings of vocabulary words from context. This makes particular sense given that students often fail to infer the meanings of unfamiliar vocabulary even when there are many and rich context cues (e.g., Jenkins, Stein & Wysocki, 1984; McKeown, 1985).

Having students practice deriving meanings from context seems to have a small effect on their ability to learn from context. Carnine, Kameenui & Coyle (1984) found that 4th-, 5th- and 6th-graders were better able to provide word definitions after studying target words in context than in isolation, with older students correctly identifying more word meanings than younger ones. These authors also found that all contexts were not equal with respect to promoting vocabulary acquisition. Specifically, learning was optimal when the distance between the unknown word and contextual information was minimal (i.e., three to ten words), and when contextual information was presented in synonym format rather than inference format. However, even when contextual information was presented in an optimal format, 6th-grade students were only able to identify the correct meaning of an unfamiliar word about 40% of the time, suggesting that students need to be provided with more than just instruction about external context clues to acquire vocabulary effectively. We encouraged teachers to integrate instruction about external context clues with the other formats of vocabulary instruction outlined in this chapter.

Better yet is to teach students strategies for making a guess about the meanings of words and testing their guesses (e.g., Patberg, Graves & Stibbe, 1984). For example, Jenkins, Matlock and Slocum (1989) taught students to use a sequence of strategies which can be summarized with the acronym SCANR:

- Substitute a word or expression for the unknown word.
- Check the context for clues that support your idea.

- Ask if the substitution word fits all context clues.
- Need a new idea—a new substitution word?
- Revise your idea to fit the context, probably resulting in a different substitution word.

In their study, the teacher provided vocabulary instruction to the class as a whole. First, the teacher presented the class with a sentence containing an unfamiliar word (e.g., "She remained totally *unflappable* despite the angry crowd," "The danger with her becoming queen is that she would be a *tyrant*"). The teacher read the sentence aloud and asked students to speculate about possible word meanings. The teacher encouraged the students to use the SCANR procedure to check whether their guesses fit sentence context. The teacher also modeled using the SCANR strategy to derive word meaning, with this process continuing until students offered at least one appropriate substitution. Next, the teacher presented the class with another sentence containing the same unfamiliar word, with the students instructed to repeat the SCANR procedure to derive possible word meanings. After students had provided a number of possible word substitutes, the teacher provided the class with the correct definition and reviewed how this meaning made sense in the two practice sentences.

Students who were instructed to use the SCANR strategy demonstrated superior word knowledge (as measured by their ability to identify word meanings in isolation, context and multiple-choice tests) relative to their peers who received conventional vocabulary instruction (i.e., providing students with unfamiliar words and their definitions and having them use these words in sentences). However, for students to use this strategy effectively, substantial practice is needed—the strategy should be introduced over a long period of time, with teachers nudging students to use it whenever new words are encountered in their reading.

As we recommend teaching students to generate hypotheses about the meanings of unfamiliar words and checking on their derived meanings, teachers need to be aware that there has been relatively little work on deriving word meanings from context clues. Our best advisement at this point is to provide a great deal of support as students attempt to learn and use strategies such as SCANR (e.g., wall charts listing the steps, practice using the approach during a variety of different readings in the various content areas).

Teach Students to Derive Meanings from Internal Context Clues [SSR]

A promising contextual approach is to teach students how to derive word meanings by examining their internal contextual features (White, Power & White, 1989). Students can be taught about the usefulness of internal cues in deciphering the meaning of unknown words. Suppose the task is to infer the meaning of the word *dissimilarity*. The word is probably unfamiliar to most young children. But many children know that the prefix *dis-* means "not," the root *similar* is a word meaning "the same as," and the suffix *-ity* is often used to form abstract nouns. These cues might be combined to infer that *dissimilarity* refers to the property of "not being the same as." This inference would be correct.

There have been several studies of morphological instruction. Graves and Hammond (1980) taught seventh-graders nine prefixes over a three-day period. There were reliable differences between the group taught the prefixes and a control group on a test of the prefixes taught and on a transfer test requiring students to use their knowledge of the prefixes taught to infer the meanings of novel words containing the prefixes. These results were obtained both immediately following teaching and three weeks after instruction had ended. In a related study, Nicol, Graves and Slater (1984) found similar results with fourth- , fifth- and sixth-graders of high, middle, and low ability.

Pressley, Levin, Woo, Sinclair, and Ahmad (1985) provided elementary school students with mastery learning instruction (i.e., to study until they are 100% correct) of some root words. Students learned roots such as *dorm*, meaning "sleep," *chrom*, meaning "color," and *taph*, meaning "tomb." When later asked to remember that *dormeuse* means "a sleeping carriage," that *chromatosis* means an "unnatural coloring of the skin," and that *cenotaph* means "a monument to a person buried elsewhere," these internal-context mastery subjects were far superior to control subjects who were not given the previous internal-context instruction. Such a finding suggests that remembering new vocabulary can be facilitated through students' capitalizing on previously learned word parts.

Semantic Mapping [T]

Semantic mapping is a teaching strategy that has proven effective in improving vocabulary learning (e.g., Johnson, Pittelman, Toms-Bronowski & Levin, 1984; Johnson, Toms-Bronowski & Pittelman, 1982;), especially with weaker students (e.g., Margosein, Pascarella & Pflaum, 1982; Pittelman, Levin & Johnson, 1985). Basically, semantic mapping involves presenting students with the to-be-learned vocabulary and having them brainstorm about related vocabulary. The teacher and the students then organize these related associations into meaningful categories. See Figure 4-1 for an example of a semantic map.

Using a very simple variation of this approach, Margosein and her colleagues (1982) presented 71 new vocabulary items (i.e., items that were familiar to about 70% of tenth-graders but not younger students) to seventh- and eighth-graders over the course of eight weeks. Vocabulary sessions were held three times a week, with three words being introduced during each lesson. Each session lasted for approximately 16 minutes.

Each word was introduced in combination with three other words that were similar in meaning and whose meanings were assumed to be familiar to students. For example, the target word *solitude* was presented with three familiar words: *quiet, lonely* and *alone*. The teacher also presented students with questions designed to elicit the meaning of *solitude* (e.g., What does it mean to be alone? How does being alone differ from being lonely?), with students being required to provide a definition for each of the familiar words. In order to help students form predictions about the definition of the target word, similarities and differences between the familiar concepts were also recorded on the semantic map. Finally, dictionaries were used to check the accuracy of students' predictions about the unfamiliar words.

Figure 4-1
Semantic map for horse.

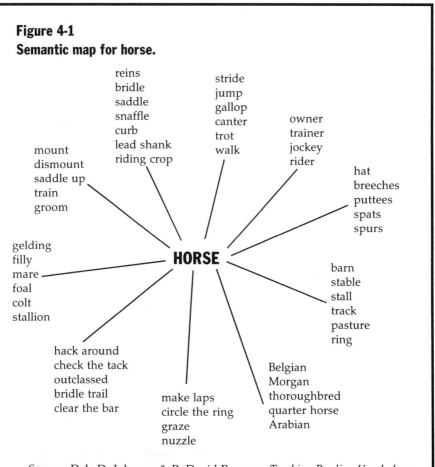

Source: Dale D. Johnson & P. David Pearson, *Teaching Reading Vocabulary* (2nd ed.), New York: Holt, Rinehart and Winston, p. 162. Copyright @1984 by Holt, Rinehart and Winston, Inc.., reprinted by permission of the publisher.

Students who received semantic map instruction demonstrated superior immediate and long-term retention for target vocabulary relative to their peers who studied the same words "in context" (i.e., these students were provided with short explanatory passages that contained clues about the meaning of the target word). Not only did students who received semantic map instruction demonstrate superior knowledge of target vocabulary items, they also demonstrated superior performances on the Gates-MacGinitie vocabulary subtest. This latter finding suggests that the benefits associated with semantic map instruction may extend to general vocabulary acquisition.

The Keyword Method [T & SSR]

The keyword method is a mnemonic technique based on mental imagery which can facilitate associative aspects of learning such as learning associations between new vocabulary and their meanings (Bower, 1972; Paivio, 1971). It was originally developed for learning foreign language vocabularies (Atkinson, 1975; Atkinson & Raugh, 1975: Raugh & Atkinson, 1975), but has since been successfully adapted to acquisition of first-language vocabulary (Levin, 1981), with new demonstrations of its effectiveness continuing to accumulate (Levin, 1993).

The keyword method consists of two stages, an "acoustic-link" stage and an "imagery-link" stage (Pressley, Levin, & McDaniel, 1987). In the acoustic-link stage, the individual acquires a "keyword," which is a familiar English word (assuming that the student's first language is English) that (a) sounds like a salient part of the unfamiliar word and (b) is visualizable through a mental image. In the imagery-link stage, the learner forms a visual image in which the keyword and the definition interact (see Table 4-1).

A few examples from Spanish illustrate the keyword method. In Spanish the word *caballo* means horse. The pronunciation of the Spanish word contains a sound that resembles the English word *eye*. Employing the English word *eye* as the keyword, one might form a mental image of a Cyclopean eye in the forehead of a mythical horse or, alternatively, a horse rearing up and kicking at a giant eye. As another example, the Spanish word for duck is *pato*. Using the English word *pot* as the keyword, one could imagine a duck hiding under an overturned flower pot, with its webbed feet and tufted tail sticking out below.

The keyword method has a solid foundation in learning theory. Psychological "principles" drawn upon by the keyword method are that

a. meaningful stimuli are far more reliably encoded than nonmeaningful stimuli;
b. interacting items are more reliably associated than noninteracting items;
c. the greater the similarity between two stimuli, the more

reliably one will evoke the other; and
d. thematic interactions are reliably retrieved from appropriate cues (Levin, 1981).

The keyword method has been empirically tested with grade-school children in many studies by Levin, Pressley, and their colleagues (Levin et al., 1982; Levin et al., 1979; Pressley & Levin, 1978; Pressley, Levin, & Delaney, 1982). The method has been compared both to control conditions in which no explicit instruction is given and to several variants of the learning-from-context method. The keyword method has always proven to be at least as effective as, and usually more effective than, the alternative methods against which it has been compared.

For example, in a study with fourth- and fifth-grade children, Levin et al. (1984) compared two groups of children, one receiving the mnemonic keyword method and the other group receiving a contextual-analysis strategy. The contextual-analysis strategy required that students search for clues contained in short paragraphs, clues that supposedly enable unfamiliar word meanings to be inferred. For

---

Table 4-1
Stages of the Keyword Method

Take an unfamiliar word.
For example, "persuade" and "surplus" are unfamiliar words that one may want fourth grade students to know.

Acquire a familiar English word as a keyword.
Keywords should:
  a) sound like a salient part of the unfamiliar word, and
  b) be readily visualizable through a mental image
For example, "purse" is a suitable keyword for "persuade" while "syrup" is an appropriate keyword for "surplus."

Form a link between keyword and unknown word.
Students should be instructed to associate the keyword and the unfamiliar word by visualizing them interacting.

Using the example of "persuade" as the unfamiliar word and "purse" as the selected keyword, one may form a picture of a woman being persuaded to buy a purse.

Similarly, using the example of "surplus" as the unfamiliar word and "syrup" as the selected keyword, one may form a picture of a boy pouring a lot of syrup on pancakes because there is a surplus of it in the cupboard.

Examples cited in Pressley, Levin, & McDaniel (1987)

example, the following passage was used to provide contextual support for the word *angler* (a person who likes to go fishing):

> The *angler* carried a lot of things down to the stream. He carried a net and a tackle box, as well as his fishing pole. He hoped to catch a lot of fish that afternoon.

The experimenter pointed out the specific fishing and fisherman-related words within the paragraph (e.g., *stream, he* [to signify that an angler is a person], *fishing pole*) that could furnish clues for deducing and confirming the word's meaning. Children who were assigned to the keyword condition were introduced to the word *angler* via an illustration in which an angel (a keyword for *angler*) was depicted fishing.

Students who were provided with keyword illustrations remembered about 50% more when required to recall the definitions given the vocabulary words than did students in the contextual analysis condition. This held for both high and low-achievers (Levin et al., 1984).

In another study, Pressley, Ross, Levin, and Ghatala (1984) demonstrated that the keyword mnemonic was superior to another contextual approach frequently used in schools. Ten- to 13-year-olds were presented a list of 22 low-frequency English nouns and their definitions. Half of the items were studied via the keyword method, and half were studied by constructing sentence contexts with the target words used appropriately. After one learning trial, the keyword method advantage was substantial: definitions of 51% of the keyword items were recalled in contrast to 8.5% of the context definitions. Definition recall of keyword items exceeded that of context items for 93% of the children.

Pressley, Levin and their associates have provided ample documentation that effective keyword mnemonic interventions can be engineered (e.g., Pressley, Samuel, Hershey, Bishop & Dickinson, 1981), although it is not until the late grade-school years that children are able to generate keyword images proficiently, if given the vocabulary words, keywords, and definitions (Pressley & Levin, 1978). Positive keyword benefits are not limited to normal populations either. Pressley, Levin, and McDaniel (1987) summarized the evidence that the keyword method can promote vocabulary learning in poor learners, including learning disabled students (e.g. Mastropieri, Scruggs, & Levin, 1985), low verbal ability children (McGivern & Levin, 1983), and mentally retarded children (Scruggs, Mastropieri, & Levin, 1985).

The method is adaptable to materials possessing diverse characteristics. Children can use the method to learn verbs, abstract nouns, and adjectives (Levin, McCormick, Miller, Berry, and Pressley, 1982). Levin et al. (1982) used words provided by the editor of a national children's magazine—ones not selected for keyword-method compatibility (e.g., easy-to-generate keywords). The fourth-grade students in that study learned items like *persuade, hesitate, sect,* and *intend,* achieving much better learning in comparison to fourth-grade students in a no-strategy condition.

Michael Gruneberg (1994a, 1994b, 1994c, 1994d) has published several books to aid students in learning a foreign language, each based on the "link word" system, a mental imagery approach much like the keyword method. Students are presented with a word and its definition: "The Spanish for *cat* is *gato.*" Students are to form an image between the definition and a word which sounds like the new word. For example, they may be asked, "Imagine a *cat* eating a lovely *gateau.*" They are told to think of the image for about ten seconds before moving on to the next word. For example, for the German word *nur*, which means "only," Gruneberg suggested imagining thinking "If I only knew her," a sentence including the meaning and a phrase acoustically similar to the to-be-learned item ("knew her" for *nur*). Although there are only preliminary data to support this method (Gruneberg, Nov. 1987, personal communication to M. Pressley), it is provisionally recommended because it is based on the same principle as the keyword method. On the face of it, Gruneberg's books should be helpful from the late grade-school years on, a proposition that deserves serious scientific study, given that these books are being disseminated widely.

Processing New Vocabulary in Multiple Ways [T]

Students can be taught vocabulary by having them process to-be-learned words in multiple ways, including generating associations to new words, constructing meaningful sentences containing new words, matching words with their definitions, playing games requiring knowledge of meaning, and using the words outside of class (e.g., Beck et al., 1982; McKeown et al., 1985).

Working with 4th-graders, McKeown and her colleagues (McKeown et al., 1985) found that when students received vocabulary instruction in which target words were incorporated into multiple activities and settings, learning of vocabulary was superior to when students received language arts instruction based on textbook exercises and activities (e.g., having students form simple associations between each word and its definition or synonym). As part of McKeown et al.'s (1985) intensified vocabulary program, a small number of target words (between eight and ten) were introduced to children on a weekly basis. During the first day of instruction, students were provided with the target words and their definitions. Students then participated in a word association activity during which the teacher presented "clues" for each new word (e.g., the clue word *crook* might be used to elicit the target word *accomplice*). Students were required to explain why the clue word and the target word belonged together.

Students completed a number of activities using the target words for the remainder of the week. For instance, students were instructed to generate sentences using the target words and to complete other activities using the meanings of the words. Students played competitive games which required them to quickly match words with their definitions. They also generated contexts or situations appropriate for each of the target words. Teachers continued to develop students' understandings of the new words by asking them thought-provoking questions (e.g., "Could an *accomplice* be a *novice*?"). Throughout the instructional session, students could earn the distinction of "word wizard" by sharing their encounters with and use of target words outside of the classroom. At the end of the week, students completed a multiple-choice test assessing their knowledge of vocabulary meanings.

The more frequently students encountered words across multiple settings and activities, the better their retention and understanding of them. Both McKeown and Beck found that students who were frequently exposed to target words (ranging from 12 to 40 exposures within a 5-day cycle) performed better on a number of measures, from definitional knowledge and fluency to sentence verification and story recall, relative to students who had minimal experiences with the target words (ranging from four to 18 exposures). Therefore, teachers are encouraged to be resourceful when introducing students to new vocabulary, making sure to provide numerous opportunities for students to experience and use words in creative manners.

Concluding Comments

Students can develop their vocabularies by reading extensively, especially if they are active in their pursuit of word meanings, analyzing external and internal context clues. Although progress has been made in understanding how to teach students to make the most of content clues, it is disappointing there is so little work on teaching such analytical skills. One simple way of increasing students' vocabulary is to present word definitions to them, especially definitions they can understand. At least some of the time—for example, when a keyword in the vocabulary is obvious—mnemonic methods can also be applied to learning vocabulary-definition associations. In short, there are strategies for all aspects of vocabulary acquisition, from figuring out the meanings of words to learning meanings once they are available. Given the extensive vocabulary a competent adult must possess, learning and using the various strategies for vocabulary acquisition outlined in this chapter is sensible.

REFERENCES

Atkinson, R.C. (1975). Mnemotechnics in second-language learning. *American Psychologist, 30*, 821-828.

Atkinson, R.C., & Raugh, M.R. (1975). An application of the mnemonic keyword method to the acquisition of a Russian vocabulary. *Journal of Experimental Psychology: Human Learning and Memory*, 123-

133.

Beck, I.L., Perfetti, C.A., & McKeown, M.O. (1982). The effects of long-term vocabulary instruction on lexical access and reading comprehension. *Journal of Educational Psychology, 74*, 506-521.

Blachowicz, C.Z. (1987). Vocabulary instruction: What goes on in the classroom. *Reading Teacher, 2*, 132-137.

Blackwell, C.L.Z. (1987). Vocabulary instruction: What goes on in the classroom? *The Reading Teacher, 41*, 132-137.

Bower, O.H. (1972). Mental imagery and associative learning. In L.W. Gregg (Ed.), *Cognition in learning and memory*. New York: John Wiley & Sons.

Carnine, D., Kameenui, E.J., & Coyle, G. (1984). Utilization of contextual information in determining the meaning of unfamiliar words. *Reading Research Quarterly, 19*, 188-204.

Cunningham, A.E., & Stanovich, K.E. (1991). Teaching the unique effects of print exposure in children: Associations with vocabulary, general knowledge, and spelling. *Journal of Educational Psychology, 83*, 264-274.

D'Anna, C.A., Zechmeister, E.B., & Hall, J.W. (1991). Toward a meaningful definition of vocabulary size. *Journal of Reading Behavior, 23*, 109-122.

Dickinson, D.K., & Smith, M.W. (1994). Long-term effects of preschool teachers' book readings on low-income children's vocabulary and story comprehension. *Reading Research Quarterly, 29*, 105-122.

Durkin, D. (1978-79). What classroom observations reveal about reading comprehension instruction. *Reading Research Quarterly, 14*, 481-533.

Eller, R.G., Pappas, C.C., & Brown, E. (1988). The lexical development of kindergartners' learning from written context. *Journal of Reading Behavior, 20*, 5-24.

Elley, W.B. (1989). Vocabulary acquisition from listening to stories. *Reading Research Quarterly, 24*, 174-187.

Graves, M.F., & Hammond, H.K. (1980). A validated procedure for teaching prefixes and its effect on students' ability to assign meaning to novel words. In M.L. Kamil & A.V. Moe (Eds.), *Perspectives on reading research and instruction*. Washington, DC: National Reading Conference.

Gruneberg, M.M. (1994a). *French by association*. Lincolnwood, IL: Passport Books.

Gruneberg, M.M. (1994b). *German by association*. Lincolnwood, IL: Passport Books.

Gruneberg, M.M. (1994c). *Italian by association*. Lincolnwood, IL: Passport Books.

Gruneberg, M.M. (1994d). *Spanish by association*. Lincolnwood, IL: Passport Books.

Jenkins, J.R., & Dixon, R. (1983). Vocabulary learning. *Contemporary Educational Psychology, 8*, 237-280.

Jenkins, J.R., Matlock, B., & Slocum, T.A. (1989). Two approaches to vocabulary instruction: The teaching of individual word meanings and practice in deriving word meaning from context. *Reading Research Quarterly, 24*, 215-235.

Jenkins, J.R., Stein, M.L., & Wysocki, K. (1984). Learning vocabulary through reading. *American Educational Research Journal, 21*, 767-787.

Johnson, D.D., Pittelman, S.D., Toms-Bronowski, S., & Levin, K.M. (1984). *An investigation of the effects of prior knowledge and vocabulary acquisition on passage comprehension* (Program Report No. 84-5). Madison, WI: University of Wisconsin, Center for Education Research.

Johnson, D.D., Pittelman, S.D., Toms-Bronowski, S., & Levin, K.M. (1984). *An investigation of the effectiveness of semantic mapping and semantic feature analysis with intermediate grade level students* (Program Report No. 83-3). Madison, WI: University of Wisconsin, Center for Education Research.

Johnson, D.D., Toms-Bronowski, S., & Pittelman, S.D. (1982). *An investigation of the effectiveness of semantic mapping and semantic feature analysis with intermediate grade level children* (Program Report N. 83-3). Madison, WI: Wisconsin Center for Education Research.

Leung, C.B. (1992). Effects of word-related variables on vocabulary growth through repeated read-aloud events. In C.K. Kinzer & D.J. Leu (Eds.), *Literacy research, theory, and practice: Views from many perspectives* (pp. 491-498). Chicago: National Reading Conference.

Leung, C.B., & Pikulski, J.J. (1990). Incidental learning of word meanings by kindergarten and first-grade children through repeated read-aloud events. In J. Zutell & S. McCormick (Eds.), *Literacy theory and research: Analyses from multiple paradigms* (pp. 231-239). Chicago: National Reading Conference.

Levin, J.R. (1981). The mnemonic '80s: Keywords in the classroom. *Educational Psychologist, 16*, 65-82.

Levin, J.R. (1993). Mnemonic strategies in the

classroom: A twenty-year report card. *Elementary School Journal, 94,* 235-244.

Levin, J.R., Johnson, D.D., Pittelman, S.D., Hayes, B.L., Levin, K.M., Shriberg, L.K., & Toms-Bronowski, S. (1984). A comparison of semantic- and mnemonic-based vocabulary-learning strategies. *Reading Psychology, 5,* 1-15.

Levin, J.R., McCormick, C.B., Miller, G.E., Berry J.K., & Pressley, M. (1982). Mnemonic versus non-mnemonic vocabulary-learning strategies for children. *American Educational Research Journal, 19,* 121-136.

Levin, J.R., Pressley, M., McCormick, C.B., Miller, G.E., & Shriberg, L.K. (1979). Assessing the classroom potential of the keyword method. *Journal of Educational Psychology, 71,* 583-594.

Margosein, C.M., Pascarella, E.T., & Pflaum, S.W. (1982, April). *The effects of instruction using semantic mapping on vocabulary and comprehension.* Paper presented at the annual meeting of the American Educational Research Association, New York.

Mastropieri, M.A., Scruggs, T.E., & Levin, J.R. (1985). Maximizing what exceptional children can learn: A review of research on the keyword method and related mnemonic techniques. *Remedial and Special Education, 6,* 39-45.

McGivern, J.E., & Levin, J.R. (1983). The keyword method and children's vocabulary learning: An interaction with vocabulary knowledge. *Contemporary Educational Psychology, 8,* 46-54.

McKeown, M.G. (1985). The acquisition of word meaning from context by children of high and low ability. *Reading Research Quarterly, 20,* 482-496.

McKeown, M.G. (1993). Creating effective definitions for young word learners. *Reading Research Quarterly, 28,* 16-31.

McKeown, M.G., Beck, I.L., Omanson, R., & Pople, M.T. (1985). Some effects of the nature and frequency of vocabulary instruction on the knowledge and use of words. *Reading Research Quarterly, 20,* 522-535.

Miller, G.A., & Gildea, P.M. (1987). How children learn words. *Scientific American, 257,* 3.

Nagy, W.E., & Anderson, R.C. (1984). How many words are there in printed school English? *Reading Research Quarterly, 19,* 304-330.

Nicholson, T., & Whyte, B. (1992). Matthew effects in learning new words while listening to stories. In C.K. Kinzer & D.J. Leu

(Eds.), *Literacy research, theory and practice: Views from many perspectives* (pp. 499-503). Chicago: National Reading Conference.

Nicol, J.E., Graves, M.F., & Slater, W.H. (1984). *Building vocabulary through prefix instruction.* Unpublished manuscript, University of Minnesota.

Paivio, A. (1971). *Imagery and verbal processes.* New York: Henry Holt.

Patberg, J.P., Graves, M.F., & Stibbe, M.A. (1984). Effects of active teaching and practice in facilitating students' use of context clues. In J.A. Niles & L.A. Harris (Eds.), *Changing perspectives in research in reading/language processing and instruction* (pp. 146-151). Rochester, NY: National Reading Conference.

Petty, W., Harold, C., & Stoll, E. (1968). *The state of knowledge about the teaching of vocabulary.* Champaign, IL: National Council of Teachers of English.

Pittelman, S.D., Levin, K.M., & Johnson, D.D. (1985). *An investigation of two instructional settings in the use of semantic mapping with poor readers* (Program Report No. 85-4). Madison, WI: University of Wisconsin–Madison, Wisconsin Center for Education Research.

Pressley, M., & Levin, J.R. (1978). Developmental constraints associated with children's use of the keyword method of foreign language vocabulary learning. *Journal of Educational Psychology, 26,* 359-372.

Pressley, M., Levin, J.R., & Delaney, H.D. (1982). The mnemonic keyword method. *Review of Educational Research, 52,* 61-92.

Pressley, M., Levin, J.R., & McDaniel, M.A. (1987). Remembering versus inferring what a word means: mnemonic and contextual approaches. In M.O. McKeown & M.E. Curtis (Eds.), *The nature of vocabulary acquisition.* Hillsdale, NJ: Lawrence Erlbaum Associates.

Pressley, M., Levin, J.R., Woo, G., Sinclair, C., & Ahmad, F. (1985). *The effect of root-word mastery on vocabulary learning.* Unpublished manuscript. University of Western Ontario, London, Ontario.

Pressley, M., Ross, K.A., Levin, J.R., & Ghatala, E.S. (1984). The role of strategy utility knowledge in children's strategy decision making. *Journal of Experimental Child Psychology, 38,* 491-504.

Pressley, M., Samuel, J., Hershey, M.M., Bishop, S.L., & Dickinson, D. (1981). Use of a mnemonic technique to teach young children foreign language vocabulary. *Contemporary Educational Psychology, 6,* 110-

116.

Raugh, M.R., & Atkinson, R.C. (1975). A mnemonic method for learning a second-language vocabulary. *Journal of Educational Psychology, 67,* 1-16.

Reinking, D., & Rickman, S.S. (1990). The effects of computer-mediated texts on the vocabulary learning and comprehension of intermediate-grade readers. *Journal of Reading Behavior, 22,* 395-411.

Robbins, C., & Ehri, L.C. (1994). Reading storybooks to kindergartners helps them learn new vocabulary words. *Journal of Educational Psychology, 86,* 54-64.

Scruggs, T.E., Mastropieri, M.A., & Levin, J.R. (1985). Vocabulary acquisition of retarded students under direct and mnemonic instruction. *American Journal of Mental Deficiency, 89,* 546-551.

Shake, M.C., Allington, R.L., Gaskins, R., & Marr, M.B. (1987). *How teachers teach vocabulary.* Paper presented to the National Reading Conference.

Stahl, S.A., Richek, M.A., & Vandevier, R.J. (1991). Learning meaning vocabulary through listening: A sixth-grade replication. In J. Zutell & S. McCormick (Eds.), Learner factors/teacher factors: Issues in literacy research and instruction (pp. 185-192). Chicago: National Reading Conference.

Stanovich, K.E., & Cunningham, A.E. (1993). Where does knowledge come from? Specific associations between print exposure and information acquisition. *Journal of Educational Psychology, 85,* 211-229.

Sternberg, R.J. (1987). Most vocabulary is learned from context. In M.G. McKeown & M.E. Curtis (Eds.), *Nature of vocabulary acquisition.* Hillsdale, NJ: Lawrence Erlbaum Associates.

Toms-Bronowski, S. (1993). An investigation of the effectiveness of selected vocabulary teaching strategies with intermediate grade level students (Doctoral dissertation, University of Wisconsin–Madison). Dissertation Abstracts International, 44, 1405A (University Microfilms, No. 83-16238).

White, T.G., Power, M.A., & White, S. (1989). Morphological analysis: Implications for teaching and understanding vocabulary growth. *Reading Research Quarterly, 24,* 283-304.

CHAPTER 5

Spelling

Correct spelling is often associated with educational attainment, accuracy, neatness, and cultivation. Spelling inability, on the other hand, is often associated with illiteracy, and may adversely affect a person's occupational status (Allred, 1984; Graham & Miller, 1979; Weisberg, 1985). There is a lot of motivation to spell well, an ambition that is within reach because good spelling requires a relatively small amount of learning. Spelling vocabularies between 2,800 and 3,000 words are sufficient for fluent and intelligent communication in both children and adults (Fitzgerald, 1951a; Graham, 1983; Horn, 1926, 1967; Rinsland, 1945; Thomas, 1972). For example, about 50 words accounted for almost half (49%) of the words that elementary-grade children use in writing (Thomas, 1979). Five hundred words accounted for 80% of the words used in written communication; 1,000 words for 86%; 2,000 words for 92%; and 3,000 words for 95%. A surprisingly small number of words (approximately 300) account for more than half the words children misspell in their writing (Allred, 1984; Thomas, 1979).

How do children obtain such spelling vocabularies? Although the exact mechanisms by which children acquire spelling knowledge are still unknown (and probably vary across individuals), we do know that spelling skills develop in an orderly fashion in most children, even handicapped students (Hall, 1984). Researchers have documented three basic stages or types of spelling errors evidenced by the majority of children as they develop spelling competence, with these errors occurring in a particular developmental order.

In the first stage, known as the *prephonetic* stage, the child's spelling attempts consist of only one or two salient letter sounds, usually the beginning or ending consonants. Prephonetic stage spellers use phoneme-grapheme relations, or sound-letter patterns, to spell (Drake & Ehri, 1984). For example, the letters "HKN" might be used to represent the word *chicken*. Prephonetic spellers are typically in kindergarten or grade 1, know their letters, and are just beginning to read and spell (Zutell, 1979).

Stage 2 spellers, or *phonetic* spellers, adopt a sequential sounding-out strategy and represent individually articulated sounds with letters that share acoustic similarity (e.g., FET = *feet*, TABL = *table*). These children will master the majority of phoneme-grapheme relationships, and are developing and improving their ability to segment pronunciations into sequences of phoneme patterns. Typically, stage 2 spellers are either late grade 1 or grade 2 readers (Zutell, 1979).

The third stage, known as the *transitional* stage, is characterized by attempts to replace phonetic spellings with conditional letter patterns and/or morpheme (meaning) spelling patterns. The transitional speller has abandoned the belief that one letter is required for every sound (Drake & Ehri, 1984). For instance, to represent the word *watched*, the transitional speller might spell "woched." Children usually reach the transitional stage after the second grade.

Some researchers (Beers & Henderson, 1977; Henderson & Beers, 1980) believe there is a fourth stage, characterized by the acquisition of correct spellings. However, this can only be considered a relative stage since children may be able to spell some words correctly (e.g., frequently seen words), but not others. For instance, phonetic-stage spellers may spell *looked* correctly because they have frequently encountered the word and have subsequently memorized it (Drake & Ehri, 1984). On the other hand, the same children may misspell the less familiar word *watched* as "wocht."

Children's perceptions of spelling ability are not consistent with this sequence of developmental improvement. Downing, DeStefano, Rich, and Bell (1985) investigated the spelling perceptions of students across the first to sixth grades. From grade two onward, children's perceptions of themselves as good spellers declined. For instance, by grade three, less than half the students interviewed considered themselves to be "good spellers." When asked why some children spell poorly, many children responded that poor spelling resulted from the lack of study and/or practice, or that poor spelling was precipitated by a failure to pay attention to the teacher during class. Other children, especially those in grade three, were particularly reluctant to discuss this topic. Although the majority of the children felt spelling was an important skill, many children reported negative emotions associated with spelling instruction. The authors found that the spelling strategy most frequently used by these children in everyday writing situations involved the analysis of words according to their phonetic units (i.e., spelling words by sounding them out). The authors concluded that most children overemphasized the importance of phoneme-grapheme relations.

Radebaugh (1985) studied 17 children in the third and fourth grades. Based on spelling tests and teachers' judgments, nine of these children were considered to be poor spellers, while the other eight were good spellers. Each child was asked to elaborate on the tactics he/she would use when spelling two easy-to-spell words (words whose spellings were known) and two hard-to-spell words (words whose spellings were unknown). Both good and poor spellers claimed that the spellings of the easy words came automatically. When asked about the specific strategies used to spell these words, good spellers reported being able to visualize the words, while poor spellers relied on sounding the words out.

When children were asked how they would spell the hard words, the poor spellers retained the sounding-out strategy. Specifically, these children divided the words into syllabic parts and sounded out each part of the word unit. In other words, the poor spellers used a letter-by-letter phonetic strategy when spelling. For example, one poor speller spelled the word *cautiously* as "koshisle." In contrast, good spellers relied on a variety of spelling strategies to spell the hard words. One strategy reported by good spellers involved breaking the words into units (not necessarily syllables) and trying to visualize how these units looked. For instance, one child reported recalling how she had printed the word "squirrel" on her crayon box earlier in the year (i.e., imagery strategy). Another strategy reported by the good spellers involved breaking the words into smaller parts and using the spelling pattern of a known word as a substitute for the spelling of the unknown word part (i.e., analogy strategy). For example, one child who used the analogy strategy spelled the word *dinosaur* as "dinosoar." Alternatively, some good spellers reported relying upon memorized spelling rules.

Overall, poor spellers mentioned using fewer strategies than did good spellers. Poor spellers also used more phonetic strategies than did good spellers and did not make use of imagery techniques. Marino (1980) and Olson, Logan and Lindsey (1988) drew similar conclusions concerning the strategies used by good and poor spellers. Marino found that as spellers became more proficient, they became more aware of sound-letter correspondences, but they also became more aware of the many constraints within each correspondence. Good spellers demonstrated awareness of common letter patterns and letter rules. Poor spellers, however, failed to display such knowledge.

Particularly relevant for this chapter on spelling instruction, good spellers reported using techniques (e.g., imagery, analogy) that research has demonstrated to be very effective in promoting spelling. Poor spellers, on the other hand, tended to be overly dependent on using phonetic strategies, strategies that do not seem to promote spelling acquisition to the degree that imagery, analogy, and other nonphonetic strategies do (Yee, 1969).

The Status of Spelling Instruction in the Classroom

Spelling is a mainstay of the elementary school curriculum. Yet many school-aged children have difficulties spelling, particularly those children who are either learning disabled or mentally delayed (Gerber & Lydiatt, 1984). In addition, there is growing concern that today's students are poorer spellers than students of 30 to 40 years ago (Graham & Miller, 1979). Why do children have difficulties acquiring spelling skills? While there does not appear to be any one answer to this question, it is probable that less than adequate teaching materials and instructional techniques may exacerbate students' difficulties.

Almost twenty years ago, Cohen (1969; cited in Graham, 1983) methodically analyzed the contents of popular spelling texts. Many of the texts contained activities that were irrelevant and inappropriate to acquisition of spelling skills. For instance, some texts included exercises that actually interfered with acquisition of spelling patterns, such as activities involving phonetic re-spelling. In addition, the texts rarely allowed students to generate spelling words in response to their own needs.

Today, it still appears that the majority of spelling instruction depends on commercial texts (90% in Cronnell & Humes, 1980). In itself, this is not particularly disturbing. However, Cronnell and Humes also found that the more widely used texts tended to concentrate upon the teaching of individual words and not the teaching of spelling patterns *per se*.

In addition, spelling instruction is not always done efficiently. Over a period of five to eight consecutive visits, Hillerich (1982) observed 34 spelling periods in six elementary school classes (grades 2, 3, 6, 7, and 8). Hillerich found that the majority of teachers devoted approximately 40 minutes per day to spelling activities—despite the empirically supported fact that the majority of children do not benefit from more than 60 to 75 minutes of spelling instruction per week (Allred, 1977; Reith et al., 1974). More disturbing, anywhere between 30% to 80% of spelling instruction time was used for irrelevant administrative or instructional activities (disciplining students, giving mechanical directions, grading papers). The correction of spelling workbook exercises was the next most popular activity, an activity not centrally relevant to learning.

Hillerich observed little instruction about how to acquire spelling skills, nor did teachers recommend or model strategies that could be used to study spelling words. In most classes, students were assigned exercises from their workbooks and then graded based on the results of spelling tests. Dictation of these spelling tests comprised between 4% and 18% of the total instructional time. Only one teacher provided students with immediate feedback by correcting the spelling tests orally. The remaining teachers collected the students' work, graded the tests, and handed the results back to students during the next instructional period.

In most classrooms, spelling instruction is based on traditional methods and not empirical research (Graham, 1983). In fact, investigators have found that some empirically supported methods, like presenting to-be-learned spelling words in list form or having students correct their own spelling tests, are rejected by a large number of teachers (Fitzsimmons & Loomer, 1977).

The purpose of this chapter is to inform teachers of effective spelling strategies that enjoy empirical support, and provide examples of how these techniques have been successfully implemented in the classroom. The strategies covered are those most appropriate for students at the elementary level. For examples of strategies appropriate for more mature students, see Hodges (1982) or Templeton (1983).

The discussion of spelling strategies will be divided into four sections. In the first, *organizational* and *instructional* hints are presented. These hints are intended to help teachers design effective spelling curricula and maintain students' interest. The second section is devoted to discussion of spelling strategies that are demonstrably useful in the *acquisition* of spelling skills. These strategies can be used when teaching children how to learn and remember word spellings. Third, effective strategies for *correcting* spelling are presented. The correction and analysis of spelling errors provides an excellent opportunity for the student to acquire new spelling skills and allows the teacher to monitor students' spelling progress. The fourth section summarizes *proofreading* tactics designed to help the student detect and correct their own spelling errors.

ORGANIZATIONAL AND INSTRUCTIONAL HINTS [T]

Organizational and instructional hints that can enhance the daily instruction of spelling are summarized in Table 5-1. All of these teaching strategies have been shown to enhance spelling instruction (Allred, 1977; Allred, 1984; Graham, 1983; Graham & Miller, 1979; Thomas, 1979). Teachers are encouraged to implement these general recommendations into their daily instructional activities.

Assess Readiness for Spelling

Prior to any spelling instruction, the student's readiness for instruction should be assessed. Spelling instruction should only be administered to those children who are able to write and name all the letters of the alphabet. Children should be able to copy words accurately, be able to spell their names correctly, and be able to enunciate words clearly. Children who are prepared for spelling instruction are able to recognize common letter-sound combinations, recognize that words are composed of different letters, ask for words they are in doubt about, write a few words from memory, and are able to express a few thoughts in writing. These children are usually reading at a second-grade level or better. Finally, but equally important, the child should express some interest in spelling (Allred, 1984; Graham & Miller, 1979). If the child does not display these characteristics, then the child is not a suitable candidate for spelling instruction.

Teachers who encounter students that do not present themselves as ready for formal spelling instruction are referred to a book by Hildreth (1956). In her book, Hildreth outlines activities designed to foster *spelling instruction readiness*.

Teachers need to impart the importance of spelling in both formal and social communications. To help maintain students' interest and motivation, spelling instruction should concentrate on words that are in the students' present, or near future, listening and reading vocabu-

Table 5-1

Organizational and instructional hints for teaching spelling

A. Assess student's readiness for spelling instruction:
1. Can child write and name all the letters in the alphabet?
2. Can child copy words accurately?
3. Can child correctly spell his/her name from memory?
4. Can child enunciate words clearly?
5. Can child recognize common letter-sound combinations?
6. Can child recognize that words are composed of different letters?
7. Can child ask about words he/she is in doubt about?
8. Can child write a few words from memory?
9. Can child express a few thoughts in writing?
10. Can child read at the second-grade level or better?
11. Does child express some interest in spelling?

B. Maintain students' spelling interest and motivation.
1. Stress importance of correct spelling in formal and social communication.
2. Concentrate spelling instruction on words that are in students' present, or near future, listening and reading vocabularies.
3. Encourage pride in correctly spelled papers and praise students' spelling progress.
4. Occasionally supplement spelling instruction with spelling games (e.g., Masterspeller, Hangman, spelling bingo).

C. Devote about 60-75 minutes a week to spelling instruction.

D. Limit the use of phonic instruction.

E. Teach spelling rules that apply to a large number of words and have only a few exceptions.

F. Present spelling words in lists rather than in context.

G. Study spelling words as whole units versus syllabified forms.

H. Use the test-study-test method versus the study-test method.
1. Administer spelling pretest to students.
2. Spelling instruction concentrates on only those words spelled incorrectly.
3. Spelling test administered including both words spelled correctly and incorrectly at pretest.

I. Have students monitor their own spelling progress.

J. Individualize spelling instruction.
1. Be responsive to the unique needs of individual students.
2. Choose students' spelling materials to match their personal needs.
3. Plan, monitor and modify spelling instruction according to the needs of the individual student.

K. Teach spelling as part of general language study.

laries (Thomas, 1979). Teachers should constantly encourage students' spelling attempts, encourage pride in correct spelling, and praise spelling progress. To help maintain students' interest, the occasional use of spelling games such as Masterspeller, Hangman, and Spelling Bingo are recommended (Graham, 1983). However, games should be used to supplement instruction only; they should not substitute for primary instruction. For examples of spelling games and references, see Graham, Freeman, and Miller (1981) and Thomas (1979).

How much time should be designated to spelling? Sixty to 75 minutes per week (approximately 15 minutes per day) is a sufficient amount of time (Allred, 1977; Allred, 1984; Horn, 1960, 1967; Reith, et al., 1974; Thomas, 1979). Short periods of spelling instruction are recommended because there is evidence that extended study periods lower student interest and motivation (Horn, 1960; cited in Thomas, 1979). However, it is important that this is time for promotion of efficient and meaningful spelling activities—students should be allowed to focus on their own special spelling needs. This time should not be devoted to discipline, administrative, or other such activities.

Perhaps one of the greatest controversies regarding effective spelling instruction concerns the use of phonics. *We recommend that teachers limit the use of phonic instruction when teaching spelling skills.* In part, arguments against the use of phonics instruction are derived from the fact that the English language has one of the largest and most complex vocabularies in the world. In English, the 26 letters of the alphabet represent approximately 44 sounds; there are silent letters; there are variant and invariant sounds; and there are 300 different letter combinations that represent 17 vowel sounds. To help place these complexities into perspective, consider that, when spelled phonetically, there are over 396,000,000 different spellings for the word "circumference" (Graham & Miller, 1979).

In comprehensive reviews of the spelling literature, Graham (1983) and Graham and Miller (1979) explain that phonic instruction can be problematic for several reasons. First, most sounds can be spelled more than one way and most letters spell many sounds. Second, many misspellings are phonemically correct. Over one-third of the words in the dictionary have more than one accepted pronunciation but only one correct spelling. More than half of the words in the dictionary contain silent letters, and one sixth of these words have double letters. In addition, unstressed syllables prove difficult to spell phonetically.

A related argument against the use of phonic instruction originates from the high proportion of phonetic errors committed by students. For example, research carried out in Alberta with 449 fourth- through sixth-grade students revealed that over 50% of a total of 5301 spelling errors involved phonetic substitutions, letter omissions, and errors resulting from inaccurate pronunciations (Thomas, 1979). Further, teachers consistently ranked phonetic substitutions and omissions as the first and second most common type of spelling error committed by students. In addition, research indicates that poor spellers tend to rely upon phonetic strategies, while good spellers use more effective strategies (e.g., Downing et al., 1985; Radebaugh, 1985).

On the other hand, there are researchers who contend that phonic instruction is valuable, considering the regular nature of some sound-symbol relationships (Gillingham & Stillman, 1969; Hanna et al., 1967). For example, Ball and Blachman (1991), Foorman et al. (1991), and Tangel and Blachman (1992) have demonstrated improvements in students' spelling performances as a result of phonemic instruction, especially when this training includes instruction in the relationships between sound segments and letter patterns (see the discussion of Sound Categorization Training in Chapter 2 of this volume). Nonetheless, evidence in support of phonics is mixed at best (Cramer, 1969; Block, 1972; Hahn, 1964; Horn, 1969; Ibeling, 1961; Personke & Tee, 1971; Tee, 1969). Therefore, like others (e.g., Allred, 1984; Graham, 1983; Graham & Miller, 1979), *we recommend only the provisional use of phonics instruction and that teachers supplement spelling instruction with other empirically supported strategies.*

Spelling Rules

Should children be taught spelling rules? Because of the number of irregularities and exceptions that exist within the English language system, only a limited number of spelling rules have proven valuable to spelling instruction (Blake & Emans, 1970; Graham & Miller, 1979; Thomas, 1979). Specifically, only those rules or generalizations that apply to a large number of words and have only a few exceptions are useful when teaching spelling skills. These rules are listed in Table 5-2. Teachers are reminded, however, that when teaching rules, emphasis needs to be placed on the development and use of the rule and not upon the memorization of the verbal statement (Thomas, 1979). In other words, students need to be provided with practical situations in which they can apply these rules.

Spelling Mnemonics

Mnemonics are memory strategies that help students remember specific information. Although students should not be taught to rely exclusively on mnemonics for the spelling of unfamiliar words, mnemonics can help students acquire the spellings of especially challenging words (e.g., irregular words). Whenever possible, students should be encouraged to develop their own mnemonics (Scott, 1993). There are many types of mnemonics, including ones based on semantics (e.g., "your princi*pal* is your *pal*"), imagery (e.g., visualizing the *t* in *witch* as a witch's hat), and sound (e.g., pronouncing the word *scissors* as "skissors" to remember the silent *c*). Readers who are interested in learning more about spelling mnemonics are referred to texts by Mastropieri and Scruggs (1991), Suid (1981), and Tarasoff (1990).

Table 5-2
Spelling Rules suitable for instruction.

1. Rules governing the addition of suffixes and inflected endings:
   a. When a word ends in *e*, the *e* is usually dropped when a syllable beginning with a vowel is added.
       bake   baking
       make   making
   b. When a word ends in *e*, the *e* is usually kept when a syllable beginning with a vowel is added.
       bake   baker
       make   maker
   c. When a root word ends in *y* and is preceded by a consonant, the *y* is changed to *i* when suffixes and endings are added, unless they begin with an "i".
       fly   flies   fly   flying
       study   studies   study   studying
   d. When a noun ends in *y* and is preceded by a consonant, the plural is formed by changing the *y* to *i* and adding *es*.
       baby   babies
       puppy   puppies
   e. When a root word ends in *y* and is preceded by a vowel, the root word is not changed when a suffix or ending is added.
       play   playful
       monkey monkeys

   f. Words that end with a consonant and are preceded by a single vowel usually require that the consonant be doubled before adding an ending.
       run   running
       sit   sitting
2. Capital letters are used in the following situations:
   a. The first word of a sentence (He went home)
   b. The letter "I" when used as a word (Jimmy and I went fishing)
   c. Proper names (Tommy, Jane, Canada)
   d. Words derived from proper names (Canadian, French)
   e. Titles before proper names (Sir Winston Churchill)
   f. The first and all important words of a book title, story, etc. (*The Return of the Native*)
3. Apostrophes are used in the following situations:
   a. An apostrophe and *s* to show possession after a single noun (the boy's coat)
   b. An apostrophe alone to show possession after a plural noun ending in "s" (the girls' coats)

Table 5-2 (cont.)
Spelling rules suitable for instruction.

      c. An apostrophe and "s" to show possession after a plural noun not ending in "s" (the children's coats)

      d. An apostrophe to show the omission of a letter or letters in a contraction (isn't, I'll)

4. Rules about the letter "s" and plurals.

      a. When adding "s" to words to form plurals or to change the tense of verbs; "es" must be added to words ending with hissing sounds. (x, s, sh, ch)

            glass   glasses
            watch   watches

      b. When "s" is added to words ending in a single "f" to form plurals, the "f" is changed to "v" and "es" is added.

            wolf   wolves
            half   halves

5. Most abbreviations end with a period.

      Ont.
      Nov.

6. The letter "q" is always followed by "u" in common English words.

      queen
      quiet

7. No English words end in "v".

      glove
      move

8. The letter "i" usually comes before "e" except after "c".

      receive
      receipt

Taken from Allred (1984) and Thomas (1979).

Spelling Lists

Another common misunderstanding in spelling instruction concerns the utility of the "list method" (i.e., learn a list of 10 new words this week) versus presenting words in context. Presenting words in a line or column is advantageous in that it focuses students' attention on each word (Allred, 1984; Graham, 1983; Graham & Miller, 1979; Smith, 1975; Thomas, 1979). Word lists may be developed on the basis of similar sounds (e.g., *pain, rain, sail*), rhyming patterns (e.g., *must, trust, dust*), or complex sound patterns (e.g., *bishop, blush, mission, pressure*; Scott, 1993). By grouping words according to shared vowel patterns or rhyming parts, students can be encouraged to use an analogy approach to spelling unfamiliar words. By grouping words on the basis of sound patterns, students may come to realize that they are spelling the same sound despite differences in visual appearance (Scott, 1993). Moreover, presenting spelling words in lists can be complemented by giving the meanings of the words. For instance, many teachers who use the list method first pronounce the words out loud, read sentences that include the words, and then read the words aloud again (Horn, 1967). Reading words in sentences presumably provides students with the opportunity to acquire the words' meanings via context. (See Chapter 4 for evidence that children do not acquire vocabulary meaning through context.)

Pronounce Words Clearly

Students often misspell words that are not pronounced clearly (e.g., *pumpkin, environment, library, probably*; Scott, 1993). Therefore, students should be encouraged to articulate words carefully and to pay close attention to sounds that are not easily heard. Similarly, teachers should model such speech for their students, occasionally exaggerating hard-to-hear sounds (e.g., chocolate, shepherd, subtle, laboratory). Because many students panic when they are required to spell multisyllabic words, they should be encouraged to break such words into smaller units (e.g., syllables, prefixes and suffixes; Scott, 1993). In order to learn where such breaks occur in words, students need to repeat word sounds and syllables regularly (examples of such repetitive activities include clapping out the syllables in words, or tossing a ball back and forth to the beat of each syllable).

Teach Whole Words

Spelling words are also better studied as whole words than in syllabified form (Allred, 1977; Allred, 1984; Graham, 1983). Students' attention should be focused on each word as a whole and not just the "hard-to-spell" spots. Visual attention directed to the whole word is presumed to aid in the formation of correct visual images which, in turn, enhance overall spelling retention.

Teach Unknown Words, Not Mixed Lists

The study of unknown words only (i.e., test-study-test method, with only words misspelled on the first test retained for study) is superior to the study of both known and unknown words (i.e., study-test method; Allred, 1977; Allred, 1984; Fitzgerald, 1951b, 1953; Yee 1969; Graham & Miller, 1979). Prior to formal spelling instruction, a spelling test for potential target words is administered. The selection of spelling words should include those words that are frequently used by children in that grade so students will have meaningful opportunities to apply the words throughout the school year (see Thomas, 1979 for a review of the 3000 most common words used in elementary-grade children's writings). Words that are correctly spelled are not included in spelling instruction. If a spelling pretest is not administered, it is very likely that words currently part of students' spelling repertoires will be included in study. This, in turn, may lower students' motivation to acquire spelling skills. After study, students are again administered a spelling test. This spelling test should include both previously known and unknown words. The periodic testing of mastered words will help ensure spelling maintenance (Neef, Iwata, & Page, 1977). Misspelled words are then noted and incorporated into future lessons.

It is extremely important that teachers monitor and praise students' achievements. It has been recommended that students should monitor their own spelling progress (Wallace & Kauffman, 1978). For instance, students could record both the number of words correctly spelled at pretest, and the number of words spelled correctly at post-test. Self-monitoring can help provide students with motivation for learning spelling skills and help them gain a better sense of their spelling strengths and weaknesses and, at the same time, aid teachers in planning the course of future instruction (Graham, 1983; Thomas, 1979). Self-monitoring may be especially useful when working with children who do not have a clear sense of their own progress (i.e., learning disabled or mentally delayed children). In his book, Thomas (1979) provides examples of suitable record forms for students in elementary and senior grades.

Individualize Spelling Instruction

The importance and necessity of individualized spelling instruction cannot be overemphasized (e.g., Graham, 1983; Graham & Miller, 1979; Rowell, 1972). According to Graham (1983), individualized instruction implies that teachers be responsive to the unique needs of every student in their class, that teachers carefully choose materials that match the needs of individual students, and that the content of spelling programs be personalized. Furthermore, instruction should be planned, monitored, and modified on the basis of the individual student's performance. The teacher must assess the current strengths and weaknesses of every student, carefully monitoring both progress and changing needs. Spelling instruction should then be adapted to those needs.

We realize that with the large number of students in classrooms today (each of whom are uniquely different), the recommendation for individualized spelling instruction is not an easy one to carry out. Yet these suggestions can reduce the costs of personalized instruction. For example, by having students study only those words they spell incorrectly at pretest (i.e., the test-study-test method), teachers can ensure suitable study materials for each student without expending additional time testing any one student. (This is true because students are given the same spelling pretest and post-test but are instructed to study only those words they spelled incorrectly at pretest.) Similarly, by having students monitor their own spelling achievements, teachers can reduce their own record keeping, yet still have access to valuable information concerning each student. Individualized instruction does not imply that students need to work alone. Rather, it is recommended that students studying identical skills be instructed as a group (van Oudenhoven, Berkum, & Swen-Koopmans, 1987).

Use the Microcomputer

The microcomputer promises to be a helpful aid in the delivery of individualized spelling instruction (Allred, 1984; Sears & Johnson, 1986). Not only can computers store and present large amounts of information, but children find using computers rewarding and fun. It is very probable that computers will soon be used to help provide individualized spelling drills and practice, diagnose spelling errors, and provide study direction (Allred, 1984).

Integrate Spelling in Written Work

Finally, it must be remembered that correct spelling is not an end unto itself. Rather, spelling is an integral part of writing and should be taught in the context of general language study (Allred, 1984; Graham, 1983; Horn, 1967). It is important that students be given the opportunity to apply spelling skills they've learned to written work. A variety of instructional materials and approaches should be used. For instance, students can be asked to spell words in response to a picture or spell the word that completes a sentence. Children should be allowed to concentrate on personally required spellings (i.e., self-generated spellings) instead of copying words from a text. For example, students can be asked to develop spelling vocabularies that pertain to their special interests and hobbies (Thomas, 1979).

SPELLING ACQUISITION STRATEGIES

One very clear finding in the spelling literature is that children should not be left to their own devices to acquire effective spelling strategies (Allred, 1977; Allred, 1984; Gilstrap, 1962; Graham, 1983; Graham & Freeman, 1986; Graham & Miller, 1979). Teachers can help students acquire and maintain spelling competence by imparting effective spelling strategies that can be used to master both materials encountered in the spelling curriculum as well as those encountered outside of the classroom. According to Graham and Miller (1979), an effective spelling strategy leads to the acquisition of the whole word, requires careful pronunciation of the word, promotes visual imagery, provides auditory and/or kinesthetic reinforcement, and involves systematic testing of recall. Not surprisingly, there is no single best method for teaching spelling (Blair, 1975; Gerber & Lydiatt, 1984; Thomas, 1979). In the following section, empirically supported spelling techniques are outlined and discussed. Ultimately, it is the teacher's decision which strategy or strategies should be taught. Depending upon the unique characteristics of the students in the classroom, it is very likely that certain strategies will be more appropriate for some students than for others.

Imagery Strategies [SSR]

Mental imagery facilitates various types of learning. For instance, Paivio and Yuille (1967) demonstrated that imagery instructions enhanced learning of paired associates as long as the pair members were depicted in a common interaction. Similarly, research conducted within the last two decades has demonstrated that instructions to code sentence content imaginally enhance the retention of sentences (Anderson & Hidde, 1971; Pressley et al., 1987) and prose passages (Anderson & Kulhany, 1972; Rasco, Tennyson, & Boutwell, 1975). The use of imagery also improves acquisition of spelling skills (e.g., Sears & Johnson, 1986).

Radaker (1963) was among the first investigators to test whether mental imagery might aid children's acquisition of word spellings. Radaker trained 60 fourth-grade children to use an imagery strategy while studying spelling words. Radaker found that the children who were instructed to use mental imagery demonstrated superior spelling performances on subsequent spelling tests relative to children who were not instructed to use mental imagery.

When evaluated (Stanford Achievement Test, Form M) prior to imagery training, the spelling scores of students instructed to use mental imagery did not differ from the scores of students who were not given imagery training. However, after training, students instructed to use mental imagery displayed superior spelling performance on a test of similar difficulty (Stanford Achievement Test, Form N). Only a few training sessions were required to teach the mental imagery study strategy adequately (i.e., performance scores were essentially equal whether students participated in two 45-minute imagery training sessions or six such sessions). Even more impressive, imagery-instructed children continued to demonstrate superior spelling achievements *one year* after training. Finally, Radaker's work confirmed the findings of other researchers who concluded that mental imagery was an effective study tool when learning to spell (e.g., Fitzgerald, 1951a; Gilstrap, 1962; Horn, 1919, cited in Graham & Miller, 1979) and suggested that instructions to use mental imagery can facilitate spelling performance over long periods of time.

The specific instructions used by Radaker are outlined in Table 5-3. Prior to imagery instruction, target words were selected that were unique in pattern, low in frequency, and relatively unfamiliar to the students. Students assigned to the imagery condition were instructed in groups of five and participated in either two or six training sessions, each of which lasted 45 minutes. Students assigned to the control condition were not directed to use any specific spelling study strategy other than the one they were currently using and were assigned to six sessions of free play and social conversation.

In the first phase of imagery training, the children were presented with flash cards that displayed the printed target words. The flash cards were presented one at a time. The children were instructed to read each word carefully, paying special attention to the word's letter sequence. The children were then instructed to close their eyes and try to imagine the word being projected on a large outdoor screen. The word was to be imagined as printed in large, glossy black letters. When the children had created their mental image of the word, they were instructed to stabilize the image by holding it in their minds for as long as possible. The objective was to hold each image for one minute.

If students experienced difficulty stabilizing their images, they were instructed to imagine that they were nailing each letter of the word onto the theater screen. To help improve retention, all the students were instructed to imagine themselves applying paste to the back of the letters and gluing the words onto the screen. The children were instructed to nail and/or paste each letter of the word as it appeared

---

Table 5-3
Imagery training instructions

1. Select appropriate words for spelling instruction.

2. Imagery Training.
   - a. Present words individually on flash-cards.
   - b. Instruct students to read each word carefully, paying special attention to the word's letter sequence.
   - c. Instruct students to close their eyes and imagine the word projected on a large outdoor screen in large, glossy black letters.
   - d. Instruct students to hold their images in their minds for as long as possible.
   - e. Instruct students who are experiencing difficulties stabilizing their images to imagine that they were nailing each letter of the word onto the theatre screen.
   - f. Instruct students to imagine that they are pasting the letters of the word onto the theatre screen.
   - g. Instruct students to image a floodlight illuminating the word letters so brightly that the letters will not fade until they dissolve their image of the word.

3. Instruct students to use the imagery technique whenever they were studying spelling words.

From Radaker (1963).

sequentially. Students were also told to imagine that a floodlight was illuminating the words with such brightness that the words would not fade until the students dissolved their images. At the end of the training sessions, it was recommended that students use this imagery technique whenever they were studying spelling words.

To reiterate, Radaker found that children trained to use mental imagery spelled more words correctly on subsequent spelling tests relative to children who were not trained to use imagery, and that instructional gains were maintained at least one year following training. Further, only a brief instruction time was required to teach students the imagery strategy.

Although the instructions used by Radaker are appropriate for younger grade-school children, teachers may want to use alternative imagery instructions with older students. Tables 5-4 and 5-5 outline instructions used by Horn (1919, cited in Graham & Miller, 1979) and Fitzgerald (1951b). Essentially, both Fitzgerald and Horn instructed students to read spelling words carefully and then imagine the words in their minds. Without looking at the printed original, students were required to write the words down on paper. Each student then checked the accuracy of his or her spelling with the original. If any word was spelled incorrectly, the process (look, visualize, cover, write, check) was repeated. Both older and younger students can be taught to use these imagery techniques when studying to-be-learned spelling items (e.g., Thomas, 1979). Older students in particular may prefer these later strategies to Radaker's "nail-and-paste" method.

Word Analogy Strategy [SSR]

The general rationale underlying the use of an analogy strategy is that the identification and use of known orthographic patterns will aid attempts to spell unknown words. Studies investigating the spelling skills of mature students have found that older students readily extract orthographic patterns of known words to spell unknown words

---

Table 5-4

Imagery instructions

1. Look at the word and say it to yourself.
2. Close your eyes and visualize the word.
3. Check to see if you were right (if you were wrong, begin at step 1).
4. Cover the word and write it.
5. Check to see if you were right (if you were wrong, begin at step 1).
6. Repeat steps 4 and 5 two more times.

From Horn (1919), cited in Graham & Miller (1979)

Table 5-5
Imagery strategy

1. Look at the word carefully.
2. Say the word.
3. With your eyes closed, visualize the word.
4. Cover the word and then write it.
5. Check the spelling.
6. If the word is misspelled, repeat steps 1 to 5.

From Fitzgerald (1951a).

(Hodges, 1982; Juola, Schadler, Chabot, & McCaughey, 1978). There is also evidence that by the second grade, some students spontaneously use familiar word patterns to help them spell unknown words (Beers, 1976; cited in Englert, Hiebert, & Stewart, 1985). Mildly handicapped students, however, appear to have difficulties spontaneously recognizing and using word patterns when attempting unknown spellings (e.g., Carpenter & Miller, 1982). Fortunately, with special training, these students can be taught to use analogy strategies successfully. For instance, Englert et al. (1985) found that when mildly handicapped children were taught to use analogy strategies, both the number of correct word spellings and the readability of misspellings were substantially improved. These authors advocate that spelling programs should include word classification activities and teach students to generate new words according to the orthographic patterns of known words.

Table 5-6 outlines the analogy instructions used by Englert et al. (1985). Twenty-two students participated in this study. Eighteen students were classified as learning disabled (verbal and performance WISC-R IQ = 90 or above), while the remaining four students were classified as educable mentally retarded (verbal and performance WISC-R IQ = 50-70). All the students lacked skills in reading and spelling. The only criterion for participation in the study was that students scored at least 80% on a rhyming pretest. Half the students were randomly assigned to an *imagery plus analogy training* condition while the other half were assigned to a control condition that entailed *imagery training* only.

Selecting the words for a pretest. Prior to training, 50 words were selected for acquisition. These core or target words were common words that rhymed and shared similar orthographic pattern with at least five other words. For each of the 50 target items, five rhyming and orthographically similar words were selected to be used as practice and transfer words. Thirty teachers were asked to review the sets of five rhyming words and choose from each set the one word that they considered to be the least common in the reading and spelling

Table 5-6
Analogy Strategy

1. Administer a pretest to select suitable target, practice, and transfer words for spelling instruction.

2. Have children learn and memorize the "Rhyming Rule".
   a. Tell the child that when two words rhyme, the last part of the words often are spelled the same.
   b. Provide examples of this rule.
   c. Have the child identify word from a word list that rhymes with an orally presented word.
   d. Have the child identify the letters that the two words share according to the Rhyming Rule

3. Have children learn target rules via an imagery strategy.
   a. Child reads and spells out loud word.
   b. Child spells word out loud from memory (if word is spelled incorrectly, printed word is presented).
   c. Child writes word twice from memory (if word is spelled incorrectly, printed word is presented).
   d. Delayed spelling test is given.

4. Instruction and training using the analogy strategy.
   a. Child given word list that contains the studied target words.
   b. Child is required to pick target word that rhymes with an orally presented practice word.
   c. Child is required to identify the letters that the two words share.
   d. Child is encouraged to spell the practice word using the rhyming elements of the target word.

5. Expansion of analogy skills.
   a. The child is asked to complete cloze sentences using the practice words (children are allowed to look at their word list to help them do this).
   b. The child is asked to write the practice word without looking at their word list.
   c. If practice word is spelled incorrectly, a verbal prompt is given to think of words that rhyme with the practice word and how they are spelled.
   d. If verbal prompt is insufficient to produce correct spelling, the word list is given back to the child and they are asked to search for the target word that rhymes with the practice word.
   e. The procedure is reiterated until the practice word is spelled correctly.

6. Spelling test is given for target words and rhyming transfer words.

From Englert, Hiebert, & Stewart (1985)

vocabularies of second-grade children. These words became the noninstructed transfer words used to measure strategy generalization. The remaining four words from each set became the practice words used to teach the analogy strategy.

All the students were then administered a spelling pretest. The spelling abilities of the students assigned to the imagery plus analogy and imagery only training conditions did not differ significantly. Using the information acquired from the pretest, 15 misspelled target words and their respective practice and uncommon transfer words were selected for each student assigned to the imagery plus analogy training condition. Thirty misspelled target words were selected for each student assigned to the imagery only condition. Teachers held individual sessions with their students three times weekly, with sessions of approximately ten minutes apiece. The training program lasted four weeks.

To start the *imagery plus analogy* session, children were taught that *when two words rhyme, the last part of the words are often spelled the same*. Teachers provided demonstrations of this rule, and students were required to memorize and demonstrate an understanding of the rule. Instruction continued until students could accurately indicate which word from a list rhymed with an orally presented word, and could indicate which letters the two words shared according to the rhyming rule.

Teaching the imagery strategy. When the children had successfully demonstrated understanding of the rhyming rule, they were taught to use an *imagery strategy* to study the target spelling words (i.e., common words chosen from the spelling pretest). In this phase, the students were first asked to read and spell out loud three to four words. The children were then required to spell the words out loud from memory and write them twice without looking at the printed original. If a student misspelled a word, the child was again presented the printed version of the word and the procedure was repeated. Each student was given a delayed spelling test (at least one minute after the last word was presented) for all the target words. Training continued until each student could spell 15 words that he or she had been unable to spell at pretest.

Teaching the analogy strategy. During the third stage, students received instruction and training concerning *the use of the analogy strategy*. Students were asked to find items from a word sheet (the word sheet consisted of the target words learned via the imagery strategy) that rhymed with an orally presented practice word (i.e., rhyming words selected at pretest). The children were also asked to identify the letters in both words that were spelled the same. (This procedure is identical to that used in phase 1, where students were taught the rhyming rule.) Students were encouraged to spell the practice words using the rhyming elements of the target words.

In the final phase of training, students expanded their analogy skills. First, the children were asked to complete cloze sentences with the practice words. The children were allowed to consult their target word list to help them complete this task. Second, the children were asked to write the practice words without looking at their word list. If a practice word was spelled incorrectly, the student was prompted to think of words that rhymed with the practice word and how they were spelled. If the verbal prompt was insufficient to produce correct spelling, the student was shown his target word list and asked to search for the target word that rhymed with the problematic practice word. Once the student identified the appropriate target word, the procedure was repeated. Thus, the primary emphasis throughout the experimental sessions was to search for orthographic similarities between known and unknown words that rhymed, and to use shared letter patterns when spelling novel words.

Imagery-only instructions. Students assigned to the *imagery-only* condition were treated similarly, with the exception that they were not given analogy training. In the first phase, children in this group were instructed to listen as the teacher read each of the 30 target words out loud. Next, they said the target words out loud in unison with their teacher, and finally, repeated the target words on their own.

In the second phase (i.e., the imagery training phase), the students were asked first to spell the target words out loud while looking at printed versions, and then to write the words from memory. If a word was misspelled, the printed word was shown to the student and the procedure was repeated. The procedure continued until the student wrote the target words successfully from memory twice and spelled the words correctly on a delayed test of recall.

Finally, students assigned to the imagery-only condition practiced completing sentences with the target words and were encouraged to spell the words from memory. Again, if a word was spelled incorrectly, the list of the target words was presented to the student, who was then required to copy the correct spelling of the word that completed the sentence.

The post-training spelling test. A spelling test for both the selected target words (common words) and transfer words (uncommon words) concluded the training sessions. The number of correct spellings and the quality of errors committed by students given imagery plus analogy strategy training was compared to the spelling performances of students given imagery training only. Both groups improved in their ability to spell target words after training. This is not surprising considering that both groups were instructed to use an imagery strategy while studying the target words. By the end of the training session, students in the *imagery plus analogy training* group spelled significantly more transfer words correctly than did students in the imagery only group. Students instructed to use the *imagery plus analogy* strategy also demonstrated substantial improvement in the quality of spelling errors committed relative to students in the imagery only group. Specifically, at the time of pretest, 50% of the students in both groups were performing at the prephonetic spelling stage. The other 50% displayed errors characteristic of early transitional stage spelling. At post-test, however, only the students in the *imagery plus analogy* group showed advancement across the developmental stages. Over two-thirds of the *imagery plus analogy* students displayed either transitional stage errors or, even better, correct spellings.

Analogy training is an effective spelling strategy that can be used to help students generalize their knowledge of known orthographic patterns when spelling novel words. Without analogy training, control subjects improved their spellings of target words only; they did not transfer their newly acquired knowledge to orthographically similar words. Although Englert and her colleagues worked with mildly handicapped students, there is no apparent reason why their training program would not also benefit the spelling performances of poor spellers who do not spontaneously use analogy skills. Overall, the results support the authors' recommendation that educators teach students that when trying to spell an unknown word, it is sometimes helpful to think of the orthographic pattern of a known word. We also feel that analogy instruction is an effective and appropriate spelling strategy for the acquisition of words with common letter patterns, but that other strategies, such as imagery, are also required when words do not have this characteristic.

Simultaneous Oral Spelling Method [T]

The Simultaneous Oral Spelling method (Bradley, 1981; Hume & Bradley, 1984) involves presenting words to children in written form. The word is spoken by another person, with the child then writing the word and pronouncing each letter as the word is written. Then the child reads the written word. An especially critical part of this process seems to be the motor behaviors involved in writing the word, with children's acquisition of spelling words much better when they handwrite words than when they "write" using little letter tiles or type the words on a computer (Cunningham & Stanovich, 1990; Hume & Bradley, 1984).

Morphological Strategies

One common approach used to improve children's spelling is to encourage them to look for meaningful parts of larger words (Scott, 1993). Such instruction can also provide students with insights about the logic of the spelling system. Chomsky and Halle (1986) argue that English spelling is optimal for such instruction because many underlying morphemic structures remain the same across variations in phonemic form. For instance, the meaning and orthography of numerous root words are unaffected by adding a suffix (e.g., *sign—signal, signature; sane—sanity*). Furthermore, when suffixation does produce orthographic changes, these changes are usually governed by adjustment rules (e.g., change *y* to *i* before adding *-ed*). Finally, the spelling of suffixes remain constant despite how they may sound (e.g., /t/ *talked*, /d/ *rolled*, /id/ *waited*; Sterling & Rusby, 1986).

Wong (1983; cited in Wong, 1986) successfully trained eight sixth-grade students (all of whom qualified for remedial spelling instruction) to use morphological structures when spelling 33 unfamiliar words. Four days a week, the students met for half-hour spelling sessions. During the first session, students completed a pretest. For the second session, they were introduced to five or six new words, with another five words introduced on the third day. The students completed a post-test for these words on the fourth day. The training sessions continued for three weeks.

As part of the training sessions, the teacher wrote the target words on the blackboard, pronounced them and explained their meanings. The teacher also explained the concept of a root word and a suffix. Students were also instructed to complete a spelling grid for the target words. Specifically, students were to record the target word, the number of syllables in the word, the base word, the suffix, and any changes in the spelling of the word that resulted from adding the suffix. Every week, the teacher used the first two training words to model how to complete the grid. For example, for the target word *education*, students recorded 4 syllables (*e-du-ca-tion*), the base word *educate* and addition/suffix *-tion*, and that the *-e* in the base word was dropped when adding the suffix. Students were also provided with the cue card containing seven general spelling questions and statements (see Table 5-7). These questions and statements encouraged students to use their knowledge of morphology or phonics when spelling unfamiliar words and to feel positive about their strategic spelling efforts.

In order to assess students' learning, they completed a spelling test consisting of eleven unfamiliar words both before and after the training sessions. Before training, students spelled 27% of the test words correctly. One week following the training sessions, students' accuracy increased to 78%. Students maintained these high performance scores two weeks following training, spelling 79% of the test items correctly.

Despite these positive findings, there is limited research investigating the use of morphological strategies to enhance students' spelling. Therefore, we encourage teachers to use this approach cautiously in their classrooms. Although there is no reason to suspect that morphological strategies would not improve all students' spelling, it would be advisable to pilot this strategy with a select group of students prior to using it with a whole class.

Table 5-7
Seven general spelling questions statements.

1. Do I know this word?

2. How many syllables do I hear in this word? (Write down the number.)

3. I'll spell out the word.

4. Do I have the right number of syllables down?

5. If yes, is there any part of the word I'm not sure about the spelling? I'll underline that part and try spelling the word again.

6. Now, does it look right to me? If it does, I'll leave it alone. If it still doesn't look right, I'll underline the part I'm not sure of the spelling and try again. (If the word I spelled does not have the right number of syllables, let me hear the word in my head again, and find the missing syllable. Then I'll go back to steps 5 and 6.)

7. When I finish spelling, I tell myself I'm a good worker. I've tried hard at spelling.

From Wong (1983; cited in Wong, 1986).

Multiple Spelling Strategy Instruction

So far, we have reviewed several individual strategies that have been demonstrated to enhance students' spelling (e.g., imagery, analogy, morphological). There is recent evidence that students also benefit from instruction about multiple spelling strategies (Kernaghan & Woloshyn, in press; Woloshyn & Thomas, 1995). Instruction about multiple strategies is critical if students are to develop a repertoire of effective spelling strategies (repertoires that are characteristic of good spellers; Hodges, 1982; Marino, 1980). However, learners can only use such strategies effectively if they possess detailed metacognitive knowledge about how, when and where to use them (Harris & Pressley, 1991; Pressley, Borkowski & Schneider, 1987, Winograd & Hare, 1988). Therefore, it is essential, when providing students information about multiple spelling strategies (or for that matter, individual ones), to also provide metacognitive information about the target strategies.

In one such multiple strategy instruction study, Kernaghan and Woloshyn (in press) improved the spelling performances of first-grade students by providing them with explicit information about phonetics, imagery and analogy. Students who participated in this study were assigned to one of three study conditions: strategy instruction with metacognitive information, strategy instruction alone, and traditional language arts. Spelling instruction occurred over the course of four weeks, with learners meeting in small groups (four to five students) once a week for approximately 25 minutes. Students who were assigned to the strategy conditions received instruction about each technique as described by Ball and Blachman (1991), Radaker (1963) and Englert et al. (1985), respectively (see previous section). Strategies were introduced individually, with the students' teacher modeling how to practice carrying out each strategy. Students were then provided opportunities to carry out each strategy independently. When students demonstrated proficiency in the use of one strategy, the next technique was introduced.

Some of these students also received metacognitive information about each strategy (e.g., that analogy was an appropriate strategy to use when an unfamiliar word sounded like a known one, or that using imagery would help prevent them from forgetting the spelling of a new word). These students also participated in discussions about the importance of good spelling as it related to educational attainment, literacy and their everyday lives.

Students in the language arts condition completed two lesson plans from a spelling series. As part of these lessons, students completed worksheet exercises including copying words, identifying rhyming words and creating sentences. Prior to the spelling lessons, all students completed a spelling dictation test for twenty unfamiliar words. Fifteen of these words were subsequently used during training, with the remaining five being used as transfer items. After the training sessions, students rewrote the original spelling dictation test. For the training words, students who received instruction in multiple spelling strategies outperformed their peers who completed traditional language arts activities. For the transfer words, only those students who had received metacognitive information in addition to strategy instruction outperformed those who completed language-arts activities. This later finding underlies the importance of providing students with metacognitive information—without such information, students are unlikely to transfer or generalize their knowledge of spelling strategies. Woloshyn and Thomas (1995) had similar success introducing third-grade students to a combination of morphological, syllabic segmentation and imagery strategies.

We encourage teachers to provide students with information about a number of spelling strategies. However, this information must be presented in a systematic manner. Specifically, students should be introduced to only one strategy at a time, and should demonstrate some proficiency with that strategy before another new one is introduced. Care should also be used when selecting strategy combinations so that only those strategies that are unknown and appropriate to students' current needs are introduced.

SPELLING CORRECTION STRATEGIES

Correct-Your-Own-Test Strategy [T]

The "correct-your-own-test" or "corrected-test" procedure has been acclaimed to be the *single* most effective strategy in teaching children to spell (Graham & Miller, 1979; Thomas, 1979). In this strategy, students, under the supervision of their teachers, correct their own errors immediately after completing a spelling test (Kuhn & Schroeder, 1971; Allred, 1977; Hall, 1964; van Oudenhoven, Berkum, & Swen-Koopmans, 1987). Typically, the teacher will either spell the test words out loud as students correct their own work, or write the proper spellings on the blackboard while students mark and correct any letter errors they may have committed (Kuhn & Schroeder, 1971; Hall, 1964). Older students may be instructed to check their work with words contained in a spelling textbook (Thomas, 1979).

The correct-your-own-test spelling procedure is probably among the first spelling strategies to be systematically researched and empirically tested. In 1946, Horn determined that self-correction procedures alone accounted for 90% to 95% of spelling gains that resulted from combined pronunciation exercises, self-test correction exercises, and study (cited in Graham & Miller, 1979; Hall, 1964; Thomas, 1979). Results of more recent research confirm that this method is an effective aid to learning spelling for both normal and learning disabled students (e.g., Allred, 1977; Hall, 1964; Kuhn & Schroeder, 1971; Stowitschek & Jobes, 1977).

Traditionally, use of the self-correction method requires students to correct their spellings as the teacher orally presents the correct spellings (e.g., Hall, 1964). Alternatively, there is evidence available suggesting that additional gains may be acquired if the correct spellings are presented in more than one sensory modality. For example, the teacher may use visual aids, such as cue cards, to point out the letters in the word while reading the correct spelling out loud (Stowitschek & Jobes, 1977). In such a situation, students can simultaneously see and listen to the proper word spellings while they correct their errors (Stowitschek & Jobes, 1977).

In one study investigating the spelling skills of 188 fourth- and sixth-grade students, Kuhn and Schroeder (1971) demonstrated that greater spelling gains were achieved when children were given combined visual and auditory feedback than when they were given auditory feedback only. Specifically, when students were provided with visual and auditory feedback, they displayed a consistent two-word spelling advantage relative to when they were just given auditory feedback. This was true for both students in the fourth and sixth grades, for both males and females, and for both high and low achievers (as measured by the Iowa Tests of Basic Skills). The authors speculated that over an extended period of time, the number of words mastered by individuals provided with both visual and auditory feedback would be substantial.

The correct-your-own-test method is believed to facilitate spelling performance in a twofold manner. First, the method presents the opportunity to discover which words are difficult to spell and, specifically, to locate the part(s) of those words that are particularly problematic. Second, the method demonstrates how to correct misspellings via the presentation of the correct spellings (Graham & Miller, 1979). Allowing students to monitor and correct their own spellings may also prove to be a motivating experience for students and provide them with an opportunity to self-diagnose their spelling progress (Thomas, 1979).

Occasionally, teachers will need to examine students' self-corrected tests. By examining the corrected work, teachers can check the accuracy of marking and supervise and assist those children who are having difficulties. Examination of a student's self-marked tests can also provide the teacher with information regarding the type of errors that the student is making. This information, in turn, may help the teacher decide upon the most appropriate course of future instruction.

Allowing students to monitor and correct their own spelling errors is a useful strategy that can be used in combination with other strategies. Whenever possible, the presentation of correct spellings should be in more than one sensory modality.

Imitation Strategy [T]

Spelling performances of learning-disabled and mentally delayed children have been improved when teachers imitated students' incorrect spellings in addition to providing the correct spellings (Gerber, 1984, 1986; Kauffman, Hallahan, Haas, Brame, & Boren, 1978). The training techniques used by Kauffman et al. (1978) are outlined in Table 5-8. The researchers instructed teachers to administer daily spelling instruction (i.e., phonic drills for phonetically regular words, drills with flash cards for irregular words, and practice writing all words on the chalkboard) and daily spelling tests for words that children spelled incorrectly at pretest. Teachers worked with the students on an individual basis for the first four days of the school week. Ten words, consisting of five new words and five review words (excluding Monday when ten new words were given), were taught and tested each day. On Friday a spelling test was administered for all 20 words studied throughout the week.

Teachers were told to imitate and help students correct spelling errors during the daily testing of target words. If the student correctly spelled a word, he or she was immediately given praise. If, however, the student committed an error, the teacher both imitated the student's incorrect spelling and presented the correct spelling. Specifically, the teacher erased the student's spelling from the chalkboard (students wrote all words on the chalkboard), reprinted the student's incorrect spelling, and printed the correct spelling to the side. The teacher highlighted the incorrect letter(s) by boxing it. The child was then required to write the word correctly.

Kauffman et al. (1978) found that children who were shown their incorrect spelling, as well as the correct spelling, improved in their overall spelling skills. For example, one student demonstrated 92.5% spelling accuracy following error imitation plus correct spelling training, relative to 82.5% spelling accuracy when he was shown the correct spelling only. The authors found that the positive effects of imitating students' errors in addition to showing them the correct spelling were more striking for phonetically irregular words than for phonetically regular words.

Gerber (1984, 1986) recently found additional evidence in favor of presenting students both incorrect and correct spellings. Like Kauffman et al. (1978), Gerber restricted his investigation to children who were either learning-disabled or mentally delayed. Gerber found that children who were shown their misspellings in addition to the correct spellings, and who continually practiced spelling target items until they reached 100% spelling accuracy, displayed fewer spelling errors on a subsequent list of rhyming and structurally similar words. Not only did these children make fewer errors in their attempts to spell novel words (compared to their initial spelling performance for the target items), but the quality of their errors was markedly improved (i.e., students abandoned phonetic spellings for more plausible and conventional representations), and fewer trials were required to reach 100% spelling accuracy.

There are several reasons why the presentation of both incorrect and correct spellings should facilitate overall spelling performance. First, the presentation helps to focus the child's attention on how his spelling attempt differs from the correct spelling. (This rationale is identical to the principles underlying the correct-your-own-test technique.) In addition, Kauffman et al., argue that when phonetic rules do not apply to the spelling of unknown words, children must rely more heavily on visual memory. The visual presentation of the correct spelling probably improves the students' visual memory for the word, which in turn enhances spelling performance. Also, for most children five years of age and older, error imitation is an adverse situation, especially when accompanied by other actions that indicate that the behavior is inappropriate. Therefore, children will be more motivated to avoid such situations by producing correct spellings. The imitation technique may also be motivating to students because it reinforces that they have only one or two letters to learn for each word, as opposed to the entire word (Scott, 1993). Finally, like most forms of concept learning, spelling acquisition should be enhanced by the presentation of negative instances followed by positive instances (Kauffman et al., 1978).

Despite the apparent success of this strategy, we know of no investigations using the imitation method with non-disabled students. This does not imply, however, that the imitation strategy cannot be successfully used in regular classrooms. For instance, Scott (1993) used this method as an opportunity to introduce fifth-grade students to specific spelling strategies on the basis of their spelling errors. Students were encouraged to reflect about which strategies were most appropriate for correctly spelling various words (e.g., using a phonetic strategy to spell the word *department*, or a mnemonic strategy, "Where's the biscuit *u* ate?", to remember the silent *u* in *biscuit*). Our position is that some degree of caution should be used prior to implementing this strategy in regular classrooms. It might be advisable to use this technique with a few students (to ensure that the method is suited for the needs of the particular children in the class), and then implement the technique on a larger scale. It is also possible that parents could be trained to administer the imitation and correction procedure with their children, alleviating some of the time teachers are required to spend with individual students.

SPELLING CONSCIOUSNESS: ERROR DETECTION AND CORRECTION [T]

The ultimate purpose behind teaching children how to spell is that they generalize the knowledge and skill acquired during instructional periods to daily writing situations (Schell, 1975). Aside from teaching

---

Table 5-8
Error imitation plus self-correction training method

1. Daily instruction and testing for words spelled incorrectly at pretest.

2. Spelling tests were given immediately after instruction. The student was required to print his responses on the chalkboard.

3. If the student spelled the word correctly, praise was given.

4. If an error was made, the teacher said "No, that's wrong" and erased the incorrect word.

5. The teacher then wrote the student's incorrect spelling on the board saying "Here's the way you spelled it".

6. The teacher wrote the correct spelling of the word beside the incorrect spelling and said "This is the way it is correctly spelled"

7. The teacher highlighted the incorrect letters by drawing a box around them.

8. The student was required to copy the correct spelling.

From Kauffman, Hallahan, Haas, Brame, & Boren (1978)

acquisition and correction strategies, another way we can help children spell accurately on a daily basis is to foster and promote strategies that allow them to know when a word is spelled either correctly or incorrectly, or to know when there is reason to be doubtful of a word's spelling (Valmont, 1972). Collectively, these skills are referred to as *spelling consciousness* and occur, ideally, during or after writing (i.e., proofreading).

As early as the 1920's, educators acknowledged the importance of developing spelling consciousness (e.g., Pryor & Pittman; 1921 cited in Valmont, 1972). However, research conducted in the area was primarily concerned with assessing the amount of spelling consciousness subjects possessed. In general, persons of all ages lacked the ability to identify misspelled words, although the amount of spelling consciousness varied across different writing situations (Valmont, 1972).

Approximately twenty-five years ago, Personke and Lester (1967) developed a training program designed to facilitate proofreading skills. They empirically tested the effects of their program on spelling performance. Their project was based on the observation that the desire to spell correctly and the use of a dictionary were insufficient if individuals did not possess strategies for finding the spellings of unknown words.

The authors recruited 40 sixth-grade children from two schools and randomly assigned them to either an experimental or control group. Prior to the training program, the children's IQ and spelling achievement scores (based on standardized tests given in the previous school year) were compared. There were no significant differences between the scores of children assigned to either the experimental or control groups. Throughout the course of the training sessions (fourteen lessons), students assigned to the experimental group practiced underlining words whose spellings were uncertain. Experimental students were also taught dictionary skills. The specific lesson plans used by the authors are listed in Table 5-9.

The training program was initiated by showing students in the experimental group a proofreading film and introducing the skills that would be taught in the lessons to follow. The children were instructed not to erase their spelling errors, but rather, to cross out any misspellings and write the correct spelling above the error. The next four lessons were devoted to improving dictionary skills and consisted of practicing alphabetical arrangements, using guide words, and finding synonyms. For the sixth lesson, students were given a spelling chart containing common spellings of English sounds and were instructed how to use the chart when spelling difficult words. The chart was an enlargement from a page of a dictionary similar to the one displayed in Table 5-10. The children practiced using the chart by looking for errors inserted into a prepared manuscript. For the remaining lessons, the students wrote and proofread dictated passages as well as their own compositions. Before papers were collected, students were given time to proofread their work and were encouraged to make use of the sound spelling charts when seeking correct spellings. The program terminated with

Table 5-9
Lesson plans for proofreading training program

Lesson 1   Presentation of proofreading film and introduction to techniques to be used in subsequent lessons.

Lesson 2   Development of dictionary skills via practice in alphabetical arrangements, use of guide words, and finding synonyms.

Lesson 3   Same as Lesson 2.

Lesson 4   Same as Lesson 2.

Lesson 5   Same as Lesson 2.

Lesson 6   Introduction in how to use the common sounds spelling chart when looking for the spelling of unknown words. Specifically, use the chart by taking the first best sound alternative. If this does not work, use the second best sound alternative and so on.

Lesson 7   Practice looking for errors in a prepared manuscript which contained errors designed to give children practice using the sounds spelling chart.

Lesson 8   Practice writing and proofreading a dictated paragraph.

Lesson 9   Practice writing and proofreading a personal composition, in this case a book report.

Lesson 10   Practice writing and proofreading a dictated paragraph containing difficult spelling words.

Lesson 11   Practice proofreading lists of spelling words selected as being particularly difficult for elementary school children. Words selected also provided the opportunity for children to use either the first or second sound choice according to their spelling charts.

Lesson 12   Same as Lesson 11.

Lesson 13   Practice proofreading a personal composition of a summary of a story read in their basal readers.

Lesson 14   Practice writing and proofreading a letter that will be mailed to a friend.

From Personke & Lester (1967).

children writing and proofreading a letter to mail to a friend.

Children assigned to the control group were provided with equal writing opportunity and dictionary practice. Students in the control group, however, were not instructed how to use the common sounds spelling chart or told about the importance of proofreading. The stories were then used to assess the frequency of spelling errors between the two groups.

The percentage of spelling errors was computed for each paper by dividing the number of spelling errors by the total number of running

Table 5-10
Spelling Sound Chart

KEY TO PRONUNCIATION

ā	as in fāte, āle, ā'corn, be-rāte', nat''u-ral-i-zā'tion.
ä	" " fär, fä'ther, ärch, mär'shal, cär-toon'; also as in whät, wänt.
à	" " fàst, glàss, a-làs'; also as in so'dà, à-dapt'à-ble.
a̦	" " fa̦ll, pa̦w, a̦w'ful, ap-pla̦ud'.
ă	" " fi'năl, sea'măn, tol'er-ănt, men'ăce.
ã	" " cãre, ãir, mil'i-tãr-y, de-clãre'.
a	" " at, ac-cord', com-par'i-son, car'ry.
ē	" " ēve, mēte, hē, Ē'den, in-ter-vēne'; also as in hēre, drēar'y.
e̦	" " pre̦y, e̦ight, o-be̦y'.
ẽ	" " hẽr, vẽrse, sẽr'vice, in-tẽr'.
e	" " met, ebb, en-dorse', mon'e-tar-y, dis-tend'.
ee	" " feed, pro-ceed', lee'way.
ī	" " pīne, I-de'a, īce'berg, de-cīde', al-lī'ance.
ɪ	" " clɪque, ma-rɪne'; also as in Mar-tɪ'ni.
ĩ	" " bĩrd, stĩr, ex'tĩr-pate, fĩrm'a-ment.
i	" " it, hit, re-mit', cit'y; also as in pos'si-ble, grav'i-ty, pu'pil.
ō	" " nōte, ōat, sō, ō'pen, hel-lō'; also as in ren'ō-vate, prō-pel'.
ŏ	" " mŏve, prŏve, tŏmb.
o̦	" " lo̦ng, cro̦ss, off, o̦rb, fo̦r-bid', do̦r'mer.
ŏ	" " at'ŏm, plŏv'er; also as in ac'tŏr, wŏrd, wŏrk.
o	" " not, for'est, non'sense; also as in dog, broth, cost; also as in con-fess', con-cur'.
o̦o̦	" " mo̦o̦n, co̦o̦, fo̦o̦d, bro̦o̦d'er.
oo	" " book, hood, foot, look, cook'y.
ū	" " ūse, fūse, ū-til'i-ty, fū'tile, im-mūne'.
u̦	" " bu̦ll, pu̦t, fu̦l-fil', boun'ti-fu̦l.
ú	" " brúte, jù'ry; also used for the German ü.
ũ	" " tũrn, fũr, bũr-lesque', de-mũr'.
u	" " up, rub, sun'set, in-sult'.
y̆	" " cry̆, ey̆e.
y	" " myth, cit'y.
ç	" " çat, to-baç'ço.
ç	" " ma-çhine'.
c	" " ace, ce'dar.
ch	" " church.
çh	" " çhord.

ġ	as in ġem.
ñ	" " añ'ger, sphiñx.
ṅ	" " French boṅ.
ng	" " ring.
ş	" " mi'şer, aş.
th	" " this.
th	" " thin.
z̧	" " az̧ure.
au	" " umlaut.
aw	" " straw.
ou	" " out.
oi	" " oil.
oy	" " boy.
ew	" " new, few.
ow	" " now.
-tūre	as -chĕr (in picture).
-tion / **-sion**	as -shun (in nation, tension).
-ciăn / **-tiăn** / **-siăn**	as -shun (in Martian, Melanesian, mortician).
-şiăn / **-şion**	as -zhun (in Persian, fusion).
-liŏn	as -lyun or -yun (in million).
-ceous / **-(s)cious**	as -shus (in cretaceous, delicious, conscious).
qu	as kw (in queen).
-ous	as -us (in porous).
ph-	as f- (in phone, etc.).
-le	as -l (at end of syllable, as in able, cycle, etc.).
-ià	as -yà (in pharmacopoeia).
wh-	as hw- in whale, etc.
kh	as in German doch (dokh).

words. Children in the experimental group made significantly fewer spelling errors than did children in the control group. Even though the experimental group had less writing time than did the control group (due to time allotted for proofreading), the number of running words did not differ between the groups. Although some caution must be used when interpreting these results (i.e., the pre-training and post-training spelling measures were not equated for difficulty; there was no measure of vocabulary level or the number of different words written), the study suggests that using a dictionary alone is not sufficient to enhance proofreading for spelling errors. Instead, children need to be explicitly told about the importance of proofreading and given strategic instruction concerning how to use the dictionary when finding words with unknown spellings. The authors conclude with the recommendation that proofreading instruction be included as part of the regular spelling curriculum.

Although the Personke and Lester (1967) study represents one of the few empirical investigations addressing the development of spelling consciousness, many untested recommendations and suggestions have been proposed. Because it is important to promote spelling consciousness, we have listed some of these suggestions in Table 5-11, including ensuring high-quality spelling instruction, providing adequate time for proofreading and correcting activities, promoting strategic approaches when finding unfamiliar spellings in a dictionary, and encouraging the use of other spelling resources. Remember that the following are only suggestions, and that their impact on spelling consciousness has not been systematically evaluated yet. Therefore, caution should be used prior to implementing any of these in the classroom. We suggest that teachers test the suitability of the activity in question with a small number of students prior to involving the whole class.

CONCLUDING COMMENTS

Although spelling has been studied extensively, there is currently nationwide concern that primary school students are not being taught the basics of spelling. It is a well-known fact that many school-aged children experience difficulty spelling, especially students who are learning disabled or mentally delayed. It is likely that less-than-adequate teaching materials and instructional methods increase students' difficulties. Unfortunately, empirically validated instructional techniques are often neglected in favor of more traditional teaching methods (Graham, 1983). Changes can occur in the spelling curriculum if teachers are made aware of spelling strategies that really work. Those techniques were reviewed here. The gap between spelling research and classroom instruction can be narrowed. Teachers can include well-validated strategies into their classrooms; researchers can extend their efforts to inform teachers about new findings. In addition to chapters

Table 5-11
Summary of proofreading recommendations and suggestions

1. Ensure that initial spelling instruction is of a high quality; use empirically validated organization, acquisition, and correction spelling strategies. The quality of initial spelling instruction is believed to effect children's later abilities to proofread.

2. Stress the importance of accurate spelling and proofreading in both formal and social communications.

3. Provide adequate time for students to proofread, correct, and copy assignments before they are collected.

4. Have students "tag" potential spelling errors. Students can tag words that they think are spelled wrong by underlining or circling them. The process of confirming uncertain spellings will strengthen recognition for correctly spelled words and provide feedback regarding misspelled words. Help children find spelling errors that are not tagged by placing a mark on the line the error occurs.

5. Familiarize children with the structure of dictionaries (i.e., alphabetical orderings and the use of guide words) and instruct children on how to use the dictionary when looking for an unfamiliar word's spelling. For example, instruct students to listen to the beginning sound of the word in question and try to locate the word based on this sound. If this fails, try to think of other letters that represent the sound.

6. Help students create and use other resources. For instance, creating a personal dictionary with index cards, using a class list of frequently misspelled words, or asking a friend to edit an assignment.

7. Help maintain students' interests with the occasional use of proofreading games. For suggestions see Graham, Freeman, and Miller (1981) and Hodges (1982).

8. Have children use computer software packages when editing written work. See Devant (1984) for comments on suitable computer packages.

From Bamburg (1977), Barnard Kendrick (1980), Lydiatt (1984), and Schell (1975)

like this one, there are other materials available to help bridge the gap between teaching and research. One of the best of these is a journal, *Spelling Progress Quarterly*. Both teachers and researchers can benefit from reading and contributing to such resources.

In the past decade, the evidence is growing that spelling should not be thought about as an isolated skill, but rather as an outgrowth of reading. A number of investigators have documented associations between instruction that develops phonemic awareness and/or phonics instruction and later competence in spelling (e.g., Ball & Blachman, 1991; Griffith, 1991; Nelson, 1990; Uhry & Shepherd, 1993), a sensible connection given that better decoders are also better spellers (Dreyer, Shankweiler & Luke, 1993). Thus, our next-to-last recommendation for developing better spellers is to teach for phonemic awareness and to develop decoding competence by teaching the letter- and word-level skills featured in Chapter 2. One payoff of such instruction is better spelling in the years ahead.

Because skilled decoding makes reading easier, it also permits more reading, which in turn permits extensive exposure to correctly spelled words. Not surprisingly, children who read a great deal are better spellers than those who do not (e.g., Cunningham & Stanovich, 1991; Olson, Logan & Lindsey, 1988). An especially powerful mechanism for building spelling competence is to encourage more reading which increases exposure to correctly spelled words (see Bradley & King, 1992, for evidence that exposure alone to correct spellings is a powerful mechanism for teaching spelling). Thus, our last suggestion for improving student spelling is to encourage them to read extensively. In short, there are important connections between reading and spelling competencies, with it likely that both decoding instruction and increased amounts of reading have causal impact on spelling competence.

REFERENCES

Allred, R. (1977). *Spelling: The application of research findings.* Washington. D.C. National Education Association.

Allred, R. (1984). *What research says to the teacher: Spelling, trends, content, and methods.* Washington, D.C.: National Education Association.

Anderson, R.C., & Hidde, J.L. (1971) Imagery and sentence learning. *Journal of Educational Psychology, 63,* 242-243.

Anderson, R.C., & Kulhavy, R.W. (1972). Imagery and prose learning. *Journal of Educational Psychology, 63,* 242-243.

Bamberg, B. (1977) *Putting correctness in its place.* Study prepared at the University of Southern California. 12 P. Available ERIC ED 162 340.

Ball, E.W., & Blachman, B.A. (1991). Does phoneme awareness training in kindergarten make a difference in early word recognition and developmental spelling? *Reading Research Quarterly, 26,* 50-66.

Barnard, D.P., & Kendrick, R. (1980). If you want to improve student spelling. *The Clearing House, 54,* 164-167.

Beers, J.W., & Henderson, E.H. (1977). A study of developing orthographic concepts among first graders. *Research in the Teaching of English, 11,* 133-148.

Blair, T. (1975) ERIC/RCS. *Reading Teacher, 28,* 604-607.

Blake, H., & Emans, R. (1970). Some spelling facts. *Elementary English, 47,* 242-249.

Block, J. (1972). But will they ever lern to spel korectly? *Educational Research, 14,* 171-178.

Block, K.K., & Peskowitz, N.B. (1990). Metacognition in spelling: Using writing and reading to self-check spellings. *The Elementary School Journal, 91,* 151-164.

Burbe, W. (Ed.) *Spelling Progress Quarterly.*

Carpenter, D. & Miller, L. (1982) Spelling ability of reading disabled LD students and able readers. *Learning Disability Quarterly, 5,* 65-70.

Chomsky, N., & Halle, M. (1968). *The sound*

pattern of English. New York: Harper & Row.

Cramer, R. (1969) The influence of phonic instruction on spelling achievement. *The Reading Teacher, 22,* 499-503.

Cronnell, B., & Humes, A. (1980). Elementary spelling: What's really taught. *The Elementary School Journal, 81,* 59-64.

Devail, T. (1984) Using the computer to strengthen spelling. *The Computing Teacher, 19,* 19-21.

Downing, J., DeStefano, J., Rich, G., & Bell, A., (1985). Children's views of spelling. *The Elementary School Journal, 85,* 185-198.

Drake, D., & Ehri, L. (1984). Spelling acquisition: Effects of pronouncing words on memory for their spellings. *Cognition and Instruction, 1,* 297-320.

Englert, C., Hiebert, E., & Stewart, S. (1985) Spelling unfamiliar words by an analogy strategy. *The Journal of Special Education, 19,* 291-306.

Fitzgerald, J. (1951a) *A basic life spelling vocabulary.* Milwaukee: Bruce Publishing Co.

Fitzgerald, J. (1951b). Methods of teaching spelling. *The teaching of spelling.* Milwaukee: Bruce Publishing Co.

Fitzgerald, J. (1953) The teaching of spelling. *Elementary English, 30,* 79-84.

Fitzsimmons, R., & Loomer, B. (1977). *Spelling research and practice.* Iowa City: Iowa State Department of Public Instruction and The University of Iowa.

Foorman, B.R., Francis, D.J., Novy, D.M., & Liberman, D. (1991). How letter-sound instruction mediates progress in first-grade reading and spelling. *Journal of Educational Psychology, 83,* 456-469.

Gerber, M. (1984) Techniques to teach generalizable spelling skills. *Academic Therapy, 20,* 49-58.

Gerber, M. (1986) Generalization of spelling strategies by LD students as a result of contingent imitation/modeling and mastery criteria. *Journal of Learning Disabilities, 19,* 530-537

Gerber, M., & Lydiatt, S. (1984). Research and practice in teaching spelling. *Academic Therapy, 20,* 5-10.

Gillingham, A., & Stillman, B. (1969) *Remedial training for children with specific disability in reading, spelling and penmanship.* Cambridge, Mass.: Educators Publishing Service.

Gilstrap, R. (1962). Development of independent spelling skills in the intermediate grades. *Elementary English, 39,* 481-483.

Graham, S. (1983) Effective spelling instruc-tion. *Elementary School Journal, 83,* 560-568.

Graham, S. & Freeman, S. (1986). Strategy training and teacher-vs-student-controlled study conditions: Effects on LD students' spelling performance. *Learning Disability Quarterly, 9,* 15-22.

Graham, S., Freeman, S., & Miller, L. (1981). *Spelling Games and Activities.* Department of Education, Washington, D.C. Available ERIC *ED 208 425.*

Graham, S., & Miller, L. (1979) Spelling research and practice: A unified approach. *Focus on Exceptional Children, 12,* 1-16.

Hahn, W. (1964). Phonics: A boon to spelling. *Elementary School Journal, 64,* 148-157.

Hall, N. (1964). The letter mark-out corrected test. *The Journal of Educational Research, 58,* 148-157.

Hall, R. (1984). Orthographic problem-solving. *Academic Therapy, 20,* 67-75.

Hanna, P., Hanna, J., Hodges, R., & Rudorf, E. (1967). Linguistic cues for spelling improvement. *Elementary English, 44,* 862-865.

Harris, K., & Pressley, M. (1991). The nature of cognitive strategy instruction: Interactive strategy construction. *Exceptional Children, 28,* 392, 403.

Henderson, E.H., & Beers, J.W. (1980). Developmental strategies of spelling competence in primary school children. *Developmental and cognitive aspects in learning to spell: A reflection of word knowledge.* Newark, DE: International Reading Association.

Hildreth, G. (1956). Beginnings of spelling. *Teaching spelling: Guide to basic principles and practices.* New York: Holt & Company, Inc.

Hillerich, R., (1982). That's teaching spelling??? *Educational Leadership, 39,* 615-617.

Hodges, R.E. (1982). *Improving spelling and vocabulary in the secondary school. Theory and research into practice (TRIP)* Urbana, IL. National Council of Teachers of English. Available ERIC. *ED 218 645.*

Horn, E. (1926). *A basic vocabulary: 10,000 words most commonly used in writing.* Iowa City: University of Iowa.

Horn, E. (1967) *Teaching spelling: What research says to the teacher.* Washington DC. American Educational Research Association.

Horn, T. (1969) Research critiques. *Elementary English, 46,* 210-212.

Horn, T., & Otto, H. (1954) *Spelling instruction: A curriculum-wide approach.* Austin: University of Texas.

Ibeling, K. (1961) Supplementary phonics instruction and reading and spelling ability. *Elementary School Journal, 63*, 152-156.

Juola, F., Schadler, M., Chabot, R. & McCaughey, M. (1978). Development of visual processing skills related to reading. *Journal of Experimental Child Psychology, 25*, 230-240.

Kauffman, J., Hallahan, D., Haas, K., Brame, T., & Boren, R. (1978) Imitating children's errors to improve their spelling performance. *Journal of Learning Disabilities, 11*, 33-38.

Kernaghan, K., & Woloshyn, V.E. (in press). Providing grade one students with multiple spelling strategies: Comparisons between strategy instruction, strategy instruction with metacognitive information and traditional language arts. *Applied Cognitive Psychology.*

Kuhn, J., & Schroeder, H. (1971). A multisensory approach for teaching spelling. *Elementary English, 48*, 863-869.

Lydiatt, S. (1984) Error detection and correction in spelling. *Academic Therapy, 20*, 33-40.

Marino, J. (1980) What makes a good speller? *Language Arts, 57*,173-177.

Mastropieri, M.A., & Scruggs, T.E. (1991). *Teaching students ways to remember: Strategies for learning mnemonically.* Cambridge, MA: Brookline Books.

Mcllroy, K. (1976) *Helping the poor speller.* Auckland: Heinemann Educational Books.

Neef, N., Iwata, B., & Page, T. (1977) The effects of known item interspersal on acquisition and retention of spelling and sight word reading. *Journal of Applied Behavior Analysis, 10*, 738.

Olson, M.W., Logan, J.W., & Lindsey, T.P. (1988). Orthographic awareness and gifted spellers: Early experiences and practices. *Roeper Review, 10*, 152-155.

Paivio, A., & Yuille, J.C. (1967). Mediation instructions and word attributes in paired-associate learning. *Psychonomic Science, 8*, 65-66.

Personke, C., & Lester, K. (1967). Proofreading and spelling: A report and a program. *Elementary English, 44*, 768-774.

Personke, C., & Tee, A. (1971) *Comprehensive spelling instruction: Theory, research, and application.* Scranton: Intext Educational Publishers. Available ERIC *ED 052 204.*

Pressley, M., Borkowski, J.G., & Schneider, W. (1987). Cognitive strategies: Good strategy users coordinate metacognition and knowledge. In R. Vasta and G. Whitehurst (Eds), *Imagery and related mnemonic processes: Theories, individual differences, and applications* (pp. 274-301). New York: Springer-Verlag.

Pressley, M., McDaniel, M.A., Turnure, J.E., Wood, E., & Ahmad, M. (1987) Generation and precision of elaboration: Effects on intentional and incidental learning. *Journal of Experimental Psychology: Learning, Memory, and Cognition, 13*, 291-300.

Radaker, L. (1963) The effect of visual imagery upon spelling performance. *The Journal of Educational Research, 56*, 370-372.

Radebaugh, M. (1985) Children's perceptions of their spelling strategies. *The Reading Teacher, 38*, 532-536.

Rasco, R.W., Tennyson, R.D., & Boutwell, R.C. (1975) Imagery instructions and drawings in learning prose. *Journal of Educational Psychology, 67*, 188-192.

Reith, H., Axelrod, S., Anderson, R., Hathaway, F, Wood, K., & Fitzgerald, C. (1974) Influence of distributed practice and daily testing on weekly spelling tests. *Journal of Educational Research, 68*, 73-77.

Rinsland, H. (1945) *A basic vocabulary of elementary school children.* New York: Macmillan Co.

Rowell, G. (1972) A prototype for an individualized spelling program. *Elementary English, 49*, 335-340.

Sears, N., & Johnson, D. (1986) The effects of visual imagery on spelling performance and retention among elementary students. *Journal of Educational Research, 79*, 230-233.

Schell, L. (1975) B+ in composition: C- in spelling. *Elementary English, 52*, 239-257.

Schoephoerster, H. (1962). Research into variations of the test study plan of teaching spelling. *Elementary English, 39*, 460-462.

Scott, R. (1993). *Spelling: Sharing the secrets.* Toronto: Gage Educational Publishing.

Smith, H. (1975) Teaching spelling. *British Journal Educational Psychology, 45*, 68-72.

Sterling, C., & Rusby, S. (1986). Evidence of morphemic spelling of novel derivatives by 12-year-old children. *First Language, 6*, 133-147.

Stowitschek, C., & Jobes, N. (1977). Getting the bugs out of spelling: Or an alternative to the spelling bee. *Teaching Exceptional Children, 9*, 74-76.

Suid, M. (1981). *Demonic mnemonics.* California: David S. Lake Publishers.

Tangel, D.M., & Blachman, B.A. (1992). Effect of phoneme awareness instruction on kindergarten children's invented spelling. *Journal of Reading Behavior, 24*, 233-261.

Tarasoff, M. (1990). *Spelling strategies that you*

can teach. Victoria: Pixelart Graphics.

Templeton, S. (1983) Using the spelling/meaning connection to develop word knowledge in older students. *Journal of Reading*, 8-14.

Thomas, V. (1972). The basic writing vocabulary of elementary school children. *The Alberta Journal of Educational Research, 18*, 243-248.

Thomas, V. (1979). *Teaching spelling: Canadian word lists and instructional techniques. Second Edition.* Gage Publishing Limited.

Valmont, W. (1972). Spelling consciousness: A long neglected area. *Elementary English, 49*, 1219-1265.

van Oudenhoven, J., Berkum, G., Swen-Koopmans, T. (1987) Effect of cooperation and shared feedback on spelling achievement. *Journal of Educational Psychology, 79*, 92-94.

Wallace, G., & Kauffman, J. (1978) *Teaching Children with Learning Problems.* Columbus, Ohio: Charles E. Merrill Publishing Company.

Webster's New Universal Unabridged Dictionary, Deluxe Second Edition (1983). New York: New World Dictionaries/Simon and Schuster.

Weisberg, P. (1985). *Teaching Spelling to the Learning Disabled in Traditional and Remedial Approaches: A Workshop.* Paper presented at the International Conference of the Association for Children and Adults with Learning Disabilities, San Francisco, CA. Available ERIC. ED *256 118*.

Winograd, P. , & Harris, V.C. (1988). Direct instruction of reading comprehension strategies: the nature of teacher explanation. In E.T. Goetz, P. Alexander, and C. Weinstein (Eds), *Learning and study strategies: Assessment, instruction and evaluation* (pp. 121-140). New York: Academic Press.

Wong, B.Y.L. (1986). A cognitive approach to teaching spelling. *Exceptional Children, 53*, 169-173.

Woloshyn, V.E., & Thomas, J. (April, 1995). Providing grade three students with multiple spelling strategies in a whole language environment. Paper to be presented at the American Educational Research Association (AERA), San Francisco, CA.

Yee, A. (1969) Is the phonetic generalization hypothesis in spelling valid? *Journal of Experimental Education, 37*, 82-91.

Zutell, J. (1979) Spelling strategies of primary school children and their relationship to Piaget's concept of decentration. *Research in the Teaching of English, 13*, 69-80.

CHAPTER 6

Writing

Ask a 10- to 12-year-old student who has had little instruction in writing to write a short essay on a topic. Will the student produce a compelling piece of writing? Readers of this book who are teachers know that the answer is no. Researchers interested in students' natural composition processes have documented in detail a range of deficiencies that undermine student writing. These include the following:

- Students often fail to establish clearly what their writing goal is. They do not think about what the writing is expected to accomplish (e.g., describe, persuade). They do not think about who the readership will be and, thus, fail to craft an essay that will make sense to and convince its readership.
- Students not provided instruction in writing typically do not generate enough content. Often, they do not search their long-term memories for information that would be relevant to include in the essay. Other times they do not make use of readily available information in their environments.
- Rather than planning and organizing their essay, they tend to "knowledge tell" (Scardamalia & Bereiter, 1986).
- Their sentence construction, spelling, and handwriting (or keyboarding) skills are weak, with students expending so much mental energy on these low-level skills that they can forget to make the essay make sense.
- Students not taught how to write will treat their first draft as a final draft, rather than something to be revised until it communicates well.
  (Bereiter & Scardamalia, 1987; Case, Mamlin, Harris & Graham, 1994; Harris & Graham, 1992a, 1992b; Langer, 1986; Scardamalia & Bereiter, 1986)

Given recognition of these deficiencies, it is not surprising that researchers were also interested in writing instruction in the 1980s (Hillocks, 1984). Before that, children were expected to learn how to write following instruction in the mechanics of writing (e.g., spelling, punctuation, and sentence format) with little, if any, attention given to higher-order writing strategies. It was assumed that students learned to write from reading and analyzing published texts and noting their structure and organizational features. The learner's role was to discover what was expected, with little guidance from the teacher. In contrast, *the process-oriented approach to writing highlighted in this chapter provides a new role for teachers—to develop young writers who can construct coherent text* (Applebee, 1982; Dominic, 1983). The student learns strategies for text construction, recognizing that the first draft is not the finished product and that teachers and peers can provide feedback as to how to improve the document.

New Process Models of Writing

One of the earliest models of strategic writing was presented by Rohman (1965), who portrayed writing as involving three stages: pre-writing (planning), writing (composing the draft), and rewriting (editing and revising). This theory was criticized in the 1970s because it was a linear model that failed to incorporate the *recursive* nature of the writing process. That is, writing does not occur in a strict plan–write–rewrite order. Rather, writing involves a series of feedback loops, with revisions requiring new planning, new writing and rewriting before a finished draft is constructed. It is a *recursive process*.

Much of writing instruction is based on Flower and Hayes' (1986) theory. According to this model there are three units involved in mature writing: the writer's long-term memory, the environment of the writer, and writing itself, which can be further broken down into three processes: planning, translating, and reviewing. *Planning* involves three sub-processes: a) generating— the retrieval of items from memory and from the environment (e.g., library resources); b) organizing—the selection of the most useful of the materials retrieved by generating; and c) goal-setting—the judging of materials retrieved by generating as to whether they serve the current purpose of writing. *Translating* involves taking the material gathered and organized during planning and transforming it into acceptable written English sentences. *Reviewing* involves improving the quality of the translated material using two sub-processes: a) reading (i.e. reading the segment of the text being reviewed); and b) editing—the detection and correction of violations in writing conventions and of inaccuracies of meaning, and the evaluation of materials with respect to the writing goals.

Because this is a recursive model, planning, translating and reviewing processes and subprocesses may be executed in any order (e.g., one may backtrack from translating to planning; review can occur before anything has been written on paper). See Figure 6-1 for an example of planning, translating, and reviewing.

Figure 6-1
Processes of Writing

Question: What did you do on your summer vacation?
"OK, let's see. I have to write about my summer vacation. What do I want to say. I went to the beach with my parents for a week. *(planning)* Actually, I went to the cottage is probably a better thing to say. *(reviewing)* When we were at the cottage we had a big bonfire down by the lake with some of the other cottages. I also went to a day camp and played games and made crafts. *(planning)* Yes, now I've planned what I want to say and I can write."

Written Text:
During my summer vacation I went to the cottage with my family. We did alot of exciting things. My favorite was the big bonfire at the lake with all the other cottages. For the rest of the summer I went to a day camp where we did crafts and played games. I had a fun summer. *(translating)*

"OK, let's see what I have. Oops, I've made some mistakes, better fix those up. *A lot* is two words and *did crafts* should be *made crafts.* Maybe I should write a little more about the cottage. *(reviewing)* What else did I do? Oh yeah, we went swimming and at the bonfire we roasted hot dogs and marshmallows, plus we got to stay up late, that's why it was my favorite thing. What about the new friend that I made at camp. Yeah, I should talk about Jenny. *(planning)* All right, uhm, maybe I won't include just the swimming at the cottage, I should add a few more things and then say that the fire was my favorite. *(reviewing and planning)* We also went into town and had pizza one night and then there were the daily trips to the store for ice cream. *(planning)* OK, I'm ready to write again."

Revised Text:
During my summer vacation I did some interesting things. At the beginning of the summer I went to the cottage with my family for one week. While we were there we did a lot of exciting things like swimming, going for pizza, getting ice cream and having a bonfire. I liked having the bonfire the best because we roasted wieners and marshmallows and we got to stay up really late.
During the rest of the summer I went to a day camp. We played a lot of fun games and made crafts. I met a girl named Jenny. She just moved into the neighborhood and is now going to my school. My summer was special because I made a new friend. *(translating)*

"Yes, I think that is exactly what I want to say."

From Flower & Hayes (1980).

Why Many Children Still Write So Poorly—
Despite the Writing Process Revolution

One of the biggest problems writing researchers have faced is trying to understand why many children who have a command of the language are such poor writers. One reason is that writing and speaking are separate, distinct processes. For example, writers do not have the audience they would if they were speaking. When speaking, a person receives feedback from the listener, such as head nods to continue, or quizzical looks and questions that suggest a need for clarification. In writing, however, the writer must *anticipate* the questions of the reader and answer any questions that may arise (McCutchen & Perfetti, 1983; Scardamalia & Bereiter, 1986). In addition, many times the motivation to learn how to write coherent prose is low due to the evaluation criteria used in schools. For instance, Odell (1980) believes that students are implicitly taught that writing is not important since competence in school is often documented by performance on multiple-choice and short-answer questions. When writing is taught, there seems to be undue concern about lower-level mechanics of writing such as spelling and punctuation (e.g., Scardamalia, 1981), rather than on higher-order organizational skills.

In order to decide how writing instruction should be changed, it is necessary to understand how the quality of writing varies with instruction. In a descriptive study of 10 classrooms, Perl (1983) found that *writing is better in classrooms where writing is taken more seriously.* The nature of writing is often viewed as social in these classes, in that children can share their writing with the class (a less critical audience than the teacher or parents) or children can collaborate on a piece of writing. There are connections made between reading, writing, and literature, with these literacy skills taught as interrelated. There is negotiation between the teacher and the student, including control over the written product. Finally, good writing teachers reflect on the instructional methods used in the classroom. The fact that writing is better overall in some classrooms than in others suggests that differences in teaching might be engineered to produce improved writing.

Although much of the writing improvement research has been conducted with very weak child writers, no children are highly proficient writers. Even those who are writing at an above average level for their age still have a lot to learn (Scardamalia & Bereiter, 1986). Thus, writing strategy instruction is appropriate for a broad range of writing abilities.

Cognitive Strategy Instruction in Writing [T & SSR]

Englert, Raphael, Anderson, Anthony and Stevens (1991; see also Englert and Raphael, 1988) have developed a program which focuses on teaching writing strategies to fourth- and fifth-grade students through verbal modeling. This program is based on three different approaches to writing instruction developed over the past few years.

The first of these approaches is a process-writing approach that emphasizes motivation and includes (1) daily writing on topics selected by the students, (2) peer evaluations through group presentations and editing, (3) publication of student papers, and (4) writing conferences (Bos, 1988; Graves, 1983). Students' motivation to write increases since they are able to choose topics which are of particular interest to them. The major criticism of this approach, when presented in isolation, is that children are left on their own to learn how to write without much teacher intervention.

Thus, Englert and her colleagues amalgamated these motivational features with another instructional model that attends more explicitly to the "hows" of writing. *Schema-building* involves providing students with information about text structure so they may build up the knowledge of what is required when writing (e.g., a narrative story). This is consistent with Fitzgerald and Teasley's (1986) finding that teaching fourth-grade children the structure of narrative stories increases their ability to write organized and coherent stories.

Englert and her associates refer to the resulting composite intervention as Cognitive Strategy Instruction in Writing (CSIW). CSIW includes a lot of explanatory monologues. When teachers use think-alouds (verbal modeling) when writing (i.e., make their thought processes transparent as they write), the children are provided an opportunity to observe the processes that guide a good writer.

CSIW is summarized in Figure 6-2. The first step in the program is to introduce children to text structure and strategies through the use of various examples. These examples range from poorly structured text to ones that are well structured. While reading a passage aloud, the teacher verbalizes questions about the passage. These are questions that might not be clear from reading alone (e.g., "I wonder how the author got into this situation?"). In generating these questions and overtly grappling with them, the teacher makes clear that it is not possible to know what is happening unless the information is written as part of the story.

Teachers then introduce "think-sheets" that guide students through the process of writing. These "think-sheets" provide an external copy of questions that should be posed as part of writing. The external availability of questions presumably frees some cognitive capacity that might otherwise be used to try and remember the questions.

- The plan think-sheet (Figure 6-3) allows the children to *think of their audience* ("Who am I writing for?"; "Why am I writing this?"), *activate their background knowledge* ("What do I know about this topic?"), and *organize their ideas prior to and during the writing process* ("How can I group my ideas?").
- The organization think-sheet (Figure 6-4) allows children to

Figure 6-2
Cognitive Strategy Instruction in Writing (CSIW)

Step 1
Introduce children to text structure and strategies through the use of various examples.

Step 2
Introduce the plan think-sheet.

Step 3
Introduce the organization think-sheet.

Step 4
Have children create the first draft.

Step 5
Introduce the edit think-sheet.

Step 6
Introduce the editor think-sheet and have the children evaluate each other's papers.

Step 7
Introduce the revise think-sheet and have the children revise their writing.

focus on text structure with questions such as "What is being explained?" and "In what order do things happen?"

Once children have used these sheets to create their first draft, they are asked to edit their own text critically. At this point another think-sheet is introduced.

- The edit think-sheet (see Figure 6-5) allows students to focus on both the content and the organization of the paper. Since the check for organization section (*Question Yourself*) can be related back to the organization think-sheet, students are able to monitor their progress.
- The next step involves peer evaluation with the editor think-sheet (see Figure 6-6). This process is the same as the editing process except that it is now done by a peer instead of the person who wrote the text.
- In the final step the children review the editorial comments and revise as necessary (see Figure 6-7).

Children's memory of these processes is facilitated with the acronym

Figure 6-3
Plan "think-sheet

Name _____ Date _____

Topic _____

WHO: Who am I writing for?

_____

_____

WHY: Why am I writing this?

_____

_____

_____

_____

WHAT: What do I know? (Brainstorm)

1. _____

2. _____

3. _____

4. _____

5. _____

6. _____

7. _____

8. _____

HOW: How can I group my ideas?

_____

How will I organize my ideas?

___Comparison/Contrast   ___Problem/Solution
___Explanation   ___Other

Figure 6-4
Organization "think-sheet"

Explanations

What is being explained?

_____

_____

In what order do things happen?

First, _____
(1st)

Then, _____
(2nd)

Then, _____
(3rd)

Then, _____
(4th)

Finally, _____
(last)

Clues: who does it, things you need, how you do it

_____

_____

_____

Figure 6-5
Edit "think-sheet"

EDIT (Explanation)

Name _____ Date _____

Read. Reread my paper.
    What do I like best? (Put a * by the parts I like best)
    What parts are not clear? (Put a ? by unclear parts)

Question Yourself. Did I:

Tell what was being *explained*?	YES	sort of	NO
Tell what things you need?	YES	sort of	NO
Make the *steps* clear?	YES	sort of	NO
Use *keywords* (first, second)?	YES	sort of	NO
Make it *interesting*?	YES	sort of	NO

Plan. (look back)
What parts do I want to change?

1. _____

2. _____

Write two or more questions for my editor.

1. _____

2. _____

3. _____

Talk. (Talk to the editor.)
Read your paper with your editor. Then the editor should read the Paper
and complete the Edit(or) page. Next, meet and talk about your answers.

Figure 6-6
Editor "think-sheet"

EDIT(OR) (Explanation)

Name _____ Date _____

Read. Read the paper.
  What's the paper about?

  _____

  _____

  _____

  What do you like best? Put a "*" by the parts you like best.

  What parts are not clear? Put a "?" by unclear parts.

Question Yourself. Did the author:

Tell what was being explained?	YES	sort of	NO
Tell what things you need?	YES	sort of	NO
Make the steps clear?	YES	sort of	NO
Use keywords (first, second)?		YES	sort of	NO
Make it interesting?	YES	sort of	NO

Plan.
  What two parts would you change?

  1. _____

  2. _____

  One thing that would make it more interesting is

  _____

  _____

Talk. Meet with the author.
  (1) Compare your comments on the Edit and Edit(or) pages.
  (2) Talk about how to fix up the paper. Help the author, if he
      or she wants help.

Figure 6-7
Revise "think-sheet"

Name _____ Date _____

1. What suggestions did your editor give?

    a. _____

    b. _____

    c. _____

    d. _____

Put a check next to the suggestions you will use.

2. How will you make your paper more interesting?

_____

_____

_____

3. Go back to your first paper and make your revisions.

REVISION SYMBOLS

Type of Revision	Symbol	Example
Add words	^	little The girl is my sister.
Take words out	—	The woman ~~has~~ tried to give
Change order	∽	He had go to home
Add ideas here	⌐	The dog is friendly. Tell <u>which</u> dog.

"P.O.W.E.R." (Plan, Organize, Write, Edit, Revise; Stevens & Fear, 1987). Acronyms can be useful in reducing the dependency on "think-sheets" once students understand how to plan, organize, write, edit, and revise.

The research and analyses of CSIW were diverse, although it was quite clear in Englert et al. (1991) that the intervention improves the quality of student writing. The essays of CSIW students include more of the elements covered on the "think-sheets" and do so in more coherent ways than do the essays of non-trained controls. Compared to students not receiving CSIW, the texts of CSIW students were more sensitive to the needs of readers, as reflected by more interesting introductions, explicit statements of purpose, anticipations and responses to potential reader questions, and explicit author voice indicating that personal opinions were being expressed. The writers' personalities were injected into CSIW essays in various ways, more so than in essays produced without CSIW. CSIW students have more metacognitive knowledge about the writing process than students not receiving CSIW: for example, they can talk about writing as a process involving planning, writing, and revising. They understand the importance of essay organization (e.g., putting closely related ideas in the same paragraph), and that revising is necessary to establish coherence, rather than simply to correct grammar and spelling. Thus, CSIW covers important information about writing and seems to promote children's knowledge and use of strategies for writing. Students' awareness that they can become efficient writers also increases.

Self-Regulated Strategy Development [SSR]

Steven Graham, Karen Harris, and their colleagues at the University of Maryland (e.g., Care et al., 1994; see Harris & Graham, 1992a, 1992b) have developed a writing program for learning disabled students that includes self-instruction, self-assessment, and self-reinforcement. The program follows specific step by step instructions (see Table 6-1) and has been used to teach poor child writers how to improve their compositional skills (Harris & Graham, 1985), write better stories (Graham & Harris, 1987), write better essays (Graham & Harris, 1988), and revise written essays (Graham & MacArthur, 1988). Discussion of the essay writing intervention (Graham & Harris, 1988) illustrates the method and its effects.

The students in the program were 12 years old and were achieving two years below their age/grade level in one or more academic areas. Students were taught individually by an instructor for 45 minutes a day, two or three days a week, for two or three weeks. Instruction continued until students met the criteria for each step. The steps were as follows:

Table 6-1
Self-Instructional Strategy Training

Step 1: Introduce Task-Specific Strategy (Pre-Training)
In this step a mnemonic for the strategy is introduced and its meaning mastered through various activities. The strategy is first introduced through a chart which provides a definition.

Step 2: Review Current Performance Level and Training Rationale
The instructor and the student examine how the student was performing on the targeted skill before the intervention began and discuss why training is important and how the strategy will improve performance.

Step 3: Describe the Learning Strategy
A small chart is used to introduce a learning strategy. The student is then asked to write down two or three creativity self-statements on paper and to practice using them.

Step 4: Model the Strategy and Self-Instruction
The instructor models the learning strategy (using all the necessary materials for that particular strategy), writes a story or an essay, thinking aloud as he/she does so. In thinking aloud, the instructor models not only the creativity self-statements but also self-instructions on how to (a) get started, (b) write the story, and (c) evaluate the story. The student then records examples of the self-instructional strategies that he/she would use.

Step 5: Mastery of Strategy Steps
The student is required to memorize the strategy plan. Once learned, paraphrasing of the strategy is allowed. The student is also required to memorize each type of self-instruction.

Step 6: Controlled Practice of Strategy Steps and Self-Instruction
The student practices the strategy using the visual aids, if necessary, and receives feedback from the instructor. While practicing the strategy the student is also required to use the creativity self-statements.

Step 7: Independent Performance
Students write independently, using the strategy and the self-statements. Feedback is provided and the transition to instinctive self-instruction is encouraged.

Step 8: Generalization and Maintenance Components
Students are encouraged to discuss these strategies with their parents and teachers as well as with the instructor in order to understand the benefits of using this strategy outside of the study. If necessary, behavioral contracts and cooperative planning with other teachers can be used to facilitate generalization and maintenance.

Step 1: Pretraining

The definition and generation of good essay components are discussed using a chart summarized by the mnemonic TREE (see Figure 6-8). After discussing the meaning of each of the prompts the student practices the mnemonic and the meaning of each of the prompts until it is memorized.

Step 2: Review Current Performance Level

The instructor and the student discuss the quality of the student's essays before the intervention begins. They then discuss the goal of the intervention (i.e., to write better essays) and why it is important. At this time a contract is filled out in which the student commits to learning the strategy for writing better essays and understands that once the course is complete, the student's best essay will be shared with the parents and the principal.

Step 3: Describe and Discuss the Composition Strategy

First, there is a check to determine if the student understands what it means to plan. The instructor then explains that she is going to teach a strategy that will help the student to plan and write better essays. A three-step strategy card for planning and writing is provided (see Figure 6-9).

The first part of the strategy involves thinking about who will read the essay and why the student is writing the essay. In the second step the student is taught that it is important to plan what it is that is going to be said in the essay. In order to help plan the essay, the student is instructed to use the TREE mnemonic that was learned in pretraining. For example, if the question of the essay was, "Should boys and girls play sports together?", notes would first be made summarizing the student's belief about the topic. Next, the student writes down the reasons for the beliefs that are held. During this time the use of self-statements is encouraged (e.g., Let my mind be free to think of all the reasons). Once all of the reasons have been written down, it is important

---

Figure 6-8

Essay parts (Self-instructional strategy training)

T - Note <u>Topic</u> Sentence

R - Note <u>Reasons</u>

E - <u>Examine</u> Reasons. Will my reader buy this?

E - Note <u>Ending</u>

for the student to examine each one. Weak reasons that would not be believed by the readers are crossed out. Then, a good ending for the essay is written. The actual writing of the essay follows, using the notes that were constructed previously. As the student writes, he/she may think of more things to write and should be encouraged to do so (i.e., say more).

Step 4: Model the Strategy

The three-step strategy chart is placed in front of the student and the instructor models out loud how a good essay should be written (for an example, see Table 6-2). The instructor then discusses the self-statements that were used and points out that these do not need to be spoken aloud (i.e., they can be thought of or whispered).

Step 5: Mastery of Strategy Steps

Students practice the three-step strategy and TREE until it is memorized. A procedure called *rapid fire* (a form of rote memorization) is useful in that it helps the children memorize the steps quickly. The teacher instructs the child that the purpose of this session is to memorize the steps used in writing. She then explains that the child is to say the steps as quickly as possible and, if stuck, can use the charts as a cue. The child is allowed to make use of the charts at the beginning. When the charts are removed the teacher provides prompts, as the child requires. Once the three steps have been learned, the process is repeated with TREE. The teacher makes certain that the child knows the steps and TREE, and understands them before moving to controlled practice of the strategy.

Figure 6-9
3 steps for planning and writing

1. THINK
   Who?
   What?

2. PLAN
   T - Note Topic sentence
   R - Note Reasons
   E - Examine Reasons. Will my reader buy this?
   E - Note Ending

3. WRITE and SAY MORE

Table 6-2
Modeling

Question: Is it better to be an only child or to have brothers and sisters?

OK, what is it that I have to do? I have to write an essay about whether it is better to be an only child or have brothers and sisters. First I will think about WHO and WHY. When I ask myself *who,* I am asking who will read my paper. [Name of student] will read my paper, so I will write it for him/her. Next, I need to ask myself *why,* or what is my goal. I want to do it to convince [name of student]. I want him/her to believe what I do. That's great.

I did a good job thinking about *who* and *why*. Now I will plan what I want to say. To help me plan what I want to say I will use TREE (*write in keyword that goes with each letter, i.e., Topic, Reasons, Examine, Ending*). First, I need to make notes for my topic sentence; I need to state what I believe. Well, I think it is better to be an only child (*write note: "Better to be an only child"*). Now, is this what I really believe? (*pause*) Yes, it is, so now I need to think of as many reasons as I can for why it is better to be an only child. I want to be sure that I can think of at least 3 or 4 reasons.

To help me think of reasons I will let my mind be free and I will take my time. (*Generate 7 or 8 reasons, some good and some bad, but do not evaluate as you generate. Reinforce yourself occasionally.*)

Now I need to examine the reasons to see if my reader, [name of student], will buy them. (*Use student-reader as much as possible, use self-evaluative and self-reinforcing statements as much as possible, and cross out poor ideas.*)

Now the last thing that I need is a good ending sentence. (*Say a sentence out loud; reject the first one. Say another sentence; accept and reinforce yourself. Make notes for planning on paper.*) Well, this is a good job, it will convince [name of student] that it is better to be an only child.

Now I need to use my plans to help me write my essay. As I write, I may think of other good things to say and I will want to be sure to use them in my essay. (*Take out a piece of paper and write the essay while thinking out loud. Be sure to use planning, definition, evaluation, and reinforcement statements. Examples: "What do I need to do next?"; "Will my reader understand this?"; "Can I say more?"; "Great, I did a good job!"*)

From Graham & Harris (1988).

Step 6: Controlled Practice

The student and the instructor compose essays together using the three-step strategy to a) *Think,* b) *Plan,* and c) *Write and Say More,* in conjunction with the self-statements (e.g., *"Let my mind be free"* and

"Take my time"). It should be noted that the instructor directs and monitors the progress of the student but does not actually write the essay. The strategy charts (Figures 6-8 and 6-9) are provided as prompts. When providing corrective feedback, the instructor comments on what was done incorrectly and makes certain that the student corrects the work. The teacher is positive and encouraging at all times, however.

Step 7: Independent Performance

Given a topic sentence, the student composes essays independently with corrective feedback provided by the instructor. The charts (Figures 6-8 & 6-9) are used in the beginning if necessary, but are faded by the end of this step so that the student can write an essay using the strategy independently. Practice continues until the student has demonstrated that the strategy can be used effectively.

Step 8: Generalization

The student is praised for doing a good job in learning the strategy to write better essays. The importance of using the strategy at all times is reinforced. Students are questioned on how this strategy could be used for classroom assignments. They are reminded that when writing essays, one must *Think, Plan, Write,* and *Say More.* The students are asked to share with their teacher and classmates what it was that they learned over the past few weeks.

The quality of the student essays was assessed using a holistic rating scale. That is, the persons grading the writing read the stories and rated them for overall quality using marks of 1 to 7, with 1 being the poorest quality and 7 the highest. Samples of low, medium, and high quality essays were provided as guidelines. Graham and Harris's (1988) program improved the quality of students' composition. The essays produced by trained students were longer and included the elements of a complete argument (i.e., premise, reasons, and conclusions). A high proportion of the information in the essays of trained students was relevant to the argument. In addition, students' perception of the criteria for a "good" essay increased.

Self-instructional strategy training has also been developed for revising (Graham & MacArthur, 1988). Students are taught to self-instruct themselves to *read* their essay, *find* the sentence that tells "what you believe," *ask* "Is it clear?", *add two reasons* why they believe it to be true, and *SCAN* (an acronym like TREE) each sentence to ask "Does it make Sense?"; "Is it Connected to your belief?"; "Can you Add more?"; *Note* errors, make changes, reread essay, and make final changes. This strategy is taught using the same eight-step plan that Graham and Harris (1988) used, only modified for revising an essay that was already written. Evaluation of this approach revealed that this strategy increases the number of revisions and results in a much longer, better-quality final product (Graham & MacArthur, 1988).

We emphasize that Graham and Harris (1987) believe that these strategies should not be used in a "recipe" fashion. Every student is an individual. The guidelines and the program of instruction should be tailored to the needs of each student. Though Graham and Harris have focused on the learning disabled population in their research, these strategies can be used in regular classrooms with modifications made for average and above average readers. Characteristics that may determine the explicitness of instruction are age and maturity, cognitive capacity and capabilities, language development, learning style, tolerance for frustration, attitudes and expectancies, whether children already use private speech to direct their activities, and initial knowledge state and strategies that students already possess (Harris, 1985).

In a larger sense, regular classroom teachers may wish to experiment with grouping students with similar writing-related performance to use this program with the small groups in their classrooms. Future research should identify the strategy needs of the regular classroom and evaluate self-instructional strategy training as part of the writing curriculum.

STRATEGIES DIRECTED AT SPECIFIC ASPECTS OF THE WRITING PROCESS

Writing research is now very analytical, with some researchers focusing on either planning or translating or revising. Not surprisingly, strategies targeted specifically at these subprocesses of writing have emerged. We review in this section some of the most prominent and effective ones with elementary students.

Planning

Many children find it hard to begin writing because they either cannot think of what to write about or, once given the topic, can think of nothing to say. Various idea generation strategies can be used in the classroom (Scardamalia & Bereiter, 1986).

Idea-generating questions have been recommended in order to get the children thinking about the types of things they could include in writing (e.g., object description, sequence of events, and arguments of the author; Humes, 1983). See Table 6-3 for a list of possible questions.

Providing *sentence openers* can also prompt children to think of things to write. A sentence opener is a phrase that a writer can use to begin a sentence (e.g., "One reason...", "Even though...", "For example...", "I think..."). Bereiter and Scardamalia (1982) discovered that children from grades 4 to 8 consistently reported that *sentence openers helped them think of things to write*. In providing writers with sentence openers, teachers are providing the cue to get started. This cue could either help the student who already has an idea to begin writing about

Table 6-3
Idea-Generating Questions

Describe an object
    1. What does it look like (i.e., size, shape, color)?
    2. What does it smell like?
    3. What does it sound like?
    4. What does it feel like?
    5. What does it taste like?

Sequence of Events
    1. What happened first?*
    2. What happened next? Next?*
    3. What happened last?*
    4. When did it happen?
    5. Where did it happen?
    6. Whom did it happen to?

Facts on a Topic
    1. What is the topic?
    2. Why is the topic important?
    3. What part of the topic should I write about?
    4. How can I illustrate the topic?
    5. What other questions can I ask about the topic?
    6. What are the answers to these questions?
    7. Do I have any problems with this topic?
    8. What are the solutions to these problems?

Arguments or Opinions
    1. What opinion can a person have about this topic?
    2. Which of them is my opinion?
    3. What reasons can others have about this topic?
    4. What reasons can I give them to show that my opinion is right?
    5. What can I say to prove my reason is a good reason?

* For older children, these three questions can be replaced by the following two questions:
1. What is the problem?
2. What is the solution to the problem?

From Humes (1983).

it, or prompt an idea based on the sentence opener (e.g., the writer may not have thought about providing an opinion, but the sentence opener "I think" provides an opportunity to do so).

    Once children have identified a writing topic, it is then necessary to generate a number of pieces of information that should be included in the essay. Students can be asked to write down all the single words they can generate that might be used in their composition. Anderson, Bereiter, and Smart (as discussed in Bereiter & Scardamalia, 1982) showed that this type of training encouraged longer essays.

For planning of narratives, Harris and Graham (e.g., 1992a, 1992b) recommend that students be instructed to ask themselves a set of questions for generating a narrative with conventional story grammar (Harris & Graham, 1992a, 1992b):

- Who is the main character?
- Who else is in the story?
- When does the story take place?
- Where does the story take place?
- What does the main character do or want to do?
- What do other characters do?
- What happens when the main character does or tries to do it?
- What happens with other characters?
- How does the story end?
- How does the main character feel?
- How do the other characters feel?

In short, researchers have devised a number of ways to encourage students to generate the content needed for writing. We are struck that greater attention has not been given to organizing information generated. Classroom teachers should emphasize both generation and organization to their students as part of the planning process.

Translating

There are many writing style manuals, most of which are filled with technical rules, detailing everything from when to use a semi-colon to how to cite a reference. It would be easy to get the impression from such sources that good writing only requires knowledge and application of grammar and punctuation rules, a perspective reinforced for years by many educators. However, knowledge of such rules does not produce good writers, or even people who can translate a writing plan into good prose. In fact, overconcern with such rules might actually interfere with the construction of text that conveys what the author wants to say. There has been ample documentation that students often receive negative feedback about technical problems in their writing, with such negative feedback discouraging additional attempts to write (Daiker, 1983, 1989; Dragga, 1986; McCarthy, 1987; Rose, 1985, 1989). When too much effort is channeled into punctuating and capitalizing correctly, a writer can forget what he or she wanted to say. Therefore, it is important that teachers do not focus instruction on writing technicalities. That is not to say that teachers should never provide instruction and guidance about important writing conventions, such as when to use particular forms of punctuation, but rather that a careful balance must be struck between written content and form (see Bereiter & Scardamalia, 1987,

Chapter 4).

Instruction about writing mechanics can be done painlessly and in the context of whole texts. For example, one of the greatest difficulties in writing for many elementary students is producing complex sentences. Lawlor (1983) has demonstrated that grade school children can be taught rather easily to combine simple sentences to create complex sentences and, hence, more interesting prose. For example, the two sentences "Joey had a dog" and "The dog's name was Sam" can be combined to produce "Joey had a dog named Sam." Lawlor's specific approach was to provide students with worksheets consisting of paragraphs containing simple sentences. Students were instructed to combine the sentences so that the paragraph flowed smoothly. Overall, practice in combining sentences improved the syntactic skills of students from grade school to college (Lawlor, 1983). Our guess is that most teachers will be able to spot plenty of simple sentences in the essays of individual students, which in turn can provide opportunities for students to practice the sentence-combining strategy.

The real challenge is teaching students how to produce text that expresses the intended meaning. In doing so, authors must respect what Nystrand (1986) refers to as the *reciprocity principle*. In constructing a text that makes sense, the author must be aware of what the potential reader knows already. Good writers keep their audience in mind as they construct text. Because the reader is not there to ask questions of the author as the composition is created, the author must anticipate the questions that readers might have and answer those questions as part of constructing the text (see McCutchen & Perfetti, 1983; Scardamalia & Bereiter, 1986). Educational psychologists refer to this process as *social cognition*: Good writers are aware of the state of the readers' minds and adjust their writing so that readers can understand the meaning intended by the writer. Throughout writing instruction, teachers should send the message to students to think about the reader: *Will the reader understand the text?* This question should be at the forefront during initial translation of the writing plan into text and during revision.

Revising

A number of studies have been conducted in which writers have been required to think aloud as they revise. Fitzgerald (1992) summarized how good writers approach the task. First, they keep in mind the overall meaning of a text and what the reader needs to obtain from it (Berkenkotter & Murray, 1983; Hayes, Flower, Schriver, Stratman & Carey, 1987). If there is a particular writing style they want reflected in the writing, it is considered prominently throughout revision (e.g., Graves, Slater, Roen, Redd-Boyd, Duin, Furniss & Hazeltine, 1988). Good writers concentrate more on the overall organization of the text than on the construction of individual sentences (Hayes et al., 1987). Although attention to higher-order meaning takes precedence, expert revisers also evaluate grammar and spelling and some writing maxims, such as to use parallel constructions and to avoid wordiness (Hayes et al., 1987; Hull, 1987). They acknowledge that concern about mechanics of writing alone does not result in effective revisions (e.g., Graham, Schwartz & MacArthur, 1991; MacArthur & Graham, 1987; MacArthur, Graham & Schwartz, 1991), but an essay is not complete until the mechanics are in order. In short, expert revisers have a repertoire of strategies they apply while revising, from those directed at the main message of a text to others directed at details of grammar, spelling, and punctuation.

Throughout Fitzgerald's (1992) review of revision, she keeps returning to Nystrand's (e.g., 1986) reciprocity principle: that good revisers are aware of the needs of the reader. For that reason among others, a popular instruction option is for students to revise in small groups, with peers reading each other's work and reacting with constructive criticism. As they do so, students should keep in mind the following points, listed here in their order of importance:

- Keep the overall meaning in mind.
- Will the meaning get across to the intended audience?
- Is the style consistent with the style desired? For example, if writing a factual piece, is it written in a matter-of-fact style throughout? If a story is being written, does it follow the classic story grammar approach of presenting character and setting information first, followed by information about problems in the story and attempts to solve the problems, culminating in a resolution and an ending?
- Are the sentences grammatical and complete? Is the punctuation correct? Are there spelling errors?

Beyond this global approach, some more specific recommendations for encouraging revision of text have been presented in the literature in recent years.

Writing More

It has been found that a lot of student writers stop their writing when they still have more ideas to convey. It seems that the main problem in generating content is accessing and giving order to ideas (Bereiter & Scardamalia, 1982). The writer does not have the verbal feedback of an audience who can prompt access to additional ideas. When teachers prompt children to write more by asking them to clarify an idea, or by simply advising them to write more, children do in fact write more (Scardamalia & Bereiter, 1985). This simple strategy may be helpful with students who are prematurely ending their compositions. At first the prompt may come from the teacher but eventually, with guidance, the student should be able to internalize a self-instruction to write more (especially if instructed to do so; e.g., Graham & Harris, 1987), and thus produce more elaborate written material.

Improving Student Monitoring of Text Quality

Why do young writers sometimes fail to revise? Often it is because they do not detect that there are problems with the text (Beal, 1987, 1989). Writers may fail to identify problems because they lack adequate criteria about what constitutes effective written communication (e.g., McCormick, Busching & Potter, 1992). For example, based in much of the feedback about writing given in school, students sometimes accept text as adequate if the mechanics of the writing (i.e., spelling, punctuation, capitalization) are correct and the writing is neat. Alternatively, they may be seduced by interesting details. For example, they may believe a text is communicative because they like the examples used in the text (e.g., anecdotes about pets), failing to recognize that the anecdotes are not very good illustrations of the phenomena being explained in the text.

More positively, students can be taught to monitor whether there are inconsistencies in a piece of writing. For example, Beal, Garrod and Bonitatibus (1990) taught third-, fifth- and sixth-graders to self-question themselves about drafts of narratives using a set of questions that should be answered in any complete and consistent narrative:

- Who are the people in the story and what are they like?
- What is happening in the story?
- Why are they doing what they did?
- Where does the story take place?
- When does the story take place?

Over a 30-minute session, students were instructed to pose these questions to themselves and to determine whether a piece of writing included answers to the questions. Specifically, the instructor provided students with cue cards containing the questions. The instructor also modeled question answering before the students tried to answer the questions on their own. Students taught to use self-questioning detected more errors and constructed more revisions, relative to students in a control group not receiving self-questioning instruction. Even more effective detection and revision was obtained with grade-3 students when the instruction they were given about revision included exposure to example stories containing parts that should be revised. In summary, Beal et al. (1990) provided compelling evidence that detection of problems in stories can be taught so that young children can identify when to make revisions.

Teaching Addition, Deletion, Substitution, and Rearrangement Skills

More than detecting problems in a text is required for efficient written communication. Fixing the problems detected is also important. Thus,

Fitzgerald and Markham (1987) taught average writers in grade 6 to revise during thirteen 45-minute lessons over a one month period. There were four 3-day cycles, with day 13 being a review of the previous 12 sessions. Each cycle focused on one of the four types of revision: *additions, deletions, substitutions,* and *rearrangements* (Faigley & Witte, 1981). The instructions for the group centered on teaching revision as a problem solving process. In this way the teacher modeled detecting mismatches between written and intended text, decided how to change this text, and then changed it. On Day 1 of each cycle, the teacher referred to the chart describing the type of revision to be discussed. She then used think-alouds to model the revision strategy to the children. After this, the class practiced revision. On Day 2, the material from Day 1 was reviewed, and the children worked in pairs revising a portion of text by using a handout that led them through the problem solving process of revision. The children then wrote a brief story. Day 3 also included review. Then the children revised a portion of a story given to them by a teacher. They also revised the story that they had written the day before. Throughout all lessons, the children were taught to think of revising as a problem solving process. (For an example of a typical cycle, see Figure 6-10.)

Fitzgerald and Markham (1987) found that their program led sixth grade children to identify discrepancies between written and intended text and to be specific in identifying the changes that needed to be made. Compared to children not instructed about revision, trained children made more revisions, and the quality of their papers increased throughout the program. Unfortunately, the final quality of the essays was not, on average, strikingly better than the quality of the non-trained students' essays after the same period of time.

In short, revision strategies are being devised and tested. The tactics studied to date have failed to improve overall writing performance beyond the level of non-trained control students, although more subtle changes in literary skills have been obtained. The importance of revision will motivate more work on the topic. Very few first drafts would not benefit from effective revision. In fact, many revisions would benefit from additional, more effective revisions.

Deciding to Revise or Rewrite

Sometimes a text will seem so problematic that it is questionable whether it makes sense to revise. Thus, an important skill to teach students is how to decide whether to revise or rewrite. Hayes and Flower (1987) provided some guidelines that students should learn:

> Rewrite if:
> - it is not important to save the original text,
> - there are so many problems with the original text that diagnosing the problem would waste more time than rewriting, or

Figure 6-10
Revision

Introduction:
The teacher explains that revisions means to identify problems, make decisions about how to change the text, and have knowledge on how to make these changes.

Modeling Stage (Day 1)
The teacher first announces that there will be revisions made to various parts of the composition and while making these revisions the teacher will talk out loud so that the students can see how she thinks. While the transparency of the composition to be revised is presented to the children, the teacher may say the following:
"Let's say I've written this story. Now I think to myself, I want my readers to have an eerie feeling about what happened to the husband and the brothers. My goal is to add mystery and make my readers feel uncomfortable. I think this part where it says 'left and never came back' isn't mysterious or eerie." The teacher points to *Locate a problem* on the chart. "This is locating a problem. Now I think to myself, how could I change it?"
The teacher describes possible ways to change the passage, then points to *Decision: Decide how it could or should be changed* on the chart and says: "This is deciding how it can be fixed."
The teacher then explains that once the decision about what to add has been made, it is time to *Change: Make the change.* Finally, the teacher summarizes the problem-solving way of thinking about revision, reiterating that writers locate problems, decide how to make changes, and actually make changes on paper.

Guided Practice (Day 2)
With the help of the teacher, the students attempt to practice their revision strategy and to share their experiences by working in pairs. A handout is given to the children outlining what they learned on day one to help them through the revision process. The text to be revised should be rigged such that there is ample room for revision. If the area of concentration is addition, then there should be a stress on additions; if the concentration is on deletions, then there should be plenty to delete, etc. After the pairs are finished, the class shares their revisions. During the discussion it is important that the reasons the children made the changes that they did be discussed. At the end of the session the teacher then reviews the problem solving approach to revision.

Independent Application (Day 3)
First, the students individually revise a passage given to them by the teacher. Finally, the students write and revise their own compositions.

From Fitzgerald & Markham (1988).

- the purpose of the text is clear, so that extracting an idea and writing a new text with this idea is easy.

Revise if:
- it is important to save as much of the original text as possible,
- the diagnosis of the errors is easy, or
- the purpose of the text is unclear, so extracting an idea and using it to rewrite the text is not possible.

Closing Comment about Planning, Translating, and Revising Strategies

Planning boils down to coming up with content and organizing it. Translating is taking that organization and generating a draft. Every good writer knows that a first draft is far from a finished product, that most of writing is revision. Hence, there has been more research on revision than on planning or translation, and more revision strategies developed than planning and translation strategies. The next section appropriately covers what is perhaps the greatest aid to revision ever devised—the word processor.

WORD PROCESSING AND WRITING [SSR & T]

Most contemporary writers compose on word processors. Fortunately, most schools can now afford one or more computers per classroom, providing the opportunity for students to be introduced to word processing. There are a variety of documented advantages to word processing over handwritten composition, with these affecting planning, translating and revising (Cochran-Smith, 1991; Daiute, 1985):

- Planning is facilitated because word processing permits students more time to think about planning, since time-consuming writing by hand is eliminated. Because it is possible to change a document on a word processor without much hassle, planning does not need to be as extensive before writing begins.
- Translating is a more public process when it occurs at the classroom word processor. Collaborative possibilities emerge as a group of children compose a story at a word processor. That translation is easier in a word processing environment is obvious from the length differences of student essays when word processed versus handwritten, with word processed essays generally being longer (e.g., Collier, 1983; Daiute, 1986).
- Revising is probably the writing process most affected by

word processors. The word processor makes changes easier, and thus it is not surprising that more revisions occur in a word processing environment than in a paper-and-pencil environment (e.g., Collier, 1983). The word processor permits exploration of options, permitting students to see what difference this or that change would make in the composition. Depending on the word processing program in use, assistance with spelling checks and grammar checks is often available. On the other hand, some revision activities might be impeded by word processing. When working with paper, it is easy to juxtapose the beginning and end of a composition. Not so with working with screens that must be viewed one at a time. (Of course, the solution to this problem is to print out the draft so as to be able to have both the advantages afforded by hard copy and the advantages provided by the electronic environment.)

The decision to teach writing in a word processing environment is not without its costs. Learning to use word processors, including acquisition of keyboarding skills, requires some effort (McArthur, 1988). When all things are considered, however, the advantages of teaching students to write in such environments are massive, including that their attitudes toward writing are better when word processing (see Cochran-Smith, 1991). Moreover, with every passing year, there are better and better word processing programs, with many new features to support student writing (Hunt-Berg, Rankin & Beukelman, 1994).

Even so, we emphasize that putting students on the machine alone—even one loaded with an excellent word processing program—is not a way to teach writing. The way to teach children to write is to develop their planning, translating, and revising skills, including the overarching understanding that writing is comprised of planning, translating, and revising. An important research goal in the coming years is to understand how students can best be taught to plan, draft and revise with a word processor.

CONCLUSION

Graham and Harris (1988, 1989; Harris & Graham, 1992a, 1992b) recommend the following for implementing a writing program in the classroom, and we concur:

1. Write at least four times a week (i.e., allocate time).
2. Expose students to a broad range of writing tasks.
3. Create a social climate conducive to writing.
4. Integrate writing with other academic subjects.

5. Aid students in developing the processes central to writing—that is, the three recursive processes identified by Flower and Hayes (1980); planning, translating, and reviewing should be taught as well as the task-specific and metacognitive strategies described in earlier chapters.
6. Automatize the skills for getting language onto paper. If writers have not mastered the techniques of spelling, punctuation, and sentence production, these lower-level writing elements can interfere with higher cognitive processes such as content generation. Direct instruction of lower-level skills is helpful in that once they become automatized, writers can perform them with little conscious attention (i.e., this "frees" their attention for higher-level aspects of writing).
7. Writing programs should include examples of various writings (e.g. narrative and expository) so that students can learn the attributes of various types of writing.
8. Help students develop the skills and abilities to carry out more sophisticated composing processes. This can be accomplished by teaching writers the various strategies outlined in this chapter.
9. Assist students in the development of goals for improving their written products.
10. Avoid instructional practices that do not improve students' writing performance. Systematic teaching of grammar and usage and *overemphasis* on low-level writing errors (e.g., spelling, punctuation) do not help. Although instruction in low-level skills is important, they should not be taught in isolation. Persistent attention to low-level errors is probably especially harmful. It tends to make students focus on their shortcomings rather than on their strengths (Hillocks, 1984) and thus has the potential for undermining motivation to write. In contrast, most of the procedures reviewed in this chapter should enhance motivation to write.

The plan-translate-revise strategy is a general composition strategy emphasized in this chapter. Although we focused on writing as composition in this chapter, planning, translating and revising occur whenever something is being composed, whether it is a sculpture, a play, or the school bake sale. Students should be taught to plan before they act, to try out their plans, and to revise as needed. Indeed, it was the insight that much of human behavior involves planning, translating and revision that inspired the information processing revolution that resulted in the development of the strategy instruction summarized in this book. Readers interested in the early theory that inspired planning-translating-revising and other strategies should take a look at Miller, Galanter and Pribram's (1960) *Plans and the Structure of Behavior*, a short, wonderfully readable volume.

REFERENCES

Applebee, A.N. (1982). Writing and learning in school settings. In M. Nystrand (Ed.), *What writers know: The language process and structure of written discourse.* New York: Academic Press.

Beal, C.R. (1987). Repairing the message: Children's monitoring and revision skills. *Child Development, 58,* 401-408.

Beal, C.R. (1989). Children's communication skills: Implications for the development of writing strategies. In C.B. McCormick, G. Miller, & M. Pressley (Eds.), *Cognitive strategy research: From basic research to educational applications* (pp. 191-214). New York: Springer-Verlag.

Beal, C.R., Garrod, A.C., & Bonitatibus, G.J. (1990). Fostering children's revision skills through training in comprehension monitoring. *Journal of Educational Psychology, 82,* 275-280.

Bereiter, C., & Scardamalia, M. (1982). From conversation to composition: The role of instruction in a developmental process. In R. Glaser (Ed.), *Advances in instructional psychology* (Vol. 2, pp. 1-64). Hillsdale, NJ: Lawrence Erlbaum Associates.

Bereiter, C., & Scardamalia, M. (1987). *The psychology of written communication.* Hillsdale, NJ: Lawrence Erlbaum & Associates.

Berkenkotter, C., & Murray, D. (1983). Decisions and revisions: The planning strategies of a publishing writer and responses of a laboratory rat—or being protocoled. *College Composition and Communication, 34,* 156-172.

Bos, C.S. (1988). Process oriented writing: Instructional implications for mildly handicapped students. *Exceptional Children, 54,* 521-527.

Case, L.P., Mamlin, N., Harris, K.R., & Graham, S. (1994). Self-regulated strategy development: A theoretical and practical perspective. In T. Scruggs and M. Mastropieri (Eds.), *Advances in learning and behavioral disabilities.* Greenwich, CT: JAI Press.

Cochran-Smith, M. (1991). Word processing and writing in elementary classrooms: A critical review of related literature. *Review of Educational Research, 61,* 107-155.

Collier, R.M. (1983). The word processor and revision strategies. *College Composition and Communication, 34,* 149-155.

Daiker, D. (1983). *The teacher's options in responding to student writing.* Paper presented at the Conference on College Composition and Communication, Washington, DC.

Daiker, D. (1989). Learning to praise. In C.M. Anson (Ed.), *Writing and response: Theory, practice and research* (pp. 103-113). Urbana, IL: National Council of Teachers of English.

Daiute, C.A. (1985). *Writing and computers.* New York: Addison-Wesley.

Daiute, C.A. (1986). Physical and cognitive factors in revising. Insights from students with computers. *Research in the Teaching of English, 20,* 141-158.

Dominic, J.F. (1983). Research on writing: A response. *The Elementary School Journal, 84,* 88-92.

Dragga, S. (1986). *Praiseworthy grading: A teacher's alternative to editing error.* Paper presented at the Conference on College Composition and Communication, New Orleans.

Englert, C.S., & Raphael, T.C. (1988). Constructing well formed prose: Process, structure, and metacognitive knowledge. *Exceptional Children, 54,* 513-520.

Englert, C.S., Raphael, T.E., Anderson, L.M., Anthony, H.M., & Stevens, D.D. (1991). Making strategies and self-talk visible: Writing instruction in regular and special education classrooms. *American Educational Research Journal, 28,* 337-372.

Faigley, L., & Witte, S. (1981). Analyzing revision. *Colleqe Composition and Communication, 32,* 400-414.

Fitzgerald, J. (1992). Variant views about good thinking during composing: Focus on revision. In M. Pressley, K.R. Harris & J.T. Guthrie (Eds.), *Promoting academic competence and literacy in school* (pp. 337-358). San Diego, CA: Academic Press.

Fitzgerald, J., & Markham, L.R. (1987). Teaching children about revision in writing. *Cognition and Instruction, 4,* 3-24.

Fitzgerald, J., & Teasley, A.B. (1986). Effects of instruction in narrative structure on children's writing. *Journal of Educational Psychology, 78,* 424-432.

Flower, L.S., & Hayes, J.R. (1980). Identifying the organization of writing processes. In L.W. Gregg & E.R. Steinberg (Eds.), *Cognitive processes in writing* (pp. 3-30). Hillsdale, NJ: Lawrence Erlbaum Associates.

Graham, S., & Harris, K.R. (1987). *A components analysis of cognitive strategy training: Effects on learning disabled students' compo-*

sitions and self-efficacy. Manuscript submitted for publication.

Graham, S., & Harris, K.R. (l988). Instructional recommendations for teaching writing to exceptional students. *Exceptional Children, 54*, 506-512.

Graham, S., & Harris, K.R. (1989). Cognitive training: Implications for written language. In J.N. Hughes & R.J. Hall (Eds.), *Cognitive-behavioral psychology in the schools* (pp. 247-279). New York: Guilford Press.

Graham, S., & MacArthur, C. (1988). Improving learning disabled students' skills at revising essays produced on a word processor: Self-instructional strategy training. *Journal of Special Education, 22*, 133-152.

Graham, S., Schwartz, S., & MacArthur, C. (1991). *Learning disabled and normally achieving students' knowledge of the writing process: Attitudes toward writing and self-efficacy.* Manuscript submitted for publication consideration. College Park, MD: University of Maryland, Department of Special Education.

Graves, D. (1983). *Writing: Teachers and children at work.* Portsmouth, NH: Heinemann.

Graves, M., Slater, W.H., Roen, D., Redd-Boyd, T., Duin, A.H., Furniss, D.W., & Hazeltine, P. (1988). Some characteristics of memorable expository writing: Effects of revisions by writers with different backgrounds. *Research in the Teaching of English, 22*, 242-265.

Harris, K.R. (1985). Conceptual, methodological, and clinical issues in cognitive behavioral assessment. *Journal of Abnormal Child Psychology, 13*, 373-390.

Harris, K.R., & Graham, S. (1985). Improving learning disabled students' composition skills: Self-control strategy training. *Learning Disability Quarterly, 8*, 27-36.

Harris, K.R., & Graham, S. (1992a). *Helping young writers master the craft: Strategy instruction and self-regulation in the writing process.* Cambridge, MA: Brookline Books.

Harris, K.R., & Graham, S. (1992b). Self-regulated strategy development: A part of the writing process. In M. Pressley, K.R. Harris & J.T. Guthrie (Eds.), *Promoting academic competence and literacy in school* (pp. 277-309). San Diego, CA: Academic Press.

Hayes, J.R., & Flower, L.S. (1986). Writing research and the writer. *American Psychologist, 41*, 1106-1113.

Hayes, J.R., & Flower, L.S. (1987). On the structure of the writing process. *Topics in Language Disorders, 7*, 19-30.

Hayes, J.R., Flower, L., Schriver, K., Stratman, J., & Carey, L. (1987). Cognitive processes in revision. In S. Rosenberg (Ed.), *Advances in applied psycholinguistics: Reading, writing, and language processing.* Cambridge, England: Cambridge University Press.

Hillocks, G. (1984). What works in teaching composition: A meta-analysis of experimental treatment studies. *American Journal of Education, 93*, 133-170.

Hull, G.A. (1987). The editing process in writing: A performance study of more skilled and less skilled writers. *Research in the Teaching of English, 21*, 8-29.

Humes, A. (1983). Putting writing research into practice. *The Elementary School Journal, 84*, 53-62.

Hunt-Berg, M., Rankin, J.L., & Beukelman, D.R. (1994). Ponder the possibilities: Computer-supported writing for struggling writers. *Learning Disabilities Research and Practice, 9*, 169-178.

Langer, J.A. (1986). *Children reading and writing: Structures and strategies.* Norwood, NJ: Ablex.

Lawlor, J. (1983). Sentence combining: A sequence for instruction. *The Elementary School Journal, 84*, 53-62.

MacArthur, C. (1988). The impact of computers on the writing process. *Exceptional Children, 54*, 536-542.

MacArthur, C., & Graham, S. (1987). Learning disabled students' composing with three methods: handwriting, dictation, and word processing. *Learning Disability Quarterly, 14*, 61-73.

MacArthur, C., Graham, S., & Schwartz, S. (1991). Knowledge of revision and revising behavior among learning disabled students. *Learning Disabilities Research and Practice, 6*, 201-210.

McCarthy, L.P. (1987). A stranger in strange lands: A college student writing across the curriculum. Research in the Teaching of English, 21, 233-265.

McCormick, C.B., Busching, B.A., & Potter, E.F. (1992). Children's knowledge about writing: The development and use of evaluative criteria. In M. Pressley, K.R. Harris & J.T. Guthrie (Eds.), *Promoting academic competence and literacy in school* (pp. 311-336). San Diego, CA: Academic Press.

McCutchen, D., & Perfetti, C.A. (1983). Local coherence: Helping young writers manage a complex task. *The Elementary School Journal, 84*, 71-75.

Miller, G.A., Galanter, E., & Pribram, K.H. (1960). *Plans and the structure of behavior.*

New York: Holt, Rinehart & Winston.

Nystrand, M. (1986). *The structure of written communication: Studies in reciprocity between writers and readers.* New York: Academic Press.

Odell, L. (1980). Teaching writing by the process of discovery. In L.W. Gregg & E.R. Steinberg (Eds.), *Cognitive processes in writing.* Hillsdale, NJ: Lawrence Erlbaum Associates.

Perl, S. (1983). How teachers teach the writing process. *The Elementary School Journal, 84,* 19-24.

Rohman, G. (1965). Pre-writing: The stage of discovery in the writing process. *College Composition and Communication, 16,* 106-112.

Rose, M. (1985). The language of exclusion: Writing instruction in the university. *College English, 47,* 341-359.

Rose, M. (1989). *Lives on the boundary: The struggle and achievements of America's underprepared.* New York: Free Press.

Scardamalia, M. (1981). How children cope with the cognitive demands of writing. In C.H. Frederiksen, M.F. Whiteman, & J.F. Dominic (Eds.), *Writing: The nature, development. and teaching of written communication.* Hillsdale, NJ: Lawrence Erlbaum Associates.

Scardamalia, M., & Bereiter, C. (1986). Research on written composition. In M. Wittrock (Ed.), *Handbook of research on teaching* (3rd Edition, pp 778-803). New York: Macmillan.

Stevens, P., & Fear, K.L. (1987). *Metacognitive knowledge about writing informational text: Effects of cognitive strategy instruction.* Paper presented at the National Reading Conference, St. Petersburg, Florida.

CHAPTER 7

Mathematical Problem Solving

This chapter presents strategies for encouraging the development of mathematical problem solving abilities. Although a variety of specific strategies will be covered, a great deal of evidence will be summarized documenting that four general strategic processes consistently facilitate problem solving, ones originally summarized by the mathematician George Polya (1957).

POLYA'S MODEL OF PROBLEM SOLVING

According to Polya, in order to solve a problem, a learner should (a) first understand the problem as much as possible, (b) devise a plan consisting of a series of moves for solving the problem, (c) carry out the plan, and (d) look back to check whether the problem was in fact solved. These processes are recursive in that they do not proceed linearly from a to d, but rather the problem solver moves back and forth in the sequence. For example, as one devises a plan for solving a problem, the need to understand some aspect of the problem more fully may become apparent.

As a problem solver is carrying out the plan, the need to do additional planning may become obvious. After a plan is carried out, the problem solver may look back and realize that his or her previous understanding of the problem was in error and that the problem was not solved, necessitating the need for more planning and execution of different problem-solving strategies.

For the first edition of this book, Pressley and Associates provided a detailed review of studies of problem-solving instruction that was effective with children in grades 4 to 8. What we found was that in all of the studies reviewed, Polya's four general steps were represented, although the specific approaches for encouraging students to understand problems, devise plans, carry them out, and look back varied from study to study. For example, Polya defined the understanding phase as translating the problem into a manageable version. This always involves some restatement of the problem and explicit identification of the principal parts of the problem—the unknown, the data, and the problem conditions. In the studies of children's problem-solving strategy instruction reviewed by Pressley and Associates in the previous edition, understanding the problem was encouraged by the following activities: defining the terms in the problem, finding the question posed as the problem, identifying important information, paraphrasing the problem, drawing a diagram, making a list or a table, using objects, and reading aloud.

The second phase, devising a plan, involves identifying the operations to be used to solve the problem and their order of application. Researchers studying children's problem solving have most frequently suggested one approach for devising a plan: Find an easier problem that is like the present problem and relate this new problem to the solution of the easier problem. The third phase is carrying out the operations of the plan that was devised. The fourth stage, looking back, provides not only an opportunity to catch an error, but also a chance to reflect on the problem and its solution and thus increase what is learned about problem solving. The purpose of doing practice problems is not just to solve them, but to learn the problem patterns that are common and how similar problems can be attacked profitably. As part of looking back, researchers have identified a number of ways to check answers and reflect on problems and their solutions, including the following: carefully rechecking the problem-solving steps for accuracy, comparing the final answer with an estimated answer, solving the problem another way, summarizing the problem and the steps taken to solve it, and attempting to make a similar problem. The Polya 4-stage problem-solving sequence is summarized in Table 8-1, with the table reviewing the various operations used by researchers to encourage understanding, planning, and looking back.

The analysis of the problem-solving literature that was presented in the first edition of this book convinced us that the Polya framework was effective. Some studies were especially convincing because their instruction so closely followed the Polya suggestions. For instance, one study that continues to receive a great deal of attention was carried out by Charles and Lester (1984) in grade-5 and grade-7 classrooms. Entire classrooms were assigned either to the control condition—with these classrooms carrying on mathematics teaching as usual—or the problem-solving condition, which involved year-long teaching of a Polya-inspired approach to problem solving.

In order to understand problems they were solving, students in Charles and Lester's (1984) problem-solving condition classrooms were taught to read and reread the problem carefully, write down what is known, look for key phrases, find the important information in the problem, paraphrase the problem, and make certain they understood what needed to be determined (i.e., what the problem was). In order to generate a solution plan, these students were taught to look for patterns in a current problem resembling patterns in previous (and now

Table 7-1
Polya's Four-Stage Model

[Note: These are recursive stages rather than a strictly linear sequence.]

Stage 1: Understanding the problem
using some of the following approaches
Read the problem carefully and then reread it
Define the terms in the problem, seeking help for unknown words and
    terms
Establish what you are looking for (i. e., What is the problem?)
Identify important information in the problem
Paraphrase the problem
Draw a diagram
Make a list or table of what is known and what needs to be known
Use concrete objects to represent the problem

Stage 2: Devising a plan
Ask whether you know a similar problem, especially an easier problem with
    a now familiar solution. Relate this new problem to that problem.
Try solving part of the problem
Try solving a simpler problem
Guess at a possible solution and attempt to work the problem based on the
    guess
Write the potential solution steps in the form of equations

Stage 3: Carrying out the plan

Stage 4: Looking back
To check the answer:
    Check each step carefully
    Determine whether all of the important information in the problem was
        used during the solution process
    Estimate what the answer should be and compare the computed answer to
        the estimated answer—That is, determine whether the computed answer
        makes sense
    Solve the problem another way
To consolidate understanding of how to solve problems like the present one:
    Summarize the problem and solution sequence
    Devise a similar problem

known) problems, simplify the problem and attempt to solve the simpler problem, guess and then check the guess, and attempt to write equations. As part of looking back, students were taught to determine whether all of the important information in the problem was used in constructing a solution, decide whether the answer made sense, and check the answer. (See Table 7-1.)

The Charles and Lester (1984) problem-solving course was implemented in the context of the normal grade-5 and grade-7 curricula. The problem-solving training made a difference. By the end of the year, the students in the problem-solving condition of the study were more likely to develop a problem-solving plan than were students in the traditional instruction control classrooms, although differences between the two groups with respect to problem solving were not huge. Our interpretation of this, consistent with our perspective throughout this volume, is that effective problem-solving will not be developed in the short-term, but rather requires years of excellent instruction—which means instruction that encourages students to understand, plan, and check as part of problem solving.

Recent Support for Polya's Model of Problem Solving

Since the first edition of this book, several important new analyses have appeared substantiating the importance of the Polya approach to problem solving.

One of the most important was provided by Montague and Bos (1990). They interviewed excellent, average, weak, and mathematics-learning-disabled grade-8 students. These students were also administered reasoning tests and mathematics achievement tests. Each student was videotaped while solving five problems, with the students then watching the videotape and explaining their problem-solving to the researcher.

Several very important results were reported by Montague and Bos (1990). First, the higher students' mathematical achievement, the more of the Polya problem-solving steps observed during problem solving. Second, the higher the math achievement, the more strategic competence was reflected in the interview data. Particularly relevant here, the better able the student, the more they knew about the four Polya strategies and specific ways to operationalize the steps and the more their own problem solving reflected attempting to understand, plan, carry out the plan, and check back. Montague and Bos (1990) established a clear relationship between problem-solving achievement among grade-8 students and use of the Polya approach.

Another important study for teachers of disadvantaged students was provided by Cardelle-Elawar (1990), who taught Hispanic grade-6 students experiencing difficulties in mathematics to apply a variation of Polya's model: The students were taught first to understand a problem, translating it into questions that could be answered. Essential knowledge and algorithms needed to solve the problem were then identified and a solution plan devised. Students were taught to monitor their execution of the problem-solving plan. Control students in Cardelle-Elawar's (1990) study received more conventional instruction, emphasizing feedback about the correctness of answers to problems. There was a huge effect of this intervention on problem-solving performance on a mathematics achievement post-test (i.e., more than 3 standard deviations difference).

A much different approach to validating Polya's theory was offered by Hembree (1992). Hembree examined almost 500 studies of problem-solving and problem-solving instruction conducted in this century. He found, collapsing across data produced in the 500 studies, very strong associations between problem-solving performance and use of the four Polya strategies. (The technical details of this analysis are beyond the scope of this book and are not necessary to appreciate the findings in the investigation.) The greatest association identified by Hembree was between selecting a sound sequence of operations (i.e., planning) and problem-solving performance. The next greatest association was between understanding the problem and performance. Although much weaker, there was also a clear association between checking and problem-solving. One of the most fascinating outcomes of the Hembree (1992) analysis was that the impact of teaching the Polya strategies increased with increasing grade level. Although the relationship between teaching of the Polya approach and achievement was very modest at the middle elementary level, it increased during the middle school years and then increased greatly during the high school years. What we emphasize here, however, is that there is always benefit of teaching the four general strategies advocated by Polya.

Even so, general strategies are not enough. Students need to learn specific strategies for meeting the problem-solving demands put on them. For most of the remainder of this chapter, we present specific teaching strategies that increase students' problem-solving performance. Before doing that, however, we take up a brief discussion of the most important conceptual direction in mathematics education today, a position that we endorse for the most part—mathematics instruction that enhances understanding of mathematics.

TEACHING FOR UNDERSTANDING AS A TEACHING STRATEGY

Contemporary mathematics educators are extremely critical about how mathematics has been taught in the past. They are especially critical of memorization and drill of mathematics facts and procedures, arguing instead for instruction that emphasizes understanding of mathematics (National Council of Teachers of Mathematics, 1989, 1991). Such understanding includes knowing that mathematics is a way of representing and organizing real experiences. The person who understands mathematics knows why mathematics is important and why the concepts being learned are essential in modern life. The person who understands mathematics recognizes how math facts and procedures are related to one another and how mathematical knowledge relates to information already understood by the student. The person who understands mathematics is metacognitively sophisticated, knowing when, why, and where to apply the mathematical concepts and procedures they have learned.

The perspective that children should be taught to understand mathematics is, of course, consistent with Polya's approach to problem solving. Polya emphasizes understanding from the beginning to the end of problem solving, with students urged to understand a problem as completely as possible before attempting to devise a plan to solve it and then encouraged to review and reflect on the problem-solving process once a problem is solved. Teaching for understanding encompasses a number of teaching strategies, all of which are intended to increase student understanding of the problem-solving process and the mathematical concepts that students are learning.

Strategies for Teaching Mathematics [T]

The most important theoretical or philosophical perspective favoring teaching for understanding is exceptionally radical constructivism—the belief that knowledge is acquired best if discovered (see Moshman, 1982). This outlook has been translated into a number of specific teaching strategies by contemporary mathematics educators.

- Learning of mathematics is best when students are active problem solvers, required to self-regulate their own problem solving and learning of mathematics. Thus, *much of instruction should involve presenting problems to students to solve.* Although the teacher can and should provide support and input as needed, as much as possible students should be problem solving for themselves—discovering solutions to problems for themselves.

- Instruction should emphasize *how mathematics and mathematical operations relate to operations in the world.* For example, when the class of 25 divides a baker's dozen of cupcakes so that everyone and the teacher each have an equal share, there is an opportunity to relate the operation of addition to the real world (i.e., 25 kids + 1 teacher = 26 cupcake eaters). When the cupcakes are cut in half so that everyone has a piece, there is the opportunity to demonstrate that dividing 13 cupcakes between 26 people can be sensibly represented as 13/26, which is equal to 1/2, meaning that each cupcake should be cut into two pieces if there is to be enough to go around. School days and weeks are filled with opportunities for mathematical cognition, and the constructivist mathematics educator makes the most of these opportunities.

- Because *word problems* require students to map relationships between the world and mathematical symbols, they should be a part of problem-solving instruction at all grade levels. In making this recommendation, we also point out that recent research has suggested that even simple word problems are very difficult for preschool children (Levine, Jordan, & Huttenlocher, 1992), so that this recommendation may only make sense beginning with the elementary years.

- Mathematical situations can often be understood better if they are concretely represented with materials that can be manipulated. Thus, *use of manipulatives* is consistent with teaching for understanding. For example, presenting a row of 12 buttons, with three buttons then taken away, provides a concrete representation of 12 - 3 = 9.

- Teachers should *model problem solving*. As they do so, they should make obvious that there are alternative solutions to problems and that problem solving often is not straightforward, frequently involving false starts and errors that need to be corrected.

- As students attempt problems, teachers should *question* them about how they are going about the process and *pay attention to their answers*, since student answers are revealing about what the student understands and does not understand. The teacher can offer *support and elaborations as needed*, for example, pointing out how student thinking about specific problems is consistent with general mathematical principles being developed in the course. See Lampert (1990) for an example of outstanding teaching involving modeling, questioning, paying attention to answers, and elaborating on student responses.

- *Small group problem solving* should be encouraged. In small groups, students have an opportunity to experience diverse methods of problem solving, as different members of the group propose and experiment with alternative methods of solving problems presented to the group. Small group problem solving also makes clear that mathematics is a social and collaborative activity rather than something a person does in isolation (e.g., Schoenfeld, 1992). It must be recognized, however, that sometimes small group interactions can go awry in ways that undermine problem solving and student learning of mathematics. For example, high-ability students sometimes dominate interactions during problem solving (e.g., Dembo & McAuliffe, 1987). Students are often all too ready to go along with an errant solution offered by group members (e.g., Stacey, 1992). When groups are not gender-balanced, boys often dominate problem-solving interactions (e.g., Webb, 1984). Sometimes small grouping results in uncooperative interactions more than cooperative ones (e.g., Good, Grouws, Mason, Slavings, & Cramer, 1990; Mason & Good, 1990). More positively, Neil Davidson of the University of Maryland and his colleagues have put together a sourcebook of methods for stimulating high quality cooperative group interactions during learning of mathematics, a volume we strongly recommend to educators who want to incorporate cooperative learning methods into their mathematics instruction (Davidson & Worsham, 1992).

- Students should experience *many and diverse examples* of how the mathematical concepts and procedures they are learning can be used.

- Many of the examples should come from the everyday world, with much of *problem solving in everyday situations*. An especially exciting advance are instructional programs that stimulate solving of problems in context, with leadership in this area from the Cognition and Technology Group at Vanderbilt University (e.g., 1992; Van Haneghan, Barron, Young, Williams, Vye, & Bransford, 1992). This group has prepared a number of interactive videodisk programs presenting complex, open-ended problem, which students then attempt to solve. For example, in a recent videodisk, a young boy must prepare a dunking machine for an upcoming school fair operating within severe budgetary and time constraints. The 15-minute story presentation includes a great deal of information. Coming up with a budget involves a great deal of real-world problem solving and is very stimulating for students, especially since it is so tied to the kinds of mathematics problems that people face as they carry on their daily lives.

- Often, eliminating the need to attend to lower-order operations will foster understanding. Calculators can sometimes be used to do computations, freeing the children's minds to attend to higher-order information. For example, if the children are attempting to solve the higher-order problem of constructing a workable budget for a field trip, the addition and subtraction is not the focus of the problem-solving activity and can be handled easily with a calculator (e.g., Fey, 1990). In studies to date, use of calculators has improved children's problem solving and learning of mathematics (e.g., Szetela & Super, 1987; for a review, see Hembree & Dessart, 1986). *Technology should be used when its use increases student opportunities to attend to higher-order aspects of problem solving*.
- Students should be encouraged to understand that *problem solving* can be successful when they make efforts to understand *a problem*. In other words, children need to understand that their mathematics achievement is under their control, which should motivate problem solving (see Borkowski, Carr, Rellinger, & Pressley, 1990).
- Students need to be encouraged to *explain their problem solving*, which is important given consistent correlations between development of mathematical competence and opportunities to explain how to solve problems to others (see Webb, 1989). One of the reasons that cooperative learning makes so much sense is that it provides many opportunities for students to explain.

Evidence that Teaching for Understanding Works

Since the first edition of this text, substantial research has been carried out to determine whether and how teaching for understanding affects students' mathematics achievement. In particular, much of this work has been conducted at the primary level. In general, the research reviewing teaching for understanding has been very favorable. Paul Cobb and his colleagues (Cobb, Wood, Yackel, Nicholls, Wheatley, Trigatta, and Perlwitz, 1991) provided one of the best known of the studies validating teaching for mathematical understanding.

Cobb et al. (1991) compared performances in 10 grade-2 classrooms receiving arithmetic instruction designed to stimulate mathematical understanding and 8 classrooms receiving conventional instruction. Children in the teaching-for-understanding classrooms solved challenging problems continuously. The students were encouraged to reflect on their problem-solving activities and to construct knowledge about how to solve problems. The problem-solving generally took place in interactive, cooperative classroom groups, groups in which the role of the teacher was to provide support and gentle guidance in the direction of productive problem-solving, rather than to provide solutions or explicit instruction about how to solve problems. Students were encouraged to believe that success in mathematics was possible through individual and collective efforts and were encouraged to feel successful when they solved challenging problems.

Did teaching for understanding make a difference? It did on state-administered assessments of mathematics achievement, as well as on a researcher-produced test of mathematics achievement. Differences favoring the teaching-for-understanding students were especially notable on items requiring application of the concepts covered in the curriculum. These students also reported that they valued collaboration more than did students receiving traditional mathematics instruction. In short, there was strong support for instruction to increase student understanding of problem solving.

Even though support is growing for instruction that promotes student understanding, the claims made by the mathematics educator community about the advantages of such instruction sometimes are too strong. In particular, there are frequent claims in the mathematics educator fraternity that such instruction is the best way for students to learn mathematics. This claim is not defensible, however, for the comparison conditions in most of the relevant studies have been variations of conventional instruction—instruction assumed not to be very effective! Although instruction for understanding can beat conventional instruction, that is no guarantee it would fare well if pitted against other high-quality teaching. For example, we would like to see outstanding versions of instruction intended to stimulate "understanding" of mathematics compared to outstanding instruction based on direct explanations—that is, based on the approach most heavily favored in this book. Of course, we believe that good instruction that includes modeling, explanations, and scaffolded practice (i.e., high-quality direct explanation teaching) includes a great deal of student construction of knowledge, so that we would view such a comparison as between two types of constructivist methods (Moshman, 1982). Direct explanation begins with an explanation from a teacher as a starting point and is followed by student reflection and elaboration of the concept or process as a function of attempting to apply the procedure to new problems. Radical constructivists often fail to recognize the constructive activities that are stimulated by modeling and explanation (Harris & Pressley, 1991; Pressley, Harris, & Marks, 1992).

DIRECT EXPLANATIONS OF PROBLEM SOLVING AS A TEACHING STRATEGY

Throughout this book we favor teaching people how to do academic tasks by explaining how to do them, accompanied by modeling and followed by scaffolded practice. We favor heavy doses of explanation and modeling with respect to mathematics as well, fully aware as we do so that there are those in the mathematics educator fraternity who would disagree, believing that such explanations prevent children from discovering effective mathematics instruction on their own. The approach they favor is arranging conditions so that problem solution discovery is likely. One problem for us is that constructivist mathematics educators are generally vague about how to do that. A second problem, however, is that children's discovery of mathematical concepts is at best inefficient and commonly leads to misconceptions. Perhaps the most famous evidence of student self-discovered misconceptions was provided by vanLehn (1990), who documented over 100 subtraction strategies discovered by children that are in fact incorrect. For instance, sometimes students "borrow" from columns when it is not necessary, do not write zeroes in their answers (e.g., generating an answer of 2 9 instead of 209), or only subtract from some of the columns. Whenever we have related vanLehn's finding in classes enrolling elementary teachers, there are many nods of recognition—teachers know that students often make errant discoveries with respect to mathematical problem solving.

When done well, a teacher explanation provides students with a good start towards understanding a problem solving procedure. Students will certainly not "get it" from most initial explanations, but as they try problems on their own with help as needed from the teacher (i.e., teacher scaffolding), their understanding will sharpen and deepen. Their understanding will increase as they encounter new situations in which the problem solving approach can be used. Their knowledge of when and where to use the procedure will sharpen as they interact with other students, solving problems in cooperative learning situations. In short, our view is that the direct explanation approach is compatible with teaching for understanding, an integral part of classrooms in which students construct knowledge of mathematics by solving problems together and alone. Some direct explanations, however, are better than others.

Providing Principle-Based Direct Explanations [T]

Our view has always been that direct explanations should include a great deal of information about why the procedure being taught works (see Pressley, 1986). That is, explanations should be principled rather than simply step-by-step directions for doing something academic.

Michelle Perry (e.g., 1991) has recently provided evidence strongly supportive of our commitment to principle-based explanations.

Perry taught grade-4 and grade-5 students to solve problems of the form $4 + 6 + 9 = \_\_ + 9$. (In the absence of instruction, grade 4/5 children fail on such problems 90% of the time.) Perry varied the type of instruction provided to students. Some students received instruction that emphasized the step-by-step procedures for solving such problems:

> One way to solve a problem like this is to add up all the numbers on the left side of the problem (e.g., in the problem $4 + 6 + 9 = \_\_ + 9$, as the teacher used her hand to indicate $4 + 6 + 9$) and then subtract the number on the right side of the problem (pointing to the 9 on the right side of the equation).

Other students received instruction that emphasized the principle involved in solving such problems:

> The goal of a problem like this is to find a number that fits in the blank and makes both sides equal; that is, to make this side (pointing to the right side of the equation) equal to this side (pointing to the left side of the equation).

Still other students received instruction that included both procedural and principle information.

On a post-test covering addition problems similar to the ones used during instruction, Perry's procedure + principle students outperformed students taught only the procedures, who slightly outperformed students taught only the principle. On a transfer task, however, involving solution of multiplication problems of the form $2 \times 3 \times 4 = \_\_ \times 4$, there was a clear advantage for students who had been taught only the principle.

Perry's (1991) finding is complemented by other outcomes reported in studies of teaching advanced mathematics [e.g., college algebra, Reed (1989); problem-solving using calculators, Bibby (1992); statistics, Hong and O'Neil (1992)]. Researchers have consistently found that direct explanations emphasizing mathematical principles are more effective than direct explanations focussing on step-by-step procedures. This, of course, is strong evidence that direct explanations stimulating student understanding of mathematics is powerful instruction.

Providing Worked Examples [T]

One of the most efficient methods for learning about mathematics—and hence teaching it—is to provide worked examples. Most publishers know this, requiring textbook authors to include worked examples. In addition, many supplementary texts in mathematics are often only books of worked problems! Presenting students with worked problems and encouraging them to study worked problems is a time-tested approach that has been studied formally by researchers in the recent past.

One of the most important studies evaluating the role of examples in acquisition of problem solving was reported by Sweller and Cooper (1985). In their studies, grade-8 and -9 algebra students were either provided worked examples of problem types or practiced solving such problems on their own. The first finding was that it took subjects less time to process the worked problems than to work through the practice problems on their own—another confirmation of the direct explanation advantage over discovery with respect to efficiency in learning.

After presentation of practice problems, the participants in the study were presented identically structured test problems. The students who had been given the worked examples during practice solved these new problems more rapidly than did the students who had worked the practice problems on their own. Moreover, the students who had received worked examples made fewer errors on the test problems than did the practice control participants (see also Cooper & Sweller, 1987). However, these advantages with identically structured problems did not transfer to problems that were new in structure, even though they involved the same problem-solving operations as the practiced problems. That is, the procedural competence acquired from studying the worked examples did not generalize to new problem types in Sweller and Cooper (1985), something that has been noted in other investigations of short-term instruction as well (e.g., Eylon & Helfman, 1982; Reed, Dempster, & Ettinger, 1985).

When longer-term instruction involving presentation of worked-out examples has been studied, there has been evidence of long-term retention of skills, as well as acquisition of understandings about when the skills learned should be applied. To date, however, the effects of long-term advantages have only been studied with older students rather than with elementary- and middle-grade students (e.g., Zhu & Simon, 1987).

There are many subtle factors that can make a worked example more or less effective. Sweller (1989) warned that worked examples are effective only if the to-be-learned relationships are apparent without a lot of mental juggling—that is, in examples where the problem statement and the problem solution were in close proximity to one another. (When too much distance separates the problem statement and problem solution, or when the problem contains excessive explanation, students must divide their attention between the solution path and problem statement, increasing the difficulty in learning the approach to problem-solving represented in the problem.) In studies with high school and college students, it has been easy to demonstrate that the effectiveness of worked out examples depends on them being easy to understand (e.g., Tarmizi & Sweller, 1988; Ward & Sweller, 1990).

A type of research that has yet to be done is an evaluation of the effectiveness of worked out examples accompanied by direct explanations compared to either worked out examples or direct explanations alone. Our guess is that the combination of printed worked examples accompanied by oral direct explanations is a powerful combination. For the present, there is growing evidence that high-quality direct explanations, whether provided by a live teacher or in print, can have powerful effects on student acquisition of problem solving procedures and strategies.

THE VALUE OF PROVIDING PRACTICE AS A MATHEMATICS TEACHING STRATEGY

Many contemporary mathematics educators who identify with the perspectives endorsed by the National Council of Teachers of Mathematics do not seem to have a favorable view of student practice, in many ways equating it with rote drill and thus inconsistent with the development of understanding. There is much theory and a great deal of evidence, however, to make the case for practice as part of mathematics instruction.

Practice to Develop Knowledge of Math Facts [T]

An important insight in recent years is that when preschoolers and primary-grade students are asked to solve problems involving addition or subtraction, they are very strategic (e.g., Carpenter, Hiebert, & Moser, 1981; Carpenter & Moser, 1982). They use various counting strategies, including counting on their fingers, counting up from the larger number by the smaller number for simple addition, and counting down from the larger number by the smaller number for subtraction problems. Such strategies often produce correct answers. Every time that they do, there is the opportunity to learn that the problem in question is answered correctly by the solution obtained via the strategy—for example, that 3 + 2 = 5, since 5 was produced by putting up three fingers and then two more.

Siegler (e.g., 1989), in particular, argued that this is how knowledge of math facts (e.g., 3 + 2 = 5, 4 + 5 = 9, 7 - 2 = 5) develops. Excellent elementary schooling provides many repetitions of the facts, with students solving problems like 3 + 2 many times. Because the correct answer will be produced much more often than the incorrect answer, the strongest association between a problem and a single numerical answer is with the correct answer. Thus, although children sometimes make errors and solve 3 + 2 as equal to 4 or 6, because 5, the correct answer, is far more common, the association between 3 + 2 and 5 is much stronger than the association between 3 + 2 and either 4 or 6. Given that the evidence is strong that children acquire mathematics facts through associations, it makes a great deal of sense to provide extensive practice "solving" math fact problems.

What Siegler contends is that as students come to know math facts, they decreasingly rely on counting strategies in order to solve problems. The advantage of retrieving answers from long-term memory, rather than solving math-fact problems every time they are presented, is that the mind is freed up for other things. Thus, students can more readily complete complicated problems that rely on math-fact knowledge once the math facts are well known (e.g., Widaman, Geary, Cormier, & Little, 1989).

As we argue for such practice, it is also clear that many preschool and primary-grades children are not as strategic as they could be—they do not use counting strategies as much as they could (Geary & Brown, 1991). If Siegler is correct, failing to use strategies has long-term implications for the development of math fact knowledge. Thus we offer the following advice: *Preschoolers and primary-grades children who are not using counting strategies, including those involving concrete objects and manipulatives, should be taught to use such strategies.* We remember vividly our primary-grades teachers scolding students for using their fingers to solve addition fact problems. Instead, such addition with a ready concrete representation is to be embraced and encouraged, with students provided lots and lots of opportunities to practice using the counting strategies so that they can build up their knowledge of the math facts!!

In reading Siegler, some errantly conclude that knowledge of math facts is certain by the middle to later elementary grades. That is far from the case, with nontrivial proportions of middle school, high school, and college students not knowing their elementary addition, subtraction, multiplication, and division facts (Widaman, Little, Geary, & Cormier, 1992). Although we believe that such students should not be given steady diets of only math facts problems, it seems a good bet that practice would help, although it might require months and years of such practice to develop knowledge of the basic math facts (see Goldman, Mertz, & Pellegrino, 1989; Goldman, Pellegrino, & Mertz, 1988).

We emphasize in closing this discussion of Siegler's perspective on practice, that it applies to more than just addition and subtraction. There is clear evidence that knowledge of the multiplication facts also develops through practice, with counting strategy approaches to multiplication eventually giving way to knowledge of multiplication facts. Years of solving multiplication fact problems correctly increases the association between problems and their correct answers (e.g., the association between 4×5 and its answer, 20; Campbell & Graham, 1985).

Practice to Develop Automatic Recognition of Problem Types [T]

When a student is first presented a complicated type of problem, for example, a distance-time problem, a great deal of effort is expended figuring out a plan for solving the problem. A really good student goes about it in a Polya-esque fashion, understanding the problem (e.g., with drawings), planning a solution, carrying out the solution, and then checking and reflecting on the solution. With increasing practice, distance-time problems increasingly are recognized immediately for what they are—distance-time problems. That is, with increasing experience, the students develop a schema for distance-time problems.

Most of the mathematics word problems presented in textbooks have typical structures. For instance, Mayer (1981) analyzed beginning algebra texts and identified about 100 common problem types. Working through those problems as part of a course has an effect on long-term knowledge of problems. Schematic representations of typical problem types reside in the long-term memories of people who have done well in algebra. There is an important consequence of such schematic knowledge. Students who possess greater knowledge of problem schemata also are better able to solve such problems (e.g., Silver, 1985, 1987). That such schematic knowledge develops through practice with problems is another vote in favor of practice as part of mathematics teaching.

Practice to Develop Proceduralization of Complex Problem-Solving Procedures [T]

Whenever people learn to do a complex procedure, it starts out as a slowly executed sequence of moves. In fact, students are often taught a sequence of verbal directions to performance complex mathematics operations. For example, students can be taught to do division with two-digit divisors by being taught to (a) estimate, (b) divide, (c) multiply, (d) subtract and compare, (e) bring down one digit, and (f) repeat these operations. Although some mathematics educators might object to such teaching, we expect that it will continue.

The only way that such operations become quicker, and thus less effortful, is through practice. John Anderson of Carnegie-Mellon University has provided a theoretical framework for understanding such practice effects. According to Anderson's theory (e.g., Neves & Anderson, 1981), all procedural knowledge starts out as declarative knowledge (i.e., a verbalizable sequence of steps). When learners are first carrying out a new procedure, they are very conscious of each of the steps, perhaps even saying them aloud or at least verbalizing some of the steps. In addition, it is not unusual for there to be errors during this stage. With practice, errors become less frequent, however, and there is less and less need to verbalize overtly. Execution of the entire sequence becomes smoother until the strategy is no longer a sequence of declarative directions but one fluent procedure. The movement from declarative representation of a sequence of actions to a single procedure is known as *proceduralization*. Practice of complex procedures is essential if proceduralization is to occur.

Distributed Practice [T]

Many mathematics books have a lesson on some particular process followed by practice problems requiring application of the process. Although such lessons are consistent with the idea of practice as developed in this section, texts structured in this way do not make the most of practice, which at its best is *distributed*. If a given amount of study or practice time is distributed over several sessions, learning is greater than if the same amount of study or practice is massed into one session.

Distributed practice effects have been known for all of the 20th century, originally identified by Ebbinghaus (e.g., 1913) in his classic research on memory. The phenomenon has been demonstrated many times and across diverse materials and tasks, from basic verbal learning to acquisition of text content to motor learning (see Crowder, 1976; Dempster, 1988; Lee & Genovese, 1988). It has also been documented with children as young as preschoolers (Toppino, Kasserman, & Mracek, 1991). Educators, nonetheless, rarely seem to exploit distributed practice (Dempster, 1987, 1988).

In contrast to presenting a mass of problems of a particular type following a lesson on the problem type, practice problems could be distributed by providing a mix of problems after each lesson, some of which require the newly-taught operation and some of which require operations learned in previous lessons. Thus, if the author of a text wanted students to practice 50 addition-of-fractions problems, the problems could be presented all in one lesson; or 10 could be presented in the first lesson (with 40 problems of other types), 5 in each of the next 5 lessons (with 45 problems of other types in each lesson), and 3 in the next 5 lessons (with 47 problems of other types in each lesson). With the latter format, the students not only receive distributed practice but are also provided practice at identifying procedures associated with each problem. No such identification is required when practice is massed, with all practice problems requiring the same operation. Because being able to recognize when to apply a procedure is extremely important in mathematics, the distributed format makes much more sense. (See Shea and Morgan, 1979, for especially strong evidence that acquisition of complex procedures is improved by forcing students to practice a new procedure alternatively with other procedures.) Although we have seen some mathematics texts that distribute practice and require students to determine which operation to use (in particular, ones developed and published by mathematics educator, John Saxon; see Mathews, 1993), practice is massed in most mathematics texts.

Summary on Practice

Practice as conceived here is not drill. When students practice not-yet-known math facts, they are using strategies to solve math-fact problems, with problem-answer associations developing that transform a math-fact problem (such as 4 + 2 = ?) into a math fact (4 + 2 = 6). When students practice word problems, they are acquiring knowledge of the elements in such problems and the relationships between those elements (i.e., schematic knowledge of problem types). When students repeat complex sequences (e.g., long division), new higher-order procedures are created, replacing what was a verbally-directed step-by-step approach with a less effortful one. When practice is distributed by having students complete a variety of problems each day rather than a mass of practice problems representing the concept just taught, students must think about which procedure to apply to each problem, and thus, essential metacognitive knowledge about when and where to apply particular math procedures should develop. This type of practice is not mindless but mind-expanding!! Those mathematics educators who argue that practice does not increase understanding of mathematics do not understand the nature of practice at its best.

SPECIFIC STRATEGIES FOR INCREASING MATHEMATICAL PROBLEM-SOLVING ABILITY

Many specific strategies have been identified that are helpful at some point in children's mathematics education. In this section, we review some of the more salient ones that have been researched in recent years.

Instruction of the Part-Part-Whole Strategy [SSR]

Any number can be decomposed into parts (e.g., Resnick, 1983; Riley, Greeno, & Heller, 1983). Thus, 15 can be decomposed into a 10 and a 5. The number 9 can be decomposed into a 4 and a 5, or alternatively into three 3's, or thought of as 10 minus 1. For the child who does not know that 15 + 9 is 24, the problem can be solved easily as (10 + 5) + (10 - 1) = 10 + 10 + (5 - 1) = 10 + 10 + 4 = 24. Instruction of part-part-whole can increase children's understanding of basic arithmetic operations.

For adult readers who need a demonstration of the power of thinking of numbers in terms of their parts, try multiplying 27 X 38 in your head. After making such an attempt, reconstrue the problem as (20 + 7) X (30 + 8) and apply the associative principle (i.e., [a + b] X [c + d] = ac + ad + bc + bd) to compute the product of 27 and 38 in your head. With a little reflection, it will be obvious that thinking of numbers in terms of their parts is a powerful strategy for computation, a strategy that can be taught profitably beginning in the primary-grades years.

For example, Fischer (1990) taught kindergarten children the first seven whole numbers using a part-part-whole approach. Two kindergarten classes received 25 days (20 minutes a day) of part-part-whole instruction. The children receiving the part-part-whole curriculum also counted sets of objects, but in doing so they were required to create subsets (e.g., if counting 5 objects, to create 2 subsets). The exercises emphasized counting various combinations of subsets in order to establish that whole numbers can be decomposed into components and that however decomposed, the parts sum to the whole. The children were also required to verbalize and point corresponding numerals for both sets and the subsets. Two control condition classes experienced a curriculum based on counting, saying, and writing the first 7 whole numbers. Basically, children in these classrooms counted objects in sets, verbalized the totals and printed the corresponding numerals. There was no emphasis on identifying or creating subsets of the sets. There was an equal amount of instruction about the whole numbers from 1 to 7 in the experimental and control classrooms.

At the end of the instruction, students receiving part-part-whole instruction were better able to do word problems than control students. They were better able to understand and solve problems such as the following (Carpenter, 1985):

> Sam had 2 books. Mom gave him 4 more. Now how many books does Sam have?

> The cat has 9 kittens. Six are brown and the rest are white. How many white kittens are there?

It takes only a little thought to recognize that awareness of how parts combine to produce wholes could facilitate representation and solution of such problems.

There is also evidence that learning of the basic number facts can be facilitated by conceptualizing the instruction as part-part-whole instruction, by reconstruing new math facts in terms of known math facts [T]. In Thornton (1978) had grade 2 students (22 control, 22 strategy-instructed) learn basic addition and subtraction facts while grade 4 students (20 control, 23 strategy-instructed) learned multiplication and division facts. The study lasted 8 weeks. The teachers in the control classrooms followed the conventional curricula. The strategies groups were taught the addition and multiplication facts in a specific order, emphasizing the relation of harder facts to easier known ones so that new math fact problems can be reconstrued as consisting of known parts.

For addition facts, the order was: doubles (e.g., 5 + 5); doubles + 1 (e.g., 5 + 6); sharing numbers, which differ by two and can be related to doubles by subtracting one from the larger addend and adding one to the smaller addend (e.g., 6 + 8 can be reconstrued as [7 - 1] + [7 + 1] = 7 + 7 + [1-1] = 14); additions to 9, whose result is one less than adding 10 to a number (e.g., 9 + 5 can be reconstrued as [10 - 1] + 5 = 10 + [5 - 1] = 14); and finally the facts not covered by any other strategy (e.g., 2 + 5). To solve subtraction problems, strategy-trained students were encouraged to think of the related addition problem—and reconstrue the components of the subtraction problem into parts that can be easily computed.

At the grade-4 level, multiplication facts were presented in the following order: products of 2's (e.g., 2 x 8); products of 5's (e.g., 5 X 4); products of 9's (e.g., 9 X 7); squares (e.g., 4 X 4), and the facts not included in these categories. To solve new division problems, strategy-trained students were encouraged to relate problem to known multiplication facts.

The results in the Thornton (1978) study were very clear. Students acquired math facts more quickly and certainly when they were taught to use the strategy of relating new to-be-learned facts to known facts. In extending these results, others (e.g., Steinberg, 1985) have added some additional relationships, such as doubles ± 2: When adding two numbers that differ by 2, double the smaller and add 2 or double the larger and subtract 2 (e.g., 5 + 7 = [5 + 5] + 2 or [7 + 7] - 2).

Of course, there is nothing inconsistent between part-part-whole based instruction and practice of math facts, with a number of math educators explicitly recognizing the value of combining the two, albeit with math facts presented conceptually, before there is much emphasis on practice of them (e.g., Wood & Dunlap, 1982). This is a perspective that we find sensible. Understand a math problem and then practice doing it.

Increasing Teacher Knowledge of Elementary Mathematics [T]

Some teachers lack important mathematical understandings (Fennema & Franke, 1992)!! For example, many primary teachers do not have exhaustive understanding of the strategies that can be used to solve simple addition and subtraction problems, strategies such as part-part-whole (Carpenter, Fennema, Peterson, & Carey, 1988). It is difficult to imagine how people who do not understand such mathematical concepts would be able to teach them to students (Ball, 1988; Fennema & Franke, 1992; Stein, Baxter, & Leinhardt, 1990).

One important teacher strategy to enhance teaching of mathematics is to learn as much as possible about mathematics. It will make a difference in the classroom. For example, Carpenter, Fennema, Peterson, Chiang, and Loef (1989; Peterson, Carpenter, & Fennema, 1989) presented evidence that improving grade-1 teachers' knowledge of the mathematics taught in grade 1 does much to affect teaching and achievement. They provided a 1-month institute during which National Council of Teachers of Mathematics' perspectives on addition and subtraction were presented (e.g., how to reconceptualize addition and subtraction as problems of operating on parts and wholes; the informal knowledge of addition and subtraction grade-1 children bring to school; and different types of addition and subtraction problems, as outlined earlier in this chapter). When the teachers attending the institute returned to their classrooms, they were more likely to use word problems in their classrooms, an approach known to increase grade-1 students' understanding of mathematics, than were teachers who did not attend the sessions (i.e., control condition teachers). When they used word problems, institute teachers were more likely to discuss the problems with the class as a group, whereas control teachers assigned the problems to individual students. The institute teachers were also more aware than control teachers of what their students knew about mathematics, perhaps reflecting that they were monitoring their students' understanding as a guide in deciding what and how to teach. The institute teachers spent less time than control teachers rote-drilling students on addition and subtraction facts. In short, problem solving occurred more frequently and was more salient in the classrooms of the institute teachers than the control teachers. Various indicators of mathematics achievement collected at the end of the academic year, including the ability to solve word problems, favored the students in classrooms of institute teachers. Increasing teacher knowledge of mathematics should be a high priority as part of the reform of mathematics instruction in schools.

Encourage Parents to Help Students With Homework [T]

Parental assistance with homework improves achievement. An especially important point is that assignment of homework is not nearly as powerful a variable in improving student learning of mathematics as is parental assistance with homework (Hembree, 1992). One possibility is that when students complete problem-solving exercises with their parents, they are more likely to receive explicit instruction about the thought processes required to solve the problems than when they solve the problems independently. An alternative possibility is that when students work problems with parental assistance, they must explain their problem-solving explicitly to their parents: Explaining how one solves problems to another person is a powerful way to increase understanding of a problem-solving process (Webb, 1989).

Encourage Computer Experiences [T & SSR]

Although the effects are not large nor consistent, students in the middle-school grades (i.e., 7 and 8) seem to especially improve in problem solving if they experience instruction and practice in *computer programming*. Experiences with *instructional computer programs* aimed at improving particular mathematical competencies also seem to work (e.g., Edwards, 1992).

One particularly interesting direction is computer programs that permit student-teacher interaction and personalization of the computer experience for the student. For example, Anand and Ross (1987) reported that computer-assisted lessons on problem solving were more effective with elementary students if the problems were personalized for the students using the program. Thus, Joseph, a student in Mrs. Williams' room, received this problem in mid-December that included reference to his favorite type of candy bar:

> Joseph's teacher, Mrs. Williams, surprised him on December 15 when she presented Joseph with 3 Hershey Bars. Joseph cut each of them in one-half so that he could share the birthday gift with his friends. In all, how many pieces of Hershey Bars did Joseph have for his friends?

Such programs have high potential for scaffolding of instruction, with teachers able to provide feedback to students and present problems that are neither too easy nor too difficult. Our enthusiasm for this and other mathematics instructional programs is due in part to recent analyses documenting that computer-mediated mathematics instruction is cost-effective (i.e., effective in boosting performance and less expensive than other forms of instruction; e.g., Fletcher, Hawley, & Piele, 1990).

A final point about computers is that with the implementation of interactive computer networks into schools (e.g., Internet), many new possibilities for large-scale cooperative interactions develop (Scott, Cole, & Engel, 1992). Although there is insufficient research to make any clear claims about how such networks can affect problem solving, we encourage teachers to explore with their students these interactive nets, perhaps by taking on joint problem-solving ventures with schools in distant lands.

Encouraging Students to Watch Educational Programming Designed to Stimulate Mathematical Knowledge and Problem-Solving Skills [T]

Watching *Sesame Street* and *Electric Company* increases children's under-standing of important numeracy concepts (Comstock & Paik, 1991, Chapter 3). A recent addition to public television is *Square One*, which was designed specifically to stimulate positive attitudes and enthusiasm for mathematics in 8- to 12-year-olds. The program encourages devel-opment of problem-solving processes and presents important math-ematical content. Math is presented via enjoyable detective stories. Children who watch the program manifest a greater variety of problem-solving behaviors in reaction to math problems, offering solutions that are both more complete and sophisticated than the solutions proposed by same-age students who have not watched the program (Hall, Esty, & Fisch, 1990). Encouraging students to watch programming like *Square One* makes a great deal of sense.

Accelerated Instruction for Mathematically Gifted Children [T]

Accelerating mathematics instruction for gifted grade-school children can have positive effects many years later (e.g., Swiatek & Benbow, 1991), including affecting grades in college and the likelihood that students will elect advanced mathematics courses. Swiatek and Benbow found that young adults (approximately 23 years of age) who had participated in an accelerated mathematics program—one in which students progressed through algebra, plane and analytic geometry, and trigonometry in less than 14 months—were more likely to attend prestigious undergraduate institutions and pursue graduate studies than were similarly gifted students who did not participate in the accelerated program. It makes good sense to make certain that the best and the brightest mathematics students receive instruction that challenges them, that provides opportunities that less talented children would not benefit from.

Summary

One message in this section is to fill students' worlds with people who are knowledgeable about mathematics, are positive and excited about mathematics, and are helpful to students as they learn mathematics. The second overarching message is that there is a great deal of new technology with great potential for improving students' mathematical competence and understanding of problem solving. The effective mathematics educator will include such technology in their teaching strategies and teach students to coordinate use of technology such as calculators with other problem-solving strategies.

GOOD INFORMATION PROCESSING IN MATHEMATICS: A SUMMARY OF MODERN PERSPECTIVES

Polya definitely believed that excellent problem solvers know both general and specific problem-solving strategies, are aware of when and where to use the strategies they know (i.e., possess extensive metacognition about the strategies they know), use strategies in conjunction with knowledge of mathematics facts and concepts, and possess motivational beliefs that support problem-solving efforts (Polya, 1954a, 1954b, 1957, 1981; for an analysis, see Pressley, 1986, or Pressley with McCormick, 1995, Chapter 13). Important contemporary mathematics educators also argue that excellent problem solving is good information processing, involving interactions between strategies, metacognition, mathematical and world knowledge, and motivation (e.g., Schoenfeld, 1992).

This chapter addressed how to arrange education to stimulate effective problem solving that is good information processing. Consistent with the perspective represented throughout this book, we believe that the answer is years of high quality instruction, teaching that includes strategy instruction. There are many excellent teaching strategies that can be used in the service of developing such good information processing. In order to make the suggestions in this chapter more memorable, we organize them around three general themes.

A Problem-Solving Curriculum

Polya's assumption was that most of mathematics instruction should be directed at solving problems. The 4-phase strategy he proposed—based on understanding, planning, carrying out the problem-solving plan, and checking—can be applied to a variety of problems. It only works, however, if students possess knowledge about mathematics and the world that is needed to solve the problem. Thus, applying the Polya approach can help in solving a budgeting problem, but such a problem also requires extensive knowledge of how the to-be-budgeted resources relate to one another and the nature of cost trade-offs (e.g., labor hours to do a job manually versus the cost of a machine that does the same task). It also requires some proficiency in the four basic mathematical operations of addition, subtraction, multiplication, and division.

Consistent with Polya, contemporary mathematics educators believe in a problem-centered mathematics curriculum. Increasingly that means problems that are realistic in scope and interesting to students—for example, the complex problems presented via videodisk in the curriculum produced by Bransford and his colleagues. Even if a classroom is not equipped with a videodisk player, the school world permits plenty of opportunity for problem solving. We recently observed students figuring out how much a lunch ticket should cost in their school if the cafeteria is to break even, with the students appraising all of the costs of preparing lunch as part of determining the daily per student contribution required to keep the cafeteria at a break-even level. These students even figured in the federal and state lunch subsidies. The excellent mathematics educational environment is filled with meaningful problems.

The solving of such problems is part of an overall emphasis on understanding of mathematics, coming to know both how mathematical concepts relate to one another but also how mathematical ideas relate to the real world. Yes, there is practice in such classrooms, but practice is in the service of the development of additional mathematical insights and knowledge. Practice is not boring drill, but rather students honing skills that they recognize as important as they build knowledge through reflection, with this occurring in an instructional world emphasizing motivating mathematical problems.

Social Support of the Development of Mathematical Competence

A salient social object in mathematics instruction is the teacher, who models problem solving, explains it, questions students about their problem solving, listens to their responses, and scaffolds students' problem-solving efforts. In doing so, the teacher aims to develop both general and specific strategies in his or her students as well as important mathematical concepts. The teacher structures the world so that students have diverse experiences with important problem types and encourages students to reflect on these experiences in order for them to get the most out of their problem-solving efforts. The excellent mathematics teacher also encourages the development of healthy self-concepts in students, sending the message that students can problem solve and do things mathematical. The excellent mathematics teacher projects that students can succeed if they exert efforts toward understanding, planning, carrying out plans, and checking mathematical work. That is, the excellent mathematics teacher does much to ensure that students are motivated to learn mathematics and do things mathematical.

In excellent mathematics instructional environments, peers are also supportive of the development of math competencies. Cooperative learning opportunities are common in modern mathematics classrooms. In such classrooms, all students participate in peer modeling of problem solving, explaining how they are solving problems, listening to the problem-solving explanations of fellow students, questioning other students about their problem solving, and offering assistance to classmates as needed. In short, in excellent mathematics instructional environments, the students support the learning of mathematics in much the same way that the teacher does.

After the student leaves school, parents can be an important source of support and input. Students definitely benefit from parental assistance with homework.

Beyond the immediate social supports, the larger society can also support excellent mathematics instruction. This can occur at a number of levels. Publishers can produce excellent materials, including texts filled with easy-to-understand solved problems that convey the operations often used by good problem solvers as they encounter mathematics problems. Worked problems at their best provide clear explanations of why the solution steps are taken. The media can contribute programming that encourages the development of mathematical cognition, with the contributions of public television particularly noteworthy. Government can fund resources like the Internet and provide means for schools to participate in the advanced conversations that can occur across the country and throughout the world, so that students can collaborate with others, comparing notes about how to solve important problems. In short, there is a world of social resources that can support the development of mathematical cognition in students, from the classroom teacher to agemates half a world away to media executives sitting on Michigan Avenue.

Technological Support for the Development of Mathematical Competence

Modern technology provides the modern student with many means for providing pedagogically significant mathematical experiences that were not available to previous generations. Calculators, including ones with sophisticated graphing capabilities, are now available at affordable prices. Computers accompanied by powerful instructional software are increasingly common in schools. Interactive videos permit students the opportunity to explore and re-explore worlds that can be presented using this technology. In contrast to the vast wasteland that is much of television programming, there are some notable oases filled with opportunities for viewers to experience mind-expanding problem solving, such as *Square One*.

Beyond its pedagogical value, technology can eliminate some burdensome, low-level aspects of problem solving, allowing students to attend more to the higher-order aspects of problem solving. Both hand-held calculators and microcomputers are increasingly available for routine computations.

Final Comment

The excellent mathematics teacher teaches strategies, but just as important, employs the overarching strategy of aligning curriculum; teachers, peers, and parents; and technology in the service of promoting students' understanding of mathematics.

The theory is that years of such excellent instruction and years of practicing problem solving can produce students who are habitually excellent problem solvers, who recognize routine problems immediately and solve them easily, and who tackle challenging problems strategically through understanding, planning, and reflecting.

REFERENCES

Anand, P. D., & Ross, S. M. (1987). Using computer-assisted instruction to personalize arithmetic materials for elementary school children. *Journal of Educational Psychology, 79,* 74-78.

Ball, D. L. (1988). *Knowledge and reasoning in mathematical pedagogy: Examining what prospective teachers bring to teacher education.* Unpublished doctoral dissertation. Michigan State University.

Bibby, P. A. (1992). Mental models, instructions, and internalization. In Y. Rogers,

A. Rutherford, & P. A. Bibby (Eds.), *Models in the mind: Theory, perspective, and application* (pp. 153-172). London: Academic Press.

Borkowski, J. G., Carr, M., Rellinger, E. A., & Pressley, M. (1990). Self-regulated strategy use: Interdependence of metacognition, attributions, and self-esteem. In B. F. Jones (Ed.), *Dimensions of thinking: Review of research* (pp. 53-92). Hillsdale NJ: Erlbaum & Associates.

Campbell, J. I. D., & Graham, D. J. (1985). Mental multiplication skill: Structure, process, and acquisition. *Canadian Journal of Psychology, 39*, 338-366.

Cardelle-Elawar, M. (1990). Effects of feedback tailored to bilingual students' mathematics needs on verbal problem solving. *Elementary School Journal, 91*, 165-175.

Carpenter, T. P. (1985). Learning to add and subtract: An exercise in problem solving. In E. A. Silver (Ed.), *Teaching and learning mathematical problem solving: Multiple research perspectives* (pp. 17-40). Hillsdale NJ: Erlbaum & Associates.

Carpenter, T. P., Fennema, E., Peterson, P. L., & Carey, D. A. (1988). Teachers' pedagogical content knowledge of students' problem solving in elementary arithmetic. *Journal for Research in Mathematics Education, 19*, 385-401.

Carpenter, T. P., Fennema, E., Peterson, P. L., Chiang, C-P, & Loef, M. (1989). Using knowledge of children's mathematics thinking in classroom teaching: An experimental study. *American Educational Research Journal, 26*, 499-531.

Carpenter, T. P., Hiebert, J., & Moser, J. M. (1983). The effect of instruction on children's solutions of addition and subtraction word problems. *Educational Studies in Mathematics, 14*, 55-72.

Carpenter, T. P., & Moser, J. M. (1982). The development of addition and subtraction problem-solving skills. In T. P. Carpenter, J. M. Moser, & T. A. Romberg (Eds.), *Addition and subtraction: A cognitive perspective* (pp. 9-24). Hillsdale, NJ: Erlbaum & Associates.

Charles, R. I., & Lester, F. K., Jr. (1984). An evaluation of a process-oriented instructional program in mathematical problem solving in grades 5 and 7. *Journal for Research in Mathematics Education, 15*, 15-34.

Cobb, P., Wood, T., Yackel, E., Nicholls, J., Wheatley, G., Trigatti, B., & Perlwitz, M. (1991). Assessment of a problem centered second-grade mathematics project. *Journal for Research in Mathematics Education, 22*, 3-29.

Cognition and Technology Group at Vanderbilt (1992). The Jasper series as an example of anchored instruction: Theory, program description, and assessment data. *Educational Psychologist, 27*, 291-315.

Comstock, G., & Paik, H. (1991). *Television and the American child*. San Diego: Academic Press.

Cooper, G., & Sweller, J. (1987). Effects of schema acquisition and rule automation on mathematical problem-solving transfer. *Journal of Educational Psychology, 79*, 347-362.

Crowder, R. G. (1976). *Principles of learning and memory*. Hillsdale NJ: Erlbaum & Associates.

Davidson, N., & Worsham, T. (Eds.) (1992). *Enhancing thinking through cooperative learning*. New York: Teachers College Press.

Dembo, M. H., & McAuliffe, T. J. (1987). Effects of perceived ability and grade status on social interaction and influence on cooperative groups. *Journal of Educational Psychology, 79*, 415-423.

Dempster, F. N. (1987). Time and the production of classroom learning: Discerning implications from basic research. *Educational Psychologist, 22*, 1-21.

Dempster, F. N. (1988). The spacing effect: A case study in the failure to apply the results of psychological research. *American Psychologist, 43*, 627-34.

Ebbinghaus, H. (1913). *Memory*. New York: Teachers College.

Edwards, L. D. (1992). A comparison of children's learning in two interactive computer environments. *Journal of Mathematical Behavior, 11*, 73-81.

Eylon, B., & Helfman, J. (1982, February). *Analogical and deductive problem-solving in physics*. Paper presented at the annual meeting of the American Educational Research Association, New York.

Fennema, E., & Franke, M . L. (1992). Teachers' knowledge and its impact. In D. A. Grouws (Ed.), *Handbook of research on mathematics teaching and learning* (pp. 147-164). New York: Macmillan.

Fey, J. T. (1990). Quantity. In L. A. Steen (Ed.), *On the shoulders of giants: New approaches to numeracy* (pp. 61-94). Washington DC: National Academy Press.

Fischer, F. E. (1990). A part-part-whole curriculum for teaching number in the kindergarten. *Journal for Research in Mathematics*

Education, 21, 207-215.

Fletcher, J. D., Hawley, D. E., & Piele, P. K. (1990). Costs, effects, and utility of microcomputer assisted instruction in the classroom. *American Educational Research Journal*, 27, 783-806.

Geary, D. C., & Brown, S. C. (1991). Cognitive addition: Strategy choice and speed-of-processing differences in gifted, normal, and mathematically disabled children. *Developmental Psychology*, 27, 398-406.

Goldman, S. R., Mertz, D. L., & Pellegrino, J. W. (1989). Individual differences in extended practice functions and solution strategies for basic addition facts. *Journal of Educational Psychology*, 81, 481-496.

Goldman, S. R., Pellegrino, J. W., & Mertz, D. L. (1988). Extended practice of basic addition facts: Strategy changes in learning-disabled students. *Cognition and Instruction*, 5, 223-265.

Good, T. L., Grouws, D. A., Mason, D. A., Slavings, R. L., & Cramer, K. (1990). An observational study of small-group mathematics instruction in elementary school. *American Educational Research Journal*, 27, 755-782.

Hall, E. R., Esty, E. T., & Fisch, S. M. (1990). Television and children's problem-solving behavior: A synopsis of an evaluation of the effects of Square One TV. *Journal of Mathematical Behavior*, 9, 161-174.

Harris, K. R., & Pressley, M. (1991). The nature of cognitive strategy instruction: Interactive strategy construction. *Exceptional Children*, 57, 392-404.

Hembree, R. (1992). Experiments and relational studies in problem solving: A meta-analysis. *Journal for Research in Mathematics Education*, 23, 242-273.

Hembree, R., & Dessart, D. (1986). Effects of hand-held calculators in precollege mathematics education: A meta-analysis. *Journal for Research in Mathematics Education*, 17, 83-99.

Hong, E., & O'Neil, H. F. (1992). Instructional strategies to help learners build relevant mental models in inferential statistics. *Journal of Educational Psychology*, 84, 150-159.

Lampert, M. (1990). When the problem is not the question and the solution is not the answer: Mathematical knowing and teaching. *American Educational Research Journal*, 27, 29-64.

Lee, T. D., & Genovese, E. D. (1988). Distribution of practice in motor skill acquisition: Learning and performance effects reconsidered. *Research Quarterly for Exercise and Sport*, 59, 277-87.

Levine, S. C., Jordan, N. C., & Huttenlocher, J. (1992). Development of calculation abilities in young children. *Journal of Experimental Child Psychology*, 53, 72-103.

Mason, D. A., & Good, T. L. (1990). *The effects of two small-group models of active teaching and active learning on elementary school mathematics achievement* (Technical Report No. 478). Columbia MO: Center for Research in Social Behavior, University of Missouri.

Mathews, J. (1993). Psst, kid, wanna buy a... used math book? *Newsweek*, March 1 1993, 62-63.

Mayer, R. E. (1981). Frequency norms and structural analysis of algebra story problems into families, categories, and templates. *Instructional Science*, 10, 135-175.

Montague, M., & Bos, C. S. (1990). Cognitive and metacognitive characteristics of eighth grade students' mathematical problem solving. *Learning and Individual Differences*, 2, 371-388.

Moshman, D. (1982). Exogenous, endogenous, and dialectical constructivism. *Developmental Review*, 2, 372-384.

National Council of Teachers of Mathematics (1989). *Curriculum and evaluation standards for school mathematics*. Reston, VA: National Council of Teachers of Mathematics.

National Council of Teachers of Mathematics (1991). *Professional standards for teaching mathematics*. Reston, VA: National Council of Teachers of Mathematics.

Neves, D. M., & Anderson, J. R. (1981). Knowledge compilation: Mechanisms for the automatization of cognitive skills. In J. R. Anderson (Ed.), *Cognitive skills and their acquisition* (pp. 251-272). Hillsdale, NJ: Erlbaum.

Perry, M. (1991). Learning and transfer: Instructional conditions and conceptual change. *Cognitive Development*, 6, 449-468.

Peterson, P. L., Carpenter, T., & Fennema, E. (1989). Teachers' knowledge of students' knowledge in mathematics problem solving: Correlational and case analyses. *Journal of Educational Psychology*, 81, 558-569.

Polya, G. (1954a, 1954b). *Mathematics and plausible reasoning: (a) Induction and analogy in mathematics and (b) Patterns of plausible inference*. Princeton, NJ: Princeton University Press.

Polya, G. (1957). *How to solve it*. New York: Doubleday.

Polya, G. (1981). *Mathematical discovery* (combined paperback edition). New York: Wiley.

Pressley, M., Harris, K. R., & Marks, M. B. (1992). But good strategy instructors are constructivists! *Educational Psychology Review, 4,* 3-31.

Pressley, M., with McCormick, C. B. (1995). *Advanced educational psychology for educators, researchers, and policymakers.* New York: HarperCollins.

Reed, S. K. (1989). Constraints on the abstraction of solutions. *Journal of Educational Psychology, 81,* 532-540.

Reed, S. K., Dempster, A., & Ettinger, M. (1985). Usefulness of analogous solutions for solving algebra word problems. *Journal of Experimental Psychology: Learning, Memory, and Cognition, 11,* 106-125.

Resnick, L. B. (1983). A developmental theory of number understanding. In H. P. Ginsburg (Ed.), *The development of mathematical thinking* (pp. 109-151). New York: Academic.

Riley, M. S., Greeno, J. G., & Heller, J. I. (1983). Development of children's problem-solving ability in arithmetic. In H. P. Ginsburg (Ed.), *The development of mathematical thinking* (pp. 153-196). New York: Academic Press.

Schoenfeld, A. (1992). Learning to think mathematically: Problem solving, metacognition, and sense making in mathematics. In D. A. Grouws (Ed.), *Handbook of research on mathematics teaching and learning* (pp. 334-370). New York: Macmillan.

Scott, T., Cole, M., & Engel, M. (1992). Computers and education: A cultural constructivist perspective. In G. Grant (Ed.), *Review of Research in Education, 18* (pp. 191-251). Washington DC: American Educational Research Association.

Shea, J. B., & Morgan, R. L. (1979). Contextual interference effects on the acquisition, retention, and transfer of a motor skill. *Journal of Experimental Psychology: Human Learning and Memory, 5,* 179-187.

Siegler, R. S. (1989). Hazards of mental chronometry: An example from children's subtraction. *Journal of Educational Psychology, 81,* 497-506.

Silver, E. (Ed.) (1985). *Teaching and learning mathematical problem solving.* Hillsdale, NJ: Erlbaum & Associates.

Silver, E. A. (1987). Foundations of cognitive theory and research for mathematics problem solving instruction. In A. Schoenfeld (Ed.), *Cognitive science and mathematics education* (pp. 33-60). Hillsdale NJ: Erlbaum &

Associates.

Stacey, K. (1992). Mathematical problem solving in groups: Are two heads better than one? *Journal of Mathematical Behavior, 11,* 261-275.

Stein, M. K., Baxter, J. A., & Leinhardt, G. (1990). Subject-matter knowledge and elementary instruction: A case from functions and graphing. *American Educational Research Journal, 27,* 639-663.

Steinberg, R. M. (1985). Instruction on derived facts strategies in addition and subtraction. *Journal for Research in Mathematics Education, 12,* 165-178.

Sweller, J. (1989). Cognitive technology: Some procedures for facilitating learning and problem solving in mathematics and science. *Journal of Educational Psychology, 81,* 457-466.

Sweller, J., & Cooper, G. A. (1985). The use of worked examples as a substitute for problem solving in learning algebra. *Cognition and Instruction, 2,* 59-89.

Swiatek, M. A., & Benbow, C. P. (1991). A 10-year longitudinal follow-up of participants in a fast-paced mathematics course. *Journal for Research in Mathematics Education, 22,* 138-150.

Szetela, W., & Super, D. (1987). Calculation and instruction in problem solving in grade seven. *Journal for Research in Mathematics Education, 18,* 215-229.

Tarmizi, R. A., & Sweller, J. (1988). Guidance during mathematical problem solving. *Journal of Educational Psychology, 80,* 424-436.

Thornton, C. A. (1978). Emphasizing thinking strategies in basic fact instruction. *Journal for Research in Mathematics Education, 9,* 214-227.

Toppino, T. C., Kasserman, J. E., & Mracek, W. A. (1991). The effect of spacing repetitions on the recognition memory of young children and adults. *Journal of Experimental Child Psychology, 51,* 123-138.

Van Haneghan, J., Barron, L., Young, M., Williams, S., Vye, N., & Bransford, J. (1992). The Jasper series: An experiment with new ways to enhance mathematical thinking. In D. F. Halpern (Ed.), *Enhancing thinking skills in the sciences and mathematics* (pp. 15-38). Hillsdale NJ: Erlbaum & Associates.

vanLehn, K. (1990). *Mind bugs: The origins of procedural misconceptions.* Cambridge MA: MIT Press.

Ward, M., & Sweller, J. (1990). Structuring effective worked examples. *Cognition and*

Instruction, 7, 1-39.

Webb, N. M. (1984). Sex differences in interaction and achievement in cooperative small groups. *Journal of Educational Psychology, 76,* 33-34.

Webb, N. M. (1989). Peer interaction and learning in small groups. *International Journal of Educational Research, 13,* 21-39.

Widaman, K. F., Geary, D. C., Cormier, P., & Little, T. D. (1989). A componential model for mental addition. *Journal of Experimental Psychology: Learning, Memory, and Cognition, 15,* 898-919.

Widaman, K. F., Little, T. D., Geary, D. C., & Cormier, P. (1992). Individual differences in the development of skill in mental addition: Internal and external validation of chronometric methods. *Learning and Individual Differences, 4,* 167-214.

Wood, M., & Dunlap, W. P. (1982). Applications of drill and practice. *Focus on Learning Problems in Mathematics, 4,* 15-21.

Zhu, X., & Simon, H. A. (1987). Learning mathematics from examples and by doing. *Cognition and Instruction, 4,* 137-166.

CHAPTER 8

Science

Approximately 30 years ago, inspired by the launching of Sputnik, the United States acknowledged that it faced a crisis in science education. There was general concern that students did not possess the adequate scientific knowledge or skills needed to cope in an increasingly technological society (Staver & Small, 1990; Yager & Penick, 1987). In an attempt to resolve this crisis, science curricula were modified to emphasize hands-on activities and process skills that emulated those carried out by real scientists (McIntosh & Zeidler, 1988). However, despite pouring over $1.5 billion into science education, many educators and researchers would agree that students' knowledge and performance in science-related domains remains in a state of crisis.

Simply allocating greater educational funds does little to promote a society that truly understands and appreciates science (Yager & Penick, 1987). One important aspect of reform involves reevaluating how science is presented to students. Science classrooms need to include instructional methods that have been empirically demonstrated to enhance students' acquisition of both scientific knowledge and skills. The primary purpose of this chapter is to review learning techniques (both teacher-directed ones and student-directed ones) that promote such scientific understanding.

The Current Status of Science Instruction

Science is a mainstay of the elementary school curriculum. Yet many students demonstrate inadequate understanding of basic science concepts, even after extensive classroom instruction (e.g., Hackling & Treagust, 1984). Furthermore, many students do not view themselves as future scientists, believing that science is, "something to be done by someone other than themselves" (Welch, Klopfer, Aikenhead, & Robinson, 1981). This pessimistic attitude is translated into the low numbers of young people obtaining college degrees in the sciences (Fitzgerald, 1990; National Center for Education Statistics, 1990). Why are more students not motivated to pursue advanced studies and careers in the sciences? While there does not appear to be one answer to this question, improving teaching materials and instructional techniques should increase some students' motivation for the sciences.

In one survey of over 12,000 science teachers, between 90% and 95% of the participants reported relying on texts for curriculum and instruction (Yager, 1983; cited in Lloyd, 1990). Unfortunately, most commercial texts do little to facilitate student learning. Science textbooks increase in content orientation with increasing grade in school. For example, in grade three students are introduced to approximately 300 new terms and concepts per text, with there being over 3000 terms and symbols in a tenth-grade text (Woodward & Noell, 1991). Furthermore, these texts are filled with activities and questions that foster only superficial learning, exercises promoting retention and comprehension more than higher order thinking skills, including application, analysis, synthesis, and evaluation (Bloom, Englehart, Hill, Furst, & Krathwohl, 1956).

Many commercial texts also fail to elaborate or embellish critical concepts. The texts for low ability students in particular often contain few examples and little elaboration. This is particularly disturbing since these students are unlikely to possess relevant background knowledge or activate the knowledge they do possess when reading (Schneider & Pressley, 1989).

Science classroom interactions, like textbook learning, can also fail to stimulate higher-level thinking processes (Mergendoller, Marchman, Mitman, & Packer, 1988; Sanford, 1987; Tobin, 1987; Welch et al., 1981). Even though students are presented with challenging questions (ones that require application, analysis, synthesis, or evaluation of science concepts), answers often are "worked out" for the whole class (e.g., by the teacher completing a problem-solving exercise on the blackboard), with students being responsible for copying out procedures and correct answers. Students often fail to understand that worked examples are intended to demonstrate the logic or conceptual underpinnings of a problem rather than promote simple memorization or repetition (rewriting). When students are asked challenging questions, they are often provided with a variety of "safety-nets" that ensure task success (Sanford, 1987). For example, greater credit may be assigned to the completion of memory and procedural components than to higher-level ones so that a passing grade is not dependent on successfully completing the latter. While many teachers believe in the merits of inquiry and discovery methods in science, they also believe that they are constrained to teaching "facts" or "the basics" (Yager & Penick, 1987; Welch et al., 1981). In fact, many teachers view science as the mastery of previously stipulated words and terms, a belief that is internalized by students who come to understand science as static, consisting of a collection of unrelated facts and ideas (Songer & Linn, 1991).

Fortunately, there is a brighter side to science education. There are numerous instances of exemplary science instruction (e.g., Tobin & Fraser, 1990), classrooms in which teachers implement many of the learning strategies and teaching approaches described in this chapter and throughout this text. Students in these classrooms are actively engaged in the scientific process.

Because students who are successful lifelong learners possess a repertoire of effective learning strategies and study techniques, and because not every strategy is suitable for all students across all contexts, it is recommended that educators use a variety of the science strategies in their classrooms. In addition, because success in science is usually contingent on possessing effective reading, writing and study skills, the science strategies contained in this chapter should be taught in conjunction with other effective learning strategies reviewed in this book (Pressley, 1995).

Inquiry-Based Learning [T]

During the 1960s and 1970s, science programs underwent massive restructuring to develop what has been referred to as the "new science curriculum." Although never clearly defined, this curriculum was associated with inquiry methods and process objectives where learning *how* to do science was valued over the acquisition of factual information (Ajewole, 1991; Shymansky, Kyle & Alport, 1983). In a meta-analysis of 81 empirical studies involving more than 40,000 kindergarten through 12th-grade students, Shymansky and colleagues (Shymansky et al., 1983; Shymansky, Hedges, & Woodworth, 1990) concluded that the new science curriculum enhanced students' science achievement and process skills, as well as positively affecting their attitudes about science relative to traditional textbook-based programs.

Science Laboratories [T]

Laboratory activities where students design investigations and predict outcomes have been part of science instruction since the 19th century. Ideally, laboratory activities should promote deep understanding, creative thinking, and problem-solving (Hofstein & Lunetta, 1982). They should provide students with opportunities for experimentation, prediction, and independent interpretation rather than be "cookbook exercises" during which students follow a prescribed set of procedures (Fuhrman, Lunetta, Novick, 1982; Lederman & O'Malley, 1990). In this sense, they are the epitome of "learning by doing."

There is substantial evidence that having learners carry out laboratory exercises facilitates their learning to the same extent or better than having them participate in didactic instruction (that is, receiving instruction consisting of teacher descriptions or demonstrations e.g., Coulter, 1966; Glasson, 1989; Hall & McCurdy, 1990; Russell & Chiappetta, 1981; Saunders & Dickinson, 1979; Yager, Engen, & Snider, 1969). For example, Shymansky and Penick (1981) assigned students to either educator-structured or student-structured laboratories. In educator-structured laboratories, the teacher purposefully and directly instructed students about what to do, when to do it, and how to do it. Students were provided with explicit feedback about the correctness of their performances. In student-directed laboratories, learners were not provided with explicit instructions or feedback from the teacher. Instead, the teacher's primary role was that of facilitator, challenging students with thought provoking questions about their activities.

Elementary and junior high school students who participated in educator-structured laboratories were more dependent on their teachers and peers than were students who participated in student-directed ones. They tended to view science as a collection of correct answers that were beyond their interpretation. Learners exposed to student-directed instruction, on the other hand, believed that science was an evolution of knowledge and explanations and that scientists were creative individuals who used the scientific process to solve problems—attributes which they viewed themselves as possessing (Shymansky & Penick, 1981).

Participating in laboratory activities appears to be especially beneficial for lower-ability or disadvantaged students (Bredderman, 1985; Odubunmi & Balogun, 1991; Shymanksy & Penick, 1981). For instance, when working with grade eight students, Odubunmi and Balogun (1991) found that average and low ability students (as determined by performance scores on a number of standardized tests measuring verbal reasoning, numerical ability and spatial skill) benefited from participating in interactive laboratory-based science classes relative to their peers whose teachers relied on the lecture method. Students of above average ability performed similarly well regardless of whether they attended laboratory-based or lecture-based classrooms. Bredderman (1985) drew similar conclusions in his review of over 50 research studies evaluating the effectiveness of laboratory-based versus lecture-based science classrooms—elementary school students who were of low economic status, low ability or who resided in inner city and rural areas acquired more content knowledge and process skills following laboratory activities than traditional science instruction.

Cooperative Learning [T & SSR]

Cooperative learning involves having students work in small heterogeneous groups of four to six individuals (Watson, 1991). Johnson and Johnson (1990a) outlined five critical elements of effective cooperative learning:

1. positive interdependence (individuals' successes are dependent on group success),
2. face-to-face positive interaction (e.g., sharing, understanding, and developing group knowledge),
3. individual accountability,
4. interpersonal and small-group skills (e.g., communication, conflict-resolution, decision-making), and
5. reflection (both of academic and social processes).

In general, cooperative learning improves students' academic performances, social behaviors, and attitudes toward school (Davidson & Shearn, 1990; Gabbert, Johnson, & Johnson, 1986; Sharon, 1990; Watson, 1991). Having students work together encourages them to conceptualize materials in new ways by generating examples and translating new information into familiar terms (Bargh & Schul, 1980). In addition, collaborative efforts expose learners to new and alternative points of view. Verbal interactions facilitate the correct use of scientific vocabulary (Champagne, Klopfer & Gunstone, 1982). By working together, learners can share and discover information that is beyond their existing knowledge.

Cooperative learning procedures can be especially beneficial in the science classroom (e.g., Humphreys, Johnson & Johnson, 1982; Okebukola, 1985; Okebukola & Ogunniyi, 1984; Watson, 1991). For example, Okebukola (1985) assigned over 600 eighth-grade students to either cooperative or individual learning groups. There were two formats for the cooperative learning conditions: pure cooperation and competitive-cooperation.

In the pure cooperative learning group, students completed tasks together and helped each other as much as possible. Students were encouraged to seek help and guidance from each other versus their teacher. There were no comparisons made between the learning performances of students working within the same group or between students belonging to different groups. Teachers provided praise and rewards to groups as a whole rather than to individual students.

In the competitive-cooperative learning group, students worked cooperatively on tasks within their group, with each group competing against the other groups in the class for first place. Students were taught to rely on each other for guidance and for clarification. Teachers provided praise and rewards to groups, with the achievements of one group being recognized over those of other groups.

In the individual learning group, each student competed with his or her peers for class position. Students did not complete tasks together nor were they encouraged to seek assistance from each other. Rather, students were instructed to consult their teacher for clarification, with teachers praising the individual efforts of students rather than groups.

Following instruction, all students completed a multiple-choice test to assess their learning (with half the examination items testing recall and recognition and the remaining items testing application, synthesis and evaluation). Students assigned to the cooperative learning conditions (pure cooperative and competitive cooperative) outperformed their peers assigned to the individual study condition, with competitive-cooperative students demonstrating greater learning than pure cooperative students (Okebukola, 1985).

In order for high quality collaboration to occur, each element of the cooperative process must be explicitly taught, modelled and practiced—a process that requires substantial instructional time. Students must also possess relevant prior knowledge to participate in group discussion effectively (Basili & Sanford, 1991). When students lack critical background knowledge, the teacher plays an especially important role. Exemplary science teachers constantly monitor students' understanding, clarify their misunderstandings and prompt relevant extensions of their thinking (Tobin & Fraser, 1990). That is, they scaffold student learning in cooperative groups.

Computers and Related Technology [T]

Computers and related technology present science teachers with unique opportunities for advanced instruction, often combining elements of science laboratories and cooperative learning procedures. The microcomputer allows students to explore, experiment, and manipulate scientific concepts and realities (Simmons, 1991). In contrast to the laboratory experiment which typically permits only one trial (most often by the classroom teacher), the computer allows for multiple repetitions of experiments and for student redesign of experiments. The computer also provides the opportunity for experimentation that otherwise would be either too expensive, too dangerous or too costly to carry out in the classroom (Simmons, 1991). Finally, the computer is more time efficient than having students complete traditional laboratories (e.g., Choi & Gennaro, 1987).

Unfortunately, there have been relatively few studies investigating the effectiveness of computer-based instruction (with many of these studies failing to use stringent experimental procedures, or being restricted to very select groups of students). Furthermore, the available findings are mixed, with some studies reporting that computer-based instruction is no more effective than traditional laboratory exercises (e.g., Beichner, 1990; Choi & Gennaro, 1987; Morrell, 1992). Merely having students complete computer exercises (as in the case of science laboratories) does not guarantee that students will demonstrate sophisticated problem solving or other scientific skills (Nachmias & Linn, 1987; Slack & Stewart, 1990). The following is a review of a few computer programs that enjoy some empirical support (for an extended review of such computer software, see Simmons, 1991).

Microcomputer-Based Laboratories and Graphing Packages [T]

As part of a five-year project to improve science education, the Microcomputer-Based Lab (otherwise known as MBL) at the Technical Education Research Centers developed software to assist students in experimental data collection and analyses (Mokros & Tinker, 1987). The software is designed to be used in conjunction with an actual experiment. Specifically, the computer is interfaced with probes that measure physical phenomena (e.g., temperature, light, force, sound). As the experiment progresses, students are provided with immediate feedback about the phenomena in the form of an evolving graph. The students are expected to make predictions about the future shape of the graph and to clarify any discrepancies between their predictions and the graph.

For example, the software package *Heat and Temperature* graphs the evaporation of water and alcohol. One temperature probe is placed in water for approximately 20 seconds and the other in alcohol. When the probes are removed, the liquids on the probes evaporate. The computer records provide immediate feedback to the students about the temperatures of the probes (Krajcik, 1991).

Microcomputer-based laboratory experiences not only increase student comprehension of science materials and graphing skills, but also student confidence in their knowledge and skill (e.g., Brasell, 1987; Linn & Songer, 1991; Mokros, & Tinker, 1987). For instance, after completing a five-day unit during which learners constructed graphs representing the motion of a toy car and their own movements, grade six students demonstrated a firm understanding of distance and velocity graphs and could successfully match written descriptions to graphs (Mokros & Tinker, 1987). Furthermore, students were very confident in their interpretations of these graphs. Consider what happened when one teacher tried to pass off to the students an incorrect interpretation of a graph:

> The girls made a velocity graph of a cart that was speeding up, and correctly demonstrated a positive slope. As they completed their work sheet questions, the teacher told them their graph was wrong. "No, it's not," replied one of the girls, "see how it gets faster, that's why the graph keeps going up." "It should be level," said the teacher. "No, it shouldn't!" insisted the girls. "Level would mean that it is going the same speed." The teacher shrugged and walked off. "We got it right," said one of the girls, and the others nodded knowingly.
> (Mokros & Tinker, 1987, p. 374)

Microcomputer Simulations of Microworlds [T]

Interactive microcomputer models provide students with the opportunity to safely and efficiently view scientific models that are difficult to observe firsthand. Often, scientific models can be simplified in microworlds by omitting superfluous details or by speeding up or slowing down time (Krajcik, 1991).

White and Horwitz (1988) had grade-six students participate in one of two classroom structures. In the first, students completed activities on the computer software package *Thinker Tools* as part of a two-month unit addressing Newtonian physics. In the latter, students received the standard curriculum which did not include computer time. As part of the computer program, simplified microworlds (e.g., one where friction and gravity did not affect the behavior of objects) were initially presented to students so that they could acquire basic understanding of

Newtonian principles, with these microworlds increasing in complexity over time.

At the end of the unit, all students completed a pen-and-paper test measuring their understanding of Newtonian mechanics as applied to "real-world" problems. Students who interacted with the microworld program consistently outperformed their peers who received standard instruction. More impressively, on selected test items, the grade-six students performed equally as well or better than a group of high school physics students who also received standard instruction (e.g., when asked about the trajectory of a ball that has been kicked off the edge of a cliff, the majority of 6th-graders responded correctly whereas the majority of high school students responded incorrectly).

Videodisks [T]

Videodisks combine picture, animation, graphics and computer-based instruction, allowing students to witness reactions that would be otherwise be too expensive, hazardous or time consuming to observe. For instance, with videodisks students can safely view the noxious reaction between liquid bromine and aluminum foil or the reaction between sodium and water. Unfortunately, research is not yet available investigating the effectiveness of videodisk technology with elementary school students, or for that matter, with any other level student. Given that videodisk technology provides students with experiences similar to microcomputer laboratories and simulations (e.g., visual representation of phenomena, repetition, immediate and corrective feedback), we are cautiously optimistic about the efficacy of this technology.

Concept Maps [T & SSR]

Concept maps, otherwise referred to as semantic maps or entailment meshes (Johnson, Pittleman, & Hiemlich, 1986 and Pask, 1975; cited in Schmid & Telaro, 1990), are essentially diagrams where hierarchical relationships between ideas or "concepts" are expressed vertically and interrelations between concepts are expressed horizontally (Schmid & Telaro, 1990). Concepts are often isolated by circles and are arranged with the most general ideas listed at the top of the page and more specific and less inclusive concepts listed below these. Concepts are connected by lines which are labelled with "linking words" that describe how the concepts are related to each other. Two or more concepts that are semantically linked (are related by meaning) are referred to as a proposition. In its simplest form, a concept map would consist of two linked concepts. For example the statements, "sky is blue" or "grass is a plant" contain the concepts "sky", "blue", "grass" and "green", and the link, "is" (Novak & Gowin, 1984). Learning occurs when students create and recognize new propositions.

Novak and his colleagues (e.g., Novak, 1976; Novak & Gowin, 1984;

Novak, Gowin, & Johansen, 1983) advocate the use of concept maps in the science classroom. Prior to concept map instruction, however, students must be able to identify concepts, recognizing that although basic definitions of concepts will be the same across individuals, each person's definition will be unique (i.e., each person will think of something a little different when provided concepts like "dog" and "cat" based on their prior experiences). Students must also learn to identify linking words and be given opportunities to use them to combine concepts and form propositions. Once students demonstrate an understanding for concepts and links, they are ready for map instruction.

While there is no one way to teach students about concept maps, Novak and Gowin (1984) and others (e.g., Malone & Dekkers, 1984) have provided some general guidelines for instruction (see Table 1.) First a stand-alone topic (e.g., genetics, atomic theory) must be identified. Students are then required to generate concepts for this topic (perhaps by brainstorming or reading selected text). Ideally, no more than 20 concepts should be identified for any one topic.

Students must then rank the concepts in order of their importance or generality. Ranking may be done individually, in small groups, or as a class (Because it is unlikely that group consensus will be reached with respect to concept ordering, teachers should take this opportunity to reinforce the idea that there are multiple ways to conceptualize concepts). Students may also be provided with ranking aids such as the scoring procedure outlined in Figure 8-1 (Malone & Dekkers, 1984).

Concepts are then physically arranged in a hierarchical order (Novak and Gowan recommend using paper rectangles that can be moved easily), with linking words used to join concepts first vertically and then horizontally. Finally, students are encouraged to reconstruct

---

Table 8-1
Directions for Constructing Concept Maps

1. Identify a stand-alone topic.

2. Generate no more than 20 concepts for topic.

3. Rank concepts in order of importance or generality.

4. Physically arrange concepts in hierarchical order.

5. Edit concepts maps to ensure symmetry and accuracy between concepts.

Adapted from Malone and Dekkers (1984) and Novick and Gowan (1984)

Figure 8-1
Ranking aid used for concept map ordering.

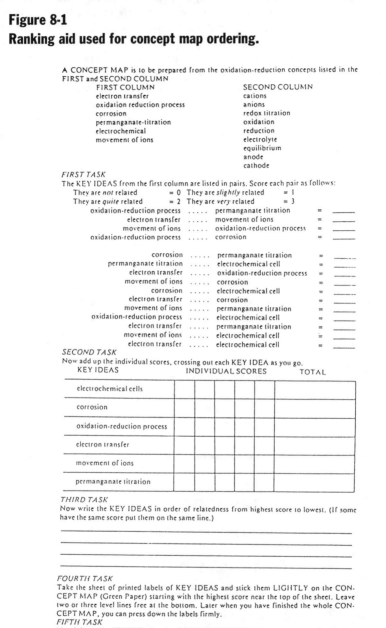

A CONCEPT MAP is to be prepared from the oxidation-reduction concepts listed in the FIRST and SECOND COLUMN

FIRST COLUMN	SECOND COLUMN
electron transfer	cations
oxidation reduction process	anions
corrosion	redox titration
permanganate-titration	oxidation
electrochemical	reduction
movement of ions	electrolyte
	equilibrium
	anode
	cathode

FIRST TASK
The KEY IDEAS from the first column are listed in pairs. Score each pair as follows:
They are *not* related   = 0   They are *slightly* related   = 1
They are *quite* related   = 2   They are *very* related   = 3

oxidation-reduction process ..... permanganate titration	=	_____
electron transfer ..... movement of ions	=	_____
movement of ions ..... oxidation-reduction process	=	_____
oxidation-reduction process ..... corrosion	=	_____
corrosion ..... permanganate titration	=	_____
permanganate titration ..... electrochemical cell	=	_____
electron transfer ..... oxidation-reduction process	=	_____
movement of ions ..... corrosion	=	_____
corrosion ..... electrochemical cell	=	_____
electron transfer ..... corrosion	=	_____
movement of ions ..... permanganate titration	=	_____
oxidation-reduction process ..... electrochemical cell	=	_____
electron transfer ..... permanganate titration	=	_____
movement of ions ..... electrochemical cell	=	_____
electron transfer ..... electrochemical cell	=	_____

SECOND TASK
Now add up the individual scores, crossing out each KEY IDEA as you go.

KEY IDEAS	INDIVIDUAL SCORES						TOTAL
electrochemical cells							
corrosion							
oxidation-reduction process							
electron transfer							
movement of ions							
permanganate titration							

THIRD TASK
Now write the KEY IDEAS in order of relatedness from highest score to lowest. (If some have the same score put them on the same line.)

_____

_____

_____

FOURTH TASK
Take the sheet of printed labels of KEY IDEAS and stick them LIGHTLY on the CON-CEPT MAP (Green Paper) starting with the highest score near the top of the sheet. Leave two or three level lines free at the bottom. Later when you have finished the whole CON-CEPT MAP, you can press down the labels firmly.
FIFTH TASK
Now join up the KEY IDEAS and write SENTENCE WORD(s) on each connecting line between the KEY IDEAS. Try to cross link as much as possible.
SIXTH TASK
GO BACK TO THE TOP OF THE PAGE. THE SECOND COLUMN on the map using your sheet of printed labels. TRY and place all these as the most important ones on the higher levels and others on the lower levels. Then try to join all the key ideas up with SEN-TENCE LINES. (Remember to put SENTENCE WORDS on each line!).
YOU HAVE NOW COMPLETED YOUR MAP

Taken from Malone and Dekkers (1984) .

their maps to establish better symmetry and accuracy between concept clusters, a practice that most students are reluctant to complete but one that is essential if they are to maintain complete and accurate maps over the course of a unit.

There is substantial evidence supporting the effectiveness of instructing students to use concept maps for science instruction (e.g., Jegede, Alaiyemola & Okebukola, 1990; Okebukola, 1990; Okebukola & Jegede, 1988; Pankratius, 1990; Soyibo, 1991;). This evidence is especially strong for low-ability students (probably because these students are unlikely to use their prior knowledge to elaborate and organize new concepts unless instructed to do so; e.g., Schmid & Telaro, 1990; Stensvold & Wilson, 1990). Willerman and Mac Harg (1991) found that eighth-grade students who received concept map instruction demonstrated greater learning of the physical and chemical properties of compounds (as measured by an end-of-unit multiple choice test) than their peers who received standard instruction for the unit. Ideally, concept map training should occur over a sustained interval (Pankratius, 1990; also see Stensvold & Wilson, 1990, for an example of where insufficient instructional time minimized concept-map learning gains), with some students being able to acquire mapping skills in about two weeks (Schmid & Telaro, 1990; Willerman & Mac Harg, 1991).

There are several characteristics of concept maps that make them an attractive learning strategy. Concept mapping may reduce students' anxieties about science (Jegede et al., 1990). Concept maps allow individualized learning, as scientific concepts can be accurately represented by more than one hierarchy. Concept maps can be used as formative and summative evaluation tools (see Novak and Gowin,1984, and Malone and Dekkers, 1984, for examples of scoring procedures that can be used to grade students' concepts maps). Students can use concept maps to organize text, lecture and laboratory materials across several content areas (Novak & Gowin, 1984). Finally, concept maps are cost-effective—they require no materials over those commonly found in school.

Overcoming Students' Inaccurate Science Beliefs [T & SSR]

A number of effective teaching techniques and learning strategies that enhance elementary school students' knowledge and understanding of science content have been reviewed here. Collectively, these strategies enhance learning because they require learners to activate relevant prior knowledge when studying information, seek out interrelations between new concepts, and make meaningful connections between new information and old concepts. However, learners often possess ideas about the world that clash with scientific viewpoints. Generally, these inaccurate beliefs are pervasive, resistant to change under normal classroom instruction, and often impede the acquisition of science concepts (e.g., Roth, 1990). For example, prior to reading a passage about photosynthesis, one student expressed the following beliefs about how plants obtain food:

> Food (for plants) can be sun, rain, light, bugs, oxygen, soil, and even other dead plants. Also warmness or coldness. All plants need at least three or four of these foods. Plus minerals (Roth, 1990, p. 145).

After reading the science passage, the student continued to express these beliefs in combination with those written in the textbook. The student responded in the following manner when asked about plants and food:

> Whew, from lots of places! From the soil for one, from the minerals and water, and from the air from oxygen. The sunlight for the sun, and it would change chemicals to sugars. It sort of makes its own food and gets food from the ground. And from the air (p. 145).

Even when students answer conventional tests and standardized assessments correctly following instruction, their errant preconceptions may endure (Arnaudin & Mintzes, 1985), largely because of multiple sources of support for errant beliefs. For example, students can acquire errant knowledge from their conversations with peers and elders, watching television, reading, or everyday experiences. Some misconceptions may even be perpetuated by teachers and textbooks when they do not help students differentiate between scientific concepts and everyday experiences (Barrass, 1984). More positively, we review here three ways to overcome errant scientific beliefs.

Conceptual conflict plus accommodation [T]

Many science educators believe that the learning process consists of *assimilation*, incorporating new information with existing knowledge, and *accommodation*, restructuring and reorganizing existing knowledge on the basis of new information (e.g., Hewson & Hewson, 1982; Posner, Strike, Hewson & Gertzog, 1982). Of the two, accommodation is the more difficult to stimulate, but it is necessary for students if they are to replace misconceptions with scientific beliefs. Posner et al. (1982) argue that for accommodation to occur, learners must express some dissatisfaction with their existing beliefs and must be provided with an intelligible and plausible alternative that is clearly superior to their existing beliefs. In other words, educators need to create circumstances that convince students to abandon their inaccurate beliefs in favor of scientific ones.

Nussbaum and Novick advocate explicitly creating conceptual conflict in the classroom. Students should be made aware of their existing misconceptions to motivate their acquisition of scientific concepts. Specifically they should be exposed to something that requires them to acknowledge and rationalize their existing beliefs. Students are then provided with a discrepant experience which cannot be explained by their erroneous beliefs. Finally, the educator must support students' search for scientifically accepted concepts. That is, teachers must assist students in restructuring their old understandings and comparing their new understanding with their old ones (Krajcik, 1991; see Figure 8-2 for a model of conceptual change).

Nussbaum and Novak (1982) have had some success in changing 6th-, 7th-, and 8th grade students' faulty beliefs about particle theory and gases by using conceptual conflict. Many students possess misconceptions about gas particles including the belief that substances like air, bacteria and oxygen exist between them. These statements underlie another inaccurate belief that matter is continuous when in fact only empty spaces exist between gas particles (Novick & Nussbaum, 1978; Lee, Eichinger, Anderson, Berkheimer, Blakeslee; 1989). Students were shown a demonstration in which air was sucked from a flask with a hand pump. In order to promote students' awareness of their existing beliefs, they were instructed to draw "before and after pictures" of the flask (see Figure 8-3 for examples of students' drawings), with the instructor selecting several of these drawings as well as the scientifically

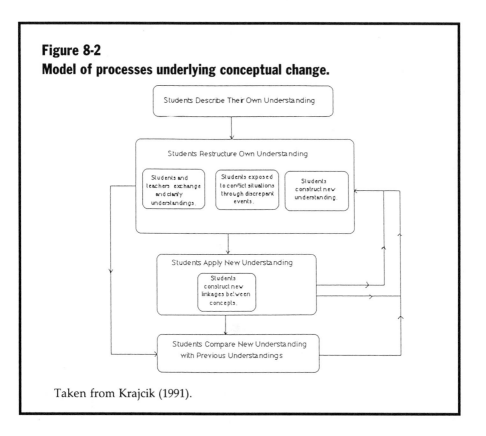

Figure 8-2
Model of processes underlying conceptual change.

Taken from Krajcik (1991).

Figure 8-3
Students' before and after drawings of gaseous particles of air being removed from a flask.

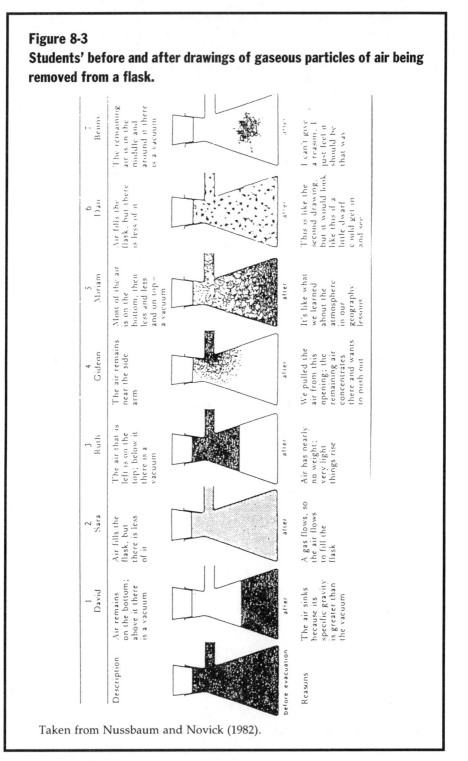

Taken from Nussbaum and Novick (1982).

correct empty-space model for class discussion.

A discrepant event was then introduced. Equal amounts of oxygen and water were compressed in syringes. Students were asked to reflect why it was possible to compress the oxygen syringe but not the water one (i.e., What special properties do gases have that liquids and solids do not?). Students then attempted to use their drawings to explain the compression of air. The instructor's task was to help students realize that, despite the strangeness of the idea, the empty space theory was the only model that could explain both the evacuation of air from the flask and the compression of air in the syringe.

Unfortunately, the accommodation model suggested by Novak and Nussbaum can only be cautiously recommended. To date, support for the model is in the form of enthusiastic reports from teachers who have used the approach. Although these reports are encouraging, they are not sufficient to establish program effectiveness or to warrant large-scale classroom implementation (Pressley, Woloshyn, Lysynchuk, Martin, Wood, & Willoughby, 1990). Instead, teachers should initially use this approach on a small-scale basis, carefully monitoring students' reactions.

Analogies [T]

Analogical thinking is a common characteristic shared by many scientists (Glynn, 1991). For instance, Kepler used a clock analogy to describe planetary motion, while Campbell argued that particles of kinetic gases behave similar to billiard balls (Pressley, 1995). A good analogy defines similarities between a new concept and a familiar one in order to make the new concept more meaningful. Educators can also use analogies to explain scientific concepts to novice scientists (Brown, 1992; Clement, Brown, Camp, Kudukey, Minstrell, Palmer, Schultz, Schimabukuro, Steinberg & Veneman, 1987; Stavy, 1991), with some case study support for analogies at the elementary school level (e.g., Joshua & Dupin, 1987). For example, the concept of a glacier may be better understood if an analogy is made to a river of ice.

There are at least four limitations associated with using analogies in the classroom, however. First, a great deal of care and effort are needed when searching for analogies, as many analogies that appear intuitive to instructors do not appear so to students (Clement et al., 1987). Second, students must understand the analogue situation for the analogy to work. When students do not possess adequate knowledge about the analogy or possess inaccurate information about it, they are likely to develop misconceptions about the target concept (see Gentner & Gentner, 1993 for an example where college students possessed inaccurate beliefs about a water flow which fostered misconceptions about the electrical flow the analogy was intended to clarify). Third, the type of analogy used influences students' thinking about a target concept. Dupin and Joshua (1989) observed that high school students possessed different thoughts about electricity following analogy training based on heat flow versus on a mechanical train. Fourth, the use of a single analogy may be incomplete, misleading or insufficient to focus students' attention on critical information.

More optimistically, simply warning learners about the limitations of an analogy may be sufficient to improve their learning (Glynn, 1991). Highlighting the limitations of an analogy may also focus students' attention to the unique features of the target concept (Pressley with McCormick, 1995). The use of multiple analogies may reduce some of the obstacles associated with single analogies. Multiple analogies may be more convincing to students, highlighting different attributes of the target concept and providing them with insights that a single analogy cannot (Pressley with McCormick, 1995).

Elaborative interrogation [T & SSR]

There is evidence that elaborative interrogation (see Chapter 9 of this volume) facilitates students' learning of content consistent with prior knowledge as well as content clashing with it (for a review see Pressley, Wood, Woloshyn, Martin, King, & Menke, 1992). Basically, elaborative interrogation requires learners to use their background knowledge to make supportive inferences and elaborations about new information by answering a "why" question (i.e., Why is that fact true?).

In recent studies, Woloshyn and her colleagues (Woloshyn, Paivio & Pressley, 1994; Woloshyn & Stockley, in press) demonstrated that instructing grade-six and grade-seven students to answer why questions facilitated their learning of science facts. The training instructions provided to students were simple and brief. Students were taught to use relevant prior knowledge from their classes, readings, and everyday experiences to answer why scientific statements were true. Students were told that there was no right or wrong answer and that they should generate as many reasons as possible for each statement. The following are examples of statements used in these studies:

Maple keys and milkweed pods are fruits. (Statement consistent with most students' prior knowledge).

The larger an animal is, the more oxygen it needs to live. (Statement consistent with most students' prior knowledge).

The light of the sun is made of every color including blue and violet. (Statement inconsistent with most students' prior knowledge).

Not all plants have roots. (Statement inconsistent with most students' prior knowledge).

Instructing students to answer why questions enhanced their learning of the science facts (as measured by recall and recognition tests) relative to when they were instructed to read for understanding or to select their own method of study, with the learning gains maintained up to six months following the training session.

Elaborative interrogation is an especially promising learning strategy for helping students overcome their inaccurate science beliefs since it can be easily implemented in the classroom. Teachers merely need to instruct students to use their relevant prior knowledge to answer why a given statement is true when they study science materials. One limitation associated with this strategy, however, is that students must possess relevant prior knowledge about to-be-learned concepts (see Woloshyn, Wood, & Willoughby, 1994, for a review of the importance of prior knowledge when using elaborative interrogation).

CONCLUDING COMMENT

Teachers should "experiment" with the strategies presented here, combining and integrating approaches whenever appropriate. Teachers can also continue to read about effective science strategies in journals such as *The Journal of Research in Science Teaching* (*JRST*). The development of new approaches for overcoming student misconceptions is an especially active area of research now, with new ideas about how to do so frequently covered in *JRST*.

REFERENCES

Ajewole, G.A. (1991). Effects of discovery and expository instructional methods on the attitude of students in biology. *Journal of Research in Science Teaching, 28*, 401-409.

Arnaudin, M.W., & Mintzes, J.J. (1985). Students' alternative conceptions of the human circulatory system: A cross-age study. *Science Education, 69*, 721-733.

Bargh, J.A., & Schul, Y. (1980). On the cognitive benefits of teaching. *Journal of Educational Psychology, 72*, 593-604.

Barrass, R. (1984). Some misconceptions and misunderstandings perpetuated by teachers and textbooks of biology. *Journal of Biological Education, 18*, 201-206.

Basili, P.A., & Sanford, J.P. (1991). Conceptual change strategies and cooperative group work in chemistry. *Journal of Research in Science Teaching, 28*, 293-304.

Beichner, R.J. (1990). The effect of simultaneous motion presentation and graph generation in a kinematics lab. *Journal of Research in Science Teaching, 27*, 803-815.

Bloom, B.S., Englehart, M.D., Hill, W.K., Furst, E.J., & Krathwohl, D.R. (1956). *Taxonomy of educational objectives, Handbook I: Cognitive Domain.* New York: McKay.

Brasell, H. (1987). The effect of real-time laboratory graphing on learning graphic representations of distance and velocity. *Journal of Research in Science Teaching, 24*, 385-395.

Bredderman, T. (1985). Laboratory programs for elementary school science: A meta-analysis of effects on learning. *Science Education, 69*, 577-591.

Brown, D.E. (1992). Using examples and analogies to remediate misconceptions in physics: Factors influencing conceptual change. *Journal of Research in Science Teaching, 29,* 17-34.

Champagne, A.B., Klopfer, L.E., & Gunstone, R.F. (1982). Cognitive research and the design of science instruction. *Educational Psychologist, 17,* 31-53.

Choi, B.S., & Gennaro, E. (1987). The effectiveness of using computer simulated experiments on junior high students' understanding of the volume displacement concept. *Journal of Research in Science Teaching, 24,* 539-552.

Clement, J., Brown, D.E., Camp, C. Kudukey, J., Minstrill, J., Palmer, D., Schultz, K., Shimaburkuro, J., Steinberg, M., & Veneman, V. (1987). Overcoming students' misconceptions in physics: The role of anchoring intuitions and analogical validity. In J. Novak (Ed.), *Proceedings of the Second International Seminar: Misconceptions and Educational Strategies in Science and Mathematics, Vol. III,* Cornell University, Ithaca, NY.

Coulter, J.C. (1966). The effectiveness of inductive laboratory, inductive demonstration, and deductive laboratory in biology. *Journal of Research in Science Teaching, 4,* 185-186.

Davidson, N., & Shearn, E. (1990). Use of small group teaching and cognitive development instruction in a mathematical course for prospective elementary school teachers. In M. Brubacher, R. Payne, and K. Rickett (Eds.), *Perspectives on small group learning.* (pp. 309-327). Oakville, Ontario: Rubicon Publishing Incorporated.

Dupin, J.J., & Joshua, S. (1989) Analogies and "modelling analogies" in teaching: Some examples in basic electricity. *Science Education, 73,* 207-224.

Fitzgerald, S.H. (1990). Responding to national concerns: A university/secondary school/business partnership in mathematics and science education. *School Science and Mathematics, 90,* 629-636.

Fuhrman, M., Lunetta, V.N., & Novick, S. (1982). Do secondary school laboratory texts reflect the goals of the "new" science curricula? *Journal of Chemical Education, 59,* 563-565.

Gabbert, B., Johnson, D., & Johnson, R. (1986). Cooperative learning, group-to-individual transfer, process gain, and the acquisition of cognitive reasoning strategies. *The Journal of Psychology, 120,* 265-278.

Gentner, D., & Gentner, D. (1983). Flowing waters or teeming crowds: Mental models of electricity. In D. Gentner and A. Stevens (Eds.), *Mental models* (pp. 101-129). Hillsdale, NJ: Erlbaum & Associates.

Glasson, G.E. (1989). The effects of hands-on and teacher demonstration laboratory methods on science achievements in relation to reasoning ability and prior knowledge. *Journal of Research in Science Teaching, 26,* 121-131.

Glynn, S.M. (1991). Explaining science concepts: A teaching-with-analogies model. In S.M. Glynn, R.H. Yeany, & B.K. Britton (Eds.), *The psychology of learning science* (pp. 219-240). Hillsdale NJ: Erlbaum & Associates.

Hackling, M.W., & Treagust, D. (1984). Research data necessary for meaningful review of grade ten high school genetics curricula. *Journal of Research in Science Teaching, 21,* 197-209.

Hall, D.A., & McCurdy, D.W. (1990). A comparison of a biological sciences curriculum study (BSCS) laboratory and a traditional laboratory on student achievement at two private liberal arts colleges. *Journal of Research in Science Teaching, 27,* 625-636.

Hewson, P.W., & Hewson, M.G., (1984). The role of conceptual conflict in conceptual change and the design of science instruction. *Instructional Science, 13,* 1-13.

Hofstein, A. & Lunetta, V.N. (1982). The role of the laboratory in science teaching: Neglected aspects of research. *Review of Educational Research, 52,* 201-217.

Humphreys, B., Johnston, R.T., & Johnson, D.W. (1982). Effects of cooperative, competitive, and individualistic learning on students' achievement in science class. *Journal of Research in Science Teaching, 19,* 351-356.

Hynd, C.R., & Alvermann, D.E. (1986). The role of refutation text in overcoming difficulty with science concepts. *Journal of Reading, 29,* 440-446.

Jegede, O.J., Alaiyemola, F.F., & Okebukola, P.A.O. (1990). The effect of concept mapping on students' anxiety and achievement in biology. *Journal of Research in Science Teaching, 27,* 951-960.

Johnson, D., & Johnson, R. (1990a). What is cooperative learning? In M. Brubacher, R. Payne, and K. Rickett (Eds.), *Perspectives on small group learning.* (pp. 68-80). Oakville, Ontario: Rubicon Publishing Incorporated.

Joshua, S., & Dupin, J.J. (1987). Taking into account student conceptions in instructional strategy: An example in physics. *Cognition and Instruction*, 4, 117-135.

Krajcik, J.S. (1991). Developing students' understanding of chemical concepts. In S.M. Glynn, R.H. Yeany, & B.K. Britton (Eds.), *The psychology of learning science* (pp. 117-147). Hillsdale NJ: Erlbaum & Associates.

Lederman, N.G., & O'Malley, M. (1990). Students' perceptions of tentativeness in science: Development, use, and sources of change. *Science Education*, 74, 225-239.

Lee, O., Eichinger, D.C., Anderson, C.W., Berkheimer, G.D., & Blakeslee, T.D. (1989). *Changing middle school students' conceptions of matter and molecules.* Paper presented at the Annual Meeting of the American Educational Research Association (AERA), San Francisco, CA.

Linn, M.C., & Songer, N.B. (1991). Teaching thermodynamics to middle school students: What are appropriate cognitive demands? *Journal of Research in Science Teaching*, 28, 885-918.

Lloyd, C.V. (1990). The elaborations of concepts in three biology textbooks: Facilitating student learning. *Journal of Research in Science Teaching*, 27, 1019-1032.

Malone, J., & Dekkers, J. (1984). The concept map as an aid to instruction in science and mathematics. *School Science and Mathematics*, 84, 220-231.

Mastropieri, M.A., & Scruggs, T.E. (1991). *Teaching students ways to remember: Strategies for remembering mnemonically.* Cambridge, MA: Brookline Books.

McIntosh, W.J., & Zeidler, D.L. (1988). Teachers' conceptions of the contemporary goals in science education. *Journal of Research in Science Teaching*, 25, 93-102.

Mergendoller, J.R., Marchman, V.A., Mitman, A.L., & Packer, M.J. (1988). Task demands and accountability in middle-grade science classes. *The Elementary School Journal*, 88, 251-265.

Mokros, J.R., Tinker, R.F. (1987). The impact of microcomputer-based labs on children's ability to interpret graphs. *Journal of Research in Science Teaching*, 24, 369-383.

Morrell, P.D. (1992). The effects of computer assisted instruction on student achievement in high school biology. *School, Science and Mathematics*, 92, 177-181.

Nachmias, R., & Linn, M.C. (1987). Evaluations of science laboratory data: The role of computer-presented information. *Journal of Research in Science Teaching*, 24, 491-506.

National Center for Education Statistics (1990). *Who majors in science? College graduates in science, engineering, or mathematics from the high school class of 1980.* Washington, DC: U.S. Department of Education.

Novak, J.D. (1976). Understanding the learning process and effectiveness of teaching methods in the classroom, laboratory, and field. *Science Education*, 60, 493-512.

Novak, J.D., & Gowin, B. (1984). *Learning how to learn.* Cambridge University Press: Cambridge.

Novak, J.D., Gowin, B., & Johansen, G.T. (1983). The use of concept mapping and knowledge vee mapping with junior high school science students. *Science Education*, 67, 625-645.

Novick, S., & Nussbaum, J. (1978). Junior high school pupils' understanding of the particulate nature of matter: An interview study. *Science Education*, 62, 273-281.

Nussbaum, J., & Novick, S. (1982). Alternative frameworks, conceptual conflict and accommodation: Toward a principled teaching strategy. *Instructional Science*, 11, 183-200.

Odubunmi, O., & Balogun, T.A. (1991). The effect of laboratory and lecture teaching methods of cognitive achievement in integrated science. *Journal of Research in Science Teaching*, 28, 213-224.

Okebukola, P.A. (1985). The relative effectiveness of cooperative and competitive interaction techniques in strengthening students' performance in science classes. *Science Education*, 69, 501-509.

Okebukola, P.A. (1990). Attaining meaningful learning of concepts in genetics and ecology: An examination of the potency of the concept-mapping technique. *Journal of Research in Science Teaching*, 27, 493-504.

Okebukola, P.A., & Jegede, O.J. (1988). Cognitive preference and learning mode as determinants of meaningful learning through concept mapping. *Science Education*, 72, 489-500.

Okebukola, P.A., & Ogunniyi, M.B. (1984). Cooperative, competitive, and individualistic interaction patterns - effects on students' achievements and acquisition of practical skills. *Journal of Research in Science Teaching*, 21, 875-884.

Pankratius, W.J. (1990). Building an organized knowledge base: Concept mapping and achievement in secondary school physics. *Journal of Research in Science Teaching*, 27, 315-333.

Posner, G.J., Strike, K.A., Hewson, P.W., & Gertzog, W.A. (1982). Accommodation of a scientific conception: Toward a theory of conceptual change. *Science Education, 66,* 211-217.

Pressley, M., with McCormick, C.B. (1995). Science. *Advanced educational psychology for educators, researchers and policy makers.* New York: Harper Collins.

Pressley, M., Woloshyn, V. Lysynchuk, L.M., Martin, V., Wood, E., & Willoughby, T. (1990). Cognitive strategy instruction: The important issues and how to address them. *Educational Psychology Review, 2,* 1-58.

Pressley, M., Wood, E., Woloshyn, V., Martin, V., King, A., & Menke, D. (1992). Encouraging mindful use of prior knowledge: Attempting to construct explanatory answers facilitates learning. *Educational Psychologist, 27,* 91-109.

Roth, K.J. (1990). Developing meaningful conceptual understanding in science. In B.F. Jones and L. Idol (Eds.), *Dimensions of thinking and cognitive instruction.* Hillsdale, NJ: Lawrence Erlbaum Associates.

Russell, J.M., & Chiappetta, E.L. (1981). The effects of a problem solving strategy on the achievement of earth science students. *Journal of Research in Science Teaching, 18,* 295-301.

Sanford, J.P. (1987). Management of science classroom tasks and effects on students' learning opportunities. *Journal of Research in Science Teaching, 24,* 249-265.

Saunders, W.L. & Dickinson, D.H. (1979). A comparison of community college students' achievement and attitude change in a lecture-only and lecture-laboratory approach to general education biological science courses. *Journal of Research in Science Teaching, 16,* 459-464.

Schmid, R.F., & Telaro, G. (1990). Concept mapping as an instructional strategy for high school biology. *Journal of Educational Research, 84,* 78-85.

Schneider, W., & Pressley, M. (1989). *Memory development between 2 and 20.* New York: Springer-Verlag.

Sharon, S. (1990). The group investigation approach of cooperative learning: Theoretical foundations. in M. Brubacher, R. Payne, and K. Rickett (Eds.), *Perspectives on small group learning* (pp. 168-184). Oakville, Ontario: Rubicon Publishing Inc.

Shymansky, J.A., Hedges, L.V., & Woodworth, G. (1990). A reassessment of the effects of inquiry-based science curricula of the 60's on student performance. *Journal of Research in Science Teaching, 27,* 127-144.

Shymansky, J.A., Kyle, W.C., & Alport, J.M.

(1983). The effects of new science curricula on student performance. *Journal of Research in Science Teaching, 20,* 387-404.

Shymansky, J.A., & Penick, J.E. (1981). Teacher behavior does make a difference in hands-on science classrooms. *School Science and Mathematics, 81,* 412-422.

Simmons, P.E. (1991). Learning science in software microworlds. In S.M. Glynn, R.H. Yeany, & B.K. Britton (Eds.), *The psychology of learning science* (pp. 241-256). Hillsdale, NJ: Erlbaum & Associates.

Slack, S.J., & Stewart, J. (1990). High school students' problem-solving performance on realistic genetics problems. *Journal of Research in Science Teaching, 27,* 55-67.

Songer, N.B., & Linn, M.C. (1991). How do students' views of science influence knowledge integration? *Journal of Research in Science Teaching, 28,* 761-784.

Soyibo, K. (1991). Impacts of concept and vee mappings and three modes of class interaction on students' performance in genetics. *Journal of Educational Research, 33,* 113-120.

Staver, J.R., & Small, L. (1990). Toward a clearer representation of the crisis in science education. *Journal of Research in Science Teaching, 27,* 79-89.

Stensvold, M.S., & Wilson, J.T. (1990). The interaction of verbal ability with concept mapping in learning from a chemistry laboratory activity. *Science Education, 74,* 473-480.

Tobin, K. (1987). Forces which shape the implemented curriculum in high school science and mathematics. *Teaching and Teacher Education, 3,* 287-298.

Tobin, K., & Fraser, B.J. (1990) What does it mean to be an exemplary science teacher? *Journal of Research in Science Teaching, 27,* 3-25.

Ward, M., & Sweller, J. (1990). Structuring effective worked examples. *Cognition and Instruction, 7,* 1-39.

Watson, S.B. (1991). Cooperative learning and group educational modules: Effects on cognitive achievement of high school biology students. *Journal of Research in Science Teaching, 28,* 141-146.

Welch, W.W., Klopfer, L.E., Aikenhead, G.S., & Robinson, J.T. (1981). *Science Education, 65,* 33-50.

White, B.Y., & Horwitz, P. (1988). Computer microworlds and conceptual change: A new approach to science education. In P. Ransden (Ed.), *Improving learning: New perspectives* (pp. 69-80). London: Kegan

Paul.

Willerman, M., & Mac Harg, R.A. (1991). The concept map as an advanced organizer. *Journal of Research in Science Teaching, 28,* 705-711.

Woloshyn, V.E., Paivio, A., & Pressley, M. (1994). Use of elaborative interrogation to help students acquire information consistent with prior knowledge and information inconsistent with prior knowledge. *Journal of Educational Psychology, 86,* 79-89.

Woloshyn, V.E., & Stockley, D.B. (in press). Helping students acquire belief-inconsistent and belief-consistent science facts: Comparisons between individual and dyad study using elaborative interrogation, self-selected study and repetitious reading. *Applied Cognitive Psychology.*

Woloshyn, V.E., Wood, E., & Willoughby, T. (1994). Considering prior knowledge when using elaborative interrogation. *Applied Cognitive Psychology,*

Woodward, J., & Noell, J. (1991). Science instruction at the secondary level: Implications for students with learning disabilities. *Journal of Learning Disabilities, 24,* 277-284.

Yager, R.E., Engen, H.B., & Snider, B.C. (1969). Effects of the laboratory and demonstration methods upon the outcomes of instruction in secondary biology. *Journal of Research in Science Teaching, 6,* 76-86.

Yager, R.E., & Penick, J.E. (1987). Resolving the crisis in science education: Understanding before resolution. *Science Education, 71,* 49-55.

CHAPTER 9

Learning Facts: The Value of Always Asking Yourself Why and Other Mnemonic Strategies

Although many educators deny it, schooling requires learning many facts. Fact-recall tests are common at all levels of education, beginning in elementary school. We were remiss in the previous edition of this book not to confront these realities. By offering a chapter on comprehension but not fact learning, we inadvertently sent the errant message that comprehension alone is sufficient to ensure memory. That this is not the case can be demonstrated easily. Read each of the following sentences, rating how well each one is comprehended on the following 1 to 5 scale:

1——Not understood at all
2——Understood a little bit
3——Understood moderately well
4——Understood fairly well
5——Very well understood

Ready? Here are the sentences you are to read and rate:

The short man bought the broom.
The brave man gave money to the robber.
The fat man read the sign.
The tall man bought the crackers.
The thin man found the scissors.
The rich man picked up the chair.
The sad man looked at his new boat.
The kind man ate dinner.
The smart man went to work.
The bald man used the phone.
The artistic man put down the knife.

The frightened man ironed the sheet.
The sleepy man bought the mug.
The evil man wound up the clock.
The blind man hit the flea.
The bearded man threw out the coupon.
The crippled man flicked the switch.
The dying man used a feather.
The religious man used the saw.
The long-haired man looked for the pole.
The Irish man counted the leaves.
The weak man thanked the checkout girl.
The patriotic man memorized the words.
The dishonest man looked closely at the wrapper.
(Sentences used by Pressley, McDaniel, Turnure, Wood & Ahmad, 1987, p. 300; based on those created by Stein & Bransford, 1979)

How many of the sentences did you rate as 3 or higher? How many did you rate as 5? Most people, in fact, rate all of the sentences as 5, indicating that they did understand them well. Now without looking back at the sentences, please fill in the blanks with the appropriate adjective describing the man who performed the action:

The _____ man gave money to the robber.
The _____ man bought the crackers.
The _____ man found the scissors.
The _____ man put down the knife.
The _____ man picked up the chair.
The _____ man read the sign.
The _____ man looked at his new boat.
The _____ man ate dinner.
The _____ man bought the broom.
The _____ man went to work.
The _____ man used the phone.
The _____ man ironed the sheet.
The _____ man gave money to the robber.
The _____ man bought the crackers.
The _____ man found the scissors.
The _____ man put down the knife.
The _____ man picked up the chair.
The _____ man bought the mug.
The _____ man flicked the switch.
The _____ man used a feather.
The _____ man used the saw.
The _____ man looked for the pole.
The _____ man thanked the checkout girl.
The _____ man memorized the words.
The _____ man looked closely at the wrapper.
The _____ man wound up the clock.

The _____ man counted the leaves.
The _____ man hit the flea.
The _____ man threw out the coupon.

Even though it was easy to understand every one of the original sentences, was it easy to remember them? If you are like most people, the answer is no. Understanding material in no way implies that the material will be remembered.

Look back at the original sentences. For every one of them, it is possible to construct a rationale about why it would make sense that the particular man cited would have carried out the specific action stated. For example, it makes sense that the weak man would have thanked the checkout girl if she helped to carry his groceries. The crackers must have been on a high shelf, so that only a tall man could reach them. Maybe the religious man was using the saw to construct a cross or help build a church. When people construct such rationales, their memories of the sentences improve dramatically (e. g., Pressley et al., 1987; Stein & Bransford, 1979). The reason these sentences were so hard for most readers to remember is that typically people do not construct elaborative explanations about how each of the *man* facts could make sense.

When people are reading facts, whether they are required to remember them or not, they are unlikely to relate them to their prior knowledge, or at least not as completely as the facts could be related to prior knowledge. That is, they are unlikely to make sense of the facts as completely as they might make sense of them and thus, the facts are not as meaningful or memorable as they might be. (For a detailed review of the evidence pertaining to this point, see Pressley, Wood, Woloshyn, Martin, King, & Menke, 1992). One simple way to encourage people to relate new facts to their prior knowledge is to ask them to explain why each new fact makes sense. Thus, people expected to learn the *man* facts could be asked to pose and answer questions such as, "Why would the wicked man wind up the clock?", "Why would the tall man buy the crackers?", and "Why would a sad man be looking at his new boat?" Asking and answering why-questions has come to be known as elaborative interrogation.

Elaborative Interrogation [SSR]

Elaborative interrogation as an approach to improving fact recall has been validated by researchers with many different types of materials. People using this strategy are interrogated or interrogate themselves, with the questions they pose intended to produce elaborations of the to-be-learned facts. Hence, when learners approach facts by asking themselves why each fact is true, they are said to be engaged in elaborative interrogation. In most of the studies carried out to date, the materials learned have been isolated facts, although there are also demonstrations that elaborative interrogation can improve memory of facts embedded in text (e.g., Woloshyn, Willoughby, Wood, & Pressley, 1990). Elaborative interrogation can be used by students working alone or by small groups of students (Kohl & Woloshyn, in press; Woloshyn & Stickley, in press).

Learning of Isolated Facts

Woloshyn, Paivio, and Pressley (1994) demonstrated that elaborative interrogation can be useful for learning science facts. Although the facts were isolated, there were sets of them related to particular topics in science—consistent with the types of thematic units that students often encounter in elementary science. The grade-6 and grade-7 students in the study learned sets of facts pertaining to the solar system, plants, the circulatory system, and animals.

Some of the facts conflicted with common prior knowledge. That is, these were facts for which many people possess misconceptions. The other facts were ones that were consistent with the prior knowledge of most people, with the misconception and prior-knowledge-consistent status of each fact established carefully in a norming study preceding the research described here. Sometimes the facts were presented along with information signaling a potential misconception about the fact and refuting the misconception; sometimes the fact alone was presented. Here are some of the facts that students were asked to learn about the solar system:

- In space, the sun's heat cannot even roast a potato. (inconsistent with prior knowledge)
- Although some people think the size of a star is always the same, the size changes. (consistent with prior knowledge, refutation presented)
- Moon soil is made up of small pieces of rock and glass. (consistent with prior knowledge)
- Oxygen is not the same as air. (inconsistent with prior knowledge)
- The distance between the earth and the moon changes every day, although some people think it is always the same. (consistent with prior knowledge, refutation presented)
- Although some people think that the light of the sun is only red or yellow, it is made of every different color including blue and violet. (inconsistent with prior knowledge, refutation presented)
- Stars are gases, although some people think that they are solid. (inconsistent with prior knowledge, refutation presented)
- The largest known volcano is on the planet Mars. (consistent with prior knowledge)

Half of the participants in the Woloshyn et al. (1994) study were control participants who were left to their own devices to learn the facts any way that they could. The remaining participants were instructed to use elaborative interrogation to learn the facts—for each fact, they asked and answered the question, "Why is that fact true?"

There was a smashing effect for elaborative interrogation in the Woloshyn et al. (1994) study. Regardless of whether the fact was consistent or inconsistent with students' prior knowledge, or whether the fact was presented unembellished or with refutation, students using elaborative interrogation remembered more facts than control students. This was true for several different measures of memory, with learning gains maintained up to 6 months after the original presentation of the facts.

Learning of Facts in Connected Text

Wood, Pressley, and Winne (1990, Experiment 2) provided a clear demonstration that children in grades 4 through 8 can benefit from elaborative interrogation when facts are presented in connected text. The children in the study were asked to learn elementary science content pertaining to different types of animals. For each animal, they read a paragraph specifying the physical characteristics of the animal's home as well as its diet, sleeping habits, preferred habitat, and predators. For example, one animal they learned about was the Western Spotted Skunk:

> The Western Spotted Skunk lives in a hole in the ground. The skunk's hole is usually found on a sandy piece of farmland near crops. Often the skunk lives alone, but families of skunks sometimes stay together. The skunk mostly eats corn. It sleeps just about any time except between three o'clock in the morning and sunrise. The biggest danger to the skunk is the great horned owl. (Wood et al., 1990, p. 744)

Students, who were instructed to use elaborative interrogation to learn the animal paragraphs, asked and answered a series of questions for each paragraph: Specifically, for every fact presented in a paragraph, the student asked and answered why the fact made sense. For example, Why do skunks eat corn? Why do owls prey on skunks? Why is the skunk away from 3 AM until dawn? Control students were left to their own devices to learn the facts.

In another important condition of the study, students were provided reasons for each fact in the paragraphs. For example, students read the statements "The Western Spotted Skunk lives in a hole in the ground in order to protect itself and its family," and "Often the skunk lives alone, but families of skunks sometimes stay together until the young skunks are old enough and strong enough to look after themselves" (Wood et al., 1990, pp. 744-5).

Students in the elaborative interrogation condition of the study learned more than either control students or students who were provided reasons for the factual relationships. Elaborative interrogation can be used profitably by elementary- and middle-school students to learn material in factually-dense text.

Mechanisms Mediating Elaborative Interrogation Effects.

Elaborative interrogation works because people who typically do not relate new material to prior knowledge are stimulated to do so by why-questions about the sensibleness of the fact. (See Martin and Pressley, 1991, for especially strong evidence that this is the mechanism mediating the elaborative interrogation effect.) What this implies is that in order for elaborative interrogation to work as a strategy, it is necessary for the student to possess some relevant prior knowledge. (For a review of the relationship between prior knowledge and elaborative interrogation, see Woloshyn, Wood, and Willoughby, 1994.) Although the data are not completely conclusive that elaborative interrogation fails as a strategy in the absence of prior knowledge, learning is much better when learners possess prior knowledge that can be related to the to-be-learned content. Fortunately, students often possess prior knowledge about content that they are presented in school, prior knowledge that can be tapped more fully through elaborative interrogation.

We cannot emphasize enough the importance of having students think about reasons why new facts are sensible. Providing students with such explanations does little to promote learning, relative to having them generate explanations themselves. Moreover, even if people do not come up with an explanation for a fact, if the fact is from a domain in which they have prior knowledge, just attempting to generate an explanation facilitates learning (see Pressley et al., 1992, for a detailed review of this argument).

In summary, when students are learning new facts that can be related to their prior knowledge, elaborative interrogation improves learning of facts, with this holding even when students cannot come up with an explanation for the factual relation. Elaborative interrogation is an excellent way to promote *more active learning* of facts—an excellent way to transform what is often conceived of as dull and rote learning into a stimulating thinking exercise, one that makes the most of what students already know.

Representational Imagery [SSR]

There are many, many demonstrations of the potency of mental imagery. In this text, there have been already several presentations of one type of mnemonic imagery, the keyword method. When the keyword method is used to learn the meaning of a new foreign vocabulary word (e.g., *Rathaus*, the German word for town hall), a keyword proxy (i.e., stand-in) for the foreign word is created in the form of an English word or phrase that sounds like the foreign word. Thus, for *Rathaus*, a keyword might be *rat's house*. A concrete image of the keyword is combined with a concrete image of the definition in order to increase the association between the foreign word and its definition. For instance, some readers might imagine a hole in the wall of their local town hall with a rat sticking its head out of the hole. If they do, it might help them later to recall the meaning of *Rathaus*. (See Levin, 1993, for the most up-to-date discussion of keyword techniques and their effects on student learning of facts.)

One objection to keyword mnemonics is that they are artificial. We do not buy this objection entirely, aware that good thinkers have used forms of the keyword mnemonic since ancient times to assist memory. This is one strategy that good memorizers seem to use. Even so, we recognize that this criticism of artificiality may actually reflect a dissatisfaction with the method because the keyword proxies are not meaningfully related to the to-be-learned content. Moreover, the image created often will lack meaning with respect to the to-be-learned material. Learning mechanisms that orient students to the meaning of new material have more curbside appeal to many educators than memory aids that do not.

Fortunately, there are variations of mnemonic techniques that rely on proxies that are meaningfully related to to-be-learned content. Pressley and Brewster (1990) created one such representational imagery approach for learning geography content. They asked Canadian students in grades 5 and 6 to learn facts about the Canadian provinces. Thus, for the province of Nova Scotia, the students were asked to learn that it was the locale of Canada's first apple trees, first dentist, and first magazine. For Saskatchewan, they were asked to learn that employment was especially high in that province, the hottest temperature in Canadian history occurred in the province, and dinosaur bones were often found there.

One strategy they explored was asking students to think of a scene from the province in question and to relate each to-be-learned fact to that scene. That is, the stereotypical scene for the province would serve as a proxy for the province name, with the linking image involving the proxy and an imaginal representation of the to-be-learned fact. For example, Pressley and Brewster thought that students might think of the rolling wheat fields when they read about Saskatchewan. Imagining many people working in those fields could represent the province's high rate of employment. An image of a blazing sun over that same wheat field might improve their memory that Saskatchewan was the province being discussed. An image of dinosaur bones in the field could assist memory of the fact that many such bones have been found in Saskatchewan. There was only one problem: the students did not possess stereotypical images for each of the Canadian provinces.

Pressley and Brewster solved the problem by finding stereotypical pictures of each province—with calendars being their source of images.

Using these pictures, they first had students learn the association between each province and its stereotypical picture. Once this association was learned, students were instructed to learn new facts about each province by constructing an image involving its stereotypical picture for the province and a representation of the new fact. This method worked very well relative to the control students who clearly understood the new facts but were not taught a specific method for remembering them.

There are many occasions when students will have concrete representations that could be used as proxies. For example, when learning new facts about chemical elements, a balloon floating away might be a proxy for helium, a skin diver's tank a proxy for oxygen, and a piece of coal a proxy for carbon. If they were to learn about U.S. states, there are many stereotypical pictures that could be identified for each state, ones that could be used to construct images to mediate acquisition of facts about the states. The same is true of European countries.

Sometimes confusing facts can be learned via imagery without the generation of proxies at all. For example, go back to the list of man sentences. Try to generate an image representing the meaning of each one. Most people can, and when they do, their learning of the man sentences improves compared with when they simply read or attempted to memorize the sentences.

Mechanisms Mediating Representational Imagery Effects

Representational imagery approaches for fact learning have not been analyzed in as rigorous a fashion as elaborative interrogation. One important component is the "dual coding" that occurs, consistent with the time-tested conclusion that imagery and verbal codes combined are more powerful than verbal codes alone (Paivio, 1971). It seems likely that a stereotypical image of a Canadian province probably acts as an imagery peg, with a variety of other images relatable to it. Once related, they can be subsequently retrieved via that peg (e.g., when asked about the province with high employment, the phrase *high employment* cues the image of of many workers in a wheat field, the peg corresponding to Saskatchewan; Paivio, 1971). If any link in the associative chain is weak, memory may not occur, especially if students really do not have a strong association between the name of a province and the stereotypical picture/image used to represent it. Thus, teachers who are considering using the representational imagery approach described here should make certain that students have a strong association between the name of the object being studied and its pictorial/imaginal representation.

Elaborative Interrogation Versus Representational Imagery.

Learning facts via representational imagery and elaborative interrogation produce approximately equal effects on learning (Pressley et al., 1988; Wood et al., 1990). Both are attractive because they stimulate more meaningful processing of to-be-learned facts than occurs through simple learning of the facts. During elaborative interrogation, students are relating a new fact to other knowledge; during construction of representational images, students are thinking about an image representing important properties of the category being studied (e.g., wheat really is an important crop grown in Saskatchewan). Both elaborative interrogation and representational imagery are powerful methods for enhancing learning of facts.

Other Approaches to Fact Learning

Many of the methods considered in Chapter 3 for enhancing comprehension of expository text are in fact, very useful approaches for learning facts that are presented in text. Most prominently, summarization of factually-dense text requires separating the important from the unimportant ideas in text and relating the important ideas to one another. Summarization has proven consistently to increase memory of facts in text. So does self-questioning and attempting to answer self-questions (e.g., King, 1994).

Our suggestion for teachers who are interested in teaching their students how to learn factual information is that they begin by teaching them elaborative interrogation, which is very easy to do. Once elaborative interrogation has been mastered, a natural expansion is to other types of self-questioning, perhaps based on the question frames presented in Chapter 3. Because summarization is such a useful comprehension strategy empowering students to generate well-organized memories of text they have processed, it should also be taught. Finally, when the opportunity presents itself, teach representational imagery. We are certain that the opportunities for doing so are great, not only for teaching of regional geography, but also for important historical periods, scientific ideas, political events, and so on. The only materials required are stereotypical pictures that can be used as starting points for student construction of images linking a number of ideas to the historical periods, scientific ideas, or political events being studied.

REFERENCES

Kahl, B., & Woloshyn, V. E. (in press). Using elaborative interrogation in cooperative learning settings: One good strategy deserves another. *Applied Cognitive Psychology.*

King, A. (1994). Guiding knowledge construction in the classroom: Effects of teaching children how to question and how to explain. *American Educational Research Journal, 31,* 338-368.

Levin, J. R. (1993). Mnemonic strategies and classroom learning: A twenty-year report card. *The Elementary School Journal, 94,* 235-244.

Martin, V. L., & Pressley, M. (1991). Elaborative-interrogation effects depend on the nature of the question. *Journal of Educational Psychology, 83,* 113-119.

Mastropieri, M. A., & Scruggs, T. E. (1991). *Teaching students ways to remember: Strategies for learning mnemonically.* Cambridge, MA: Brookline Books.

Paivio, A. (1971). *Imagery and verbal processes.* New York: Holt, Rinehart, & Winston.

Pressley, M., & Brewster, M. E. (1990). Imaginal elaboration of illustrations to facilitate fact learning: Creating memories of Prince Edward Island. *Applied Cognitive Psychology, 4,* 359-370.

Pressley, M., McDaniel, M. A., Turnure, J. E., Wood, E., & Ahmad, M. (1987). Generation and precision of elaboration: Effects on intentional and incidental learning. *Journal of Experimental Psychology: Learning, Memory, and Cognition, 13,* 291-300.

Pressley, M., Symons, S., McDaniel, M. A., Snyder, B. L., & Turnure, J. E. (1988). Elaborative interrogation facilitates acquisition of confusing facts. *Journal of Educational Psychology, 80,* 268-278.

Pressley, M., Wood, E., Woloshyn, V. E., Martin, V., King, A., & Menke, D. (1992). Encouraging mindful use of prior knowledge: Attempting to construct explanatory answers facilitates learning. *Educational Psychologist, 27,* 91-110.

Stein, B. S., & Bransford, J. D. (1979). Constraints of effective elaboration: Effects on precision and subject generation. *Journal of Verbal Learning and Verbal Behavior, 18,* 769-777.

Woloshyn, V. E., Paivio, A., & Pressley, M. (1994). Use of elaborative interrogation to help students acquire information consistent with prior knowledge and information inconsistent with prior knowledge. *Journal of Educational Psychology, 86,* 79-89.

Woloshyn, V. E., Pressley, M., & Schneider, W. (1992). Elaborative interrogation and prior knowledge effects on learning of facts. *Journal of Educational Psychology, 84,* 115-124.

Woloshyn, V. E., & Stockley, D. B. (in press). Helping students acquire belief-inconsistent and belief-consistent science facts: Comparisons between individual and dyads using elaborative interrogation, self-selected study, and repetitious reading. *Applied Cognitive Psychology.*

Woloshyn, V. E., Willoughby, T., Wood, E., & Pressley, M. (1990). Elaborative interrogation facilitates adult learning of factual paragraphs. *Journal of Educational Psychology, 82,* 513-524.

Woloshyn, V. E., Wood, E., & Willoughby, T. (1994). Considering prior knowledge when using elaborative interrogation. *Applied Cognitive Psychology, 8,* 25-36.

Wood, E., Pressley, M., & Winne, P. H. (1990). Elaborative interrogation effects on children's learning of factual content. *Journal of Educational Psychology, 82,* 741-8.

CHAPTER 10

Getting Started
Teaching Strategies

Our hope is that readers are sufficiently intrigued by this point to want to try strategy instruction in their own classrooms. Perhaps it still seems a little overwhelming. A lot of strategies have been covered in this volume. The first chapter spelled out a rather exacting approach to teaching strategies, one demanding much of the teacher.

We believe most teachers would benefit greatly from formal training in strategy instruction, including supervised practice providing direct explanations (see Chapter 1) about strategies to students. Realistically, however, that is not an option for most teachers, at least in the short term. Thus this chapter, while not intended to substitute for formal instruction, is meant to provide some guidance to those who wish to get started teaching strategies.

1. Select a Few Strategies to Teach, Maybe Only One at a Time

No child could learn all of the strategies covered in this volume over a short period of time. That is one reason strategy instruction needs to be extended over a number of years of schooling. There are strategies appropriate for every level of schooling and for all content areas. The teacher new to strategy instruction should take what we have called a "small is beautiful" approach, inspired by Schumaker's (1973) approach to economics in the book of that name. Select a few strategies particularly relevant to the students you are teaching and make a commitment to teach these procedures well, usually one at a time (Pressley, Goodchild, Fleet, Zajchowski, and Evans, 1989).

For instance, a teacher may notice her sixth-grade students often do not seem to understand thoroughly what they are reading; in particular, they often fail to make appropriate inferences when reading. The teacher would then seek information about reading strategies to promote understanding and integration of text. Chapter 3 of this book can provide a starting point. Representational imagery was one strategy specified in that chapter as promoting construction of coherent representations of text. Teaching children to generate questions about content they read was reviewed as a promising approach to increasing inferential comprehension. Summarization, including constructing paraphrases of material covered in text, was cited as generally benefiting recall of information in text. These strategies would be a good start, with students encouraged to use all three strategies as they try to make sense of text.

Throughout this book, we have provided information only about scientifically validated strategies. Why? Because real dangers follow from instruction of strategies that do not produce the benefits purported. At a minimum, such strategies are a waste of instructional time. More seriously, they may undermine a teacher's motivation to continue teaching strategies. It is not easy to teach strategies, a theme developed in Chapter 1 and reiterated later in this chapter. If a teacher expends a great deal of effort in teaching strategies with no discernible payoff, she or he will be less likely to continue teaching the same strategy in the future—a good outcome. It is possible, however, the teacher will draw the generalization from one or a few negative experiences with strategy instruction that the entire enterprise is flawed. Even worse, consider the students, particularly weak students who are often prime candidates for strategy instruction. Such students already have low confidence. A teacher leads the child to process according to a strategy presumably capable of producing competent performance. The child has to work hard to learn how to execute most strategies. If such effort goes unrewarded, there is the great danger the child may become more convinced than ever that his academic problems really do reflect immutable factors. After all, if learning remains poor for a child using approaches supposedly producing competent performance for most people, an easy inference to draw is that nothing could help this learner. This is not the type of student thinking about "self as learner" teachers want to encourage. Teaching ineffective strategies has the potential for encouraging just such thinking. This danger is more than enough reason to avoid instruction of any strategies other than those already proven effective in believable tests.

Other considerations in selection of strategies:

(a) They should mesh with the rest of the curriculum, being compatible with the goals school is intended to promote. The strategies included in this book were selected largely with this goal in mind.

(b) Strategies teachable with materials already available in the classroom are to be preferred over strategies requiring special merchandise. Most of the strategies covered in this book can be taught with materials commonly found in all present-day schools. Because a number of publishers have offered expensive kits, workbooks, and other resources as part of strategy instruction curricula, many believe strategy instruction to be an expensive component. Keeping it economical is fiscally and professionally responsible.

(c) Why is it professional to keep strategy instruction inexpensive from a materials resources point of view? Although buying a kit offered by a publisher seems like an easy way to begin strategy instruction, our general impression is that these should never be adopted *in toto* as provided by the publisher. First, most have never been validated. Second, they may not produce much benefit if used as prescribed, for many are based on an instructional model incompatible with conditions known to enhance strategy instructional efficacy. That is, students are taught a very large number of strategies in a short period of time, with little information provided about where and when to use the approaches and no guidance in applying the strategies across the school day. When strategy instruction has worked, a few strategies were taught at a time, slowly, with plenty of information about specific contexts, and many opportunities to experience guided practice in applying the strategies to important tasks encountered across the school day.

2. Use Powerful Methods of Teaching

Virtually all successful strategy instructors are using a variation on one particular approach to the teaching of strategies. A few strategies are taught at any one time; they are taught well; and they are taught in the context of the ongoing curriculum. Teaching well operationalizes the general model of teaching strategies covered in Chapter 1 (see Table 1-2 in that chapter, a good *aide-memoire* for this approach to teaching). The model may be more meaningful at this point in the book, given the extensive review of strategies presented in the previous chapters.

- The teacher *models* the strategy for the students repeatedly, across the school day when opportunities arise. Much of this modeling can be accomplished by the teacher thinking aloud (e.g., Ericsson & Simon, 1983).
- The teacher provides *extensive explanations* to students about how the strategies can be applied to different tasks encountered at various points in the curriculum. Thus, the teacher electing to instruct imagery, question-generation, and summarization strategies for reading will make a point of letting her students know when she is trying to construct an image of the content covered in the text. She may ask students to try to do so, and have them compare their images with one another. The teacher can provide explanations when student images are errant (e.g., when mixed with fantasy elements neither actually present in the reading nor reasonably inferable).
- The teacher can also *overtly construct self-questions* as she reads the text, with this activity extended to any text that may be encountered in the course of the school day. For instance, when the school's daily announcement sheet arrives, rather than simply reading the announcements to

the class, the teacher can generate thought questions designed to stimulate complete processing of the information in the text. Thus, an announcement such as "The Girl Scouts will sell cookies in the lunch room next week" can prompt several self-questions. The teacher can ask, "Why would the Girl Scouts be selling cookies?" "Why might we want to buy Girl Scout cookies?"

Current events, a staple of many classroom morning exercises, also provides opportunity for the teacher to model self-questioning. Reading an article about athletes using steroids or other drugs can lead the teacher to pose such questions as: "Why is there a lot of attention when athletes use drugs?" "Is there a message here for ordinary boys and girls?" "Since I would have never dreamed X was using drugs, what does that tell me about who else might be using drugs?" "What good might come from an article like this one, which on the face of it seems to be aimed at discrediting prominent people in athletics?"

- Teacher modeling and explaining are not enough, however. Frequent and extensive *re-explanations* are absolutely essential, for students usually will misunderstand at least part of the strategy. Good teaching is largely good diagnosing of what it is that students do not understand, followed by explanations focusing on points of difficulty and re-explanations appropriate to the level of understanding of the student. Student practice, with re-explanations by the teacher, continues as long as necessary for the student to acquire the strategic procedure to a high level of confidence. Many strategies take some time to acquire.

Student practice in applying strategies should often occur in cooperative groups. Students experience an opportunity to explain their thinking in such groups, providing all students in the group with a window on the flexible use of strategies. Such group use of strategies is consistent with Vygotsky's theory—an individual's thinking skills benefit greatly through interpersonal interactions mirroring the intellectual skills the individual is to acquire. Whether students come to value the strategies they are learning, and thus continue to use them after instruction ends, depends largely on the students recognizing their performance improves because they are using the strategies proposed, or those that they find work for them. Thus, contemporary models of strategy instruction emphasize *students should be taught to monitor their performances*, noting improvements in performance as a function of using a particular strategy for a particular task. Sometimes, this improvement is formally plotted by students on graph paper, providing tangible evidence of improvement. Student recognition of gains due to use of strategies is a critical determinant of durable strategy use. It is important for them to come to realize that high performance is not due to immutable ability, uncontrollable luck, or simple effort, but rather effort directed through procedures well matched to the requirements of a task (Borkowski et al., in press; Clifford, 1984).

What is required is more than just continuing to use the procedure; students must *appropriately* use the strategies they learn. Students need to learn each strategy is appropriate only in certain situations or for particular tasks. Thus, a lot of *information should be provided during instruction about when and where to use strategies being acquired; students also should be given many opportunities to practice a new strategy with a range of materials,* both those which can be readily matched to it and those requiring some adjustment of the strategy. Practice with diverse materials permits firsthand opportunities for adapting strategies to new circumstances and learning when the strategy can be adapted and when adaptation will not work. *Students should be taught to size up new assignments before attempting them,* to determine whether they know a procedure that could be used to help them solve a task. One real benefit of students trying strategies in groups is that group members can reflect with one another about when and where to use strategies.

In short, strategy instruction is explicit and extensive, with a great deal of supervised student practice and feedback to students from teachers. Sometimes students practice strategies together—in fact, we recommend that this occur regularly, with teacher assistance to students working together on an as-needed basis. Teaching is encouragement to use strategies by guiding and reminding students about when and how strategies can be applied to new situations. At first, this process will be difficult for many teachers, but with practice, it will get easier. The only way to learn the types of errors students might make is to work with students; with experience, teachers will recognize errors more quickly, errors they have seen before. Teachers will also build up a repertoire of effective responses for helping students handle the many types of common errors. With practice, it will be more obvious to teachers where strategies being taught can be applied in the curriculum, so they will be in a better position with increasing teaching experience to provide information about where and when to use procedures they are teaching. As with so many areas, the more involved teachers become with strategy teaching and use, the more they will be able to think how to help the student prepare for and handle a task, and what procedures are likely to be most effective.

3. Motivate Students to Use the Strategies They Are Taught

Students need to understand that success in school and life beyond school are both largely a function of using appropriate strategies. Students should be made aware that the strategies being taught to them are those used by very good readers, writers, and problem solvers. They are not acquiring mental crutches when they learn strategies, but rather powerful cognitive tools, ones which, in the absence of instruction, are often discovered only by exceptionally good students.

Motivation will be heightened if students are taught strategies that are appropriately challenging. They should not be so difficult to learn that great effort is required to master them. Thus, the imagery, self-generated questioning, and summarizing strategies selected by the teacher can be learned by sixth-graders. They are at an appropriate level of difficulty; they are also strategies promoting learning of content important to sixth-graders, another factor potentially heightening student motivation. Throughout instruction, teachers should emphasize that errors are to be expected and are a natural part of the learning process. In diagnosing student errors in order to make corrective re-explanations, teachers should never make students feel embarrassed about their mistakes or anxious about their progress. Students should be convinced efforts made to learn strategies are investments, even if success is not immediately apparent. Failure must never be attributed to low ability—doing so could easily undermine future efforts to learn strategies.

In fact, good strategy teaching includes explicit attempts to eliminate such beliefs. For instance, many students with reading difficulties attribute their difficulties to low ability (e.g., "I am dumb"). Such self-perceptions should be replaced with ideas supporting the learning of strategies. Students should be made aware that their current processing problems are due to their lack of knowledge of the right strategies (e.g., "I could understand this text if I used the right strategy"). Borkowski and his colleagues (1990) have provided especially powerful evidence that changing beliefs about the self as a learner as part of strategy instruction can have a profound effect on the success of strategy instruction. What is most apparent from that research is that students' motivation to use strategies they are learning can be heightened dramatically if they come to believe they are capable of acquiring strategies improving performance, if they begin to think acquisition of such procedures is a more powerful determinant of performance than innate abilities.

The motivational recommendations in this section are very contemporary, emerging from research undertaken in the last five years. Many old ideas about motivation should not be ignored in designing strategy instruction, however. Students can be offered incentives and rewards for acquiring strategies. Praise should be provided throughout the process. The long-term advantages of learning strategies should be highlighted as well. Students can be reminded of the economic, social, and personal advantages accruing from effective comprehension of what is read. For instance, one school that we know which emphasizes problem-solving strategies arranges for visits from engineers, scientists, and local businessmen, who inform students of the importance of mathematics and problem solving in their professional lives.

4. Encourage Students to Believe They Can Become Good Information Processors

Students should be encouraged to believe they can grow up to be like engineers, scientists, and community business leaders—that is, effective thinkers fulfilling important roles in their community. Students must come to understand that such roles are not achieved on the basis of innate ability, but rather by learning the strategies and knowledge associated with these roles. Thus, lawyers know many lawyering strategies, physicians strategies for producing particular medical outcomes, and urban planners tactics for accomplishing striking changes in ever-changing cities. These professionals did not always know how to do these things. They learned the tactics of their profession in school. Most critically, when they were in grade 6, they were much like today's grade 6 students. Students should be encouraged to recognize that they could become like these leaders, and that a good start in pursuit of this role is to learn the academic strategies used by successful people—to acquire the reading, writing, and problem-solving strategies these people know. Make it clear to them many adults do not have these skills and lack of such skills can be a cause of adult failure. Learning important academic skills is something a grade 6 student can do to increase the odds of later success.

In short, it is important for students to believe it possible for them to become good information processors and that becoming a good information processor is an important part of developing into an effective participant in society. Believing in a possible self better than the current self can have important motivational consequences. A possible self can provide "direction and impetus for action, change, and development" (Markus & Nurius, 1986, p. 960). It can motivate learning to reduce the difference between the current self and the desired possible self. Who does not know a child who has set his sight on a long-term career goal, with much energy directed toward achieving that goal? An important part of strategy instructional education is to encourage students' understanding that acquisition of academic strategies can reduce the distance between their current selves and the possible selves to which they aspire.

Perhaps a little more concretely, students can be made aware of how the strategies they are learning in school can mediate many real-life demands. Brophy (1986) provides a nice summary of this idea:

> Basic language arts and mathematics skills are used daily when shopping, banking, driving, reading instructions for using some product, paying bills and carrying on business correspondence, and planning home maintenance projects or family vacations.... In general, a good working knowledge of the information, principles, and skills taught in school prepares people to make well-informed decisions that result

in saving time, trouble, expense, or even lives, and it empowers people by preparing them to recognize and take advantage of the opportunities that society offers... Do what you can to rekindle this appreciation in your students by helping them to see academic activities as enabling opportunities to be valued (p. 30).

In short, students should be taught they are capable of acquiring strategies important in the real world. Much of the role of education is to pass on strategies of great ecological validity. What is being taught in school is relevant now and in the future.

5. Following Initial Success in Teaching Strategies, Extend the Approach in the Curriculum Areas.

Suppose the teacher tries teaching imagery, question-generation, and summarizing strategies, and all goes well. He or she should be in a better position to continue teaching and supporting those same procedures the next year, for a lot of knowledge about students' reactions to such instruction will be acquired during the initial year of teaching. The teacher will have acquired a repertoire of routines for responding to common errors made by students in attempting to use strategies.

In addition to continuing instruction of the three reading strategies, there may be other curriculum areas in need of instructional enrichment. Typically, sixth-graders are expected to begin learning how to construct coherent essays, and are often not very good at it. The teacher might want to try instruction of strategies for improving qualitative aspects of writing. Some of the writing strategies outlined in Chapter 6 could be attempted, using the teaching sequence specified earlier in this chapter and reviewed more generally in Chapter 1. Because such writing strategies require instruction over a long period of time, the plan might be to practice them throughout the year whenever students are given an essay assignment.

Most important, having taught a strategy, teachers should now help students apply it to the different curriculum areas for which it is appropriate. The student should be encouraged to use a summarization strategy learned in English or language arts for a science or a social studies assignment. The more opportunities a student has to try out the strategy in different applications, the more he or she will see it as broadly useful beyond the context in which he learned it. This understanding is what makes strategy use a powerful experience!

Teachers experiencing success with strategy instruction in their own classrooms can often provide valuable information to teaching colleagues. In particular, a sixth-grade teacher can provide information to seventh-grade teachers about strategies taught in grade 6, and thus stimulate discussion about how the seventh-grade teachers might build upon and add to what has already been taught.

There are now quite a few schools across North America in which a number of teachers provide strategy instruction. Visits to some of them have confirmed that these teachers have a sense that they are on the cutting edge, providing instruction consonant with recommendations in the most modern curriculum outlets. This book was motivated in part by communications from these teachers that any resource providing information about well-validated strategies would be professionally useful to them. We hope that will be the case with this book.

REFERENCES

Borkowski, J.G., Carr, M., Rellinger, R., & Pressley, M. (1990). The dependence of self-regulated strategy use on attributional beliefs, self-esteem, and metacognition. In B.F. Jones & L. Idol (Eds.), *Dimensions of thinking: Review of research* (pp. 53-92). Hillsdale, NJ: Lawrence Erlbaum & Associates.

Brophy, J. (1986). *On motivating students* (Occasional Paper No. 101). East Lansing: Institute for Research on Teaching, Michigan State University.

Clifford, M.A. (1984). Thoughts on a theory of constructive failure. *Educational Psychologist, 19*, 108-120.

Ericsson, A., & Simon, H.A. (1983). *Verbal protocol analysis.* Cambridge MA: MIT Press.

Markus, H., & Nurius, P. (1986). Possible selves. *American Psychologist, 41*, 954-969.

Pressley, M., Goodchild, F., Fleet, J., Zajchowski, R., & Evans, E.D. (1989). The challenges of classroom strategy instruction. *Elementary School Journal, 89*, 301-342.

Schumaker, E.F. (1973). *Small is beautiful: Economics as if people mattered.* London: Blood & Briggs.

FOR FURTHER READING

In recent years the Pressley group has documented in great detail the nature of effective strategies teaching, especially in elementary reading. For those who wish a research-based expansion of the comments provided in this chapter, the following should be helpful.

Brown, R., & Pressley, M. (1994). Self-regulated reading and getting meaning from text: The transactional strategies instruction model and its ongoing evaluation. In D. Schunk & B. Zimmerman (Eds.), *Self-regulation of learning and performance: Issues and educational applications* (pp. 155-179). Hillsdale, NJ: Erlbaum & Associates.

Gaskins, I.W., Anderson, R.C., Pressley, M., Cunicelli, E.A., & Satlow, E. (1993). Six teachers' dialogue during cognitive process instruction. *Elementary School Journal, 93*, 277-304.

Pressley, M. (1993). Teaching cognitive strategies to brain-injured clients: The good information processing perspective. *Seminars in Speech and Language, 14*, 1-17.

Pressley, M., Almasi, J., Schuder, T., Bergman, J., Hite, S., El-Dinary, P.B., & Brown, R. (1994). Transactional instruction of comprehension strategies: The Montgomery County MD SAIL program. *Reading and Writing Quarterly, 10*, 5-19.

Pressley, M., & El-Dinary, P.B. (1992). Memory strategy instruction that promotes good information processing. In D. Herrmann, H. Weingartner, A. Searleman, & C. McEvoy (Eds.), *External memory aids: Effects and effectiveness* (pp. 79-100). New York: Springer-Verlag.

Pressley, M., El-Dinary, P.B., Brown, R., Schuder, T., Bergman, J.L., York, M., Gaskins, I.W., & Faculties and Administration of Benchmark School and the Montgomery County MD SAIL/SIA Programs (1995). A transactional strategies instruction Christmas carol. In A. McKeough, J. Lupart, & A. Marini (Eds.), *Teaching for transfer: Fostering generalization in learning.* Hillsdale, NJ: Erlbaum.

Pressley, M., in long-term collaboration with El-Dinary, P., Brown, R., Schuder, T., Pioli, M., Gaskins, I., & Benchmark School Faculty (1994). Transactional instruction of reading comprehension strategies. In J. Mangieri & C.C. Block (Eds.), *Creating powerful thinking in teachers and students: Diverse perspectives* (pp. 112-139). Fort Worth, TX: Harcourt Brace Jovanovich.

Pressley, M., El-Dinary, P.B., Gaskins, I., Schuder, T., Bergman, J.L., Almasi, J., & Brown, R. (1992). Beyond direct explanation: Transactional instruction of reading comprehension strategies. *Elementary School Journal, 92*, 511-554.

Pressley, M., El-Dinary, P.B., Stein, S., Marks, M.B., & Brown, R. (1992). Good strategy instruction is motivating and interesting. In A. Renninger, S. Hidi, & A. Krapp (Eds.), *The role of interest in learning and development* (pp. 333-358). Hillsdale, NJ: Erlbaum.

Pressley, M., Harris, K.R., & Marks, M.B. (1992). But good strategy instructors are constructivists!! *Educational Psychology Review, 4*, 1-32.

Pressley, M., Rankin, J., Gaskins, I., Brown, R., & El-Dinary, P. (in press). Mapping the cutting-edge in primary-level literacy instruction for weak and at-risk readers. In T. Scruggs & M. Mastropieri (Eds.), *Advances in learning and behavioral disabilities.* Greenwich, CT: JAI Press.

Pressley, M., Schuder, T., SAIL Faculty and Administration, Bergman, J.L., & El-Dinary, P.B. (1992). A researcher-educator collaborative interview study of transactional comprehension strategies instruction. *Journal of Educational Psychology, 84*, 231-246.

APPENDIX

Additional Sources of Information about Strategy Instruction

All of the following sources are recommended for teachers who want more information about strategies. *A* journals tend to carry articles about how to teach particular strategies; *B* journals publish formal reports of research on cognitive strategies; *C* lists recommended books that provide information about how to teach many strategies and summaries of relevant research data; and *D* lists books produced by Pressley and his associates which summarize the available scientific evidence supporting strategy training.

There is a caveat attached to the recommendation to rely on these sources for more information about strategies. None of the *A* sources or the *C* texts are based exclusively on strategies that have been validated in formal studies. Therefore, care must be exercised in accepting the recommendations in these sources.

A and B. Journals

A. Readily available to teachers, generally written for nonresearcher professionals, and regularly publishing articles about strategy instruction:

Arithmetic Teacher
Educational Leadership
Elementary School Journal
Journal of Learning Disabilities
Journal of Reading
Learning Disabilities Quarterly
Reading Teacher
Remedial and Special Education

Teaching Exceptional Children

B. More written for researcher professionals:

American Educational Research Journal
Cognition and Instruction
Journal of Educational Psychology
Journal of Reading Behavior
Journal of Research in Mathematics Education
Review of Educational Research
Reading Research Quarterly

C. Textbooks

Baroody, A. J. (1987). *Children's mathematical thinking.* New York: Teacher's College Press. The best summary of information processing-inspired mathematics instruction, with substantial commentary on theory and research provided throughout.

Devine, T. G. (1987). *Teaching study skills: A guide for teachers.* New York: Allyn & Bacon. Good source of information about strategies, although emphasis is on strategies for high school and university students. Coverage includes all major contents in the curriculum, plus writing of term papers, class notetaking, memory, and motivation.

Duffy, G.G., & Roehler, L.R. (1989). *Improving classroom reading instruction: A decision-making-approach.* New York: Random House. Covers all aspects of reading instruction, with detailed coverage of how many reading skills can be taught as strategies.

Flower, L.S. (1989). *Problem-solving strategies for writing.* New York: Harcourt Brace Jovanovich. Although intended primarily as a university freshmen-level composition text, the information-processing model of composition can be appropriately adapted to teaching younger children how to write.

Gagné, E.D. (1985). *The cognitive psychology of school learning.* Boston: Little, Brown. An excellent textbook on the cognitive approach to instruction. Covers all of the major content areas of the elementary-school curriculum.

Mayer, R.E. (1987). *Educational psychology: A cognitive approach.* Boston: Little, Brown. Another excellent textbook on cognitive approaches to teaching. Coverage similar to Gagné, although a little broader and more current.

McNeil, J.D. (1987). *Reading comprehension* (2nd edition). Glenview, IL: Scott, Foresman. The best short summary of reading comprehension strategies available. Used in many reading clinics. Very appealing because of nice expositions of the strategies, with readable commentaries about research support for strategies covered.

Tierney, R.J., Readence, J.E., & Dishner, E.K. (1985). *Reading strategies and practices: Guide for improving instruction*. Boston: Allyn & Bacon. An excellent source book for all aspects of the reading process. A great strength of this volume is its summaries of a great deal of research supporting recommendations made.

D. Other books by Pressley and his associates.

McCormick, C.B., Miller, G.E., & Pressley, M. (1989). *Cognitive strategy instruction: From basic research to educational applications*. New York & Berlin: Springer-Verlag. An up-to-date, state-of-the-art summary of cutting edge research on cognitive strategy instruction.

Pressley, M., & Levin, J.R. (Eds.) (1983). *Cognitive strategy training: Educational applications and theoretical foundations*. New York & Berlin: Springer-Verlag. This two-volume set summarizes most of the important research on cognitive strategies conducted as of 1983.

Author Index

A

Adams, M.J., 21, 24, 30, 34, 35, 38
Ajewole, G.A., 215
Allen, L., 41
Allred, R. , 116, 119, 120, 122, 123, 125, 126, 128, 140
Anand, P.D., 203
Anderson, D.R., 23, 35, 129
Anderson, R.C., 74, 79
Anderson, T.X., 2, 6
Anderson, V., 94
Applebee, A.N., 1, 154
Armbruster, B.B., 62
Arnaudin, M.W., 224
Atkinson, R.C., 2, 108

B

Baddeley, A., 45
Ball, E.W., 23, 27, 123, 139, 149
Bamberg, B., 148
Bargh, J.A., 217
Barnard, D, P., 148
Barnhart, J.E., 23
Baron, J., 2, 4, 39
Barr, R., 20, 35
Barrass, R., 224
Basili, P.A., 218
Baumann, J.F., 61
Beal, C.R., 175
Bean, T.W., 59
Beck, I.L., 19, 20, 101, 111, 112
Beers, J.W., 117
Beichner, R.J., 218
Bell, A., 85
Bereiter, C. , 6, 82, 153, 170, 171, 172, 174
Berkenkotter, C., 173
Berkowitz, S.J., 61, 62, 63
Beuhring, T., 67
Bibby, P.A., 194
Biemiller, A., 41
Blackman, B.A., 27
Blackowitz, 102
Blair, T., 128

Blake, H., 123
Block, C.C., 95
Block, J., 123
Bloom, B.S., 214
Bogatz, G.A., 23
Bond, G.L., 24
Borkowski, J.G., 2, 191, 248, 249
Bos, C.S., 157
Bower, O.H., 108
Bradley, L., 20, 24, 25, 26, 27, 136, 149
Brainerd, C.J., 11
Bredderman, T., 216
Brophy, J., 250
Brown, A.L., 227
Brown, R., 87, 89, 93, 95
Bruck, M., 24, 42
Bryant, P., 54, 59
Byrne, B., 34

C

Calfee, R., 19, 24
Campbell, P.T., 14, 23, 197
Cardelle-Elawar, M., 187, 188
Care, 164
Carnine, D.W., 104
Carpenter, P.A., 132, 201
Carpenter, T.P., 196, 201
Carver, R.P., 40
Case, R., 5, 153
Chall, J.S., 50
Champagne, A.B., 217
Charles, R.I., 185, 187
Chiesi, H.L., 79
Chipman, S.F., 13
Choi, B.S., 218
Chomsky, N., 136
Cipielewski, J., 41
Clark, M.M., 22
Clement, J., 227
Clifford, M.M., 3, 248
Clymer, T., 35, 36
Cobb, P., 191, 192
Cochran, 178, 179
Coley, J.D., 85

Collier, R.M., 178, 179
Collins, C., 82
Comstock, G., 204
Cooper, G., 195
Corley, P.J., 31
Coulter, J.C., 215
Crain-Thoreson, C., 24
Cramer, R., 123
Cronnell, B., 119
Crowder, R.G., 199
Cunningham, A.E., 8, 41, 102, 136, 149
Curtis, M.E., 19

D

D'Anna, C.A., 103
Daiker, D., 172
Dauite, C.A., 178
Davey, B., 68, 69, 72
Davidson, N., 190, 217
Dembo, M.H., 190
Dempster, F.N., 199
Denner, P.A., 68
Derry, S.J., 6, 8
Deshler, D.P., 8, 94
Dewitz, P., 80
Dickinson, D., 102
Doctorow, M., 59
Dominic, J.F., 154
Dowhower, S.L., 39, 40
Downing, J., 117, 123
Dragga, 5., 172
Drake, D., 116, 117
Dreher, M.J., 77, 149
Duffy, G.G., 8, 82, 83, 84, 95
Dupin, J.J., 227
Durkin, D., 1, 22, 101

E

Ebbinghaus, H., 199
Edwards, L.D., 203
Ehri, L., 20, 30, 31, 32, 35, 38, 42
El-Dinary, P.B., 95
Eller, R.G., 102
Elley, W.B., 102

Elliott-Faust, D.J., 6
Englert, C., 6, 132, 133, 139, 156, 157, 164
Ericsson, A., 246
Eylon, B., 195

F
Faigley, L., 176
Fennema, E., 202
Fischer, F.E., 200
Fitzgerald, J. , 116, 126, 129, 131, 157, 173, 174, 176, 177, 213
Fitzsimmons, R., 119
Flavell, J., 11, 58
Fleisher, L.S., 40
Fletcher, J.D., 204
Flower, L.S., 4, 154, 155, 180
Foorman, B.R., 123
Frederiksen, J.R., 30
Fuhrman, M., 215

G
Gabbert, B., 217
Gagne, E.D., 6
Gambrell, L.B., 64
Garner, A., 6, 8, 74, 75
Gaskins, R., 42, 43, 45, 85, 89, 90, 91
Geary, D.C., 197
Gentner, D., 227
Gerber, M., 118, 128, 141, 142
Gettinger, M., 20
Gick, M.L., 6
Gillingham, A., 123
Gilstrap, A., 128, 129
Glaser, , A., 10
Glasson, G.E., 215
Glynn, S.M., 227, 228
Goldman, S.R., 197
Goldsmith, J., 31
Good, T.L., 190
Goodman, Y.M., 21, 31
Goswami, U., 42
Gough, P.B., 34
Graham, S., 2l, 116, 118, 119, 120, 122, 123, 125, 126, 127, 128, 140, 141, 147, 164, 168, 169, 170, 174, 179
Graves, M.F., 106, 157, 173, 174
Griffith, P.L., 24, 149
Gruneberg, M., 111

H
Hackling, M.W., 213
Hahn, W., 123
Hall, E.R., 204, 215
Hall, N., 116, 140
Hanna, P., 123
Hansen, J., 79, 80
Harris, K.R., 34, 138, 153, 174, 170, 172, 179, 192
Hasselhorn, M., 4
Hayes, J.R., 6, 173
Hembree, R., 188, 191, 203
Henderson, E.H., 117
Hewson, P.W., 224
Hildreth, G., 120
Hillerich, R., 119
Hillocks, G., 153, 180
Hodges, R.E., 119, 132, 138
Hofstein, A., 215
Hong, E., 194
Horn, E., 39, 116, 122, 123, 126, 128, 129, 131
Hull, G.A., 174
Humes, A., 136, 170, 171
Humphreys, B., 217
Hunt-Berg, M., 179
Hutchins, E., 85
Huttenlocker, J., 23

I
Ibeling, K., 123
Idol, L., 77, 78, 79

J
Jegeda, O.J., 223
Jenkins, J.R., 59, 63, 103, 104
Johnson, D.D., 20, 106, 107
Johnston, P., 82
Juel, C., 24, 41
Juola, F., 132
Just, M.A., 19, 20, 30

K
Kauffman, J, 141, 142, 143
Kernaghan, K., 138
King, A., 68, 69, 70, 72, 84
Kintsch, W, 58, 59, 60, 61
Kohl, B., 237
Krajcik, J.S., 219, 225
Kuhn, J., 3, 140

L
LaBerge, D., 38, 39

Lampert, M., 190
Langer, J.A., 153
Lawlor, J., 173
Lederman, N.G., 215
Lee, K.S., 199
Lee, O., 225
Leichter, H.P., 22
Lesgold, A.M. , 19
Leung, C.B., 102
Levin, J.R., 65, 66, 67, 74, 108, 109, 110, 190, 240
Linn, M.C., 219
Lipson, M.Y. 80
Lloyd, J., 214
Logan, G.P., 5
Lundberg, I., 24, 27
Lydiatt, 5., 148
Lyman, F.T., 72, 84
Lytle, S.L., 82

M
MacArthur, C., 174, 179
Malone, J., 221, 222, 223
Mandler, J.M., 77
Margosein, C.M., 106
Marino, J., 118, 138
Markman, E.M., 8
Marks, C., 84
Markus, H., 250
Marsh, G., 42
Martin, V.L., 239
Mason, D.A., 190
Mastropieri, M.A., 110, 123
Matthews, J., 199
Mayer, R.E., 4, 6, 198
McCarthy, L.P., 172
McCombs, B.L., 3
McConkie, G.W., 30
McCormick, C.B., 65, 175
McCutchen, D., 156, 173
McDonald, J.D., 68
McGivern, J.E., 110
McIntosh, W.J., 213
McKeown, M.D., 103, 104, 111, 112
Mehan, H., 89
Meichenbaum, P.M., 2, 4
Mergendoller, J.R., 214
Miller, L., 102, 180
Mokros, J.R., 218, 219
Montague, M., 187
Morrell, P.D., 218
Morris, P.E., 2

Morrow, L.M., 21, 22
Moshman, D., 8

N
Nachmias, R., 218
Nagy, W., 102
National Center for Educational Statistics, 213
National Council of Teachers of Mathematics, 188, 196, 202
Neef, N., 127
Nelson, 149
Neuman, S.B., 21
Neves, D.M., 198
Nichol, J.E., 105
Nicholson, T., 31, 102
Nolte, R.Y., 77, 79
Novak, J.D., 220, 221, 223
Novick, S., 224, 225
Nussbaum, J., 224, 225, 226
Nystrand, M., 173, 174

O
Odell, L., 156
Odubunmi, O., 216
Okebukola, P.A., 217, 223
Olshavsky, J.E., 82
Olson, G.M., 82, 118
O'Shea, L.J., 40

P
Paivio, A., 63, 108, 128, 241
Palincsar, A.M., 68, 83, 84
Pankratius, W.J., 223
Paris, S.G., 79
Patberg, J.P., 104
Pearson, P.D., 58
Pennington, B.F., 24
Perfetti, C.A., 19, 29, 30, 39
Perl, 5., 156
Perry, M., 194
Personke, C., 123, 144, 145, 147
Peters, E.E., 67
Peterson, P.L., 42, 202
Petty, W., 101
Pflaum, S.W., 20
Pierce, J.W., 64
Pittelman, S.D., 106
Plessas, G.P., 22
Polya, G., 184, 205

Posner, G.J., 224
Pratt, A.C., 24
Pressley, M. , 1, 2, 3, 6, 8, 9, 11, 49, 50, 57, 63, 64, 74, 84, 85, 88, 89, 93, 96, 106, 108, 109, 110, 129, 138, 184, 192, 193, 205, 214, 227, 228, 235, 236, 239, 240, 241, 244
Pryor, 144

R
Radaker, L., 129, 134, 139
Radebaugh, M., 117, 123
Rahman, T., 77
Raphael, T.E., 75, 76
Rasco, R.W., 129
Raugh, M.R., 108
Rayner, K., 30
Reed, 194, 195
Reinking, D., 103
Reith, H., 119, 122
Resnick, L.B., 200
Rice, M.L., 23
Riley, M.S., 200
Rinehart, S.D., 60, 61, 62
Rinsland, H., 116
Robbins, C., 102
Rohman, G., 154
Rose, W.H., 172
Rosenshine, B., 83
Roth, S, 45, 47, 223, 224
Rowell, G., 127
Rowls, M.D., 74
Russell, J.M., 215

S
Sadoski, M., 64
Samuels, S.J., 38, 39, 40, 41
Sanford, J.P., 214
Saunders, W.L., 215
Scarborough, H.S., 24
Scardamalia, M., 6, 153, 156, 170, 173, 174
Schell, L., 14, 148
Schmid, R.F., 220, 223
Schneider, W., 5, 8, 57
Schoenfeld, A., 190, 205
Schuder, T., 85, 95
Schumaker, E.F., 244
Schwantes, F.M., 31
Scott, R., 123, 125, 126, 136, 142, 204
Scruggs, T.E., 110

Sears, N., 128, 129
Segal, J.W., 13
Shake, M.C., 101
Sharon, S., 217
Shea, J.B., 199
Short, E.J., 77, 79
Shriberg, L.K., 65
Shymansky, J.A., 215, 216
Siegler, R.S., 196
Silver, E., 198
Simmons, P.E., 218
Singer, H., 68
Slack, S.J., 218
Smith, F, 31, 125
Smith, L.C., 81
Songer, N.B., 214
Soyibo, K., 223
Spilich, G.J., 4
Spring, C., 40
Stahl, S.A., 21, 102
Stanovich, K., 24, 30, 31, 38, 41, 102
Staver, J.R., 213
Stein, M.L., 76, 202, 235, 236
Steinberg, R.M., 202
Stensvold, M.S., 223
Sterling, C., 137
Sternberg, R.J., 2, 89, 102
Stevens, P., 164
Stowitschek, C., 140
Strauss, A., 14
Stuart, M., 24
Suid, M., 123
Sulzby, E., 21
Swiatek, M.A., 205
Symons, S.E., 1
Szetela, W., 191

T
Tangel, D.M., 27, 123
Tarasoff, M., 123
Taylor, B.M., 20, 41, 59, 60, 62, 63
Teale, W., 22
Tee, A., 123
Templeton, S., 119
Thomas, V., 116, 120, 122, 123, 125, 126, 127, 128, 131, 140, 141
Thompson, A.G., 1
Thornton, C.A., 201, 202
Tobias, 5, 4
Tobin, K., 214, 218

Toms-Bronowski, 5, 106
Toppino, T.C., 199
Torgeson, J.K., 19, 28, 45
Treiman, R.A., 27
Tunmer, W.E, 34

U
Uhry, 149
Underwood, A., 19

V
Valdez-Menchaca, M.C., 23
Valmont, W., 144
Van Haneghan, J., 191
vanLehn, K., 193
van Oudenhoven, J., 128, 140

Vellutino, F.R., 20
Verschaffel, L., 34

W
Wallace, G., 127
Ward, M., 195
Warner, M.W.,
Watson, S.B., 216, 217
Weaver, C., 21
Webb, N.M., 190, 191, 203
Weisberg, P., 116
Welch, W.W., 213, 214
White, T.G., 105, 219
Whitehurst, G.J., 22, 23
Widaman, K.F., 197
Willerman, M., 223

Wilson, P.T., 79
Wimmer, H., 29
Winograd, P., 138
Woloshyn, V.E. , 138, 139, 228, 229, 237, 239
Wong, B.Y.L., 68, 137, 138
Wood, M., 202, 238, 241
Woodward, J., 214
Wyatt, J.W., 85

X-Y-Z
Yager, R.E., 213, 214, 215
Yee, A., 116
Zhu, X., 195
Zutell, J., 116, 117

Subject Index

A

alphabet reading and blending: phonological approach, 34

B

Benchmark School, 42, 85, 89
 analogy approach to decoding, 42-45

C

Cognitive Strategy Instruction in Writing (CSIW) , 157
comprehension strategies, 82
 reciprocal teaching, 83

D

Daisy Quest Program, The, 28
 analytical phonological skills, 28
 synthetic phonological skills, 28
decoding, beginning of reading, 19, 21
 whole-word vs. phonics instruction, 19
  difference in emphasis, 20
  graphemes & phonemes, relation between, 20
decoding, beyond phonemic awareness, 30
 dual-route theory, 30
 explicit teaching favored, 31
 processing of words, 30
dialogues, strategically mediated, 89-93

E

Educational Psychologist, 49
Elementary School Journal, 94

F

facts, learning of, 234
 elaborative interrogation, 236-238
  effects of, 239
  vs. representational imagery, 241
 in connected texts, 238
 in isolation, 237
 prior knowledge, 239

Illinois Center for the Study of Reading, 43, 45
imagery, 63, 246
 mental, 63
  dual-coding theory, 63

 mnemonic, 65
  keystone method, 65-67
  representational, 64
imagery, representational, 239
 meaningful proxies, 240
 mechanisms for, 241
 vs. elaborative interrogation, 241
information processing, components of, 2, 4
 activating prior knowledge, 3
 metacognitive knowledge about, 3, 11
 memorizing, 3
 mnemonic strategy, 3
 monitoring, 3
 motivation, 11
 nonstrategic knowledge base, 4, 11
 problem solving, 3
 reading procedures, 3
 strategy user, good, 2, 3, 250
  meets cognitive challenges, 2
Iowa Tests of Basic Skills, 140

J

Journal of Research in Science Teaching, 229

K

Kansas strategy intervention model, 8

M

mathematics (see problem solving)
mathematics, strategies for teaching, 189
 accelerated instruction, 205
 calculator, when to use, 191
 computer program, 203
 educational computer programs, 204
 explanation of problem solving, 193-200
  increasing problem-solving ability, 20
  increasing teacher knowledge, 202
 manipulatives, use of, 190
 problem-solving curriculum, 206
 small-group problem solving, 190
 technological support for, 208
metacognitive knowledge, 3, 5
Microcomputer-Based Laboratories (MBL), 218
 see also, science instruction
 simulations of Microworlds, 219
mnemonic strategies, 234

P

phonemic awareness, 23
    prediction of success in early reading, 24
    sound categorization training, 24
        rhyming and reading skills, relation between, 24
        sets of words used in training, 25-27
    use of computer programs to increase, 28
phonological and visual recognition, method for promoting both, 41
    encouraging more reading, 41
    computer programs, 45
        Construct-A-Word, 45-47
        Daisy's Castle, 48
        Hint & Hunt, 47
        Reader Rabbit, 48
phonological approach, 34
    alphabet reading and blending, 34
    using phonic rules, 34-35
picture training, integrated, 31
    letter-sound training, 32
    mnemonic method, 31
prior knowledge, activating of, 79-81
    cloze procedure, use of, 80
    prereading discussion, 80
    to improve reading comprehension, 79
problem solving, mathematics, 184
    strategic processes, 184
        Polya's model, 184
            four-stage sequence, 186
            support for, 187, 188
proofreading skills, 144
    lesson plans for, 145

Q

question-answering strategies, 73, 75
    lookback, 74
    relationships, 75
question-answer relationships (QAR), 75
question generation, 68, 73
    think-type (Think Trix), 68, 84, 246

R

reading competence, development of, 21
    emergent literacy, 21, 23
    home environments, support from, 22
    parental intervention, 22
reading comprehension, strategies, 57
    as learning tools, 57
    summarization instruction, 59, 62
        improvement of recall, 62
reciprocal teaching, 83
    key ingredients of, 84

research and practice, closing gap between, 13

S

science beliefs, inaccurate, 223
    accommodation, 224-227
    how to overcome, 224
science instruction, status of, 213
    analogies, 227
        limitations in classroom use of, 227
    computers, 218
    concept map, 220-223
    cooperative learning, 216-218
    elaborative interrogation, 228
    inquiry based, 215
    laboratories, 215, 216
    videodisks, use of, 220
self-generated questions, answering of, 68-73, 79, 246, 247
self-regulated strategies, 7, 8, 14
    direct teaching, interactive, 10
    interaction between, and knowledge base, 10
    metacognition about, 9
    model for teaching of, 12
    monitoring, 8, 237
    teaching in context, 10, 14
    teaching of, first step, 11
        integration with content, 12
Sesame Street, impact of, 23
sound categorization training, 24
    evaluation data, 27, 28
spelling, 117
    classroom instruction in, 118
    imagery/analogy strategies, 118
    lists, advantage of, 125
    mnemonics, 123
    phoneme-grapheme relationships, 116
    phonics, 116
    rules, 123, 124
    transitional stage, 117
spelling acquisition strategies, 128
    imagery, 128, 134, 135
        flash cards, 130
    morphological structure, 136
    multiple spelling, 138
    teaching of, 134, 135
    word analogy, 131, 133
        orthographic patterns, 131
spelling consciousness, 143
    error detection and correction, 143
    extensive reading encouraged, 149
spelling correction strategies, 140
    correct-your-own-test, 140, 141

autonomous use of, 1
dissemination of information, obstacles to, 13
research and practice, closing of gap, 13

T
task analysis, 6
importance of for communication, problem solving, vocabulary, 6
thinking, relevant models of, 2
short-term vs. long-term memory, 2, 5
think sheets, 157
transactional strategies instruction (TSI), 84, 89
becoming TSI teacher, 95
long- and short-term goals, 85, 94
summarization of, 95, 242
validation of, 93
TREE, 166, 167

V
visual recognition approach, 35
orthographic recognition, 38
automaticity theory, 38
reading by analogy, 42
repeated readings method, 39
adaptations of, 40
sight word knowledge, 35-38
vocabulary instruction, 101
computer presentation, use of, 103
encouraging extensive reading, 102
keyword method, 108, 109
acoustic-link and imagery-link stages, 108
mnemonic interventions, 110
meanings from external and internal context clues, 104, 105

morphological, 106
paucity of, 101, 102
processing new vocabulary, 111
word association, 111
revised definitions, use of, 103
SCANR procedure, 105
semantic mapping, 106, 107
strategies for guessing meanings, 104

W
word processing and writing, 178-179
writing process, specific aspects of, 170
planning, 170
idea-generating questions, 170, 171
plan-translate-revise strategy, 180
recommendation for writing program, 179, 251
revising, 173, 175, 176, 177
rewriting, 176
translating, 172
reciprocity principle, 173, 174
writing strategies, 153
cognitive strategic instruction, 156
schema-building, 157
deficiencies in, 153
essay organization, 164
plan-translate-revise, 180
P.O.W.E.R. (Plan, Organize, Write, Edit, Revise), 164
process-oriented approach, 154, 155
recursive, 154
self-regulated strategy development, 164, 165
steps in process, 166-169
think-sheets, 157, 158

About the Authors

Michael Pressley, Ph.D. is Professor in the Department of Educational Psychology at the University of Albany, State University of New York. He has studied student cognition, especially students' use of strategies, for about 20 years, including programs of research on children's imagery, mnemonics, cognitive monitoring, and reading comprehension. He is the author or co-author of more than 200 scientific publications and is considered an expert in the areas of children's memory, educational psychology, and reading comprehension. Mr. Pressley recently co-authored five books: doctoral, intermediate, and undergraduate level textbooks in educational psychology, all from HarperCollins; *Verbal Protocols of Reading: The Nature of Constructively Responsive Reading*, published by Erlbaum and Associates; and this revision of the best-selling textbook, *Cognitive Strategy Instruction that Really Improves Children's Academic Performance*, from Brookline Books.

Mr. Pressley does not shy away from controversy, as exemplified by his recent contributions to the whole-language debate, and by the editing of the August 1994 issue of *Applied Cognitive Psychology* concerned with the scientific evaluation of claims that long-forgotten memories of childhood sexual abuse can be recovered through therapy. In a nutshell, his position on whole language is that it is often not a sufficient form of instruction to ensure the development of literacy in primary-level students, especially at-risk students. He concurs with the predominant view among cognitive psychologists that it is impossible to know whether recovered memories of childhood sexual abuse are accurate, with a number of reasons to believe that therapy intended to recover memories of abuse actually produces distorted recall of childhood.

Vera E. Woloshyn is an Assistant Professor in the Faculty of Education at Brock University. Her research interests include the development and implementation of strategy programs, particularly those that provide student with explicit multiple strategy instruction. She currently holds a grant from the Social Sciences and Humanities Research Council (SSHRC). Professor Woloshyn has also co-edited the text *Cognitive Strategy Instruction for Middle and High Schools*, in which she also appears as an author.